THREE DAYS IN JUNE

JAMES O'CONNELL

monoray

First published in Great Britain in 2021 by Monoray, an imprint of
Octopus Publishing Group Ltd
Carmelite House, 50 Victoria Embankment, London EC4Y 0DZ
www.octopusbooks.co.uk
www.octopusbooksusa.com

An Hachette UK Company
www.hachette.co.uk

First published in paperback in 2022

Distributed in the US by Hachette Book Group
1290 Avenue of the Americas, 4th and 5th Floors, New York, NY 10104

Distributed in Canada by Canadian Manda Group
664 Annette St., Toronto, Ontario, Canada M6S 2C8

ISBN 978 1 91318 361 5

A CIP catalogue record for this book is available from the British Library.

Printed and bound in UK

1 3 5 7 9 10 8 6 4 2

This FSC® label means that materials used for the
product have been responsibly sourced

This **monoray** book was crafted and published by
Jake Lingwood, Sybella Stephens, Tom Bromley, Jonathan Christie,
Jeremy Tilston and Peter Hunt.

THREE DAYS IN JUNE

Dedicated to my wife Maureen

Thank you for putting up with me during this very long project.

Also to my mother and father who encouraged me to write this account, but sadly who both died before the project was finished.

And to the memory of those who gave their all on Mount Longdon.

CONTENTS

FOREWORD

by Major General Jonathan Shaw CB CBE

In 1982, Argentina invaded the Falkland Islands. A British Task Force, including The 3rd Battalion, The Parachute Regiment, was assembled to assist in reclaiming the islands. I was a 24-year-old Platoon Commander, of 6 Platoon, B Company, 3 PARA. We had no idea this was to be a defining moment of all our lives.

On Saturday 12 June I would lead my men on to Mount Longdon. Our objective was to capture the summit, codenamed Fly Half. All went well until an anti-personnel mine exploded among 4 Platoon and, almost immediately, Mount Longdon came alive. What followed next will stay with me for the rest of my life. They say, 'No plan survives first contact with the enemy.' And that is true: chaos; confusion; everything we thought we knew about the enemy turned out to be wrong. This was the most intense night of most of our lives and, since then, many of us will have fought and relived that night many times. Those memories are recorded in extraordinary detail in this book and I would like to thank Jimmy O'Connell for putting this excellent account of the battle together, and for keeping the memories alive of those men who made the ultimate sacrifice for Queen and Country.

My abiding memory of that night is that, from my platoon, more men died while trying to save their friends than trying to kill the enemy. This spirit of self-sacrifice has ever since epitomized for me the highest ideal of military service. Love is not the first emotion people think of when they think of paratroopers. But they should, and reading this book will show them why.

Lt Jonathan Shaw
Officer Commanding 6 Platoon, 1982

FOREWORD
from the privately published edition, 2013

by Lieutenant General Sir Hew Pike
KCB DSO MBE

Jimmy O'Connell has done us all a unique service, by travelling thousands of miles over the past few years to gather together the threads of this perspective – the reflections and memories of many former friends and comrades-in-arms forty years on from an extraordinary passage of arms. He has put together a wonderful record of courage, tenacity, stoicism, self-sacrifice, teamwork and, of course, humour, so that from all these personal reminiscences, a number of threads can consistently be traced, all of them timeless truths of war. The qualities of the soldiers of 3 PARA naturally dominate all else: as you read these pages about the terrible battle for Mount Longdon, you will think to yourself, 'Greater love hath no man than this, that a man lay down his life for his friends.' Striking, too, is to remember how such close bonds are formed, in the training and selection process for The Parachute Regiment and Airborne Forces, a process founded in World War II, nurtured in the decades that followed and further vindicated on operations since 1982.

The awful nature of close-quarter combat, the devastating effect of artillery and mortar fire, the confusion and setbacks of a long night battle among the rocks, tested unsparingly the resolve of the men remembered in these pages.

Jimmy has presented his own great salute to his former comrades, whose stories remind us of the qualities essential to the soldier who will prevail.

Hew Pike, Commanding Officer
3rd Battalion The Parachute Regiment, 1982

THE FALKLAND ISLANDS

The ownership of the Falkland Islands has been a long and contentious issue between Argentina and the United Kingdom, mainly due to the distance of the Islands being 300 miles from Argentina and 8,000 miles from UK. During the past 500 years the Falkland Islands have been occupied at various times by the British, French, Spanish and Argentines; however, the UK claim to sovereignty dates back to 1690, when English sailors first landed on the islands, and almost continuously since 1833 when a British settlement was established.

Argentina first raised its claim to the Falkland Islands in 1829, only to abandon it in 1850. A second attempt in the 1880s resulted in the UK ignoring the issue. However, the creation of the United Nations in 1945 brought about another opportunity; in 1960 the UN's interest in colonization presented Argentina with a third chance to reignite their claim, and in 1965 the UK found itself succumbing to the UN's demand for sovereignty negotiations.

By 1971 the dispute between Argentina and UK came down to territorial integrity versus residents' right to self-determination. The latter won and by 1972 the Falklanders had gained an effective veto over what could happen to their islands. The UK Parliament was firmly behind them and their wish to remain British – whether that was in the best interests of the islands or Britain's relationship with South America had become irrelevant.

Argentina could not accept that only the islanders could decide on the outcome. The Falklands were seen as 'Little Britain' and Argentina's frustrations would lead to a change of tactics. On 24 March 1976 an Argentine right-wing coup overthrew President Isabel Perón and a military junta (dictatorship) officially named National Reorganization Process was installed, headed by Lieutenant General Jorge Rafael Videla as President of Argentina. In December 1981 General Leopoldo Galtieri ousted Videla to become President and immediately began planning an invasion of the Falkland Islands; by this stage the economy was in deep recession and the regime was increasingly unpopular.

In May 1979 Margaret Thatcher became UK's first female prime minister, a controversial figure whom people either loathed or loved. Her election was followed by many turbulent years in the UK – the IRA was highly active in Northern Ireland and on the British mainland; there were serious riots in Brixton, Toxteth and other inner-city centres across the UK; and the Iranian Embassy fell under siege, resolved only after a decisive operation by the SAS.

On 19 March 1982 Argentine marines posing as civilians landed on South Georgia in the Southern Atlantic and raised the Argentine flag – this was followed on 2 April by a full-scale invasion of the Falkland Islands. News of the invasion was received positively in Argentina, and the anti-junta demonstrations were replaced by patriotic support of President Galtieri and his government, who believed the UK would not respond... but they were wrong.

The politics at that time, both international and domestic, will be forever debated, but in 1982, as the British Naval Task Force sailed south, all those on board were in no doubt who was the aggressor and the need to reclaim the Falkland Islands by any means possible. The British soldiers, sailors and airmen had only one thing on their mind – they had a job to do.

INTRODUCTION

This book is a testimony to the men of 3 PARA Battle Group. It is not exaggerated in any way, and is a factual account. These men and the memories of this battle have been with me since 1982, although the war has been over for nearly forty years. Every morning as I wash my face, my scars and my glass eye are constant reminders of the heroism of the men with whom I had the honour to serve, who I know never received the credit they were due. Among these men are several who saved my life in the most extraordinary circumstances and yet received nothing.

This book will give you some understanding of the bravery shown over those three days. How young men barely out of school will kill and be killed; how in the most awful of circumstances, some will break down and cry, yet others will shine and find they thrive in the mud and blood of the battlefield. It will show you the meaning of compassion, and how, while some men will lay down their lives for their friends, others will be quite indifferent to the suffering of their fellow men. This is our story.

The battle for Mount Longdon was part of a three-phase attack which it was hoped would bring about the end of the Falklands conflict with Argentina. British forces were to break through the ring of mountains surrounding Port Stanley. These mountains had been occupied by Argentine forces for ten weeks and had been turned into formidable defensive positions, with registered targets for defensive mortar, artillery and machine-gun fire on all approaches. Mount Longdon also had minefields running along the south, west and northern approaches of the feature.

The units involved on the night of 11 June 1982 were 3 PARA, 42 Cdo and 45 Cdo with all their attached arms. This book will concentrate solely on

3 PARA; they had been selected to be the first unit to initiate what was a relatively simple battle plan. After leaving the Start Line in a silent attack (until it went noisy), A and C Companies would secure an area 600 metres to the north of Mount Longdon known as Wing Forward.

With B Company leaving the Start Line and advancing east towards the mountain, the three platoons would separate to their various tasks: 6 Platoon would capture the feature known as Fly Half, then proceed to another feature known as Full Back and secure this. At the same time 4 and 5 Platoons would move along the northern edge of the mountain, clearing the lower slopes all the way to Full Back. Once Mount Longdon was secure A and C Companies would, if time allowed, capture an Argentine company position located on Wireless North (code name Rum Punch), a feature that lies north of Wireless Ridge.

The resulting battle for Mount Longdon featured some of the British Army's bloodiest and most deadly close-quarter fighting since the Korean War. 3 PARA found themselves under fire from the front, rear and sides, with enemy appearing from a multitude of hiding places on this rocky feature; the resulting casualties bear testament to a battle that was more extreme and more violent than anyone had expected.For example, the battalion was poorly equipped for the 1982 campaign, having been issued with second-hand winter clothing, which came from the King's Own Scottish Borderers who had just returned from Norway. Though their kit was ready for the bin we were issued with it and once we landed on the Falklands it quickly began to fall apart due to the extreme weather.

Also by today's standards it is almost unbelievable that the government would send soldiers to fight in war with no body armour of any kind or even an adequate helmet. At that time the Parachute Regiment were using the lightweight parachute helmet made by Thetford Moulded Products. The shell was made of fibreglass and offered no ballistic protection – in fact it probably had the same ballistic properties provided by a cycle helmet.

Many people assume that helicopters featured heavily in the Falklands War, but for this battle, severely wounded soldiers were forced to wait at least ten hours, and sadly in some cases died due to the delay. Compare that with more recent campaigns such as Afghanistan, for example, where evacuation of 'urgent' casualties to a NATO Role 2 or 3 medical facility takes less than 60 minutes, despite a NATO standard of 90 minutes. Any mission that exceeds the 60-minute limit is subject to a delayed mission report. Lt Col James M Ryan (a field surgeon during the campaign) was quoted in the *Journal of The Royal Army Medical Corps* as saying the Falklands War had more in common with the First World War or even the Boer War, than it did with a modern conflict. Despite all this, the formidable qualities of Parachute Regiment soldiers should never be underestimated: they tend to thrive in adversity and do not know when to quit. These same qualities took the battalion on a 60-mile advance over the most hostile terrain in appalling weather conditions, then to fight and win a battle against the odds, suffering the highest casualties of any land battle during the campaign, then march into Port Stanley with maroon berets on and heads held high.

My personal role during the battle was as a member of Support Company, Anti-Tank Platoon. Our platoon had been divided up between the rifle companies and my section was attached to C Company to provide extra firepower. C Company's role was to remain out of contact but to stay close enough to be able to provide support or react to any contingencies that may arise during the battle. Once Mount Longdon was captured, B Company would consolidate on the mountain and C and A Companies would push eastwards to capture Wireless Ridge North.

During the battle, although the company that I was attached to remained out of contact, it was extensively shelled with artillery and mortars and constantly swept with machine-gun fire resulting in various gunshot and shrapnel injuries. I was wounded during the occupation of our designated area. I received a glancing gunshot wound, a bullet passing from left to right clipping my face as it passed in front of my left eye, then went through the bridge of my nose, took out my right eye and cheekbone, then carried on its deadly journey. The impact also caused my teeth to bang together with such force it knocked out my top front teeth.

Experiences like mine were very common on Mount Longdon, which saw a truly shocking number of horrific casualties on both sides. As you read this book, which is written as an oral history, using extensive interviews with the soldiers themselves, you will learn of the terrible ordeals of the young men involved, many fresh from school. Although members of the British Armed Forces cannot legally be deployed on the frontline until they have turned 18, this seems to have been overlooked during the Falklands War, as many members of the Task Force serving in the exclusion zone were 17 years old;

in fact 3 PARA had a very young battalion with ten 17-year-olds, and forty-two 18-year-olds. Two of the 17-year-olds and two aged 18 would be listed among the final death toll.

Another feature of the conflict back in 1982 was the absence of aftercare for those involved. No one ever asked, 'How are you? Are you okay?' PTSD was never spoken about. It was almost as if once we returned from the war, it had never happened; we were back to barrack-room duties and military exercises. There was a huge spike in soldiers self-medicating with drink; everyone drank and fought more, including me – when I say more, I mean to oblivion – everyone was different, we couldn't really take authority. There was a general feeling of, what can you do to me that hasn't already be done? Many soldiers left within a few years. In hindsight I think every one of us was suffering from PTSD to some degree, but back then there were no mobile phones or computers – you couldn't just reach out to any agencies. Several members of the battalion took their own lives, others struggled on with their demons and although they did not take their own lives, PTSD without doubt killed them through drink and health conditions exacerbated by their poor physical or mental health. Marriages broke up; veterans ended up in jail for extreme acts of violence, even murder. Even today I think we all suffer to a certain degree, we all have our bad moments, which can often occur out of the blue and take us by surprise, we all have episodes of anger, guilt and confusion over what happened and why.

I think these two quotes sum it up very well:

'In war, there are no unwounded soldiers.' José Narosky

'Not all scars are visible and not all wounds heal.' Lisa French

When I left the army in late 1984, I found it extremely difficult getting work. I found a couple of temporary jobs, but a lot of employers simply said, 'We'd employ you but for your one eye,' which at the time was disappointing. However, a friend said, 'Why don't you try the taxis?' I said, 'But surely, the minimum requirement is two eyes to be a taxi driver?' I applied anyway to Liverpool Hackney Carriage Office and was granted a taxi licence. The job was a lifesaver for me, and I subsequently worked for twenty-three years driving a black cab around Liverpool and created a small taxi business employing five men.

In 2007, twenty-five years after the end of the war in the November, I was given the opportunity to visit the Falkland Islands as part of a 25th Falklands

War Pilgrimage, funded by the National Lottery. When I first applied to go on the trip I was told there were no places left. However, at a very late stage someone dropped out and off I went. Unbeknown to me, this trip would be something of a turning point for me, as it became the catalyst for writing this book. Finally going back to Mount Longdon with several of my colleagues was highly emotional. Walking around the mountain on a beautiful sunny day, where so much death and destruction had taken place, was just so moving for all of us; standing all these years later where my friends had died moved me so much that I decided there and then that I had to do something to keep the memories of these men alive.

I had read books that had been written about the battle for Mount Longdon and I knew that some were just plainly wrong. They had been written by historians who had relied on one man's version of events and never questioned whether it was factually correct, or by veterans of the battle who had written their own accounts of how they saw the battle. One man's perspective is limited and cannot give the overall view of a battalion attack, especially when the rifle companies and individual platoons are all fighting their own battles in different areas.

However hard I looked, I just couldn't find a book that portrayed the battle for Mount Longdon as it actually *was*.

I returned home to Liverpool thinking, how do I write a book about all of this? I'd come to the realization that if anyone was going to write this story, perhaps it was going to be me. I bought several books including titles such as *How to Write a Book*. But nothing really prepared me for the huge project I was about to take on.

In 2010 I began writing in earnest. My plan was to get it all finished so that my former colleagues could read it when the thirtieth anniversary came around in 2012.

I began contacting as many veterans of the battle as I could find, asking would it be possible to meet up for a chat, have a phone conversation or email correspondence about their memory of the battle and what role they played as it unfolded. I began travelling all around the UK, knocking on doors, drinking endless cups of tea and chatting with people I had not seen in years, about what they had seen and done. I had known, from my visit to the Falklands, that people's stories would be varied but the thing I found with all participants was how limited their view of the battle was; they all seemed to be very much in their own bubble. The fighting was so terrifying, and it was so dark – unlike the Argentine forces the British soldiers had little or no access to night-vision equipment – that they knew very little of anyone or anything that was happening within 20 metres of them, let alone what happened on the other side of the mountain. If they were in A Company they knew little of B Company, if they were in 6 Platoon they knew very little about 4 Platoon and so on.

At the end of the interview process I had spoken to over 148 veterans of the battle.

Once I had recorded my interviews, I would begin the hard job of typing everything out; as I cannot type with two hands – I am a one-finger typist – this made the task so much longer.

I think in my naivety I had underestimated how hard it would be to write a book, especially a factual account. I worked full-time on the manuscript, every day either writing, chasing someone up, visiting people or doing research, visiting museums or archives, but in hindsight I loved doing it. Meeting up, having a chat with old friends – it doesn't get better than that, and slowly seeing the whole thing come together was a fantastic two-year journey, which would not have been possible without a very understanding wife.

As I got more and more involved in the project, I found I wanted to fill in even more gaps. What happened between this moment and that moment? Where did that story originate? Who saw whom doing what? I had a brainwave, and decided to contact some veterans of the battle, asking if they would like to return to the Falklands with me to walk through their actual movement during the battle on the mountain, just as I had done on that earlier trip. This second trip provided incredible, invaluable detail. In the end I went back to the Falklands five times with different groups of men from the various rifle companies and platoons.

When visiting the Falkland Islands veterans can stay at Liberty Lodge, which can accommodate up to twelve. It is a wonderful log cabin-style building, very informal, and we veterans all mucked in with cooking. Liberty Lodge's running and maintenance costs are paid for by charitable donations, all guests making a donation at the end of their stay.

I used a Dictaphone to record my interviews. I would place it on the table alongside a large folder with all manner of photos of Mount Longdon. I was fortunate that on one of my visits I met a Royal Marine veteran in the Victory Bar, and after a few pints it turned out he now worked in the Falklands as a helicopter pilot, and agreed to take me on a flight over Mount Longdon. I was able to take many aerial photos of the various approaches to the mountain.

On one return trip to the Falklands with several members of B Company, we were on the top of Mount Longdon by the memorial cross. About 100 metres away was a group of about eight Argentine veterans, from which a young Argentine clearly too young to have been in the war made his way across to us. He said, 'Can my friends meet you? They are veterans of the battle and would like say hello.' In our group we had two amputees and two who had been wounded during the battle, but we understood that the only other people who know how hard the battle was, are our opponents, the enemy. We said, 'No problem, tell them to come over.' They came across and we shook hands, one of the Argentines had a bottle of wine and some plastic glasses, we all drank and gave a toast to absent friends; everything was translated through their young friend. At the end of the day we are all just soldiers sent to do our country's bidding. I think that is why I have no animosity to any Argentines.

As a result, some of the most important people in making this book accurate were the Argentine veterans of the battle. Lieutenant Sergio Dachary, who was the commander of the Marine Infantry Anti-Aircraft Platoon, gave the exact location of all his .50 Cal machine guns. Fortunately he had interviewed his men after the battle, and these accounts were invaluable. His input was especially generous as he had lost his brother, Lieutenant Alejandro Dachary of 601st Anti-Aircraft Artillery Group, who was killed while manning Argentine defences at Port Stanley Airport.

Another veteran, Cpl Gustavo Pedemonte, 2 Platoon, B Company, 7th Infantry Regiment, gave a fascinating eyewitness account of his part in the clash between Sgt Ian McKay VC and Argentine forces. This is a unique view from an enemy soldier of a Victoria Cross action, which is very rare in VC awards.

One of things that I discovered was that on both sides, many of these men had not spoken about their experiences; they had simply locked them away, almost as if it was something that needed to be hidden from their family. Even those that were seriously wounded had found the memory too painful to share with family, but because I was a fellow veteran we had a bond, and were able to talk informally. Slowly these stories began to come out. During this process, on several occasions tears were shed. But I pushed on, determined to save these men's stories, or their struggles and sacrifice would have all been for nothing.

The book had morphed from being an interesting idea to something I now thought was really important. All my travel and expenses around the UK to interview my colleagues, visit museums and archives and travel back and forth to the Falklands were paid for out of my own pocket, and I wouldn't have been able to afford it at all if I hadn't sold my taxi business in 2010.

I was initially writing the book for the veterans and the families of veterans who took part or were killed in the battle, and I thought if I could get 500 copies printed 'we' would buy it as something we could keep as a record. But people I showed the book to suggested I should get it published professionally, so I contacted a publisher and told them what I was doing and asked would they be interested in it. They said they would, and to keep them informed of my progress. I ploughed on.

Then, in January 2012, I was in the final stages of putting the book together when one afternoon I received a phone call telling me to attend a clinic appointment as I had recently attended the hospital for breathing problems due my nasal injuries. I wasn't unduly concerned, but it was to be a life-changing appointment: the doctor told me I had kidney cancer. I immediately asked, how long have I got? But he said we don't know, it's not until we open you up that we can see how far it has spread. It was devastating news, even more so telling my wife and boys. From working on the book almost full time, my life took a completely different route of hospitals, surgery and uncertainty, of planning for my immediate death. Fortunately, I had fantastic treatment from the NHS, my cancerous kidney was rapidly removed and it was confirmed the cancer had not spread, it had been contained in my left kidney. However, my right kidney then began to fail and I ended up on dialysis, attending hospital every other day where my blood was cleaned over a six-hour period.

During this time I finished my book and in 2013 I contacted my initial publisher and was told, they were sorry but as the thirtieth anniversary had passed they were not interested, as they had moved on to the various upcoming anniversaries. To be honest I wasn't that disappointed as I had other bigger and more pressing health problems to deal with. I did contact a number of other publishers, one of which told me that the world doesn't need another Falklands book, while another said, 'Sorry, with the anniversary passing, I'm afraid you've missed the boat.'

So, I had a 220,000-word manuscript full of incredible detail, and no publisher wanted it! But that didn't matter too much to me because the plan had always been to write this book for veterans and their families. Undeterred, I decided to self-publish the book as an ebook, just to get it out there, so people could read of the men that I had had the privilege to serve with.

Immediately the feedback from the ebook edition was fantastic, with up to 185 five-star reviews. It went to number 1 in the military Kindle charts, and then *Soldier Magazine* gave it a wonderful five-star review. People kept asking where they could buy the paperback version, so I decided to contact a local printer who printed 500 copies which sold out straight away. I began to buy batches of 200 books at a time and sell them, as I really enjoyed the feedback from fellow veterans, battlefield historians and family members of the fallen, many of whom who were grateful to read a full account of the battle for the first time and learn how their son or husband had died. This, more than anything, gave me great comfort that what I had done was right.

All this time I was still attending dialysis. If you have never experienced it, you may find it hard to understand how soul-destroying dialysis can be: it's a sort of limbo where you're not sure if you have a future or are just treading water before death. I spent four years watching fellow patients dying on a regular basis. I would attend the clinic and ask where Ted or Barbara was, only to be told, 'Oh, they died at the weekend.' And I would find myself thinking about when my turn would come.

Eventually in June 2017 I received a phone call from the transplant team telling me to make my way into the Royal Hospital Liverpool. When I arrived, they told me a kidney may be available; a young man was gravely ill and was not expected to survive. I waited two days, and then in the early hours I was rushed into surgery. I can never thank the family of that young man enough for giving me the gift of life.

In 2019 I was contacted by Jake Lingwood at Monoray publishers. He had come across the book, and suggested we publish it in time for the fortieth anniversary. And so here we are today. This edition you hold in your hands is slightly shorter than the edition I published myself. It has been edited and tidied up a little but essentially it is the same book, and a book I am incredibly proud of.

These memories are important. Something that still frustrates many veterans of the battle is the award system at the time. So many individual, selfless acts of bravery had taken place: some men were listed for awards but then received lesser awards; others were listed for major gallantry awards but were given nothing at all, and then there are in every battle those whose bravery goes unseen, who are never put forward for awards. Only those who were alongside them in the darkness know what manner of men they are.

One soldier in particular has been the focus of many veterans of the battle: Cpl Stewart McLaughlin. A campaign has been running over several years where over 150 veterans with pipes and drums, all suited and wearing medals, have marched annually along Whitehall to Downing Street with the 3 PARA Commanding Officer Sir Hew Pike leading. In previous years they have presented a signed petition at the door of 10 Downing Street calling for a retrospective award for Cpl McLaughlin, but so far it has fallen on deaf ears. Military honours or not, at least this book can be a fitting memorial to those men, alive or dead.

And for those alive, the book seemed to have a second use. What I realized was that whatever side you were on, Argentine or British, this book – which is not so much my book as theirs – has helped all of us as veterans understand our own battle, a battle that no one else really understands. I was hugely moved by the feedback I received from soldiers who served on Mount Longdon, or soldiers who were elsewhere in the Falklands who hadn't understood the scale of what was happening when they were watching the tracer fire on the mountain.

I hope that this book gives an insight into the bravery of my colleagues, every man a hero.

This is the best chance all of us have in helping you understand what we went through on those three days in June in 1982.

Pte James (Scouse) O'Connell, 2021

TIDWORTH TO MOUNT LONGDON

Thursday 8 April 1982. The battalion left their Barracks in Tidworth, Wiltshire for Southampton, where we spent our first night onboard SS *Canberra*. The next day we sailed south, and the following six-week journey involved a continuous re-training in all the basic skills of field craft, including reaction to enemy fire, target indication, fire-control orders, radio-communication skills, battlefield first aid, plus a multitude of intelligence briefings and updates. Diplomatic negotiations were ongoing throughout the journey, but after the sinking of the ARA *General Belgrano* on 2 May, followed by HMS *Sheffield* on 4 May there would be no turning back.

Friday 21 May. At 02.45hrs (zt) 3 PARA, who were now onboard HMS *Intrepid*, were sent to assault stations for the landings, but due to various delays the first wave of 3 PARA landed just before dawn, then the second wave of 3 PARA and 45 Commando landed in broad daylight. The battalion immediately secured the high ground and San Carlos settlement. A Company engaged a retreating platoon of Argentines who shot down two Gazelle helicopters, killing three crew members.

We remained in our defensive perimeter for seven days, overlooking an area which became known by the press as 'Bomb Alley' – here we witnessed the Argentine air attacks on Port San Carlos.

THE BREAKOUT FROM PORT SAN CARLOS

Thursday 27 May. 3 PARA received orders from Brigade to move at best speed to Teal Inlet. Shortly before the battalion moved out, Falkland Islander

Councillor Terry Peck made contact with 3 PARA HQ and volunteered to act as a guide. The battalion moved out at 13.15hrs (zt) carrying only 'fighting order' (carrying as much ammunition as possible and only what was needed to survive over a 24-hour period).

It was a long 45-kilometre walk to Teal Inlet, a community of only twenty people, which we eventually reached after marching over the most demanding terrain in rain, sleet and snow, arriving in the early hours of Saturday morning.

Sunday 30 May. After the battalion had rested, feet powdered and socks changed, at 14.00hrs (zt) we began our advance to Estancia House, the home of Tony and Ailsa Heathman where 3 PARA HQ would be based. This was another long 30-kilometre hard march across the most arduous ankle-breaking terrain, which proved to be a real test of endurance. Marching through biting wind, rain and blizzard conditions, this was soldiering at its most extreme and some soldiers collapsed with exhaustion, while others suffered from exposure or trench foot as a result.

Monday 31 May. The battalion stopped just short of Estancia House in a lay-up area, while D Company carried out reconnaissance patrols to establish whether any enemy were around. They reported back that no enemy had been observed, and at last light A Company advanced and secured Estancia House.

Tuesday 1 June. All three rifle companies moved up into the mountains, and with the help of the Falkland Islanders' tractors and Land Rovers, tons of supplies were moved to around Estancia House, where 3 PARA HQ was set up.

Thursday 3 June. The battalion began an impromptu 'advance to contact' towards Mount Longdon. On visiting 3 PARA to update them, Liaison Officer Lt Andrew Mills discovered they had left already – he immediately informed the Brigade Commander, who flew forward to make contact with CO Hew Pike to stop the advance.

Friday 11 June. After an extensive reconnaissance by D Company, 3 PARA mounted their assault on Mount Longdon.

3 PARA's route from Port San Carlos to Port Stanley

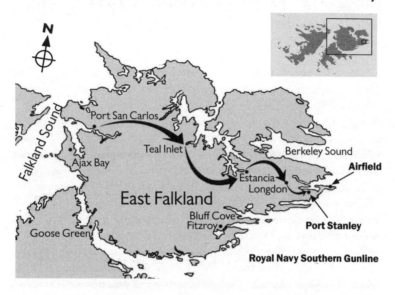

3 PARA's planned H-Hour Company positions

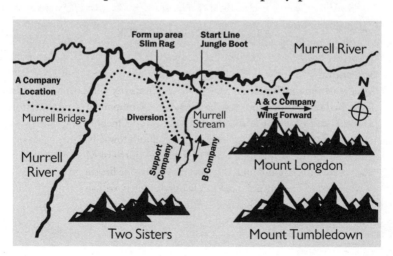

THE BRIGADE PLAN

On Friday 11 June 1982, 3 PARA took part in a three-phase plan to capture Port Stanley:

Phase 1: The capture of Mount Longdon, Two Sisters and Mount Harriet.

Phase 2: The capture of Wireless Ridge, Mount Tumbledown and Mount William.

Phase 3: The capture of Sapper Hill, subsequent phases on order.

Mount Longdon was to be the first objective and would be a silent attack in order to allow 3 PARA to get as close as possible to the objective undetected.

3 PARA PLAN OF ATTACK

A Company

After reaching the 'Battalion Start Line', A Company will wait for the rest of the battalion. Once everyone has arrived, A Company will advance to a 'form-up' area located in dead ground at grid 332764. Once here they will shake out into assault formation and then advance south towards Wing Forward, which is a position approximately 600 metres north of Mount Longdon, where they will clear and hold the ground and provide fire support as needed. In the event of the capture of Mount Longdon, they will advance east with C Company and capture Wireless Ridge (north), codenamed Rum Punch.

B Company

On reaching the Battalion Start Line at grid 314764 they will wait for the remainder of the battalion and then move in a southerly direction following the Furze Bush Stream. When they reach grid 314754, codenamed Jungle Boot, they will turn and face the western flank of Mount Longdon. The company will be positioned along the Start Line running north to south, in this order: 4 Platoon, B Company HQ, 5 Platoon and 6 Platoon.

The three platoons will assault the mountain from west to east.

4 Platoon will be the most northerly platoon, advancing and clearing the low ground to north of Mount Longdon as far as Full Back.

5 Platoon will move centrally, advancing and clearing the northern side of the main ridge as far as Full Back.

6 Platoon will be the most southerly platoon, advancing directly up the western slope, where they will capture and clear Fly Half, then advance and clear and hold Full Back.

C Company

On reaching the Battalion Start Line at grid 314764, they will wait until A Company is in position on Wing Forward, then they will move to a reserve position at grid 330760, just north of A Company. Here the company will be positioned in such a way that it is out of contact, but will remain close enough to be able to react in support of the Battalion Command's plans or contingencies. In the event of the capture of Mount Longdon, they will advance east with A Company and capture Wireless Ridge (north), codenamed Rum Punch.

D Company

During the campaign D Company are the eyes and ears of the battalion, moving ahead of the battalion during the advance across East Falklands. Once the battalion establish its Headquarters at Estancia they will provide all the battalions' information about enemy forces on and about Mount Longdon through extensive close-target reconnaissance. On the night of 11 June 1982 the company will provide guides for the rifle companies and secure the crossing point. If not tasked to accompany the rifle companies, they will be out in OPs or preparing for the following day's reconnaissance tasks.

Support Company

Support Company will be split into two groups. The first group will provide a firebase for B Company; Major Dennison will be positioned at grid 310753, codenamed Free Kick. In this location are three SF (sustained-fire) machine guns and three Milan posts. Also at this location is the primary RAP team with eighteen ammunition-bearers/stretcher-bearers. Positioned north of the main firebase is Captain Mason at grid 320760. He has two SF machine-gun detachments and one Milan post. Positioned south of the main firebase is Sgt Colbeck at grid 310749. He has one SF machine-gun detachment and one Milan post. Support Company will remain flexible and provide fire support where and when required.

The second part of the Support Company group will move as a vehicle convoy and consist of four Volvo BVs (BV202E also known as Snowcats), six tractors and trailers, one tractor with a box, a crawler tractor and sledge, along with nine civilian Land Rovers. This group will bring the mortar ammunition, Milan and GPMG ammunition. However, the vehicle convoy will not be allowed to cross the Murrell Bridge until 45 Commando have crossed their Start Line as, until then, they have priority over the only passable track leading to Mount Longdon from the Murrell Bridge. Also in the vehicle convoy are the secondary RAP team with a doctor, two medics and medical supplies, the Blowpipe Section and 2 Troop 9 Squadron RE. Once the ammunition and supplies are delivered, the Volvo BVs will evacuate any wounded to a medical reception centre set up at Estancia House (codenamed Starlight 2).

HQ Company

The company will provide logistical support, establishing a supply chain. A large number of HQ Company will be attached to the rifle companies to replace personnel suffering from various conditions such as trench foot and exposure.

Mount Longdon Western Slope

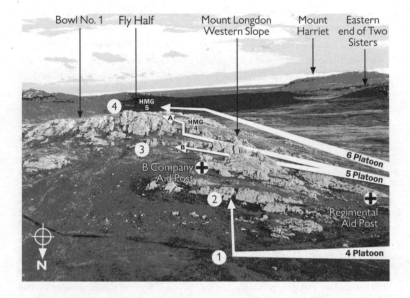

1. As 4 Platoon advance through the minefield, Cpl Brian Milne stands on an anti-personnel mine here.

2. 4 Platoon face incoming fire and make their way to the rock line on the north-west corner for the nearest cover.

3. After 4 Platoon have linked up with 5 Platoon (B) they begin to slowly push east. On reaching this area Lt Andrew Bickerdike is shot.

4. 6 Platoon go firm.

KEY

HMG   Argentinian Heavy Machine Gun Positions

✚   British Aid Posts

Mount Longdon Eastern Slope

5 Cpl Stewart McLaughlin forms a machine-gun line along the line of rocks to support Sgt Ian McKay.

6 From here Sgt Ian McKay leads his impromptu group to attack HMG (heavy machine gun) No 3.

7 The location of Argentine 3 Platoon, the local defence for the HMG situated above.

Mount Longdon Western Approach

This view shows the approach that 4, 5 and 6 Platoon take up the western side of Mount Longdon. When the mine explosion occurs, 5 Platoon rush forward, and in the darkness and confusion they form two separate groups at the rocks which divide routes **2** and **3**.

4 Platoon turn from their intended path towards the rock line on the north-west corner, then make their way across route **1** and link up with 5 Platoon (B) on route **2**.

NOTES FOR THE READER

The time zone used by British Forces throughout the Falklands campaign was Zulu Time. This was Greenwich Mean Time, which is now known as UT (Universal Time); it was four hours ahead of local time in the Falkland Islands. This was done to avoid any confusion between the Task Force and London. This would mean that during the Falklands winter of 1982, sunrise for British Forces was at approximately 10.00hrs Zulu time (zt), which equates to 6.00am local time (lt). Sunset for British Forces was at approximately 20.00hrs Zulu time (zt), which equates to 4.00pm local time (lt).

The Falklands Islands have completely different weather seasons from Great Britain. The main characteristic of the weather is that from being mild and pleasant it can change very rapidly to become cold and severe. Generally, winter begins in earnest in June and lasts until mid-October. It is extremely cold, and regularly falls below freezing. Snow and sub-zero temperatures are experienced to varying degrees, but the most distinguishing climatic factor is the wind. Temperature changes due to wind-chill can occur quickly and catch out those who are ill-prepared or ill-equipped; a gloriously sunny day can rapidly become a sub-zero blizzard.

All radio transmissions are transcribed as they were written by the various units involved. 3 PARA radio log was written at Estancia House.

All text in square brackets during speech are author comments.

A glossary of military terms used throughout the book can be found on page 453.

THE BUILD-UP

'If any of you are religious, this is the time to sit down and have a word with the man upstairs.'

FRIDAY 11 JUNE 1982

6 Platoon's role in the plan is to assault up the western slope of Mount Longdon and capture Fly Half and Full Back. However, in order to reach the objective, they must first cross a minefield that had been identified by D Company 3 PARA and 9 Squadron RE; this is approximately 500 metres in length from grid 322752 to grid 319749 running north to south. The CO stated during the Company Commanders' 'O' Group that, 'Once in the minefield the impetus must be maintained.' Once they have crossed the open ground, they will begin to advance up the western slope, a rocky steep-sided feature with large amounts of loose broken rock.

Situated at the top on Fly Half is the command post of Lt Baldini's 1 Platoon. The western slope measures approximately 300 metres from its base up to Fly Half. At the widest point, it is 80 metres wide. At this end of Mount Longdon, Infantry Marine Officer Lt Sergio Dachary has placed three .50 calibre heavy machine guns under the command of Cpl Carlos Colemil. One of the guns, 'Gun number 5', is located on Fly Half to cover the air threat from the west. The second, 'Gun number 4', is situated approximately 200 metres up from the base on the northern edge of the western slope. This gun covers to the north and north-west, providing anti-aircraft defence from aircraft attempting to fly through the Furze Bush Pass.

The third, 'Gun number 6', is located in 3 Platoon's area on the south-west corner of the mountain and completely out of sight from the western slope. This gun covers the south-west corner and provides air defence from any aircraft attempting to fly through the Moody Brook Valley. This platoon is not engaged at any time during the battle. Among the various bunkers on the western slope are 81mm mortar positions and the bunker of 25-year-old Lt Alberto Ramos, who is acting as Forward Observer Officer for 7th Mechanized Infantry Regiment (7 RI Mech). He has the vital role of directing the Argentine artillery.

At just after last light on Friday 11 June 1982, 3 PARA begins moving out from an assembly area codenamed 'Apple Flake' at grid 265767. The order of march is A Company, Battalion Tactical Headquarters, B Company, Support Company and finally C Company. The vehicle convoy will move to a holding area and wait until called forward. The approach march is a seven-kilometre night march with a river crossing. Once across the river the companies will all head for the Battalion Start Line at grid 314764, where a stream running north to south (the Furze Bush stream) will indicate the Start Line.

Major Mike Argue, 35 yrs – Officer Commanding B Company

The battalion plan had been modified in the light of intelligence, so that we would now attack two companies up and one in reserve. 2 PARA had been brought forward as Brigade reserve. A Company would be positioned on the left and B Company to the right, which would include the main feature of Longdon itself. My orders were to capture Mount Longdon and depending on resistance to exploit as far eastward as possible. Patrol Company NCOs and a local farmer would guide us through the difficult approach to the objective; thereafter it was up to the platoons. We knew that the southern slopes were mined and deliberately avoided that route.

I briefed the whole company together, before they got their detailed orders from Platoon Commanders. This was probably unwise in view of the artillery threat, but I wanted them to really understand what the attack would mean. First of all, mines which may have been strewn about the objective; secondly, the depth of the enemy position we were up against; thirdly, the artillery and mortars the enemy could call upon to bombard us with once we had moved within range, and finally the remoteness of the position from immediate medical assistance for casualties.

An hour before last light, supporting elements from echelon began to close on our position, also locally requisitioned tractors and trailers which would be used for evacuation to safe landing sites. The company shook out into formation and there was just time for a last smoke and check of equipment. We had done this many times in assembly areas on live firing exercises in places as far apart as Canada, Oman and Salisbury Plain. But this time, not everything was the same, as we knew that the targets were capable of shooting back. [Taken from a personal account written by Major Argue]

After Major Argue has spoken to B Company, CSM John Weeks also speaks to the men, trying to encourage and motivate but also explain the grim reality of what lies ahead.

CSM John Weeks, 35 yrs – Company Sergeant Major, B Company

I went up and down the line speaking to the lads, trying to reassure them: 'Listen in, you lot; this is it. It's going to be harder than you lot can imagine, tough hand-to-hand fighting; you're going be moving from trench to trench. If one of your mates is wounded, you must keep fighting through; others will treat him. It is vital that you win the firefight; that is the way you will help your mates. Try to remember all the things you've been taught in training. There's going to be things happening that you have never experienced before: live rounds will be coming at you, explosions, there will be chaos and confusion, but I know you will do well.

'There is the chance that some of you standing here will not be coming back. If any of you are religious, this is the time to sit down and have a word with "the man upstairs". I will be shortly having a quiet moment and saying a little prayer, as tonight we are all in the same boat.'

I was as nervous as them, I had never done anything like this before. Shortly after, I spoke to personal friends, among them LCpl Doc Murdoch. We shook hands and wished each other good luck.

4

Pte Dave Roe, 18 yrs – 2 Section, 6 Platoon

I remember when CSM John Weeks spoke to the company and said, 'For those of you that believe in the man upstairs, now is the time to have a few words.' It really brought home the reality of things.

LCpl Colin Edwards, 24 yrs – 2 Section, 5 Platoon

I stood there listening, and I thought, 'Although Johnny Weeks means well, he's probably terrifying the younger soldiers.'

Pte Grant Grinham, 19 yrs – 2 Section, 5 Platoon

I'd had a good think after CSM Weeks had spoken to the company. I ran through the possible outcomes in my head, and it seemed pretty straightforward; I had three options. I would survive unscathed, and in this case, there was no problem. I would be killed, in which case it was now too late for me to worry about it, although my parents would be upset. I decided they'd come to terms with it eventually, so that would be okay. The last possibility was I would be injured, but again if I survived that was okay too. These three possibilities all seemed okay to me, and it really cleared my head to do whatever was needed later.

I went and found my mate, Harry Harrison in 4 Platoon. I'd known Harry since we were kids and had been in the army cadets together. I'd never imagined back then that we'd find ourselves about to go into battle together, fighting in the same company. I had a few words with Harry; I wished him luck and after that I made my way back to start cooking a last meal before we set off. I asked Cpl McLaughlin what he wanted but he told me not to eat anything in case I got injured during the battle and needed to have an operation.

B Company moves out.

On 11 June 1982 at 17.00hrs (zt), B Company leave their company location; the order of march is 6 Platoon leading, followed by 5 Platoon, then Company HQ, followed by 4 Platoon. The battalion assembly area is at A Company's location and is a four-kilometre march; they will rendezvous there at about 20.00hrs (zt) and later, at approximately 20.30hrs (zt), just after last light, they start a two-kilometre march to the Murrell River, where the entire battalion will cross; once across they then march a further three kilometres to grid 304763. It is here that they realize that they will have to divert from their intended route of march, due to time delays caused by the river crossing and also because some of 5 and 6 Platoons have lost their way for a short while due to a navigation error. They now take a direct line to their Start Line at grid 304763. The Start Line will be indicated by white mine tape that has been marked by elements of D Company 3 PARA.

THE BATTLE

CHAPTER ONE

'CORDITE, BLOOD, SWEAT AND DEATH'

B COMPANY 6 PLATOON

1.1   'Right, guys, let's fucking go!'

FRIDAY 11 JUNE 1982

23.59hrs (zt): from C/S 29 to C/S 9: 'Now at Slim Rag.'

B Company realize that they will have to divert from their intended route of march. One of the platoons has accidentally tagged on to Support Company plus there are time delays crossing the Murrell River. They now take a more direct route to their Start Line at Grid 304763.

Cpl Jimmy Morham, 25 yrs – Anti-Tank Platoon attached to B Company

I commanded a Fire Support Section consisting of me, Pte Stewart Laing and Pte Charlie Hardwick, with their 84mm Carl Gustav; also with us was Cpl Ronnie Cooper, who was a Mortar Fire Controller and Pte Mark Dodsworth, who was a medic. We were attached to 6 Platoon HQ, to be used as required by Lt Shaw for the attack on Mount Longdon. I was carrying nothing but the essentials as we were carrying huge amounts of ammunition. [Also Pte David Furnival and Pte Tony Stott.]

B Company reach their allocated position on the Start Line approximately 20 minutes late. The order to fix bayonets is passed along the company line.

Cpl Jerry Phillips, 22 yrs – D Company Guide

The atmosphere on the Start Line was quite tense. Everyone was deep in thought about the forthcoming attack. It was a bitterly cold night as it was now the height of winter. I remember when the order was given to 'Fix bayonets'. It was a bit unnerving, when you know this is the real thing.

Sapper Sam Robson, 29 yrs – 9 Sqn RE attached to 6 Platoon

When I heard the order to fix bayonets, I thought, 'Fucking hell; this is it!'

SATURDAY 12 JUNE 1982

Major Mike Argue contacts the CO, Hew Pike, telling him that B Company have started their advance:

00.24hrs (zt): from C/S 29 to C/S 9: 'Now at Jungle Boot and moving forward.'

00.30hrs (zt): from C/S 29 to C/S 9: 'Now across Jungle Boot.'

Almost immediately the CO orders A Company to move to their form-up area north of Wing Forward:

00.30hrs (zt): from C/S 9 to C/S 19: 'Call sign 1 move now.'

Pte Dave Roe

The tussock grass was covered in frost and you could see your own breath. As we moved out, I remember it was nearly a full moon, and I felt we were quite exposed.

Pte Morgan Slade, 20 yrs – Anti-Tank Platoon attached to B Company

I was very apprehensive, but our guides had done numerous reconnaissance patrols of Mount Longdon. LCpl Doc Murdoch gave us the order to move and led us off in single file at quite a slow tactical patrol pace.

Cpl Trev Wilson, 25 yrs – 3 Section, 6 Platoon

'Right lads,' I whispered to my section, 'let's keep it together and let's do what we've come here to do.'

Lt Jonathan Shaw, 24 yrs – Commanding Officer, 6 Platoon

My platoon objective was to capture Fly Half. We made our way cautiously towards the main western slope of Mount Longdon. We were led by our D Company guides, Cpl Phillips and LCpl Wright, plus a member of 9 Squadron RE, Sapper Robson, whose job it would be to tackle any obstacles or booby traps.

Pte Simon Clark, 22 yrs – 1 Section, 6 Platoon

We were moving in file at a fairly slow pace at first. There were three or four people in front of me, and our guides were Cpl Phillips and LCpl Wright from D Company.

Pte Julian (Baz) Barrett, 17 yrs – 3 Section, 6 Platoon

Pte Stu Grey stopped in front of me. He gestured for me to come closer. 'We're in a minefield, don't stray. Pass it on.' I didn't really register the implications of the message until I had dutifully passed the message back to Pte Den Dunn, who just grunted on hearing the news.

Although there are many 17-year-olds in B Company, Baz Barrett is the youngest member of the company.

Cpl Jerry Phillips

LCpl Steve Wright and I led the platoon, with Lt Shaw following, then the rest of 6 Platoon behind him. We crossed the open ground to the front of Mount Longdon and I concentrated on taking the correct route up. We went across to the south-west corner, and advanced up the western slope in single file.

Pte Stuart Grey, 19 yrs – 3 Section, 6 Platoon

As we approached the base of Mount Longdon there was a light mist or fog. We later found out that we had bypassed enemy troops asleep in their bunkers. In the dark mass of rocks, you couldn't see where the enemy positions were and so we quietly kept moving up.

Cpl Jerry Phillips

We kept moving up to a point where I would release 6 Platoon to complete their various tasks. I reached the drop-off point and said to Lt Shaw, 'Right, there's the summit. Do you know where you're going from here, are you okay?' He said, 'I'll take it from here.'

Pte Steve Richards, 18 yrs – 2 Section, 6 Platoon

As we moved further up the mountain I noticed my breathing was getting rather heavy. I wasn't sure whether it was the weight of all the ammunition that I was carrying or just the anticipation of what was about to come. I was worried that everyone could hear me.

01.07hrs (zt): from C/S 29 to C/S 9: 'Contact wait-out.'

Lt Jonathan Shaw

We progressed up the hill at a steady pace. It was quite misty, and we couldn't see very much. We managed to get probably about three-quarters of the way up when Cpl Milne stood on a mine.

Pte Phil Simpson, 20 yrs – HQ Company attached to 6 Platoon

There was a small explosion and a scream. I knew the shit had just hit the fan. LCpl Doc Murdoch turned to us and said, 'That's it. Let's go, boys!' We began racing up towards Fly Half, which was only about 20 metres away. As we moved through it and over it we began descending on the eastern slope. Doc Murdoch signalled 'extended line', and we started advancing down the eastern slope.

Cpl Trev Wilson

I said to the lads, 'Right, guys. Let's fucking go!' Now that the mine had gone off and firing was taking place on the northern side, we switched from tactical to non-tactical and the race was on to get to the top as fast as possible. Once we reached Fly Half we advanced straight over. We were approaching the First Bowl; my section was the extreme left section and we had still not been engaged; LCpl Doc Murdoch advanced to the centre, and Cpl John Steggles was extreme right.

Lt Jon Shaw

There was small-arms fire going in all directions, screaming, shouting – absolute bedlam. Cpl Wilson's section came into contact almost immediately on reaching Fly Half. LCpl Doc Murdoch went straight over and seemed to have a clear run down the eastern slope. Cpl Steggles with 2 Section assaulted a .50 calibre heavy machine-gun position around the area of Fly Half. It was chaos.

Pte Steve Richards

We all began to run. I could hear machine-gun fire and small-arms fire. My Section Commander Cpl Steggles shouted, 'Right, 2 Section. Follow me!' There was an enemy position on the top right. We moved in pairs, me and Pte Trevor (Benji) Benjamin, basically skirmishing up the mountain until we reached a bunker with a .50 Cal heavy machine gun. We threw grenades. As soon as they exploded, we jumped in firing, but the position was empty. Cpl Steggles said, 'I know how to use this.' He told us to break out the ammunition, then loaded the gun and swung it around to face east. He started firing. Bright green tracer rounds left the barrel of the gun, and we all opened fire in the direction of the tracer rounds.

This is Cpl Carlos Colemil's heavy machine-gun position (No. 5).

Pte Stuart Grey

The noise was deafening, and everyone seemed to be shouting. There were rounds going in every direction, the Argentines were now alert to us, there were screams and shouting in Spanish. Cpl Trev Wilson was calling out fire-control orders, desperately trying to win the firefight.

Cpl Trev Wilson

One of our machine-gunners Pte Mick Lynch was having a problem with his GPMG. The gun had jammed and he couldn't clear it. LCpl Dave Scott ran forward and tried to clear the stoppage. In the end, Dave stood the gun upright and kicked down on the cocking handle. He then took over the gun and began putting down suppressive fire.

Incoming fire was all around us. Dave Scott and I slowly edged our way forward to the lip of the First Bowl; we were just behind a built-up stone bunker. I was lying next to Dave, who was putting fire into the various Argentine positions to our front. I passed my GPMG ammunition to him and shouted several fire indications – not that he needed any as he was working well, putting fire into the multitude of positions.

LCpl Murdoch's 1 Section is as yet unopposed on the eastern slope.

Pte Kevin Eaton, 19 yrs – 1 Section, 6 Platoon

I was on the extreme left. On the eastern slope, there was no one there, no enemy, no resistance. We continued for about 100 metres and reached an area just beyond the Second Bowl. In the distance, we could see Port Stanley. Behind me, I could hear small-arms fire and screaming. LCpl Doc Murdoch said, 'Right, lads. Stop here.' We all dropped to one knee, and he signalled, 'Get down.' We all lay down across the eastern slope facing the Full Back position. We now began to receive some incoming fire from Full Back. I turned the gas regulator on my GPMG up to three and started firing away.

Pte Morgan Slade

I could hear Cpl Trev Wilson's voice shouting, and I also remember hearing someone yelling, 'They've got Fester [Pte Tony Greenwood]; they've got Fester.' This was followed shortly by, 'Fester's dead.'

Pte Simon Clark

We could hear the sound of heavy contact to our left on the northern side, but for us it was still quiet. I was thinking all the time, 'When are they going to open fire?' We then lay down facing Full Back. It was after that we started receiving small-arms fire from Full Back and we began returning fire at the muzzle flashes.

Pte Phil Simpson

We had now advanced approximately 100 metres when there were muzzle flashes coming from about 300 metres away. Morgan Slade and I opened fire, then Kev Eaton began firing his GPMG. After a short while Doc Murdoch told us to stop firing, as he was on the radio trying to speak to Lt Shaw.

Back on Fly Half.

Pte Julian (Baz) Barrett
The night became a torrent of red and green tracer and flashes of light. It seemed like all the air had gone and there was just noise and a crazy light show raging against the pitch-black sky. The next thing I knew I felt like I had been drilled through the hips, tossed up in the air like a rag doll. It felt like it was happening in slow motion, but when my chin hit the ground it knocked my senses back into my head. I could hear myself screaming. The pain was overwhelming. All I could do was scream my head off. I couldn't move any of my limbs at all and I was starting to panic.

Cpl Trev Wilson
Dave Scott had stopped firing, so I turned to look at him and thought, Fucking hell, he's dead! I shouted over to Pte Harry Gannon, who was also returning fire, 'Harry, get your fucking arse over here! Dave's gone down.' I carried on firing while Harry came crawling across to check Dave.

Pte Harry Gannon, 20 yrs – 3 Section, 6 Platoon
I quickly rolled him over, but it was immediately apparent Dave was dead. I checked him for a pulse and looked for any signs of life, but Dave was definitely dead.

Pte Julian (Baz) Barrett
I could hear voices cutting through the chaos, on my forward right shouting, 'Scotty's dead!' and then, 'Fester's dead.' Den Dunn let me know he was moving forward, but I couldn't give him covering fire. Den came anyway; he ran past me, on towards where Stu disappeared to. He disappeared down into the darkness and within no time at all he had been shot in the shoulder.

Pte Nick Rose, 20 yrs – 3 Section, 6 Platoon
We were taking heavy incoming fire when Pte Tony [Fester] Greenwood shouted to me, 'Nick, stoppage!' I continued firing while Tony cleared his weapon, and then heard Tony continue firing. Shortly after this I called back to Tony, 'Changing mags!' That's when I saw him lying face down over a rock that he'd been using for cover.

Pte Dave Roe

Pte Darren Nichols and Pte Gareth Lewis were to my left when the firing started. We hit the ground, and I shouted, 'It's us, it's us!' because I wasn't sure what was happening. At one stage we jumped into an Argentine shit pit for cover, only to find a dead Argentinian already in there. We rolled him in front of us, using him as a bit of cover as tracer rounds were hitting the ground and ricocheting off in all directions.

Pte Julian (Baz) Barrett

Sgt Pete Gray, Pte Nick Rose and Pte Harry Gannon ran through the fire to treat me. They were really exposed and bloody lucky not to get hit. In an attempt to stifle the heavy enemy fire, Pete Gray, who was right by my head, pulled the pin out of a grenade and rose slightly to throw it. As he did so, he was shot in the wrist. Automatically he let go of the grenade.

Pte Harry Gannon

Pete Gray said, 'The grenade's gone off in my hand and blown it off.' I felt his wrist, and said, 'Your hand is still there, it's okay,' but I thought, Where's the fucking grenade? There was a moment of panic because there was now a rogue grenade about to explode. Luckily, it had rolled down into the First Bowl, then exploded. I then felt up his forearm, and I could feel something sticking out. I said, 'Pete, you've got a big piece of shrapnel sticking out your arm' [It was in fact bone.] I put a couple of shell dressings on his forearm and gave him morphine.

Cpl Trev Wilson

As I passed a gap in the rocks, I was opened fire upon, but wasn't hit. I took cover with Den Dunn, who had been shot in the shoulder. Just to the side of the rock I was taking cover behind, I could see human breath on the cold night air. I turned to Den and said, 'There's someone behind this fucking rock. We're going to have to sort these fucking blokes out. Brace yourself.' I pulled the pin and tossed the grenade, but it struck a rock, bounced and exploded short of its intended target. A small piece of shrapnel caught me in my right hand, causing me to curse. Den asked, 'Are you okay to throw another one, Trev?' I said, 'Fucking right I am!' I tossed another one around the corner, which exploded. Immediately I heard a groan and saw in the cold night air a large exhale of breath.

Cpl Jimmy Morham

Lt Shaw was trying to find out what was happening. We received some tracer fire from our rear coming from the southern side of the western slope; we returned fire into the position and it never fired back again. Cpl Ronnie Cooper, our MFC [mortar-fire controller], said, 'Jimmy, that was a mine explosion; someone has stood on a mine.' Just then someone shouted, 'Dodsworth, you're needed up the top!' Mark immediately began running forward with his huge Bergen full of medical supplies. His Bergen was so large it got wedged between the rocks and I had to give him a push, saying, 'Come on, Dodsy, get your arse through there, mate!'

1.2   'I don't want anyone one else going forward; it's just too fucking dangerous!'

01.28hrs (zt): from C/S 29 to C/S 9: 'All call signs in contact, but making good progress for Full Back.'

Pte Steve Richards

I heard Lt Shaw shouting over to us to stop firing the .50 Cal. He shouted, 'Stop firing that fucking gun, it's drawing fire.' He was right: a heavy volley of green tracer came down on our position. Pte Mark Dodsworth brushed by me as rounds seemed to be flying everywhere and people were screaming from both sides. Suddenly Mark Dodsworth was thrown backwards between Benji and me as a number of rounds hit him. I tried to find his wounds but couldn't work my way through his multiple layers of clothing. I found his morphine and jabbed the Syrette into his leg.

Pte Dave Roe

Pte Mark Dodsworth had been very badly wounded. I remember him telling us to 'Elevate, elevate my legs!' We couldn't take him down to the aid post at this stage as we were under a tremendous weight of fire, but Mark was still talking. I was on his left-hand side and I was trying to comfort him, but there was tracer going all over the place.

LCpl Steve Wright, 22 yrs – D Company Guide

Cpl Phillips and I started moving up towards Fly Half. Jerry and I skirmished up towards Fly Half firing the odd couple of rounds, and when we reached the top we found an unoccupied stone bunker. It was really chaotic, there were people running about, just black figures. Then a member of 6 Platoon came across to us and asked if we could help. Jerry and I now decided to separate; I crawled over onto the eastern slope with this member of 6 Platoon to try to help a number of the wounded on the forward edge of Fly Half.

Pte Steve Richards

I knew that a shell dressing held around a pint of blood and the one I had applied to Mark filled up within minutes. Dave Roe was now with us, and he was talking to Mark Dodsworth, trying to reassure him and hold his hand. Suddenly Jerry Phillips appeared. All the time this was going on there were rounds bouncing off the rocks all around us.

Lt Jonathan Shaw

I came across a group of soldiers around our company medic, Pte Dodsworth. I remember he was saying, 'I'm cold, I'm cold.' By now I had lost sight of 1 Section; they had gone out of my line of sight, so I got on the radio to LCpl Murdoch and said, 'I want you to bring your section back to my location right away.'

We now continue with 1 Section located approximately 100 metres east of Fly Half:

Pte Phil Simpson

Word got passed to me that we were now going to move back to Fly Half. We just got up and started withdrawing back the way we'd come, in extended line.

Pte Kevin Eaton

We began skirmishing up the eastern slope heading towards Fly Half. As we moved forward, we were aware of gunfire and shouting to our front, but no one was actually shooting at us, and we still hadn't seen any Argentines. We began to call out, '1 Section coming in!' The next thing I remember I was flying through the air; I had been shot in the top of my left leg.

Pte Simon Clark
On my right, Doc Murdoch had dropped down low. I shouted, 'Doc, what's up?' He replied, 'Kev Eaton's been hit.'

Pte Phil Simpson
Privates Morgan Slade, Bryn Cowley, Michael [Mushrooms] Bateman and I dropped into a shallow piece of cover on the southern side of the eastern slope, virtually opposite Kev Eaton, and began firing at any green muzzle flashes.

Pte Kevin Eaton
Doc Murdoch heard me cry out. I was lying at the side of a clump of rocks by the First Bowl, about 40 metres from Fly Half. He dropped to his knees and asked, 'Where've you been hit?' He began to take a shell dressing out of its wrapper when a round clipped him on the hand. He cried out and shook his hand and whispered, 'The wee bastards,' but continued to apply the dressing to my thigh.

Pte Simon Clark
As I reached Doc Murdoch, he was putting a shell dressing on Kev Eaton. I moved over to a gap in the rocks for some extra cover, but Doc said, 'Don't go there, I think that's where Kev got shot from.' Doc was on his knees, dealing with Kev, when suddenly he was shot in the head.

Pte Kevin Eaton
I remember Doc saying to Simon, something like, 'Clarkie, watch yourself; I think Kev got shot from that direction.' Then he murmured, 'Ah,' and slumped across me and rolled off. Doc groaned, 'Oh my eyes, my eyes, I can't see, oh mother help me!'

Pte Simon Clark
After Doc had been shot, he began asking for his mother. I crawled closer into the rock, and then about a minute later I was also shot. I was thinking, what

next? After about five or ten minutes, Doc stopped asking for his mother. The moment Doc Murdoch was shot, his mind was not on Longdon: he was somewhere else, in his childhood maybe. I truly believe Doc passed away in his own world peacefully; it was absolutely heartbreaking.

Pte Simon Clark

I now had my ankle, tibia and fibula shattered and was in a great deal of pain. I manoeuvred myself into a position keeping as low as possible. I tried to raise my damaged leg slightly, to elevate the wound as I had been trained, whilst all the time being shot at by the sniper or snipers who had now hit all three of us.

Pte Kevin Eaton

We were desperate to get out of this area but were unable to move as the rounds were striking the rocks extremely close to us. This man definitely wanted to kill us all.

Pte Phil Simpson

I could hear Kev Eaton shouting to me, 'I'm over here, Geordie, I've been hit.' I said, 'Kev, I'd help you, but I can't move myself, we're pinned down.' Pte Michael [Mushrooms] Bateman called over to me, 'There's a sniper out there.' I said, 'Well keep your fucking head down!' Mushrooms shouted back, 'I think I can see where the sniper is firing from, I'm going to try to hit him with a 66mm.' I said, 'Okay, but be careful.' Mushrooms extended the 66mm, got up on one knee, fired, and then dropped back into cover. There was an explosion. The sniper seemed to have been silenced. Mushrooms ran across to Kev, Doc and Simon. He got to within a metre of them when a round struck him in the throat.

Pte Kevin Eaton

Mushrooms fell just by the side of me. In the darkness, I thought that he had been shot in the chest because of the noises coming from him. He was lying on his back gurgling. I thought, I had better turn him on his side as it may help him with his breathing, or he might drown in his own blood.

Back on Fly Half.

Lt Jonathan Shaw

I called for anti-tank support in the shape of Cpl Jimmy Morham's team, and Pte Tony Stott and his No.2, Pte Dave Furnival.

Cpl Jimmy Morham

Very shortly after Mark Dodsworth had left us there was a call for the anti-tank team. Pte Stewart Laing, Pte Charlie Hardwick and I began running through the rocks onto Fly Half and crawled down the forward slope. The whole area was under intense enemy fire. We had broken into the enemy company defensive position and were now being engaged from almost 360 degrees, from positions in depth, and along the ridge. As I crawled forward I vaguely remember seeing Mark Dodsworth. Then we came across Dave Scott's body, and Stewart Laing said to Charlie Hardwick, 'Right, Charlie, strip his ammo.'

Pte Charlie Hardwick, 18 yrs – Anti-Tank Platoon attached to B Company

I began searching through Dave's Scott's smock. I could feel his body was still warm, and I then heard someone over on our left shout, 'Pete Gray has been shot.' I thought, 'Fucking hell! We're a bit fucking exposed out here.'

Cpl Jimmy Morham

We took cover behind the world's smallest rock on the forward edge. On our left and below us were the remnants of Cpl Trev Wilson's section: Nick Rose, Harry Gannon and Mick Lynch, they were all still firing away. Cpl John Steggles' section were also putting fire down. We were receiving fire from the First Bowl and along the ridge of the mountain and from Full Back. Members of 6 Platoon were trying to give target indications. What was evident was that a lot of the enemy were very near: a number of the anti-tank rounds we fired at them did not explode, because we were just too close. Throughout, incoming tracer was searching us out. Being on a forward slope, we were in full view of the enemy.

Cpl Jerry Phillips

I could hear Stewart Laing's voice calling out fire drills for the 84mm. Charlie Hardwick, Stewart Laing and Jimmy Morham were firing rounds like they were going out of fashion.

LCpl Steve Wright

There was a group of maybe four or five snipers – or just Argentines with very good night sights – that were taking pot shots at everything that moved. The wounded lay just in front of our position, protected by some rocks that were about two feet high. I decided to try crawling across to them, and somehow drag the wounded back to the cover of the rocks up on Fly Half. I was with a 6 Platoon bloke who knew exactly where the wounded were, and I would follow his lead.

We had gone about three-quarters of the way across, when suddenly a round hit me in my right arm, passing straight through my bicep, shattering my humerus in three places. I was trying to compose myself, expecting a second round at any moment. I instinctively continued crawling, supporting myself with my left arm. My right arm felt like it was on fire, with what I thought was the stump digging into the ground every time I put it down on the ground. Once we had reached cover, I felt along my arm to see if my hand was still there; thankfully it was.

The group I was with, I now know was Dennis Dunn, Stuart Grey and another member of 6 Platoon. There were rounds bouncing off the rocks that we were hiding behind. While I was lying there, I could hear Stewart Laing's voice, as he had a very distinctive Geordie accent, and I knew him quite well. He seemed to know where the sniper was and began firing his 84mm at the position, but due to the excellent cover that the rocks gave, he couldn't get him.

Cpl Jimmy Morham

I heard someone from 1 Section shouting, 'It's 1 Section coming in.' I then distinctly remember seeing muzzle flashes that were really close, and someone calling out, 'I'm hit, I'm hit.' We now had wounded to our front, we didn't know where in the pitch dark, but we could hear them. I heard Pte Baz Barrett shouting, 'I've been hit, and I can't fucking move!' Other voices were shouting back, 'Baz, keep quiet!' 'Baz, just hang in there!' It was a fucking nightmare. I shouted back, 'Don't worry, we're going to get you out – just stay calm and keep your head down.' But due to enemy fire it was impossible. I ran back to Platoon HQ, a few yards behind us in the rocks. I said to Lt Shaw, 'Right, what are we going to do?' He said, 'We're going firm; we are not going any further forward.'

Pte Charlie Hardwick

I remember Cpl Jimmy Morham returning; he knew that Michael Bateman and others had been wounded. Stewart Laing said, 'Right, we'll have to go out and get them.' Geordie stripped off his webbing, turned to me and said, 'Charlie, give me covering fire'. Before you knew it, he was off running into the darkness, and within seconds we heard a shot. Geordie fell down wounded, followed shortly by another shot.

Pte Phil Simpson

I heard some British voices to my left – I recognized one of them as Stewart Laing and shouted, 'Stew, watch yourself; they're fucking good, they've just shot Mushrooms.' I then heard them talking about how they were going to try to reach the wounded, and I shouted, 'Hang on a moment, Stew, and we'll give you covering fire.' However, we weren't in a position to give covering fire at that precise moment, and then suddenly Geordie ran out.

Pte Morgan Slade

We were about 40 metres from Fly Half on the southern side of the eastern slope, not far from the four wounded men who were almost opposite us, about 30 metres away on the northern side of the eastern slope. Then Stewart Laing appeared running downward from Fly Half. We warned him not to go forward as it was just too dangerous, but his only concern was for his mates. He had nearly reached them when a shot rang out. I can still hear the noise of it, to this very day.

Lt Jonathan Shaw

I shouted, 'That's it; you lot, just stay where you fucking are! I don't want anyone one else going forward; it's just too fucking dangerous!'

1.3   'We cannot go forward, and we cannot pull back'

01.50hrs (zt): from C/S 29 to C/S 9: 'Call sign 2/3 has several casualties, enemy still firing from high ground, and still advancing and clearing.'

Pte Kevin Eaton
Stewart Laing fell almost by my feet. I tried to reach out to pull him in, but every time I reached out the sniper fired.

At approximately 02.00hrs (zt), 42 Commando cross their Start Line and begin their assault on Mount Harriet and Goat Ridge.

02.00hrs (zt): from C/S 0 to C/S 99: 'Situation report from Forward Officer Commanding Mount Longdon, casualties taken, warn off Hawkeye [Wessex helicopter] for later on.' (Possibly three seriously)

The comment in brackets is as it was written in the radio log.

Cpl Jerry Phillips
I was now lying alongside Lt Shaw, trying to take out the sniper. His use of fire and movement and the rocky terrain provided very good cover for him. Then Cpl Trev Wilson asked me if I had any morphine. Fortunately, I had searched Mark Dodsworth's Bergen earlier for medical supplies and had found a case of morphine Syrettes. I said, 'Here you go, Trev, here's a boxful.'

At approximately 02.00hrs (zt), intense machine-gun fire is coming from a position on the northern side just below Fly Half. 6 Platoon are completely unaware of any problems that 4 Platoon may be having. Then a member of 6 Platoon decides, in his words, 'to shut the noisy bastard up'. He drops a white phosphorus grenade in among the machine-gun crew.

LCpl Steve Wright
I remember seeing the white light of an explosion and then someone running about screaming his head off. A voice shouted, 'Fucking shoot him! Put him out of his misery.' After that it all went quiet. I reached into my smock and pulled

out a grenade. I could only use my left hand so I tried to pull the pin out with my teeth and found that I couldn't do it, so I got one of the lads to pull it for me. I then tossed it over into the First Bowl, as I could hear Spanish voices talking, but I don't think I managed to throw it that far, as I felt some of the blast on my legs as it exploded. I then administered my own morphine. We were stuck and would have to stay here.

When asked about the following incident, Lt Jonathan Shaw had no knowledge of it. But this is not surprising due to the darkness and the chaotic nature of a night battle.

Cpl Jerry Phillips
I was trying to locate the sniper when suddenly a white phosphorus grenade exploded off to my left, and then an Argentinian came staggering in, stumbling and screaming – he was completely ablaze, and lighting the whole area up, much to everyone's alarm. He was in intense pain and screaming. Another Argentinian came running past me, so I tackled him, and said, 'Come here, you cunt.' He lashed out at me and I started punching him. He spoke English, and started babbling, 'I surrender, I surrender.' There was another prisoner that someone else had taken hold of: an idea was hatched that if one of the prisoners went forward and spoke to his colleagues they could somehow arrange a truce, and then both sides could recover their wounded. The first prisoner went forward into the darkness and never came back. Then my prisoner went forward with his hands in the air and shouting in Spanish. He fell over, turned around and ran back.

Pte Kevin Eaton
Out of the blue an Argentinian appeared without a weapon. I pointed to Stewart Laing and gestured for him to pick Stewart up. The Argentinian bent down to pick Stewart up, but two rounds were fired and he dropped dead in a heap next to Stewart.

Pte Charlie Hardwick
As the first Argentine made his way gingerly towards Stewart Laing, he was shot and killed. A second one went forward, calling out in Spanish but didn't get that far. A couple of shots were fired and he ran back to our position.

Cpl Carlos Colemil, Argentine marine, in charge of HMG Nos 4 / 5 / 6

After the alarm was raised, I went with two conscripts to our gun [HMG No. 5]; I heard gunfire and also heard a 12.7mm being fired. The enemy troops had overrun our positions and occupied the rocky areas immediately north and south of my position. I had by now lost contact with both crews soon after the battle started [HMG Gun No. 4 and HMG No. 6]. We had received orders before the battle that in case of being overrun, the .50 Cal must be destroyed and the three gun crews would then become riflemen for further actions.

We were now in the midst of enemy troops, and I concluded that if we are to continue fighting, we must first get out of here alive; we had no other option. The other gun-crew gun [HMG No. 4] had still not relocated with our section, so our force was now reduced to only one section. I could not have imagined that we would leave our gun [HMG No. 5], but it was the only logical thing to do for our safety, to get out of this place and find another area from which to continue the fight.

Appreciating that there were enemy troops in the area, I ordered the conscripts to become riflemen as planned and to follow me as closely as possible. Crawling slowly, we left our position; the heat of battle was felt everywhere, but none directed at us. Conscripts Alfredo Cardozo and Daniel Ferrandis followed me, but the other two [Luis Angel Leiva and Gerardo Ferreyra] were delayed, and we lost contact.

We began moving to the area of the 105mm recoilless gun where there were firing positions that had been dug into the ground and rocks that would provide cover. This was a prearranged meeting point, and we would wait prior to the initiation of any withdrawal.

On reaching the pre-planned position at the 105mm recoilless gun we spread out on the ground so we would provide mutual support, and contact was made by shouting loudly. We had another fallback position with Cpl Lamas at [HMG No. 3] situated in the Third Bowl, but crawling across 200 metres of no-man's land would be a dangerous thing to do.

We had lost the head-mounted night sight, and I had an M-2 FAL rifle which fires in bursts. I also had a Litton night sight, nine full magazines and about

400 rounds in a backpack. The conscripts were similarly armed, except for S/C62 Puerto Leiva; he was unarmed.

The first targets I acquired were at the top of the mountain.

A British soldier climbed over the rock which supported the accommodation bunker of the 105mm gun crew, and from here he was silhouetted. He screamed like he was giving out orders, I aimed and fired and he fell, then Conscript Ferrandis alerted me to the approach of three British soldiers on the flank. I observed with the night sight they were very close. I saw one of them was carrying a gun with bipod; he fell at the first shot and shouted. Another man approached him and I fired again and also got him.

So far, I had remained static in the same place, which would later be an error; we should have moved. The conscripts by not having night sights were firing at the silhouettes that were outlined.

Now the action became focused on the rocky area immediately north of my position. About 30 metres from me was a depression [First Bowl] in which was the HQ of Sub Lt Baldini; he had set up a tented area housing some 15 men. The enemy based on the summit constantly attacked the tents, and for this reason two or three men moved down to the tents and riddled them with gunfire and returned to the security of where they came from. Focusing on this area, my main action was against targets of opportunity. I was firing at them from a distance of 10 to 15 metres from which it was impossible to miss.

Many people fell to the ground screaming, but soon the enemy was aware of my presence and every time I fired a shot I received a great deal of fire in response. Not long after my main action I was wounded. I should not have stayed in the same place and I appreciate that now. When I poked my head above the parapet to return fire, I got hit. A round pierced my helmet – luckily it absorbed the force of the impact. My scalp opened from the centre of my forehead almost to the back of my head, my helmet flew off on impact and I did not find it again. I lost my rifle and went instinctively to the other side of the position, where I stayed for a while. I tried to find the rifle but did not find it. I looked and finally I touched someone. I tried to lift him, but he was heavy. I felt something warm running down his face, thereby discovering he was also wounded and had no helmet. I touched my own head and I felt burning, but no pain.

We could also hear the cries for help from the Rasit radar operator Sgt Roque Nista, who was wounded. I could hear Sgt Cabral, who was a sniper – he was also firing; I could hear Argentine machine-gun fire, and I could hear HMG No. 3 firing to the north [Wing Forward], but of HMG No. 6 and HMG No. 4, I now heard nothing.

There was the intense and constant noise of gunfire and great confusion. The enemy was moving among the rocks in groups of two or three men, appearing at times and then disappearing; their movements crossed, some moving and others falling back. At first there was an intense noise of combat, of machine guns; then Sterling SMG decreased and rifle fire increasingly took its place. I took aim with the sight and put the weapon on automatic and I fired a full magazine. I looked back and there was no one there, perhaps some of them were killed or wounded in that position.*

Cpl Jimmy Morham

We were desperate for some night-vision sights and I bobbed and weaved back to platoon HQ. Cpl Jerry Phillips and others were there treating some of our casualties. I borrowed Jerry's L42 sniper rifle because it was fitted with an IWS night sight and then ran back across to Charlie [Hardwick]. I now tried to engage positions using Charlie as my spotter. I would allow them to get a couple of shots off, so that I could pinpoint them, before putting one into them.

Pte Charlie Hardwick

We also fired quite a number of 84[mm] rounds. I had brought six and we had been given more while we were up there, plus a couple of 66mm which we had fired at various targets in the First Bowl and the rocks above it. We also fired down towards the Second and Third Bowls, and threw a number of grenades. We were attracting quite a bit of fire, but by now we had found a decent bit of cover.

---

* From *La 2ª Sección en Longdon* 'The 2nd Platoon on Longdon' by Lt Sergio Dachary, Marine Infantry ARA, commanding officer of the Marine Infantry Heavy Machine Gun Detachment on Mount Longdon. The order in which it was written has been rearranged to make the sequence of events clear.

Cpl Jimmy Morham

We made contact again with Baz Barrett, who said, 'I've been shot in the arse!' He could hear weapons being cocked, and shouted across to us, 'There's a bunker near me.' I said to him, 'Throw a grenade at it.' I was thinking, even if he didn't get it, the momentary flash might indicate the position. He threw a grenade and we saw the bunker in the flash; I loaded up the 84mm, but I couldn't get a sight picture in the dark and I said to Charlie, 'I can't see fuck all.' I took the scope off the 84mm and tried using the iron sights, but I still couldn't make it out with the iron sights. I folded the iron sights back along the barrel, knelt up and aimed using a simple alignment along the side of the barrel with the target. Unfortunately the round went just over the top.

Charlie loaded another round; we moved slightly to the right and popped up again and fired. It hit the bunker smack on, but did not explode – it went straight through and out the other side. The following day, I checked the bunker and found that the round had gone through the wall of the bunker and had exited through the doorway.

I heard shouting from 5 Platoon, who had by now battled their way up the feature. I am sure it was Cpl Skidmore I was shouting to. He shouted back that they thought they could see a sniper and to get our heads down as they were going to fire at him, but when they opened fire it fell into our area, and I was shouting, 'Fuckin' stop firing; it's us!'

The time is now approximately 02.30hrs (zt). Elements of 5 Platoon are on the western slope and have set up a small firebase on Fly Half with a couple of GPMGs in the light role plus a number of riflemen; they are returning fire.

B Company HQ have also arrived on the western slope: HQ Group included: Major Mike Argue; Captain Adrian Logan; CSM Johnny Weeks; Sgt Johnny Pettinger (D Coy guide); Sgt Des Fuller; Cpl Scotty Wilson (9 Sqn); Pte Duncan Daly (radio operator); Pte Martyn Clarkson-Kearsley; Pte Clifton Lewis; Pte Mark Harding (radio operator); Pte Mick O'Brien; Pte Dave Mellors; Pte Dickie Absolon (D Coy sniper) and others.

Lt Jonathan Shaw

I sent a message to Major Argue saying, 'We cannot go forward, and we cannot pull back. I will hold the position at the top of the hill, sort out my casualties and go firm here.' I then sent some members of 6 Platoon to look for anything that we could use to keep the wounded warm.

Pte Steve Richards

I was still with Mark Dodsworth when someone told me to go and find B Company HQ and locate a medic. I remember seeing CSM John Weeks and Major Argue. I told him we needed a medic, but he said they had all been deployed. I began to make my way back when Jerry Phillips appeared with an Argentine prisoner. He asked me to give him a hand as he was on his own and had found a group of Argentines. We made our way down the western slope, along with Gareth Lewis and a bloke from the Pay Corps [Cpl Victor MacDonald Evans].

Just over halfway down the slope, Jerry shouted, 'Stop!' He knelt down and opened fire. I followed his lead and we manoeuvred towards what I thought were rocky features but were actually bunkers. We made our way to the entrance of one and stood either side. I flipped open my pouch and pulled out two grenades. We both pulled the pins out, threw the grenades into the bunker and waited until the grenades exploded. Then Jerry stormed into the bunker. He must have only been in for a few seconds, but it seemed like ages. He came back out and shouted, 'Clear!'

Further down the hill, we came across another bunker. Again, we grenaded it, but this time Jerry rushed in too quickly and caught some of the back blast. It threw him backwards. I could swear he was chuckling to himself. We worked our way further down and could hear shouting in Spanish from our right and behind. We saw an Argentinian coming out of a bunker with his hands in the air; he seemed to be unarmed, so we ran towards him and dragged him to the ground. I sat astride the Argentinian, as I tried to search him. He started to panic and was thrusting his hands up at me, trying to give me his rosary beads or pray. I couldn't carry out a search while he was doing this, so I punched him in the face to subdue him, and he went silent. He seemed to now accept his fate.

We moved on to another bunker and our first Argentine prisoner began talking down into it. We heard a group discussion coming from in the ground. I only had one grenade left, and there were boxes of mortar ammunition stacked around us, so I couldn't toss it in. They didn't want to come out. A few were poked with bayonets. Jerry grabbed a few and shouted, 'Come on, you cunts, get out.' Some of the Argentines took offence. Punches were thrown and shots were fired. It all went a bit chaotic for a moment. Order was restored and we now had about five or six of them.

We came across a couple of tents and again our Argentine prisoner shouted over to them. They crawled out and put their hands up. By now we had about 15 prisoners. Someone spotted an Argentine hiding in a trench. He was quickly dragged out and pushed to the floor. A couple of the Toms frisked him and told him to roll over so they could search him from behind. One of the Toms found a pistol stuck down the back of the prisoner's trousers and said to Jerry, 'Look what this fucker's got, the cheeky bastard!'

Eventually, Jerry and our motley crew lined the prisoners up. We took them to the RAP area and left them with some members of HQ Company. We then went back up to Fly Half. Some members of Support Company had now begun to arrive. They were setting up a Milan post and SF machine guns.

Pte Gareth Lewis

At some stage we began clearing bunkers on the western slope. We went to one bunker and shouted for them to come out. One Argentine came out, and said there was someone else in there. We told his friend, 'Tell him to come out. We're not going to fuck about here, we're going to throw a grenade in.' He still wouldn't come out, so we threw a grenade. There was an explosion, loads of dust and shit flew out of the bunker. We moved on to the next.

Lt Jonathan Shaw

I started wondering where the men were that I had sent for blankets. Eventually they turned up and I said, 'You took your time, where've you been?' They said, 'Well, Sir, there's loads of the enemy down there. We've been rounding them up.' It was then that I began to realize that we had missed a load of bunkers on our way up the mountain.

Cpl Jimmy Morham

I remember thinking about the bunkers the next morning. How the fuck did we miss them?

On the southern side of the eastern slope Pte Morgan Slade, Pte Bryn Cowley and Pte Phil Simpson are still pinned down by Argentine fire.

Pte Phil Simpson

We could hear Argentine voices behind us. Bryn Cowley said, 'Shall we try moving backwards and getting back around the southern side?' 'Are you fucking stupid?' I said. 'There's fucking Argies everywhere!'

Pte Morgan Slade

At one stage I saw five or six Argentines running out of the Second Bowl, across the eastern slope and down the southern side of Mount Longdon. We didn't open fire as they were running away and had their backs to us. This was a time when I thought, What the fuck am I doing here? I decided to eat some of my rock-hard AB biscuits [Army Biscuits, or as we called them, Airborne Biscuits] since there was not much else we could do. A constant stream of automatic fire was aimed at us, the rounds just clearing the ridge above our heads. As I sat watching the tracer fading out into the distance, it looked like something out of *Star Wars*.

Pte Phil Simpson

We were stuck. I am not sure how long we were there, when I said, 'We can't just lie here; we have to try to make a run for it.' Just as we broke cover an Argentine flare went up. We ran as fast as we could up to Fly Half shouting, '1 Section coming in.'

Pte Morgan Slade

We braced ourselves, then began to sprint over the rocky ground up to Fly Half. A Schermuly [illumination rocket] went up, which may have dazzled the Argentines. Luckily the three of us made it back safely and met up with 6 Platoon HQ. Lt Jon Shaw asked, 'Where's the rest of 1 Section?' and I replied, 'Sir, this is it! We are 1 Section.'

Pte Phil Simpson

The first person I met was Cpl Trev Wilson, who said, 'Dave Scott and Tony Greenwood have been killed.' I was gutted. They were from the MT Platoon and, like me, were only attached to 6 Platoon. As I bent down to tie my boot lace, there was a terrific explosion and I was blown off my feet. I was shaken up, and my head was ringing for about 15 minutes. I remember hearing Captain Willie McCracken [Naval Gunfire Forward Observer Officer] giving fire-control orders, and I remember seeing the CO and Tac HQ turning up. They walked across Fly Half like there wasn't a problem. I thought, What the fuck are you doing?

Major Dennison and CSM Thor Caithness arrive, bringing the main foot element of Support Company. Sgt Chris Howard, Sgt Graham Colbeck, and Cpl Bert Oliver from the Anti-Tanks are setting up a Milan post. Cpl Peter Thompson and LCpl Mark Rawlings are on Fly Half firing their SF machine gun. Shortly after Support Company arrived the CO's Tactical HQ turn up, including the Commanding Officer Hew Pike; RSM Lawrie Ashbridge; Captain Kevin McGimpsey, Adjutant; Acting Captain Giles Orpen-Smellie, the Intelligence Officer; CO's bodyguard Sgt Ray Butters, Major John Patrick, RA Battery Commander; Cpl John Sibley, medic, LCpl Daryle Bunkle, radio operator; LCpl Alan (Jock) Begg, CO's radio operator; Tac HQ's protection team of Captain Matthew Selfridge, CSM Ernie Rustill and LCpl Stephen (Benny) Bentall, plus others.

Pte Morgan Slade

I saw Lt Col Hew Pike and someone else walk calmly by my position, as though nothing was happening. I thought, Perhaps I should tell them that there was enemy out there, but they were moving too quickly and had disappeared into the darkness.

Pte Charlie Hardwick

I saw movement to my front. I wasn't sure whether they were Argentines or not, but as they got closer I could hear English voices. 'You stupid bastards,' I shouted out, 'get your fucking heads down!' It turned out to be the CO, Hew Pike, who had gone forward to see what the hold-up was. Fucking hell, I thought. Good job I never shot him.

Pte Julian (Baz) Barrett

The CO arrived in front of Fly Half, out in the open. Although the battle had lulled to a degree, it still wasn't a safe place to be. He asked if I had seen Major Argue. I said, 'Sir, get down, there are snipers out there, everyone here has been shot.' In quite strong terms he told me to mind my own business. The CO was more concerned with the whereabouts of Major Argue and the momentum of the attack.

Cpl Jerry Phillips

We started to treat and evacuate our wounded. A few of us went to carry Mark Dodsworth, but he was too heavy. I shouted to Harry Gannon and a few others to give me a hand. We picked him up and took him to an aid post that had by now been established just behind some rocks, near the top of the western slope. One of the medics with Tac HQ, Cpl John Sibley, took him off us. Later, this area would be where the CO and Major Argue planned their next move.

Pte Julian (Baz) Barrett

Fly Half was turning into a strong fire position, with Support Company adding weight to the firefight. The Anti-Tank and Machine Gun Platoon detachments, along with others, congregated up there to put as much firepower down as possible. The Argentines consistently replied with their own firepower display just as intense as ours, with many of the rounds falling in and around my area. I was totally pissed off by this and blamed our blokes for annoying them. This wasn't received too well. I was told to shut up.

Cpl Jimmy Morham

The Machine Guns arrived and one detachment began setting up. I warned them that we had casualties out to the front and to be careful. We had just fired our last 84mm round when Captain Matt Selfridge came crawling down and said, 'What's happening?' He gave me a 66mm and then crawled back to update the CO. Shortly after, I decided to use the 66mm. I noticed someone passing on my right side going forward. I shouted, 'Fucking get back!' It turned out to be the CO and Tac HQ coming to see what the hold-up was. He was then on the forward edge of the battle. They quickly took our advice and pulled back. Shortly after this, two Milan missile rounds were fired over the top of us.

Pte Kevin Eaton

Sgt Chris Howard shouted to throw our grenades into the First Bowl, as we could hear Spanish voices. Even though Mushrooms was severely wounded, he managed to pass across his L2 grenades. I said to Simon Clark, 'Make sure these clear the rocks or we're fucked.' It was quite a difficult thing to do while lying down. We took turns throwing about eight grenades. There wasn't much else we could do, as all the time we were being sniped at.

Pte Charlie Hardwick

My leg had strayed out from behind my piece of cover and almost immediately a shot rang out, only just missing me. Eventually the incoming fire began to lessen. I noticed some of 6 Platoon [Steve Richards, Dave Roe and RSM Lawrie Ashbridge] moving with one of the wounded blokes [Mark Dodsworth]. They were struggling a bit, so I went over to help. During the move to the RAP, I somehow lost my weapon. Once we had left him with the medics, I immediately went back up the mountain, but without a weapon, which left me a little concerned.

Support Company informs the CO that they now have located four of 6 Platoon's wounded: LCpl Steve Wright, Pte Mark Dodsworth, Pte Stuart Grey and Pte Dennis Dunn:

03.20hrs (zt): from C/S 59 to C/S 9: 'Four casualties taken by call sign 59 stretcher party.'

Pte Stuart Grey

We were absolutely freezing and were discussing whether we should try to make a run for it. I decided that I would try first. I picked myself up and began to run slowly uphill. A burst of machine-gun fire fell just to my left and I dropped to the floor, waited for a moment before running into the cover of the rocks on Fly Half. As I moved down onto the western slope I came across the Battalion Tac HQ. One of them asked if I was okay. By now I was physically and mentally exhausted. I made my way down to the RAP where I was checked over by Dr John Burgess. Shortly after I arrived Den Dunn and Steve Wright came into the aid post and were treated by Sgt Steve Bradley and Pte John Kennedy. Alongside us in the RAP was Mark Dodsworth, who was unconscious.

LCpl Steve Wright

I decided to make a run back up to Fly Half. I took a few steps and fell over; I picked myself up and staggered up to safety. I was met by John Sibley, who put a shell dressing on my injury over the top of my smock and then put my lower arm inside the smock for support. He gave me a cigarette even though I don't smoke. I smoked it, and then someone led me down the western slope into the Regimental Aid Post area.

The CO has still not located Major Argue:

03.30hrs (zt): from C/S 9 to C/S 29: 'Can you assess the situation?'

Major Argue replies to the CO:

03.30hrs (zt): from C/S 29 to C/S 9: 'Roger, I am now with call sign 2/3 [6 Platoon]. There are a few well-sited automatic weapons but believe little resistance left. Do not think it necessary for call sign 3 [C Coy] to pass through us yet. We will keep knocking the enemy bit by bit.

Lt Jonathan Shaw

Then we received a message over the company radio net telling us to stop firing as we were endangering 5 Platoon.

Cpl Stewart McLaughlin's 2 Section are now the forward element of the battalion and are occupying the Second Bowl. They are trying to take out .50 Calibre Machine Gun No. 3, commanded by Cpl Domingo Lamas and manned by Marine Infantrymen Anselmo Franco, Diego Iriarte, Pedro Miranda and Jorge Arturo plus members of the 7th Infantry Regiment. The Argentines in this area are stubbornly holding on to their position under the most extreme artillery bombardments.

1.4 'The shit simply dropped out of the sky through the darkness'

The time is now approximately 04.00hrs (zt).

Lt Jonathan Shaw

I received another message from Major Argue saying, 'We are going to call in artillery fire, forward of your location.' I then informed Pte Eaton and Pte Clark to keep their heads down. When the rounds came in, they landed extremely short. There was an enormous explosion. It was like being in a tube station during a train crash. Luckily, no one was hurt, and thankfully, they adjusted their fire. However, it was very scary indeed.

Pte Kevin Eaton

By now, the three of us had lost quite a bit of blood. Mushrooms had slipped into unconsciousness. We received a message from Trev Wilson saying that we would probably have to wait until first light, about six hours away. We were not happy. However, we fully understood the gravity of the situation we faced. The effect of the cold cannot be overplayed. I truly thought we would freeze to death. Then the shelling started.

Pte Julian (Baz) Barrett

The artillery fire was like some sort of macabre Russian roulette game. We had our FOO, Captain McCracken, bringing it in extremely close – so close that at times I thought he might be an Argentine double agent! It was horrendous. You could hear it coming from miles away, through the local sounds of battle. When they hit the rocks they sent shrapnel everywhere, ricocheting and echoing with extraordinary violence. When they hit the boggy areas I'd get showered in mud and stone. The shit simply dropped out of the sky through the darkness. The percussion of these big rounds only added to my sense of total hopelessness.

Pte Simon Clark

The rounds landed down by the Full Back position at first, then began creeping back towards Fly Half. They were getting louder and louder. I said to Kev, 'Another 50 to 100 metres and they're going to kill us.' It seemed only a matter of time until it would be all over for us. But, thankfully, they stopped just short.

04.16hrs (zt): from C/S 41B to C/S 29FDC: 'C/S 3 End of mission ZU7920 add on 600 metres 55 rounds expended.'

At 04.16hrs (zt), Y and Z Companies of 45 Commando are to cross their Start Line and begin their attack. The Snowcat vehicles are only now allowed to cross the Murrell Bridge and drive the 2 kilometres to 3 PARA's Mortar Line to drop off their mortar ammunition, and then drive 1.5 kilometres to the RAP to start evacuating the wounded.

At approximately 04.20hrs (zt), Cpl Thompson of Support Company engages what may be the Argentine counter-attack by 1st Platoon, 10th Engineer Company commanded by 2nd Lieutenant Hugo Quiroga. They are advancing along the southern side of the eastern slope to link up with Lt Neirotti's 3 Platoon 7IR based on the south-western corner of Mount Longdon.

Pte Julian (Baz) Barrett

I was exhausted and kept 'double tapping', nodding off, falling asleep then waking up suddenly. When I went quiet the blokes would shout at me to stay awake. They wouldn't let me sleep or even pee in case I became hypothermic. Cpl Jimmy Morham talked me through much of the night. He got me spotting enemy positions to my front and kept feeding me reasons to carry on. At one point I was told to sing to keep myself awake. I sang a couple of Simon and Garfunkel songs that seemed to sum up my melancholy. It was weird lying in a firefight singing my head off, but there wasn't a great deal else to do in the situation. On a couple of occasions during the night the blokes would sprint out and cover me with a blanket. They would crawl towards me, have a bit of a brief chat, whilst waiting for a moment to crawl back.

Pte Gareth Lewis

At some point, we were asked to join 4 and 5 Platoon. CSM Johnny Weeks said, 'No, leave them, they've done well.'

Pte Charlie Hardwick

Cpl Jimmy Morham took me into the First Bowl, where I met up with more of the Anti-Tank Platoon – Cpl Phil Skidmore, Kev Connery and Jon Crow. It was great to see familiar faces. We got a brew on. There was talk of a plan to get 4 and 5 Platoon formed up to try to carry out a left-flanking manoeuvre along the sheep track leading to the Second Bowl.

The Snowcat vehicles finally arrive at 05.30hrs (zt). Four members of 6 Platoon's wounded are now loaded into the vehicles: LCpl Steve Wright, Pte Mark Dodsworth, Pte Stuart Grey and Pte Dennis Dunn.

The RAP informs 3 PARA HQ that they need a helicopter:

05.35hrs (zt): from C/S 9A to C/S 0: 'Can we confirm that large Hawkeye [Wessex helicopter] will collect casualties from about one kilometre west of Broken Arrow [Murrell Bridge]?'

Acting Captain Giles Orpen-Smellie, 22 yrs – Battalion Intelligence Officer

The CO went across to 6 Platoon to see Lt Jonathan Shaw to persuade Jonathan to make another attack along the northern side of the ridge. Jonathan was very calm and sensible [despite the casualties his platoon had suffered] in the advice he offered; suffice to say the CO accepted Jonathan's advice.

At approximately 06.15hrs (zt), HMS Glamorgan *and HMS* Yarmouth *begin their late withdrawal, leaving HMS* Avenger *on the gunline.*

Lieutenant-Commander Ian Inskip, Navigating Officer of HMS *Glamorgan*:

Our orders that night were 'to support 45 Commando and to be back on the carrier screen by dawn'. 45 Commando were delayed, and *Glamorgan* elected to stay on the gunline until 45 Commando no longer needed us. Had we left early to be back with the carriers by dawn, 45 Commando would have suffered many more casualties and may not have taken the Two Sisters mountain.

We received an updated position of the carriers, which had moved another 50 miles east overnight, an extra two hours steaming. We were thus going to be extremely late getting back. Intelligence had informed us that the Exocet [missile launcher] was based at Cape Pembroke Point: with a missile range of 20 miles, therefore a 20-mile danger arc was promulgated. To get from the gunline, we had to enter the danger zone to avoid the kelp/rocks. The decision was made to head due south, away from the danger of the Exocet, until Cape Pembroke was outside radar range. At this point we altered to 150 degrees true to make a good 50 per cent of our speed towards the carriers while still making a good 89 per cent of our speed away from the charted 20-mile danger arc, keeping outside radar range of the believed Exocet site.

The risk we took was carefully calculated, since we knew that if we lost a carrier, we risked losing the war, and while we were inshore, there was a gap in the carrier screen. Unfortunately, due to flawed intelligence regarding the launch site, our calculations based on Cape Pembroke were meaningless. Unknown to us, the missile was not located at Cape Pembroke Point, but near Hookers Point. We were still within radar range of the launch site.[*]

Cpl Jerry Phillips
I went back down the western slope and east along Route 3 towards the First Bowl, to see what I could do from this side. As I walked, I began noticing wounded and dead Argentines. It was clear that 4 Platoon had also suffered badly. I bumped into a group containing Captain Pat Butler of D Company. I said, 'I have to get into there,' indicating the Second Bowl. Butler said, 'It's still full of Argentines and too dangerous. You're coming with me to get 2 PARA and bring them in down the Murrell River.' I thought, No, I'm not, as I was still involved with 6 Platoon and did not want to leave them. I met LCpl Stephen [Benny] Bentall and he updated me on what was happening on this side. I thought, I am going to fuck off back and see Lt Jon Shaw, as not many people on the northern side seemed to appreciate the position that 6 Platoon were in. I'd started walking back when I saw a group of blokes in single file. I got down and challenged them. It was A Company 2 Platoon. Nobody replied: they just walked past me, bayonets fixed, as if they were all in a trance, intent on what was coming next for them.

---

[*] Email correspondence with Lt Commander Ian Inskip, 24 August 2011.

06.37hrs (zt): HMS Glamorgan *hit by an Exocet missile in the port side hangar and main galley; 13 men dead with 14 wounded. HMS* Yarmouth *and HMS* Avenger *go to assist. The* Glamorgan *is able to make 15 knots as all three ships return to the main carrier group. There is no more naval gunfire after this time. 29 Commando will be the sole artillery support.*

Pte Charlie Hardwick

Back up to Fly Half, I joined Cpl Mick Matthews and others, who were carrying ammunition for the SF teams. We were all struggling up and down the mountain with ammo, carrying either large sandbags full of loose ball or metal boxes of ammunition. We would carry two or three at a time, over the rocky western slope, which in the dark was extremely difficult. We also sat linking up sandbags full of the loose Argentine ammunition for the GPMGs. The whole area of the western slope seemed to be getting quite congested with members of Support Company, Tac HQ and 6 Platoon.

Brigade informs 3 PARA HQ that they intend to reinforce 3 PARA with 2 PARA:

07.28hrs (zt): from C/S 99 to C/S 0: 'We are going to reinforce you with 2 PARA, but need to know, which flank you want them on and how you will tie up with them.'

Cpl Carlos Colemil, Argentine Marine

I was separated from the conscripts and had lost contact with anyone. It was not until approximately 07.30hrs (zt) when I assessed my performance. I had caused several casualties: it gave me strength because I was surrounded by the enemy and did not think I would come out alive from the situation that I was in! I was still losing blood, but recovered fully. I ran, maybe about 2–3 metres, using the cover of the rocks. I decided to change tactics. Using the cover around my position I would crawl towards some rocks, fire at targets, then return to my original position. Lying on the ground, I fired my rifle against the shadows that were continuing to appear among the rocks. At one point, having left my position to fire again, I felt something hit the rocks, then bounce in front of me, rolling down the slope to my front. It was a grenade, thrown from an area that I had been firing at. Shrapnel and frozen peat flew over my body.*

At approximately 08.18hrs (zt.) 45 Commando reports that their objective, Two Sisters, is secure.

Cpl Jimmy Morham

At some stage before first light I met up with CSgt Steve Knights who asked me what was happening up at the front. I told him, there's a group of 6 Platoon blokes including Doc Murdoch and Mushrooms that are wounded, and we can't get to them.

Pte Dave Roe

I remember watching as A Company moved through our position. Nobody was talking. We were all in shock, had all just been through the most harrowing experience of our lives. We were all mentally and physically exhausted, and it showed on our faces, the way A Company looked at us.

Cpl Jerry Phillips

The SF teams set up and began firing in A Company. I watched for a while as Cpl [Peter] Tomo Thompson began knocking out thousands of rounds; and then decided to go down the RAP for a brew.

At approximately 08.50hrs (zt), the Machine Platoon establishes a gunline containing four GPMGs set up on SF. Point gun is Cpl Peter Thompson, Gun No. 1 Cpl Johnny Cook, Gun No. 2 LCpl Vince Bramley, Gun No. 5 LCpl Tony Peers (gun numbers 3 and 4 did not fire due to limited space on the gunline). They are directed by CSM Thor Caithness and begin firing at roughly 09.00hrs (zt). At approximately 09.27hrs (zt), a 105mm recoilless rifle located at the western end of Wireless Ridge opens fire at the gunline, the round arcing high in the air. It passes through the gunline, plunging down the western slope and impacting among a Milan crew.

---

* From *La 2ª Sección en Longdon* 'The 2nd Platoon on Longdon' by Lt Sergio Dachary.

09.27hrs (zt): from C/S 0 to C/S 9B: '4 x casualties from 59, exact number not known.'

Pte Charlie Hardwick

I was having a brew with one of our Milan teams that were in the cover of an Argentine bunker. We were only 25 metres below the skyline of the main firebase and were waiting to be called forward. Suddenly there was a huge whoosh, followed by an enormous explosion. Immediately, there were cries of 'Medic!' We rushed over to where the explosion had happened. The area was a smouldering mess. There were low moans and groans. Pat Harley dived straight in, quickly checking Cpl McCarthy and Pte Phil West. He then ran up to CSM Thor Caithness, a short distance up the hill. There were a number of other people wounded: REME Craftsman Clive Sinclair received a very bad head wound; Signaller Garry Cripps received multiple shrapnel wounds to the legs, arms and body; Pte Chris Dexter had wounds to his legs; so it was a chaotic scene. In the darkness, we were unaware that Pete Hedicker had been killed.

Cpl Jimmy Morham

Pte Pat Harley came running up saying, 'Sir, some of the blokes have been hit and I need help.' I immediately made my way down. I came across Cpl McCarthy, who was lying there. He'd received devastating injuries. I began to give him mouth to mouth resuscitation, but his injuries were too severe and he died shortly after. I turned my attention to Pte Philip West but, sadly, he had also died. There was another member of the crew killed, but at this time we did not know who it was, as his injuries were extreme. I began treating LCpl Garry Cripps [Royal Corps of Signals signaller attached to 3 PARA], who had multiple shrapnel wounds to his legs. I propped him up against a bunker and dressed his wounds.

I made my way back up to Fly Half and 6 Platoon HQ. Just before dawn there was a huge creeping barrage of artillery. I stressed to Lt Shaw that we still had wounded to our front, and they must be careful because it was landing about 70 metres from us, and probably only 50 metres from the wounded. I relayed my concerns to the CO. Now that the SF machine guns were set up and firing, there was a noticeable reduction in Argentine incoming fire.

Pte Charlie Hardwick

What I do remember, when I think back now, is how little I knew of what was going on. No one seemed to know what was happening. I didn't know anything about A Company being moved forward. I just noticed it had gone a lot quieter as the machine guns had stopped firing.

1.5 'At that moment, I felt extremely lucky to be alive'

First light approximately 10.00hrs (zt).

Lt Jonathan Shaw

It was time to go and collect our wounded. I said, 'Right. Listen in; this is what we're going to do. Half of the platoon will gather the wounded, and half will provide protection for them.' Cpl Wilson's group would provide cover while Cpl Steggles' group would deal with the wounded.

Cpl Jimmy Morham

It was now daylight and a mist had come down covering the whole of the eastern slope. Out of the mist came a stretcher party carrying my friend Michael Bateman, who looked awful. He had a shell dressing on his throat and one on his shoulder; I ran over and redressed one of his wounds, and he gave me a thumbs up. I helped carry the stretcher down to the RAP.

Pte Phil Simpson

Lt Shaw told us we were going to evacuate the wounded. My role would be to provide protection for the stretcher-bearers. Sgt Pete Gray, who had been wounded in the early hours of the battle and had refused to leave his men, was now finally evacuated, but only after all of 6 Platoon's wounded had been moved to the RAP.

Pte Morgan Slade

The wounded had been lying on the eastern slope in freezing conditions for the past ten hours with various gunshot wounds. To be honest, I thought they may

45

well have died. At that moment, I felt extremely lucky to be alive. Now we had to go back onto the eastern slope: I can't tell you how scared I was.

Lt Shaw threw a white phosphorus grenade to create a smokescreen, while the medics gathered the injured men. My heart was pumping all the time; it felt like an eternity waiting for the others to move back. As soon as the order came to move, we were off like whippets along with the stretchers. Mushrooms was just about alive, with congealed blood all over his throat. I said, 'Don't worry, Mushrooms, you'll be all right now, mate.' My words sounded hollow.

We had to get the wounded off the hill pretty quick, as we could hear the crump of Argentine artillery being fired from [Port] Stanley; the rounds were in the air as we moved off with the wounded. As I looked back to where we had just been, about 50 metres away, a load of dirt, explosions and general shit just lifted like a silent curtain. The Argentines realized they had lost the mountain and began a barrage that would last right up to the ceasefire.

Lt Jonathan Shaw
Just as we were leaving with the wounded, we could hear the whistle of incoming shells rushing towards where we had just been. We moved to the bottom of the western slope and found whatever protection we could in the enemy bunkers and whatever crevices we could find in among the rocks. Then a massive barrage began. Most of 6 Platoon attempted to get a brew going and to get some rest, or at least as best we could, as we had artillery dropping all around us.

Pte Simon Clark
After just over ten hours of lying out in freezing conditions, dawn was breaking. Pte Bryn Cowley from my section came out and picked me up. He put me over his shoulder in a fireman's lift and ran back up to Fly Half. I thought, At any moment now I'm going to get shot again. We reached Fly Half then descended down the western slope, Bryn then placed me down by members of the Anti-Tank Platoon. Pte Tony [Stretch] Dunn and Sgt Graham Colbeck looked after me. Graham dressed my wound and put me in an Argentine sleeping bag, then gave me a cup of tea. It was the best cup of tea I have ever had. I remember that my emotions at that point were so intense that I shed a tear. There were shells dropping around us, but the warmth I felt in seeing other people is hard to describe. Shortly after, Pte Dave Roe, Pte Gareth Lewis and Pte Harry Gannon

carried me down the hill, passing dead Argentines lying at odd angles with faces full of pain. I will never forget it.

Pte Dave Roe

Pte Gareth Lewis and I came across Simon Clark, who had been shot in the leg. Somebody told us to get him to the bottom of the western slope where the RAP had been established. We made a chair lift with a rifle, and tried to take him down that way. But it was very difficult due to the terrain. At this stage I was still unaware of what had happened to 4 and 5 Platoons.

Pte Kevin Eaton

I remember Lt Shaw, Cpl Steggles, Pte Kev Ames and others turning up. They had one stretcher which Mushrooms was loaded onto, and then some other blokes turned up with another stretcher. As I was placed on to it, I remember Kev Ames giving me a pair of Arctic Socks to put on my hands. I just felt so relieved, it was absolutely fantastic.

Full Back is now secure and Major Collett informs the CO, Hew Pike:

10.28hrs (zt): from C/S 1 to C/S 9: 'Now on position, very extensive position with Sp Gun at end.'

[Sp Gun = Support Gun: 105mm recoilless rifle.]

Two minutes later 42 Commando on Mount Harriet confirm their objective is secure.

Cpl Jerry Phillips

Just after first light we started to receive quite heavy incoming, Argentine 155mm. They were landing really close to us, and I honestly felt that this was it. It was just so fucking loud. The ground was shaking and I don't mind admitting I was shitting myself. I moved up towards First Bowl, where Sgt Johnny Pettinger said, 'Right, Jerry, you're back with me again.' So now I was 2ic of his patrol. He took us back down the hill and we relocated to a lay-up position known as 'Drunken Duck', about 1 kilometre away. We got some scoff and got our heads down, while Longdon was still getting stonked with defensive fire.

Pte Dave Roe

I remember Nick Rose and myself walking back up a gully. We came across this Argentinian body lying face down, but we had to be cautious in case of booby traps. I lay on him and rolled him back, while Nick watched to see if he was clear. He was dead and had terrible facial injuries. I remember the Argentine was about the same age as me, 18.

Cpl Trev Wilson

On Saturday afternoon I was asked by Sgt Des Fuller, he said it was not an order, but would I take some men and recover the bodies of members of 6 Platoon. I said that I would prefer not to, as they were extremely good friends of mine.

Pte Harry Gannon

I agreed to help recover the bodies of 6 Platoon. Gareth Lewis also came with me. I collected ID discs and helped load them into body bags with the assistance of members of 9 Squadron, who then took them away on stretchers.

Pte Dave Roe

At some time after first light, maybe mid-morning, I went to the RAP and saw CSM John Weeks. I asked him how Mark Dodsworth was; he informed me that Mark had died. I felt horrible. I still had Mark's blood on my clothes and hands. I remember sitting down by a small frozen puddle, breaking the ice and washing his blood off. I felt guilty, like I could have done more.

Pte Steve Richards

The smell of the mountain was really intense: cordite, blood, sweat and death. A smell I will never forget. CSM Johnny Weeks came to our position and asked for volunteers to collect the dead. I really couldn't face it. I didn't mind dragging the Argentine dead around but couldn't face the thought of our own blokes. Mark Eyles-Thomas told me that Jason Burt was dead. I couldn't believe it. I walked to the other side of the hill to 4 Platoon's location. There were around ten bodies laid out, all wearing British uniforms. When I reached the fourth or fifth body, I recognized it was Jason.

We lived in the same area and used to go out together when we were on leave. The last time I went out with Jason was Christmas 1981. We went to a club in Ilford and at the end of the evening they played 'Hi Ho Silver Lining' by Jeff Beck. It was meant to be a Soul Club, so Jason ribbed me mercilessly about it. Now, every time I hear the song, I always think of Jason.

Pte Phil Simpson

The platoon was moved further down to the base of the western slope. By then we were amalgamated with 4 Platoon and Sgt Des Fuller was now our Platoon Sergeant. I met up with Cpl Keith Deslandes and Pte Sulle Alhaji who were from my original MT Platoon, so we all basha'd up together. We were told there was going to be an Argentine helicopter counter-attack, so we all took up defensive positions, but nothing came of it.

A sentry system was worked out. The mail arrived, and I received the deeds for a house that I was in the process of buying. The deeds had to be signed by an officer, so I ran around the mountain trying to find an officer to sign the form. I also received a court summons for late payment of a speeding fine.

Sapper Sam Robson, 9 Sqn RE

After we'd finished rounding up prisoners, I went back down to the RAP where 2 Troop, 9 Sqn were located. It was there that I heard about the death of Cpl Scotty Wilson. I just couldn't believe it; he was a great lad and a really switched-on solider.

Pte Charlie Hardwick

I bumped into Steve Richards, whom I had joined the army with. We hugged as if we hadn't seen each other in years. I also bumped into Kev Connery, who was on his own, wandering around like a lost sheep. By then he was the only member of his Anti-Tank detachment left. I called him over. We chatted and had a brew, then we went for a mooch about.

Cpl Jimmy Morham

I met up with Cpl Terry McGlasson, 4 Platoon's MFC. We found somewhere in the First Bowl to sit, and made a great big stew in a grenade tin. Then an Argentine artillery and mortar barrage began to drop on Mount Longdon.

Major Argue said, 'Right, I want everybody down off the upper slopes.' I remember running with my pot of stew as the artillery rounds were landing on the top of the mountains, and Terry McGlasson shouting, 'Don't drop the stew!'

Cpl Carlos Colemil, Argentine Marine

I don't know what time it was when I was wounded in the calf with a 9mm bullet. Still, I did not withdraw. I was feeling sleepy, probably due to a loss of blood, and was left for dead. At about 13.00hrs (zt) in the afternoon, British medics picked me up; they treated me with the same dedication as the British casualties. I was taken by helicopter to a field hospital, where they operated on me.*

Pte Charlie Hardwick

At some time in the afternoon Pte Pat Harley, Pte Chris Parris, Cpl Jimmy Morham and I helped to recover the bodies of [Pte] Phil West and Cpl Keith [Ginge] McCarthy. It was a dreadful scene. I then basha'd up with Steve Richards in the rocks at the bottom of the western slope. We decided to go hunting for food and spoils, but when the shelling started we dived for cover among the rocks. The shells pounded in around us. They were landing within a few metres of our position, but the explosions were being absorbed by the soft ground. Then the Argies started to use airburst rounds, which would explode above our heads. Between the shelling, we would scour the hillside looking for food and anything we could use. We eventually found a ration store filled with tins of corned beef. We both dined well that night.

Pte Steve Richards

I managed to acquire two Browning 9mm pistols and a set of infrared night sights on my looting expeditions. I'd also seen numerous sets of rosary beads scattered all over the mountain, but thought I'd better not take them, as it might upset the man upstairs.

---

* From *La 2ª Sección en Longdon* 'The 2nd Platoon on Longdon' by Lt Sergio Dachary.

Pte Charlie Hardwick

I settled in for another freezing night on the mountain. During the night, I felt extremely ill, and I thought it must have been those tins of corned beef we'd eaten earlier. Then almost without warning I threw my guts up over Steve Richards.

Lt Jonathan Shaw

On the Saturday night, I woke up and was violently sick into my signaller's helmet.

Cpl Jimmy Morham

That first night, Saturday night, it was freezing and all I had managed to find to keep me warm was an Argentinian sleeping-bag liner. I lay in between Cpl Terry McGlasson and Cpl Ronnie Cooper, and unbeknown to me, I was developing appendicitis. In the early hours of the morning I started getting stomach spasms and I knew I was going to be sick. In the dark I was struggling to get out of the sleeping-bag liner and vomited onto Ronnie Cooper's face! I don't think he's ever forgiven me.

1.6 ## 'By then I'd seen enough death and destruction'

SUNDAY 13 JUNE 1982

First light approximately 10.00hrs (zt).

Pte Charlie Hardwick

It was another bitterly cold morning. There was a light layer of snow on the ground. I didn't feel too well after being sick the night before. I stayed close to the bunker. At some stage, I heard artillery or mortar rounds landing not far from my position…

Cpl Jerry Phillips, Cpl Mark Brown and Pte Dickie Absolon have all been wounded. The RAP informs 3 PARA HQ:

13.34hrs (zt): from C/S 9A to C/S 0: 'Just had more casualties. Inform Brigade this area has just had two more casualties. This is an unacceptable delay.'

13.36hrs (zt): from C/S 9A to C/S 0: 'First casualty brought in with head injury.'

Pte Charlie Hardwick

We heard terrible screaming. Steve Richards and I ran over to Cpl Jerry Phillips, who was screaming in pain. Pte Dickie Absolon had a bad head wound and was fitting. Cpl Mark Brown had been wounded in the leg. Pte Mark [Zip] Hunt was also injured. A piece of shrapnel had lodged into the Clansman radio that he was carrying on his back. He was lying face down, unable to move. As Jerry Phillips was taken away, I noticed his gloves lying on the floor. I know it sounds awful now, but I picked them up and put them straight on, thinking, He's not going to use them now, and I'm fucking freezing.

Shortly after this I decided to walk down to where the bodies were laid out. They were just away from the RAP area over at the bottom of the western slope. I was tired, and I needed a cigarette. I knew that my friend Stewart Laing, who'd been killed the day before, had a full packet of Dunhill cigarettes in his smock pocket. We had spoken about this packet of cigarettes before the battle and said we'd keep these cigarettes until the end. So I thought I'd better go and get them. I knelt down and removed the blanket that was covering him and tidied him up a bit, then opened his smock pocket to discover some bastard had already taken them!

Another artillery salvo came in, so I decided to go back to my bunker. We'd found some more Argentinian meatballs which we devoured. Not long after that my stomach condition started to worsen. I developed intense dysentery.

Pte Gareth Lewis

I remember watching as Sgt Johnny Pettinger's patrol moved towards Mount Longdon. They were coming from the west in single file through the minefield. As they moved up Route 3, they stopped for a moment. Sgt Pettinger moved away from his patrol, and then I think there was an air burst. I remember hearing Cpl Jerry Phillips screaming. I ran over to him; I was the first person to reach him. He said, 'Is my arm still there?' I said, 'Yeah, you've got a big hole in it, but you'll be okay.' I started shouting for a medic and I remember Cpl Phil Probets arriving. After that medics seem to appear from everywhere. I then watched as Pte Dickie Absolon was stretchered away.

Cpl Jimmy Morham
On Sunday evening I vaguely remember Denzil being wounded and being carried off the hill; by then I'd seen enough death and destruction. As the wounded were being rushed past us I asked who it was and someone said, 'It's Denzil.' I thought, 'Not another Anti-Tanker'.

Pte Phil Simpson
We got a further briefing from Sgt Des Fuller. Halfway through it had to be cancelled due to a mortar and artillery barrage. As the day progressed, we were moved forward into the Second Bowl. Another artillery barrage started. LCpl Vince Bramley shouted and gestured for us to come over and join them. We waited for the shells that were still in flight to impact and then ran over and sat by Vince. Another barrage began, and our old shelter was demolished by an incoming round.

Pte Morgan Slade
I remember at some stage watching 2 PARA Mortars moving up through the Furze Bush Pass to their form-up positions, carrying all their kit, while air bursts exploded high above them. During the day they moved some of our artillery up to a rocky outcrop about a mile away, I think by the Two Sisters, which were just behind Mount Longdon.

Pte Phil Simpson
That night, Dave Wakelin, Cpl Keith Deslandes, Sulle Alhaji and I were tasked to go out with Support Company to assist 2 PARA with their attack on Wireless Ridge. We stayed out all night but were never used; I was now completely exhausted and absolutely frozen stiff. We moved back in just before first light, made a brew and huddled up to try to get some warmth into us.

1.7 'No berets yet, wait until I give the order'

MONDAY 14 JUNE 1982

First light approximately 10.00hrs (zt).

Lt Jonathan Shaw

On Monday morning I attended an 'Orders' Group. We were told the battalion would now be attacking Moody Brook, then going on to Stanley. C Company would lead, followed by A Company, then B Company. The company would be broken up into 5 Platoon leading, followed by Company HQ and 6 Platoon amalgamated with 4 Platoon bringing up the rear. At some time in the afternoon we set off walking down the north side of Longdon, keeping to the dead ground, heading for Wireless Ridge. We heard that the Argentines had surrendered and to get our berets on. I must admit that it was a bit of a weepy moment.

Cpl Trev Wilson

On Monday all the Platoon Sergeants and Section Commanders gathered around Major Mike Argue to receive our orders for the forthcoming push into Stanley. During the orders, there was a brief update on casualties. When Doc Murdoch's name was mentioned it brought a tear to my eye. Suddenly the signaller stuck his head out of a bunker and said, 'Sir, they need you on the radio.' Major Argue climbed into the bunker while we stood outside, muttering to ourselves and wondering what the fuck was going on. He next reappeared with a huge grin on his face and said, 'Gentleman, it's over; it's finished, apparently there are white flags flying in Stanley.' He was then called back into the bunker, then reappeared and said, 'It is now definite that they've surrendered. We have orders to make our way into Stanley ASAP. Get hold of your guys, get your kit together, we're moving now!'

Everyone just bomb burst [quickly dispersed] to their various sections and platoons. Everyone was panicking, looking for their berets, but CSM Johnny Weeks said, 'No berets yet, wait until I give the order.' When we reached the top of Wireless Ridge looking down into Moody Brook, we could see 2

PARA followed closely by elements of A Company 3 PARA on the Ross Road. We speeded up dramatically to try to catch up. Eventually, we were stopped. 2 PARA had gathered on the racecourse and 3 PARA sat on the edges of the Ross Road wondering what would happen next. Finally, we were told to take over a bungalow.

Cpl Jimmy Morham

I remember hearing about the ceasefire from CSM Ernie Rustill, who shouted over to us, 'Berets on, lads; they've surrendered.' I pulled my beret out of my pocket, and it looked like a dried-up red sock. I remember seeing a helicopter flying in with a weighted white flag hanging underneath as we came over Wireless Ridge. We moved down into Moody Brook, passing the old Marine Barracks. It was a smoking ruin, along with a wrecked Argentine helicopter. All along the road going into Stanley were NBC boots, discarded by 2 PARA.

Pte Phil Simpson

As we passed through Moody Brook all the Argentines had gone – it was like the *Marie Celeste*. The old Marine Barracks was practically demolished and still smouldering; smoke was drifting across the road from burning bunkers. Equipment was scattered everywhere, all the signs and smells of war, but there was no one there. As we walked along the Ross Road past deserted gun positions it was a strange feeling. We came to a halt and sat at the side of the road waiting to be told what was happening next. No one seemed to know. Eventually we were allowed to take over the bungalows on the Ross Road, and pretty soon alcohol began appearing. The rest is history.

Pte Harry Gannon

As we marched in there was an Argentine sitting at the side of the road. He'd been shot in the thigh. CSM Johnny Weeks said to me, 'Gannon, get a shell dressing on that Argy.' I said, 'You're fucking joking, aren't you?' John replied, 'It's over, they've surrendered, now treat him, he's a prisoner of war.' I said, 'For fuck's sake, these cunts have been trying to kill me for the last two days!'

Pte Morgan Slade

As we moved off Mount Longdon, I looked around at the debris of war all around us: boxes of shells, sleeping bags, and boxes of this and that. Shortly after we set off the news was passed back down the line that the Argentines had surrendered; white flags were flying over Stanley. After making our weapons safe, we moved down off the hills through Moody Brook and on to a concrete road leading us into Port Stanley. There were plumes of smoke coming from various places around the area.

We eventually moved into a strip of houses alongside the road; they were bungalows made of timber and wriggly tin. The battalion was told to occupy the houses but not to trash them. My section moved into a house and was told to occupy one of the rooms. I remember the Royal Marines coming into Stanley, walking past our position. The lads were shouting, 'What kept you?' and, 'Where the fuck have you lot been?' Eventually the owners of the house arrived and lifted up some of the floor boards and produced a tin full of cakes and biscuits for us. They were so pleased to see us. They told us to make ourselves at home and use whatever we needed. The lady then went around and kissed each of us. It was the first time I could really see who and what I had been fighting for: good, decent people.

Pte Dave Roe

I remember seeing a white flare being fired up from Port Stanley. We moved cautiously towards Wireless Ridge, and before I knew it we had passed through Moody Brook and on to the Ross Road heading into Port Stanley. On the road I met up with members of 2 PARA. I bumped into Padre Derek Heaver and I told him, 'Padre, while I was on that mountain, I prayed like I had never prayed before.' He said, 'Take it from me; you were not on your own.'

I then met a lovely lady outside number 24 Ross Road, her name was Hulda Stewart. She gave us all an extremely warm welcome. She lifted up the cellar floorboards to reveal a stash of homemade cakes and biscuits. She told us that she had been saving them for that day. Forty-five of us took over her two-bedroom bungalow! We also made our way to the Post Office in Port Stanley, which was still open and working, and I sent a telegram home. They charged us! What a cheek! I think it may have been a fiver.

CHAPTER TWO

'AT THIS MOMENT MY LIFE HAD CHANGED IN AN INSTANT'

B COMPANY 5 PLATOON 'A'

The next thing I remember was someone shouting, 'Get into cover'

FRIDAY 11 JUNE 1982

During the early stages of the battle 5 Platoon split into two separate groups, 'A' and 'B'.

23.59hrs (zt): from C/S 29 to C/S 9: 'Now at Slim Rag.'

B Company divert from their intended route of march due to time delays; they will now take a more direct route to their Start Line at Grid 304763.

SATURDAY 12 JUNE 1982

The company now pause while the entire company fixes bayonets:

00.24hrs (zt): from C/S 29 to C/S 9: 'Now at Jungle Boot, and moving forward.'

00.30hrs (zt): from C/S 29 to C/S 9: 'Now across Jungle Boot.'

00.30hrs (zt): from C/S 9 to C/S 29: 'Roger.'

LCpl Lenny Carver, 22 yrs – 1 Section, 5 Platoon

On the night of 11/12 June we were late arriving at the Start Line. I was carrying about 700 rounds of GPMG ammunition, four full magazines of ball, plus 180 rounds of ball shoved into various pockets, six grenades, and two 66mm's. When we reached the Start Line, we immediately went to ground, fixed bayonets and lay there. When we were given the order to advance, we shook out. Cpl Ian Bailey was to my left. We advanced slowly and steadily towards the mountain. Suddenly there was an explosion to our forward left, followed by screaming. I turned to the two lads closest to me, and said, 'Follow me, boys, get directly behind me; we're going for the rocks.'

Pte Andy Steadman, 21 yrs – 1 Section, 5 Platoon

As we moved off the Start Line, we were in an extended line. On my left was Ben Gough and on my right was Dominic Gray. It was very quiet, and we had nearly reached the rocks at the base of Mount Longdon when suddenly there was an explosion to our left. We halted for a moment as we realized that we may be in a minefield. Then small-arms fire began to come from the mountain. The next thing I remember was someone shouting, 'Get into cover.' We all ran across to the rocks – this is when the platoon got split up. I ran towards Route 3 and ended up with Sgt John Ross.

01.07hrs (zt): from C/S 29 to C/S 9: 'Contact wait-out.'

Pte Chris Masterman, 20 yrs – 3 Section, 5 Platoon

There was an explosion, followed by a terrible scream. I remember hearing Cpl Graham Heaton say, 'Oh fuck!' I ran forward to the group of rocks that were nearest me, by the base of the main spine. It was here that the platoon seemed to split, with our group on the right side and Cpl Ian Bailey and Cpl McLaughlin's section over to the left. There was quite a lot of fire, but nothing seemed to be aimed directly at our group.

LCpl Lenny Carver

When we reached the rocks we slowly started making our way up. We paused for a moment and I took the GPMG off Pte Chris Masterman to give him a break as he was carrying quite a lot of ammunition. I came across Cpl Graham Heaton, who had a complete section. We could hear above us machine-gun fire, screaming and shouting; I now realized Cpl Bailey was not with us, but we sort of amalgamated with Cpl Heaton into a large section.

Cpl Graham Heaton, 28 yrs – 3 Section, 5 Platoon

We had reached an area about 15 metres from the base of Mount Longdon when I heard a bang and a scream. I don't remember anyone saying run for cover, we just ran for the rocks. I had my full section on the right-hand side, at the base of Route 3. I met LCpl Lenny Carver, who had half his section with him. I said, 'You might as well join me.' Sgt John Ross was on the radio trying to find out what the hell was happening. We didn't know where 4 Platoon were and there was gunfire everywhere.

Sgt John Ross, 29 yrs – 5 Platoon

At first I thought the Argentines had fucked off. Then within seconds the whole mountain seemed to open up with green and red tracer fire. I needed to find out where people were but we had almost no communications. We decided that we would push forward and just see what we could see. As we reached the rocky divide I had now lost contact with Cpl Ian Bailey and Cpl Stewart McLaughlin, who had gone up Route 2; we slowly progressed up Route 3.

Pte Terry Bowdell, 20 yrs – 3 Section, 5 Platoon

We all began to run for the cover of the rocks. It was all a bit chaotic, and some of my section was split – I lost contact with 5 Platoon as it was pitch dark. I stopped and knelt down listening and eventually heard the voice of Pte Chris Masterman and I linked up with him. We started moving forward, and we then met up with Pte Dominic Gray and our 2ic LCpl Lenny Carver. We paused here while decisions were made on what was best to do next. There seemed to be gunfire all around us.

Cpl Graham Heaton

Although there was gunfire everywhere, no one was shooting at us. It was decided by Sgt John Ross that I should take my section and LCpl Carver's half section forward and see what we could find. As we moved up, we spotted a .50 Cal firing across to the north. We decided to have a go at it, when suddenly the .50 Cal stopped firing. The barrel swung up into the air: I guess they had some sort of stoppage. We could hear Spanish being spoken excitedly and then the barrel dropped down, but it still never fired; I assume they were having problems. We decided to split into two groups – one would give fire support, while Pte Dominic Gray and Pte Ben Gough would assault.

This .50 Calibre gun position is Gun No. 4 and is manned by Marine Infantry, Luis Roberto Fernandez, Sergio Giuseppetti, Jorge Roberto Inchauspe and Claudio Scaglione.

Cpl Phil Skidmore, 25 yrs – Anti-Tank Platoon attached to B Company

No one was firing directly at us, although the noise of gunfire was tremendous and Argentine flares were now being fired. Sgt John Ross gathered the section commanders and said, 'Right, Scouse, you and Beetle Bailey take your lads up to the left and see what's happening. Graham, you take your lads further up this side and report back to me.'

B Company reports to the CO that 4 and 5 Platoons are both now in contact:

01.15hrs (zt): from C/S 29 to C/S 9: 'Call signs 2/1 and 2/2 in contact – northern edge of feature, sporadic small arms fire one casualty anti-personnel mine, artillery now hitting Full Back hard.'

Pte Chris Masterman

It was decided that our group would split into a fire-support group and an assault group: Cpl Heaton, LCpl Carver (GPMG), Pte Terry Bowdell, Pte Gary (Gaz) Juliff (GPMG), myself and others would provide fire support and Pte Dominic Gray and Pte Ben Gough would assault the gun position. As we got closer, we could hear the Spanish voices, they were shouting and very excited: I think they may have had a jammed round. At some stage Cpl Heaton was shot in the leg, but I'm not sure when or how. Quickly two 66mm's were extended, but both misfired and were cast aside, one striking me on the helmet as it was tossed away.

Pte Ben Gough, 20 yrs – 3 Section 5 Platoon

The support group at first tried firing two 66mm's but both misfired and were discarded. They then opened fire at extremely close quarters with GPMG and

SLR while Dominic Gray and I crawled up. We were now only a couple of metres away from the gun and were struggling to pull the pins from our L2 grenades, as the pins had not been crimped. We were only feet away when suddenly the firing stopped – me and Dominic looked at each other and let the safety lever of the grenades fly. We jumped out from our cover and tossed our grenades over into the stone sanger and shouted, 'Grenade!'

The excitement in the Spanish voices increased and after two or three seconds there was a muffled explosion. It wasn't loud, but it echoed, and then we heard groans. We both charged into the position, firing rapid aimed shots at anything that moved, 'double tapping'. After our short exchange one lay dead and two lay dying. The smell of cordite filled the air, my ears were ringing. We started shouting, 'Position Clear, Position Clear.'

Cpl Graham Heaton
As we were passing through the Argentine gun position, a round struck a rock by me and ricocheted off and clipped my left leg. I shouted 'Ah, I've been shot in the fucking leg.' But after checking it, I found it was only a flesh wound so I put a shell dressing on it and followed LCpl Carver, who by this stage had moved on to the western slope.

LCpl Lenny Carver
We heard rifle fire and shouts of 'Position Clear'. Passing through the position that had just been cleared, I heard a noise on my left. I saw what seemed like a small cave and immediately fired a burst of about 20 rounds, which was instantly followed by screaming and crying. An Argentine came crawling out. He was grabbed, searched and passed back to Cpl Graham Heaton's section. On the western slope we could hear Spanish radio chatter coming from a bunker. Ben Gough and Dominic both fired 66s into it; our group now began to move across the slope, clearing anything that we came across in the usual manner of grenade, rifle fire and bayonet.

This radio chatter may have come from 25-year-old Lt Alberto Ramos, who was acting as Forward Observer Officer for 7 RI Mech, at approximately 01.30hrs (zt) = 9.30pm (lt). Just after the .50 Calibre was taken out he sent a message to Artillery Group 3 saying, 'Fire illumination flares on the west and north-west of

Mount Longdon! This is hell, there are Englishmen everywhere shouting like crazy, many fall, but more come; I think we're surrounded!' He then ordered his assistant Sgt Quinteros to fall back, saying he would follow later. Lt Ramos had 6 Platoon to his rear and 5 Platoon advancing to his front. The death of Lt Ramos was a major factor in this early stage of the battle and left the Argentine artillery blind to the developing situation on Mount Longdon.

Pte Ben Gough
I fired a 66mm into a large square-shaped bunker, but it never exploded. We then crawled forward and grenaded it. We also cleared a number of tents by basically firing through them.

Pte Terry Bowdell
We [the fire-support group] moved up and came under fire from our left, from 4 Platoon. I shouted, 'Stop firing, it's 5 Platoon, do not fucking fire!' But they continued. We moved up onto the western slope moving through the .50 Cal gun position. One of the gun crew was dead and two of them were just barely alive and died very shortly after. One was dragged out; this man could speak good English and we asked him to tell us where his friends were.

Cpl Graham Heaton
I was given a prisoner who was an Argentine marine pleading in perfect English, 'Don't kill me, please don't kill me.' I told him to calm down. I explained, 'You will have to come with us, but you will get passed back to the rear shortly.' We asked him to lead the way, and tell us where the officers were, but he said, 'There are none, they've all gone into Stanley; they go every night.' He was very talkative and co-operative.

The Argentine prisoner who Cpl Graham Heaton is sure was a marine, may have been 20-year-old Claudio Norberto Scaglione of Gun Crew No. 4, who was a qualified laboratory technician and spoke fluent English.

5 Platoon HQ are now moving up, but are slightly behind LCpl Carver and Cpl Heaton.

Sgt John Ross

It was chaos as we moved up. I was still trying to contact 4 Platoon to find out where they were. It was too dangerous to advance any further forward, so we now moved on to the western slope. We passed through a .50 Cal machine gun that had already been assaulted by LCpl Carver and the rest of the section. I looked into the .50 Cal position and noticed a plastic container. I opened it and it contained a set of PNGs [passive night goggles] which I took and used throughout the night.

Pte Andy Steadman

As we moved on to the slope Sgt John Ross said to me, 'Keep our back covered, because we don't know where they are.' It was still chaos, there were blokes running here and there. I remember Ben Gough and Dominic Gray leaving our position to take on bunkers to our front and in the darkness I could hear Ben saying to Dom, 'Dom, I've got one here.' Then explosions and screams. We went firm near Fly Half as we couldn't get any further because of the amount of fire. It was around this time we met up with some members of 6 Platoon on the western slope.

Pte Kevin Connery, 20 yrs – Anti-Tank Platoon attached to B Company

It was chaos on the western slope. I heard Sgt John Ross shouting, 'Has anyone cleared those fucking tents?' I looked and saw three Argentine pup tents. I'm not sure who fired first, but quite a few blokes began firing, and I squeezed off a burst of GPMG into them. Immediately from inside the tents there was screaming, the tents shook and whoever was in them was now dead. My mind was racing; my ears were ringing. At this moment my life had changed in an instant. My eyes and ears were alert to any possible threat.

Cpl Phil Skidmore

We could hear Spanish being spoken excitedly, coming from just behind the rocks to our front, then suddenly there was a silhouette of a man standing up about 20 feet away. We were not sure whether he was one of ours or one of theirs, but the fact that he was standing up looked odd. Kev shouted something to him, and he began shouting back in Spanish. We all opened fire and the man flew backwards, and we assumed he was dead. Almost immediately another man appeared. Again we all opened fire, and the man spun backwards and fell out of sight.

A third Argentine stood up, and we all opened fire, and he fell. But he began to get up, so I and Pte Jon Crow decided to throw a grenade, just in case there were any more about to come out. Jon's grenade hit the man in the chest and fell to the ground quite close to him. He began to crawl towards it, to throw it away, when it exploded. We moved further forward, then we were fired on from behind and took cover. I had seen where the fire came from, so I said to Kev and Jon, 'Watch where I fire, and when I fire, you fire.' I then fired and Kev and Jon also opened fire in the location; no more fire came from that position.

Captain McCracken now halts the naval gunfire on Full Back and the northern side of Longdon because he is unclear where the forward locations of B Company are:

01.44hrs (zt): from C/S 41B to C/S 29FDC: 'C/Sign 3 finished ZU7920, 91 rounds; HE expended, ZU7920 + ZU7918 now unsafe.'

Sgt John Ross
We kept moving forward, and I now made contact with Cpl Graham Heaton and his section. By now he had acquired an Argentine prisoner whom we nicknamed 'Pedro'. We slowly continued up to Fly Half where we consolidated. We made contact with Cpl Trev Wilson of 6 Platoon, who were pinned down and were heavily engaged in contact. I ordered some fire onto the enemy muzzle flashes, only to be told by the guys in 6 Platoon to stop as they were right in the enemy position, and our fire was too close to them. We could not go forward because of the sheer weight of Argentine fire coming from Full Back.

It was clear to me that we needed to consolidate and get some serious indirect fire onto the enemy positions to our front. Our group had now cleared a route up to Fly Half with no serious casualties. This would be the main route too for B Company HQ and Support Company to move up, followed a short while later by Battalion Headquarters. I told the lads to set up a defensive area and get a brew on.

Pte Terry Bowdell

I held the prisoner by the arm and said, 'I bet you're fucking glad you learnt English at school.' He began pointing things out to us as he led the way up the western slope. We eventually reached Fly Half and made contact with Cpl Trev Wilson of 6 Platoon. He informed us they had taken a number of fatalities and that we should not come forward yet as it was too dangerous. They were pinned down on the left-hand side of the reverse slope of Fly Half, and Cpl Steggles' 2 Section 6 Platoon were also pinned down on the right. You couldn't put your head up for more than a second or you would have got one between the eyes, as the enemy seemed to be able to see every movement. Sgt John Ross appeared and said, 'Right, lads, let's go firm here until we find out what's happening.' We got a brew on. Eventually B Company HQ arrived with the naval gunfire officer.

It is now approximately 02.00hrs (zt). Support Company are leaving their Start Line and heading towards Longdon:

02.00hrs (zt): from C/S 59 to C/S 9: 'Now moving forward to west end of the feature.'

Captain McCracken contacts the Fire Direction Centre:

02.08hrs (zt): from C/S 41B to C/S 29FDC: 'From 41B, forward call sign moving along ridge quite well, 41B held up by small-arms fire, NGS very good over.'

Pte Kevin Connery

Myself, Jon Crow and Phil Skidmore found a bit of cover and kept our heads down and just waited. Eventually we heard the voice of CSM Johnny Weeks, shouting, 'Sgt Ross, Sgt Ross, has anyone seen Sgt Ross?' Behind him were Sgt Johnny Pettinger, Captain Willie McCracken and Major Argue; they would all now try to sort out the next move.

Sgt John Ross

It was good to see Johnny Weeks. From the minute he arrived, he was a rock, and was encouraging and reassuring all the guys around him. I gave Major Argue a quick situation report and told him we needed to blitz the enemy to our front with indirect fire, as they were in positions behind hard cover that they had spent weeks preparing.

CSM John Weeks

All this time I could hear voices of commands being shouted by various NCOs, particularly Sgt John Ross and Cpl Stewart McLaughlin. We came across one bunker that had been taken out by 5 Platoon (HMG No. 4) when I noticed a body covered with a blanket. I thought it didn't look right. I turned to a member of 9 Squadron RE [Cpl Scotty Wilson], and said to him, 'Take aim while I pull this blanket off.' When I did it revealed an Argentine holding a white phosphorus grenade in his hand. The corporal quickly opened fire and killed him.

Cpl Graham Heaton

Eventually B Company HQ arrived up on the western slope. I remember hearing someone shouting, 'It's the FOO party.' I then saw in this order: CSM Johnny Weeks; [Sgt] Johnny Pettinger; the FOO party Pte Duncan Daly; Major Argue and Captain Logan. We now handed our prisoner over to B Company HQ.

Captain Adrian Logan, 28 yrs – B Company 2ic

I can speak a bit of Spanish, and I began to ask the prisoner questions about the strength of the enemy on the mountain, where they were, etc. The prisoner was telling me everything we needed to know, even before I could finish my questions.

2.2 'It doesn't matter what fucking call sign they are, all I want you to do is grab whoever you can and push forward'

B Company HQ arrive on the western slope approximately 02.10hrs (zt). Shortly after this the prisoner (Pedro) is escorted down to the RAP area, but during this move he breaks loose and runs. Warnings are shouted, but unfortunately lethal force is used and he is shot dead. At the same time up on Fly Half, Pte Andy Steadman watches an Argentine running around on fire.

Pte Andy Steadman

I am not sure what time it was, but I do remember watching an Argentine who was running around screaming in the darkness on fire. I wasn't sure what happened to him, but I do remember him.

LCpl Lenny Carver

I remember seeing CSM Johnny Weeks and Lt Mark Cox having a discussion. Just seeing John Weeks was very reassuring to all of us. Captain McCracken had also arrived and we briefed him what we could see up on Fly Half. We took him up to Fly Half to the trench/latrine we had last occupied. Once we had all squeezed into the trench, we put our heads up and could see the incoming fire from the Full Back position. Captain McCracken said, 'Right, I'm going to call in some naval gunfire.' He busied himself giving coordinates, etc. Then 'Shot out!' followed shortly by the whistling noise of naval gunfire coming in. It dropped not far in front of us. The noise was absolutely deafening and the whole area shook violently. Immediately after the explosion, Captain McCracken turned and said, 'Run for it, there are another five more in the air.' We ran for all our worth back into cover while the shells landed *boom, boom* one after another, just above the bowl.

Captain Adrian Logan

Captain McCracken told me he was about to bring in some naval gunfire. I asked him how accurate it would be in such rough sea conditions, and he said, 'Plus or minus a kilometre.' I hoped he was joking, but when those shells exploded, I wasn't so sure.

02.31hrs (zt): from C/S 41B to C/S 29 FDC: 'This target ZU7920 is at add 600.'

Target ZU7920 is the Full Back position, add 600 [metres] these rounds will land 100 metres from the forward troops and 50 metres from 6 Platoon's wounded.

Pte Duncan Daly, 22 yrs – SP Company Signals Platoon attached to B Company HQ

Our group moved through the rocks up towards the western slope. As we progressed we could hear Sgt John Ross's voice and soon met with 5 Platoon. Shortly after we met up we received a radio message from 4 Platoon stating that their Sunray [Lt Bickerdike] was wounded and Sunray Minor [Sgt Ian McKay] was missing, and that 4 Platoon had taken casualties. Shortly after this Sgt Des Fuller from our group was despatched to see what was happening with 4 Platoon, and we now went firm for a while.

CSM John Weeks

I heard from one of the signallers that now Sgt McKay was missing. As we had a spare sergeant with us, Sgt Des Fuller, I turned to Des and said, 'Des, you're now in charge of 4 Platoon. Go and check their situation.'

Pte Martyn Clarkson-Kearsley, 20 yrs – B Company HQ

Des Fuller then went off looking for 4 Platoon, and after about five minutes came back and said, '4 and 5 Platoon are strung out all over the place, they've taken a couple of wounded and I can't find [Cpl] Ned Kelly.' Johnny Weeks replied, 'Des, I don't give a fuck who you get, it doesn't matter what platoon they're from, it doesn't matter what fucking call sign they are, all I want you to do is grab whoever you can and push forward.' With this Des calmly went off into the darkness.

Captain McCracken is now up on Fly Half:

02.35hrs (zt): from C/S 41B to C/S 29 FDC: 'Held up by sniper fire, but are trying to consolidate.'

Cpl Phil Skidmore

Looking for the sniper, we spotted a single muzzle flash quite forward of our position. I said to Kev Connery, 'Give me your gun, I'll put a burst into him.' I began to engage where I had seen the muzzle flash with the GPMG but Cpl Jimmy Morham, who had heard this, immediately began shouting, 'Fuck off, it's me, stop firing,' accompanied by 'Skidmore, you bastard!'

Pte Mark (Zip) Hunt, 20 yrs – D Company Patrol Guide for B Company

As we began moving up towards Fly Half an Argentinian appeared from behind a rock on my left, and almost before he had time to recognize me, I shot and killed him. In the dark there was just no time to take prisoners, it was him or me. As soon as we moved through the rocks a bullet struck the rock, barely missing me; 6 Platoon were indeed receiving what seemed like very accurate sniper fire.

We located a group of 6 Platoon, and spotted Lt Shaw. He looked a bit shocked, and said, 'Where've you come from?' and Sgt John Pettinger said, 'Back over there,' pointing over to the western slope. 'How many blokes have you lost? We've taken a hell of a lot of dead and wounded; Sgt Gray has just been shot, it's chaos, we've got people stuck out to our front that are wounded but we just can't reach them because of sniper fire, they've taken out two of my men who tried to rescue them; we can't move.' Sgt Johnny Pettinger told him, 'Sir, I have an excellent sniper in my patrol [Dickie Absolon] that has an IWS, let me see what we can do.' We then crawled over to the left of Fly Half, and I remember seeing the body of Pte Tony Greenwood laying there.

Pte Terry Bowdell

You could feel the blast of rounds whizzing past you; you could actually feel them passing overhead and around you. We could see Navy signaller Titch Barfoot's radio aerial and it was attracting quite a lot of fire. Willie McCracken said, 'I'm not having that,' and we could hear him saying, 'Adjust your fire, drop 200, 100 drop, add 50, fire for effect, that'll teach the bastards!' Willie was using a pair of Argentine night-vision goggles, but as soon as the aerial went up, there would be a burst of two or three rounds – they were lower than us, and we were silhouetted against the night sky.

Pte Chris Masterman

We now went forward: me, Terry Bowdell and some others. We had three GPMGs lined up on Fly Half with Kev Connery, Gaz Juliff and Dominic Gray. In front of us was Sgt Johnny Pettinger and Dickie Absolon scanning the area for any signs of movement. Dickie Absolon with his L42 sniper rifle fitted with an IWS would fire a tracer round, and we would fire at it with Johnny Pettinger calling corrections.

Sgt John Pettinger, 28 yrs – D Company attached, Guide with B Company HQ

I told Pte Connery to put that fucking gun on there [meaning, fire there], which he did, firing to the rocks to our front. We now had Captain Willie McCracken and his team up with us and he was bringing in naval gunfire. You could hear him saying, 'Drop 50', then 'Drop 50', and my eyes got a bit wider! Then he said, 'Tell your lads to get their heads down and brace.' And I thought, Fucking hell. The noise was tremendous, the ground was shaking; it was incredibly close, but he was very good at his job, and it worked.

B Company contact Support Company, asking for stretchers for 4 Platoon:

03.00hrs (zt): from C/S 29 to C/S 59: 'Have taken quite a number of casualties and require a lot of stretchers, caused by heavy firefight.'

Then the CO, who is listening in to the radio traffic, asks Major Argue for a situation report:

03.02hrs (zt): from C/S 9 to C/S 29: 'Send sit rep.'

Major Argue informs the CO what has just happened:

03.02hrs (zt): from C/S 29 to C/S 9: 'Roger, Call Sign 21 did splinter assault on enemy position, have taken several casualties and a couple of prisoners.'

The CO and Tac HQ are now making their way up the western slope trying to make contact with Major Argue and find out what is happening.

CSgt Steve Knights, 31 yrs – Support Company Anti-Tank Platoon

I was on the western slope when B Company OC came on the radio saying they had taken casualties and they required stretchers. I said, 'I don't have the stretchers any more, they are with Captain Burgess at the western end of the feature with the RAP.' Not long after, CO Hew Pike shouted across to me and said, 'Can you tell me what's happening?' I told him that basically B Company had taken the western end of Longdon. We'd set up a firebase there and were returning fire at the Full Back location, but it would appear we'd slowly ground to a halt because of the return of heavy tracer fire from the enemy.

CSM John Weeks

Sgt Fuller came back to give me a situation report, saying, 'Sgt McKay is dead, we have a number of blokes that are very badly wounded that need evacuating urgently, we also need more ammo, and we need more people back up there now.' I turned to Pte Clarkson-Kearsley and [Pte] Clifton Lewis and said, 'Right, lads, we have to go forward and collect casualties.'

Pte Martyn Clarkson-Kearsley

Des Fuller was a different man from the one I had seen earlier. His face looked completely different in some way; you could tell something terrible had happened.

Cpl Phil Skidmore

I remember Sgt Des Fuller coming back and telling us, 'Ned Kelly is dying and Ian McKay is dead, Lt Bickerdike's wounded, the platoon is fucked.' That was the first we really knew about it, and we were gutted.

Pte Duncan Daly

Major Argue now went up to Fly Half and I followed. We were all behind a large boulder with an Argentine .50 Calibre firing at it and ricocheting off in all directions. You could feel the rock vibrating. Eventually we had to move back because there was nothing we could do from this location.

Pte Andy Steadman

Support Company arrived with Milan teams and SF machine guns. The FOO officer Captain McCracken, who was not far from me, was giving his coordinates and calling in fire missions onto positions forward of Fly Half. Before long the firebase was established and they were suppressing the incoming fire.

Major Dennison now informs the CO that four of 6 Platoon's wounded are being moved:

03.20hrs (zt): from C/S 59 to C/S 9: 'Four casualties, taken by call sign 59 stretcher party.'

Pte Terry Bowdell

Everyone was firing blindly into the First Bowl, and after a while nothing came back. Either everyone was dead or had bugged out.

The CO is talking to Major Argue over the radio. They are both up on the western slope, but in the darkness it is hard to locate anyone:

03.30hrs (zt): from C/S 9 to C/S 29: 'Can you assess the situation?'

Major Argue replies to the CO:

03.30hrs (zt): from C/S 29 to C/S 9: 'Roger, I am now with Call Sign 2/3 [6 Platoon] There are a few well-sited automatic weapons, but believe little resistance left, do not think it necessary for Call Sign 3 [C Company] to pass through us yet. We will keep knocking the enemy bit by bit.'

Captain McCracken calls in more danger close [close proximity] artillery:

03.34hrs (zt): from C/S 41B to C/S 29FDC: 'C/S 3 Fire mission battery ZU7920 add 600 metres.'

Cpl Graham Heaton

Sometime after the CO turned up, we were asked to clear the First Bowl. There was no fighting as everyone appeared to be dead, but we checked positions by tossing grenades and firing a couple of 66mm's into bunkers just make sure they were clear. The FOO party now reaches the top eastern end of the First Bowl, the CO's party were also in the First Bowl with Major Argue, and my gun team and Lenny Carver's gun team were now at the forward edge of the bowl putting fire down towards Full Back.

LCpl Lenny Carver

We went into the First Bowl and I realized that there were lots of small bunkers in this very dark area, and a bunker immediately to our front had radio chatter coming from it in Spanish. Ben Gough and Dominic fire 66s into it which exploded. Our group consisting of Dominic, Ben, Terry and Gaz Juliff now moved across the bowl area, clearing the various positions in the usual manner.

Pte Duncan Daly

I remember the SF machine guns were asking for more ammunition, but we were told it was in the BVs and would not be coming until first light.

The CO locates Major Argue. The time is now approximately 03.45hrs (zt).

Acting Captain Orpen-Smellie

A short while later the CO moved forward with a much smaller group – probably himself, the Battery Commander Major John Patrick and the Mortar Platoon Commander Captain Julian James and their signallers – to join Major Mike Argue. I remained with the rump of Tac HQ in our original position on Fly Half.

2.3   'This is going to be a close one, tell your blokes to get their heads down'

04.16hrs (zt): from C/S 41B to C/S 29FDC: 'C/S 3 End of mission ZU7920 at add 600 metres 55 rounds expended.'

Captain Adrian Logan

We moved into the First Bowl. There were dead and dying Argentines lying about, moaning and groaning, asking for 'Mama'. There were a few who were completely broken gibbering wrecks, crying, and some were praying. It was awful. However, at this moment in time, we had no sympathy for them; some of the Toms told them to 'fucking shut up'. The CO said, 'Okay, Adrian, tell your guys to secure the area.'

The time is now approximately 05.00hrs (zt). CSM John Weeks has now returned from assisting 4 Platoon.

Pte Martyn Clarkson-Kearsley

I remember being in the First Bowl with Captain McCracken, and he turned to CSM Johnny Weeks and said, 'Right, this is going to be a close one, tell your blokes to get their heads down.' The naval gunfire came in, and I thought he had got it wrong it was that close; he was trying to take the .50 Cal out in the Third Bowl, which was only about 100 metres away.

LCpl Lenny Carver

CSM John Weeks said to Cpl Graham Heaton and me, 'Get your lads into positions around the edge of the bowl, just in case we get a counter-attack.' I then heard Major Argue come into the bowl with us with the CO and various head sheds, including Major Collett and Major Pat Butler. Major Argue said, 'Right, we're going to do a flanking attack along the northern side,' i.e. the sheep track. Major Argue was told in no uncertain terms that we'd been down there once, and this was not the way to go, but he insisted.

Sgt John Ross

Major Argue suggested that we form a fighting group and that we would attempt to take the enemy positions to our front by going left-flanking; I was not amused by this. I called all my Section Commanders in and told them what was happening, that we were basically going to attempt to go down the same route that Cpl McLaughlin had been before. This time we would take the naval gunfire team with us, a totally professional group of guys led by another Ulsterman, Captain McCracken. We also had our MFCs Cpl Ronnie Cooper and Cpl Terry McGlasson up with us, and I specifically remember asking Terry for a Dolly mix [white phosphorus fired after each High Explosive bomb]. They were trying to neutralize an enemy position, which when we moved was only 20 to 30 yards in front of us, an almost impossible task without taking friendly-fire casualties.

Pte Ben Gough

The next thing I remember is hearing CSM Johnny Weeks' voice. He was calling everyone in and saying, 'We're going to go left-flanking.' We were not in sections, just a large group of 5 Platoon.

Pte Chris Masterman

I remember CSM Johnny Weeks being sent to gather as many people as he could find for the forthcoming push. We had been briefed that we were now going along the northern side of the mountain. The Anti-Tanks, for some reason, were put at the front of 5 Platoon with Lt Cox who would take the lead. People were saying, 'I don't fucking like this; this is a bad idea.'

Cpl Phil Skidmore

The OC B Company said, 'I want the machine guns leading, put the support element at the front.' I said to Jon Crow and Kev Connery, 'Fucking hell, lads; I don't like the sound of this – we've got to lead 5 Platoon.'

3 PARA HQ informs Brigade:

06.10hrs (zt): from C/S 0 to C/S 99: 'At present winning firefight on last known position on eastern end of Mount Longdon, from Prisoners, there are 6 × 120mm mortars at grid 338748 our call sign investigating.'

The Argentine mortar position is situated on the south-eastern end of Full Back.

Pte Mark (Zip) Hunt

Now that Support Company were dominating Fly Half, Sgt John Pettinger located a bunker and told Pte Dickie Absolon, Pte John (Jock) Wilson and me to take cover here as he would leave us to meet up with Sgt Mac French, who was leading A Company across from Wing Forward.

CHAPTER THREE

'THERE WOULD BE NO TURNING BACK'

B COMPANY 5 PLATOON 'B'

'Once I'd stopped running I realized I was on my own'

FRIDAY 11 JUNE 1982

We continue from the Start Line with 5 Platoon B.

23.59hrs (zt): from C/S 29 to C/S 9: 'Now at Slim Rag.'

SATURDAY 12 JUNE 1982

Pte Paul Hutchinson, 23 yrs – 2 Section, 5 Platoon

Once we reached our position on the Start Line, we lay down and waited. The tussock grass was covered with white frost. It was minus 10 degrees and you could see everyone's breath in the cold night air.

Lt Mark Cox, 25 yrs – Officer Commanding, 5 Platoon

The moon rose behind the peak of Fly Half in front of us, which was a scary detail that perhaps had been completely unforeseen in the preparations – now we were actually going to be illuminated approaching the enemy's front line. I was given the order to 'Go' over the radio and gave the simple order to my Platoon, 'Right, let's go.' We all stood up and moved off in extended line. On our left was B Company HQ, and on our right was 6 Platoon. It was quite eerie as we moved silently towards Mount Longdon. There was this curious sense of being launched, and there would be no turning back.

Pte Mick Southall, 17 yrs – 1 Section 5 Platoon
I heard the order to 'Fix bayonets.' This sent me to a new level of alertness, and this was the order that really changed things for me.

Pte Grant Grinham
My Section Commander, Cpl Stewart McLaughlin, turned to me and said, 'Good luck, Grant.' It was unlike Scouse, as I didn't see him as someone who needed luck, and although I appreciated him saying it, it unsettled me a bit. For the first time I had a moment of doubt about what might lie ahead.

00.30hrs (zt): from C/S 29 to C/S 9: 'Now across Jungle Boot.'

LCpl Colin Edwards
I was so cold I was just glad to be moving and start advancing towards Mount Longdon. My section would be the point section – Cpl Stewart [Scouse] McLaughlin was in the middle, and I was on his right; we were in an extended line.

Pte Mick Southall
It seems strange now, but I was nervous and quite excited at the same time. The adrenaline was pumping. The moon was full and I could see the shape of the mountain in front of me. I knew if I had to move quickly I could, as I had only just passed out of the Depot and was very fit.

Pte Paul Hutchinson
We moved out in extended line but would shake out into arrowhead formation. 2 Section, which was my section, would be point, with Cpl Bailey's 1 Section to our rear left and Cpl Heaton's 3 Section to our rear right, with Platoon HQ with Sgt John Ross to the centre and rear and Lt Cox and his radio operator in the centre. You could have heard a pin drop. My back was aching with all the extra ammunition we were carrying.

As we neared the base of Mount Longdon I noticed that 6 Platoon, who were on our right, had now moved out of sight. There was a small explosion from among 4 Platoon, who were forward left; this was followed immediately by a terrifying scream which seemed to travel across the cold night air. We paused for a moment, and Cpl McLaughlin whispered, 'Watch out, lads, it's mines.' Now machine-gun and small-arms fire was coming off the mountain, long streams of green and red tracer heading in the direction of 4 Platoon and a distinctive heavy noise of a .50 Cal machine gun thumping away in short regular bursts of three or four rounds. We now ran as fast as we could, and when we reached the base of Mount Longdon, kept tight in against the rocks in whatever cover we could find.

3.2   'Fucking use it, and fire it at the fucking position'

Forty minutes after they begin their advance, a contact report comes from B Company HQ to CO Hew Pike:

01.07hrs (zt): from C/S 29 to C/S 9: 'Contact wait-out.'

Cpl Ian Bailey, 22 yrs – 1 Section, 5 Platoon

I ran towards the left side of the rocks on Route 2 but my 2ic LCpl Lenny Carver had gone to the right-hand side on Route 3. I was shouting, trying to pull my section together and managed to locate Pte Mick Southall, Pte Mark [Boots] Meredith and Pte Glyn [Scouse] Lloyd, but it was chaos as we were now in contact with various Argentine positions. They were just popping up or out from behind rocks.

Pte Mick Southall

There was an explosion to my left and I dropped down, wondering what to do. I seem to remember someone saying we were in a minefield, and then we came under enemy fire. Someone shouted, 'Run,' so I ran as fast as I could. Once I'd stopped running I realized I was on my own, and my heart stopped. I had ended up at the base of the main spine of Mount Longdon. I took cover and could hear British and Argentine voices. Rounds were hitting the rock in front of me and I knew I couldn't go that way. I wasn't panicking, but I knew I had to get back to my section. I started making my way back to where I could hear British voices. Everyone seemed to be shouting. I eventually got back and we started moving through the rocks, led by Cpl Bailey.

It soon became apparent that the platoon had been split in the chaos that had just ensued. We were behind a large mass of rocks, and when I peered around it I could see the outline of a man about ten metres away. I turned to Cpl Bailey and told him, and he said, 'Well, fucking fire, then!' I moved to a position where I could fire and fired four or five rounds at the man. I was almost in shock at what I had just done. Everyone in our group ran around the rocks and past the body of the Argentine soldier. Somebody said, 'Well done, Mick.' However, I just kept staring at the body, and I felt sick.

Cpl Ian Bailey

The artillery fire was now going over us in both directions, as the Argentines had begun dropping defensive fire onto their pre-arranged DFs around A Company and C Company, and our artillery was firing from Mount Kent onto Full Back. One noise in particular was the .50 Cal machine guns firing towards A Company, huge green tracer flying towards Wing Forward.

Eight minutes after the first contact report Major Argue informs CO Hew Pike that 4 Platoon and 5 Platoon are now in contact and artillery fire has been called:

01.15hrs (zt): from C/S 29 to C/S 9: 'Call Signs 2/1 and 2/2 in contact - northern edge of feature, sporadic small-arms fire one casualty anti-personnel mines, artillery now hitting Full Back hard.'

Pte Pete Hindmarsh, 22 yrs – 2 Section, 5 Platoon

We now began firing as we seemed to be getting incoming fire from all directions. It was at this stage that I was shot through the buttocks. I was in great pain, and called over to my section, 'I've been hit.' I was in a relatively exposed position, behind a rock in the open and I was under very effective fire from a position somewhere in the rocks. Cpl Stewart McLaughlin shouted out, 'Okay, Pete, where've you been hit?' I said, 'In the arse.' Cpl McLaughlin shouted, 'Do you have a 66mm?' I replied, 'Yeah.' He said, 'Well, fucking use it, and fire it at the fucking position.'

Pte Grant Grinham

Cpl McLaughlin shouted out to Pete asking where he'd been hit and Pete replied, 'In the arse,' and we all started laughing. Cpl McLaughlin turned to the section, glared and said, 'Who thinks it's fucking funny?' That shut everyone up. McLaughlin and Pte Paul Hutchinson ran down to Pete, grabbed him by his webbing and dragged him back. Watching Cpl McLaughlin do that was really reassuring to the rest of us. He didn't seem fazed by the situation at all.

Pte Pete Hindmarsh

Cpl McLaughlin said to Pte Tony Kempster, 'Right, Tony, look after him.' Tony began giving me first aid and placed shell dressings on my wounds, which at first fell off, as it's an awkward place to put a shell dressing on. As Tony was doing this Cpl McLaughlin said, 'Pete, are you okay, do you want me to leave you here for the medics or can you carry on?' I said, 'You must be fucking joking; I'm not fucking staying here on my own, I'm staying with you lot.'

Cpl Ian Bailey

There were 66mm and 84mm weapons being fired – the noise was deafening. The Argentines were to the left and right and also above us in the rocks dropping grenades. Cpl McLaughlin's GPMG gun team gave us covering fire and I shouted, 'Who's got the 84mm?' Pte Mick Southall shouted, 'Me.' I said, 'Right, you follow me.' We crawled back up to the Argentine gun position, Pte Mark [Boots] Meredith would now act as loader and Mick would fire the 84mm. Mark slid the HEAT round in, slammed the Venturi shut, braced his arms around Mick Southall and shouted, 'Ready.'

Mick shouted, 'Stand by.' Then the deafening boom followed by 'Unload.' Mick Southall tried to fire another round, but the weapon misfired, and in the heat of the moment he had forgotten what to do in the event of a misfire! I shouted, 'Throw the fucking thing away and get back into cover.' We put about four grenades into the position, which was a trench with a stone wall around it and a tent, which was blown over from the impact of the 84mm.

We then ran towards it, me and a group of Toms. We found one Argentinian just a few feet away: Meredith and I both fired with our rifles and killed him, there were two men already dead, killed by the grenades or the '84' shrapnel. We put more rounds into them to make sure they were dead.

Pte Paul Hutchinson

We began to move further up the mountain. At this stage there was gunfire from all directions. A lot of Argentine tracer coming from the eastern end was going high, but the constant rattle of machine-gun fire was deafening. The smell of cordite was everywhere and a smoky mist hung in the air – it was like bonfire night. The sight of tracer being fired in both directions, then hitting rocks and ricocheting in all directions was amazing. My eyes were constantly scanning the rocks all about me; my heart was racing.

Now 21 minutes after the first contact Major Argue informs CO Hew Pike all his call signs are in contact:

01.28hrs (zt): from C/S 29 to C/S 9: 'All call signs in contact but making good progress for Full Back.'

3 PARA HQ based at Estancia House now inform Brigade:

01.30hrs (zt): from C/S 0 to C/S 99: 'Situation report, Call Sign 1 encountered no opposition as yet, Call Sign 2 experiencing strong resistance on Mount Longdon, Artillery called at eastern end of Mount Longdon.'

Pte Paul Hutchinson

We had just emerged from out of the rock divide on Route 2 into the open area, when GPMG fire coming from our left swept immediately across our front and struck some rocks to our right-hand side. We began shouting, 'Stop, it's 5 Platoon, hold your fire.' But again machine-gun fire hit the rocks to our front and fragments of rock flew all over the place.

Pte Pete Hindmarsh

A piece of rock hit me in the head, which was very painful and stunned me, I called out, 'I've been hit,' and Cpl Stewart McLaughlin called back to me,

'Fucking hell, Pete, you're always getting hit.' LCpl John [Taff] Goreing appeared and picked me up, and took me to the B Company Aid Post.

4 Platoon and remnants of 5 Platoon now meet. The time is approximately 01.40hrs (zt).

CHAPTER FOUR

'KEEP PUSHING FORWARD'

B COMPANY 4 PLATOON

'Longdon seemed to come alive'

FRIDAY 11 JUNE 1982

Major Mike Argue, Officer Commanding B Company
We expected at least a four-hour march to the Start Line, which was a north–south-flowing stream 1 kilometre from the base of the mountain itself. Only one major obstacle was encountered en route, the Murrell River: this was crossed by the use of a ladder, put in place by 9 Squadron RE.

After two hours' marching, we stopped for a five-minute break and I walked back to check the platoons only to find half of 5 Platoon and all of 6 Platoon missing. There then followed a half-hour of frantic bird impersonations to try and make contact. We were in radio contact and a rather embarrassed Platoon Commander announced that he'd tagged on to the tail of the Anti-Tank fire-support group, taking half of B Company with him. When at last we were restored to our full number, progress was resumed.

One and a half kilometres from Longdon the enemy fired a parachute illumination shell; we all hit the deck and in the light we had our first real look at the objective. A good moon was rising behind Longdon and, as we moved through the Start Line, we could clearly see its craggy features. Frost was settling on our own helmets and backs. 6 Platoon peeled off to the right and on to the western end of the objective, while 4 and 5 Platoons with Company HQ attempted to outflank the position to capture the eastern end of the feature.

After paralleling the feature for about 100 metres there was a flash and a bang and shouts for the B Company medic; we had found the mines we most feared. Cpl [Brian] Milne, one of my most capable Section Commanders, had had his leg blown off. Almost immediately the enemy opened up with accurate heavy machine-gun fire.

Cpl Phil Probets, 24 yrs, B Company Medic

My role throughout the battle would be as 'B Company Medic' and I was to be assisted by Pte Mark Dodsworth. I decided the only way to provide medical cover for the entire company would be for Mark Dodsworth to go with 6 Platoon, as during the attack 6 Platoon would be entirely separated from 4 and 5 Platoons. I'd be acting as the sole medic for 4 and 5 Platoons.

SATURDAY 12 JUNE 1982

00.24hrs (zt): from C/S 29 to C/S 9: 'Now at Jungle Boot (Start Line) and moving forward.'

Major Argue now informs the CO Hew Pike that they have crossed the Start Line:

00.30hrs (zt): from C/S 29 to C/S 9: 'Now across Jungle Boot.'

00.30hrs (zt): from C/S 9 to C/S 29: 'Roger.'

Pte Craig (Harry) Harrison, 19 yrs – 2 Section, 4 Platoon

The atmosphere on the Start Line was quite tense. When we got the order to move, I was just pleased to be moving again. I was shivering as we moved slowly towards the north-western corner of Mount Longdon, Cpl Milne of 1 Section on our left. Then there was a flash and an explosion to my left somewhere among 1 Section, followed by the sound of someone in great pain. We hit the ground immediately and shortly after that someone said, 'I think a grenade's gone off.' Cpl Ned Kelly shouted, 'We're in a minefield, stay still!' There was a brief pause, and after that the Argentines opened fire on us. I think they were most probably waking up and getting themselves together.

LCpl Roger James, 28 yrs – HQ Company attached to 4 Platoon
When the explosion occurred, there was a brief moment when nothing happened. But shortly after that Mount Longdon seemed to come alive with small arms and a heavy machine gun being fired in our direction, and we dropped to the ground as illumination flares had also been fired. At this stage, nobody returned fire. We realized we were in a minefield, and no one wanted to move about too much. I could hear Cpl Milne in awful pain over to my left. I can't remember who gave the order, but someone shouted, 'Follow me!' And we began to move out of the minefield towards Longdon in single file, following the footsteps of the man in front.

Lt Andrew Bickerdike, 25 yrs – Officer Commanding 4 Platoon
We moved off in extended line and then 'shook out' into assault formation, which was two sections forward and one section to the rear. Cpl Milne's 1 Section was on my left. On my right was Cpl Kelly's 2 Section. I positioned myself in the centre with Pte Barlow and my signaller Pte Cullen. We reached the north-west corner, with Longdon on our right-hand side and were about 100 metres out from the rocks when there was an explosion, followed almost immediately by screaming over to my left. I ran across to see what had happened and discovered that Cpl Milne had trodden on an anti-personnel mine. He was being treated by his section, and I called for a medic. I knew I had to keep the platoon moving forward as we were in a very exposed position. In no more than a couple of minutes Argentine illumination flares were being fired and small arms and a .50 Cal machine gun started firing from the northern side of the mountain towards us. At this stage, some of the platoon became separated, taking cover in a peat bank on our left, but the bulk of the platoon was taking cover by the first rock line at the base of Mount Longdon.

The B Company radio operator reports to the CO that they are now in contact:

01.07hrs (zt): from C/S 29 to C/S 9: 'Contact wait-out.'

Pte Tony Barlow, 19 yrs – member of 4 Platoon HQ
As we were moving around the north-west corner, with Longdon now to our right, there was a very bright flash and an explosion, followed by screaming. We all dropped to one knee. Almost immediately a machine gun opened up;

it fired into our general area, and as I dropped to the ground, a round struck one of the 84mm rounds that I was carrying on my back. It ricocheted off, but it caused me to panic, as I initially thought I'd been shot. I shouted, 'I've been hit.' Sgt McKay came over to me and quickly checked me out and established that I hadn't been shot, and hissed, 'Get a fucking grip, Barlow.'

Cpl Domingo Lamas, Argentine Marine

I heard a small explosion, and CC62 Anselmo Franco shouted, 'Mine explosion!' He then called out, 'Cpl Lamas, come look, the British are coming!' I looked through the night-vision sight and could see infantry troops. I estimated there was more than one platoon moving across the minefield and a column of men cut off on the other side, who were probably about to cross the minefield.

I heard the clatter of automatic weapons in the western sector of the mountain. Franco told me: 'We are being attacked!' We came to combat positions and Cpl Roldan (HMG No. 1) informed me that his whole group was ready. I tried to make contact with Cpl Colemil, but he did not respond. Almost immediately the British artillery began to be unleashed, we (HMG No. 3) began to open fire on the column that was about to cross; we fired a stream of 12.7 tracer rounds, followed by the enemy returning gunfire.[*]

Cpl Lamas' gun position is in the Third Bowl facing north; he may be firing at A Company, as from his location he cannot see 4 Platoon.

Cpl John Lewis, 22 yrs – 3 Section, 4 Platoon

We were about 100 metres out from the cover of the rocks, when there was a small explosion followed almost instantly by a scream. I heard over the radio that we were in a minefield, and I thought, Fuck me. I turned to LCpl John (Taff) Goreing and said, 'For fuck's sake, we're in a minefield!' By now, illumination flares had gone up, and small-arms fire and tracer were coming off the mountain and going over our heads. I shouted, 'Right, we're going to make for the rocks, get in single file and follow me and watch your step.'

---

[*] From *La 2ª Sección en Longdon* 'The 2nd Platoon on Longdon' by Lt Sergio Dachary,.

CSM John Weeks, 35 yrs – B Company HQ

I dispatched Cpl Probets our medic to where the explosion had occurred to treat any wounded personnel, which was now evident by the screaming. The Argentine defenders were now awake and firing at us. We began zigzagging to a rocky escarpment for immediate cover. Most of the fire was ineffective, but pretty soon we began to receive effective fire from various Argentine positions. We gingerly started moving forward, myself, Sgt Pettinger, Captain McCracken and his FOO party and Sgt Fuller, followed by Major Argue and Captain Logan with the Company Signallers LCpl Daly, Pte Harding and Pte Cullen. Rounds seemed to be bouncing off the rocks in all directions. They must have been using night sights as we were pinned down in this position.

Cpl Phil Probets

CSM Johnny Weeks turned to me and said, 'There you go, kid, off you go.' I raced across to where the explosion had happened. When I got to the casualty I discovered it was Cpl Brian Milne. Pte Ron Duffy was with him. Brian was in extreme pain and I had to use my torch; I knew that I shouldn't use it, but I had to; people began shouting at me to 'turn that fucking torch off!' but it was the only way I could determine his injuries and administer morphine. In truth, his leg was just hanging on. I didn't want to upset Brian any more than I had to, so I put his shattered leg in an inflatable splint.

Pte Craig (Harry) Harrison

Ned Kelly said, 'Right, get in double file, follow me and Alhaji.' Sulle Alhaji led one file, and Ned led the other, saying, 'Stay back, but watch where we put our feet.' I thought at the time it was a very brave thing for them to do. I stayed behind Ned, grimly peering into the darkness to see where he had stepped.

Cpl Ned Kelly

I shouted to the rest of the section, 'Keep your distance, and watch where we put our feet.' I heard Lt Bickerdike shouting out, 'No, we need to keep pushing forward [to the east].' I turned and said, 'I couldn't give a fuck where you're going, we're going towards them fucking rocks.' I didn't give a fuck whether he came or not.

4.2 **'The position was now ablaze'**

Major Argue informs the CO that two of his call signs are in contact:

01.15hrs (zt): From C/S 29 to C/S 9: 'Call Signs 2/1 and 2/2 in contact – northern edge of feature, sporadic small-arms fire one casualty anti-personnel mine, artillery now hitting Full Back hard.'

3 PARA HQ informs Brigade:

01.15hrs (zt): from C/S 0 to C/S 99: 'Situation Report, A & B still advancing, B Coy hit mine, minor casualty.'

Pte Sulle Alhaji, 21 yrs – 2 Section, 4 Platoon
It was such a relief to reach the rocks. By now I could hear the sound of a .50 Calibre machine gun booming out in bursts of three and four rounds. It was going right over the top of us, streaks of green tracer flying off into the distance. With that and the flares lighting up everywhere, it was exciting and terrifying at the same time.

Pte Mark Eyles-Thomas, 17 yrs – 1 Section, 4 Platoon
My section was still lying on the ground. I turned to LCpl Keith Deslandes and asked him, 'What the fuck are we going to do?' and he replied, 'Right, you lead on.' So I picked myself up and began to walk slowly forward. I was terrified by the thought that every time I put my foot down I was going to lose a leg. I began to speed up. I just wanted to get clear of the minefield and find some cover. The rest of the section started shouting, 'Fucking slow down.' As they were following in my footsteps, I reluctantly slowed the pace, but when we were finally clear of the minefield all my section ran to various pieces of cover.

CSM John Weeks
We were joined by Pte Dickie Absolon. He was a D Company sniper and one of the best shots in the battalion. With his help we gradually began moving forward, but it was at a very slow pace. The rocks held a multitude of hiding places; I was constantly hearing the voices of commands being shouted by various NCOs, particularly Sgt John Ross and Cpl Stewart McLaughlin.

Pte Tony Barlow
When we reached the rocks, I remember watching Lt Bickerdike, Sgt McKay and Cpl Kelly having a heated discussion.

Lt Andrew Bickerdike
We began to reorganize at the rocks and return fire at various positions. We could hear Spanish being shouted everywhere but we couldn't be sure 'who was who', as I couldn't confirm where 5 Platoon were. I spoke to Sgt McKay, who said he had identified an enemy position, and he was going to fire a 66mm at it, which he did; the position was now ablaze, and we began moving forward.

Pte Tony Barlow
I helped Cpl Balmer as he fired the 84mm at a machine-gun position. The first round hit some rocks just in front of us and exploded; we then fired a second round but although it didn't explode, it silenced the machine gun and we now began to push forward. I remember following Pte Sulle Alhaji through some rocks moving up towards the main ridge.

Cpl John Lewis
The first line of rocks were quite large, approximately 8–10 feet tall. On the other side of them, we could hear voices in both British and Spanish, also gunfire and explosions. There was a massive flash and an explosion from that area; it may have been 5 Platoon – they seemed to be in heavy contact.

LCpl Roger James
As more and more people gathered at the rock line, they started returning fire at positions on Mount Longdon. During this phase the sections were all mixed up; eventually the last man came out of the minefield and I moved up through the rocks to catch up with the rest of the platoon. They were in small groups returning fire at various enemy positions. I joined in the firing, and we began moving slowly forward. But we soon became pinned down by very accurate sniper fire.

Sgt John Pettinger
I was located with B Company HQ, and we were positioned between 4 and 5 Platoons; with me was Pte Mark (Zip) Hunt acting as a radio operator,

Pte Richard (Dickie) Absolon, and Pte John (Jock) Wilson; we also had a civilian, Vernon Steen, who was acting as a guide. When Cpl Milne stood on the mine, my patrol along with B Company HQ headed in towards the north-west corner, skirmishing as we went. I remember Dickie Absolon firing a 66mm into a bunker which set it on fire, and we then all ran forward.

Pte Mark (Zip) Hunt – D Company attached to B Company HQ

I remember seeing Dickie Absolon fire a 66mm into a bunker, then a group of about ten or twelve of us consolidated among the rocks. There was a cave-type feature, and I remember seeing Captain Logan, the B Company 2ic in there. I was crouching with my back against the rocks watching CSM Johnny Weeks in heated discussion with Major Argue. There was loads of radio traffic going back and forth, small-arms fire all around us, and the noise of incoming Argentine artillery fire.

Captain McCracken RA reports progress to the Fire Direction Centre:

01.24hrs (zt): from C/S 41B: 'Attack going well.'

Major Argue now informs the CO that all B Company call signs are in contact:

01.28hrs (zt): from C/S 29 to C/S 9: 'All call signs in contact but making good progress for Full Back.'

Captain McCracken is busy calling in fire missions from the Fire Direction Centre:

01.29hrs (zt): from C/S 41B to C/S 29FDC: 'ZU7920 objective taken out + 2 mortar positions.'

01.35hrs (zt): from C/S 41B to C/S 29FDC: 'C/S 3 shot ZU7920.'
[C/S 3 = HMS *Avenger*]

Pte Sulle Alhaji

We all started slowly moving up towards the main ridge and returning fire at anything that fired at us. Dark figures were running about. I decided to only shoot at the green flashes because they were definitely Argentines. I'd got in close to some rocks for cover, when a body fell on me from above. I instinctively jumped back and fired a couple of rounds into it. I thought, Fucking hell, where did he come from? I was now gradually moving towards Route 2 where I could hear the voices of members of 5 Platoon.

Pte Mark Eyles-Thomas

Ahead of me I saw some peat banks where members of 1 Section had taken cover. Pte Jeff Logan shouted across to me, 'Get over here.' Alongside him was Pte John Wynne-Jones. We could hear 5 Platoon in contact ahead of us when suddenly there was a large white explosion in their area. I could hear Lt Bickerdike shouting, trying to reorganize the platoon and push forward. We decided to run fast and low for the cover of the rocks over to our right. We sprinted across and were glad to be back with the rest of 4 Platoon.

Cpl John Lewis

We could hear and see explosions coming from up on Routes 2 and 3, where 5 Platoon were heavily in contact. Thankfully, they had taken some of the attention away from us. However, we were taking fire from a large automatic weapon, and as we lay on the ground trying to see where it was coming from, chunks of earth were being ripped up around us.

Pte Craig (Harry) Harrison

In the rocky corridor running parallel to us, we could hear 5 Platoon on Route 2. They were in heavy contact, with lots of firing in both directions and grenade explosions. The noise was tremendous; fire-control orders were being shouted and then more semi-automatic fire. I could actually hear the 84mm teams shouting, 'Loaded' and 'Stand by,' followed by an explosion as the round was fired. They seemed to be right in the thick of it.

Pte Mark Eisler, 20 yrs – 2 Section, 4 Platoon

As we got nearer I could hear the voice of Pte Peter Hindmarsh from 5 Platoon, and I shouted, '4 Platoon coming in!' We then met up with Cpl Bailey and Cpl McLaughlin. We stopped here for a moment and began to sort ourselves out. Then Lt Bickerdike and Sgt McKay got all the Section Commanders together and had a discussion about what to do next.

4.3 'Come on, lads, I'm fucking bullet-proof, follow me!'

At approximately 01.40hrs (zt), 4 Platoon have made contact with twelve members of 5 Platoon. These men will stay with 4 Platoon. So far only Cpl Milne and Pte Hindmarsh have been wounded from this group.

B Company HQ are still trying to push forward, although they are coming under machine-gun fire and accurate sniper fire.

Captain McCracken reports he is still under small-arms fire, but is now unsure of the 'Forward Location of Own Troops':

01.43hrs (zt): from C/S 41B to C/S 29FDC: 'Still under small-arms fire and mortar fire FLOT still uncertain.'

01.43hrs (zt): from C/S 41B to C/S 29FDC: 'Call Sign 3 finished ZU7920, 91 rounds; HE expended Z7920 + ZU7918 now unsafe.'

The registered targets are now unsafe due to the uncertainty of the forward locations of friendly troops: ZU7920 Full Back / ZU7918 northern side of Longdon just east of Fly Half.

Pte Mark Eyles-Thomas
We reached a rocky embankment and went firm while Lt Bickerdike and Sgt McKay spoke to all the 4 Platoon Section Commanders; also included were Lt Cox, Cpl McLaughlin and Cpl Bailey of 5 Platoon who had now linked up with us.

LCpl Colin Edwards
I was with Pte Terry Mulgrew, who like me had taken cover in another Argentine shit pit, and we now had used toilet paper stuck all over us. We crawled forward and took cover in some rocks. Tony McLarnon also joined us. There was an Argentine trench about 20 metres away, but with a built-up rock wall which made it really hard to get at them. I threw a couple of grenades, but they fell short. I remember Pte Mark (Boots) Meredith putting his helmet on the end of his rifle to attract fire. This worked, and we all returned fire. My SLR

packed in so I picked up an Argentine FN and started returning fire with that. Eventually someone put an 84mm round into the bunker.

Pte Paul Hutchinson

Further east we could hear the noise of .50 Cal machine guns being fired at A Company. I sat and listened as Lt Bickerdike tried to keep the momentum going. He was constantly pushing 4 Platoon further east, shouting, 'Come on, 4 Platoon, keep pushing forward, come on', moving them along the embankment. Eventually they could get no further due to the weight of fire from a SF GPMG position that was firing down at them from high up in the rocks, just below Fly Half.

B Company OC Major Argue now informs the CO that 6 Platoon have taken casualties:

01.50hrs (zt): from C/S 29 to C/S 9: 'Call Sign 2/3 has several casualties, enemy still firing from high ground, and still advancing and clearing.'

Pte Grant Grinham

There was a SF machine gun just below Fly Half, holding up the forward movement. We were told to climb high up into the rocks to see if we could overlook the gun position, but after quite a difficult climb we still couldn't hit the gun team due to large rocks shielding them. We needed to try another way to attack it. This seemed to be the pattern all night; try one approach, get stuck, go around another way and try again. We seemed to be up, down, backwards and forwards all night. At times we weren't sure if we had killed them, or they were just lying low, as some areas we thought we had cleared would suddenly open up again.

We moved back on to the lower ground and began to make our way along the front of the feature. As we crossed over an area of open ground we were engaged by the SF gun and were forced to ground by the sheer weight of fire. We were now really pinned down. It seemed only a matter of time before we would start taking casualties.

Cpl McLaughlin must have decided he'd had enough. He stood up in the middle of all this fire and opened his arms wide either side of him. His rifle was in his right hand, and he shouted to the section, 'Come on, lads, I'm fucking bullet-proof, follow me!' He ran forward towards the gunfire, followed by Pte Tony Kempster and then the rest of the section. It was totally beyond belief that someone would stand up like that, under such heavy fire, and lead us forward. It's the bravest thing I've ever seen.

Pte Tony Kempster, 20 yrs – 2 Section, 5 Platoon

Suddenly I saw Scouse McLaughlin standing up! There was tracer going everywhere, and he looked at us and shouted, 'Come on, lads, I'm fucking bullet-proof, follow me!' I knew he wasn't asking, he was telling us to follow him and I thought, Fucking hell! I got up and the whole section followed. Quite how we weren't killed on that move I will never know. But, on that mountain, he was an inspiration.

At approximately 02.00hrs (zt), the Argentine SF position below Fly Half is firing away, and what seems to have happened next is that, as Cpl McLaughlin leads his men towards the gun position, a member of 6 Platoon who is completely unaware of 4 Platoon's plight decides to drop a white phosphorus grenade down onto the SF machine-gun position, which is situated approximately 12 feet directly below him; and he decides to toss the grenade down into the machine-gun position, in his words, 'To shut the noisy bastards up.' This grenade sets one of the Argentine gun team completely ablaze and he and his colleague both scramble up to Fly Half and into the middle of 6 Platoon.

This now allows 4 Platoon to move forward further east, just forward of Fly Half. Cpl McLaughlin's section will now go firm while 4 Platoon, who are to his left, move further east. Cpl Bailey, acting on his own initiative, has managed to crawl forward of 4 Platoon.

Cpl Ian Bailey

Pte Mark (Boots) Meredith and I crawled along the embankment, keeping as low as possible as red and green tracer was going everywhere, hitting rocks and ricocheting off in all directions. The noise was intense. Across to our right, high up on the ridge, was a .50 Cal firing in the direction of A Company. We then made our way back and told Lt Bickerdike and Sgt McKay about the .50 Cal, and after a brief discussion, it was decided by Lt Bickerdike that he and

Sgt McKay would go forward and take a look for themselves, to see if there was a way to possibly outflank this position. But shortly after Lt Bickerdike moved off, he was shot.

4 Platoon have now advanced along Route 2, they are forward of Fly Half and are in the cover of a line of rocks just below the First Bowl. Ahead of them is an SF machine gun situated high on the ridge, also further east is at least one other SF machine gun, and two .50 Cal machine guns. The main direction of the machine-gun fire is towards A Company on Wing Forward. However, the riflemen who are defending the .50 Cal in the Third Bowl are armed with second-generation night sights and are aware of British forces advancing from the west, and are putting accurate small-arms fire down in the direction of 4 Platoon. Due to the location of the .50 Cal in the Third Bowl its arc of fire is almost directly to the north, due to rock formations on the left of the gun blocking its line of fire. There is also fire coming from assorted Argentines who are popping up everywhere and firing randomly.

Lt Andrew Bickerdike

As we went forward, we were warned to watch out for snipers, which I already knew about. We started moving forward, keeping below the rock line as there was machine-gun fire coming from higher up. We reached a spot where we had to break cover. I said to Sgt McKay, 'Cover me while I move across.' I then dashed out; I remember seeing a green muzzle flash and a number of rounds zipped passed me. A round hit me in the thigh. Luckily the force of the round knocked me backwards into some cover, and some members of 1 Section dragged me into the cover of the rocks. I spoke to Sgt McKay and said, 'The platoon's yours, you're in charge now.'

Cpl John Lewis

I was sitting next to Scouse McLaughlin. He said to Lt Bickerdike, 'Don't go, you'll get fucking shot.' We then heard him getting shot. Cpl McLaughlin turned towards me and said, 'For fuck's sake!'

Lt Andrew Bickerdike

I cut open my trousers to check the wound and found a small entrance hole with a trickle of blood. I knew it wasn't arterial; the round had gone straight through and missed the bone, but it was still extremely painful. I couldn't find the exit wound. Then from out of the darkness came Lt Mark Cox. He crawled up to me and asked, 'Have you been shot?' He proceeded to check my leg whilst still wearing gloves that were covered in Argentinian faeces, which everyone including me seemed to be covered in. I shouted, 'Get off my bloody leg, you'll contaminate it!'

Lt Mark Cox

I came across Andy Bickerdike in the cover of some rocks, having just been shot in the upper-right thigh. I made a tourniquet and I remember joking with him about how, for him, the war was over.

B Company Headquarters are still making their way up towards the western slope.

CSM John Weeks

We gradually began moving forward, but it was very slow. The rocks held a multitude of hiding places. Sgt Johnny Pettinger, Pte Clarkson-Kearsley and I, along with Captain Willie McCracken and his FOO team, went forward to try to take out one particular position. We fired a number of 66s into this position to our front. The bunker exploded and caught fire. I called back to Major Argue, 'It's okay, Sir, it's now clear,' and we carried on pushing forward.

4.4   'Take that fucking trench out!'

Back with 4 Platoon.

Pte Sulle Alhaji

Shortly after Lt Bickerdike was shot, Cpl McLaughlin came up to me and said, 'Right, you, come with me now. Look, there's a bunker over there, load me.' I thought, 'Shit: we were in a quite exposed position. Cpl McLaughlin shouldered an 84mm anti-tank weapon. I quickly loaded it. He pulled the trigger but nothing happened. He tried a second time, and still nothing happened. He then shouted, 'Misfire, unload.' I quickly unloaded and reloaded, and shouted, 'Loaded.' He fired, and still nothing happened. Then he muttered,

'Fuck it' and threw the weapon away. From somewhere he produced a 66mm, which he quickly extended and fired. The bunker exploded and with that Cpl McLaughlin ran off into the darkness.

Pte Andy Stone, 20 yrs – 3 Section, 4 Platoon

After a while, I am not sure how long, it was decided that we would cross a piece of open ground below the First Bowl. Cpl Lewis said, 'Listen in, 5 Platoon are going to give us covering fire, and we are going to move forward up to the main rock face.' We shook out into extended line and began moving up the incline. There was no fire as we moved across the ground, but as we got nearer to the rock face a number of Argentine positions opened fire and Pte Taff Parry and Pte Dave Kempster were both shot.

Pte Dave Kempster, 22 Yrs – 3 Section, 4 Platoon

I remember hearing Taff Parry saying, 'Why did you kick me?' [Taff Parry had just been shot.] I replied, 'I didn't kick you.' And then a burst of enemy fire came from a high point to my right, a bullet clipped the tip of my nose and a burst of fire hit my left arm.

Pte Andy Stone

When the firing started, Cpl Lewis got into cover; Duggie Field, Simon Ward and I also found some cover. We then all began returning fire and throwing grenades. Cpl Lewis shouted across to Simon and me to 'Take that fucking trench out!' I shouted to Simon, 'I'll give you covering fire and you throw a grenade in.' I began firing left-handed around a rock; Simon then threw a grenade which fell right into the trench. There was an explosion and a scream – after that, nothing. Cpl Lewis then shouted at us to grab Dave Kempster. I shouted, 'You give me covering fire and we'll get him.' Immediately someone started firing, and I ran over and grabbed him and started pulling him back, then suddenly LCpl John [Taff] Goreing appeared and we both dragged Dave back into cover, and for some reason I said, 'I've forgotten his weapon,' and I dashed back out for it. When I came back either Cpl Lewis or John Goreing said, 'Right, you stay with Dave and sort him out.' I didn't need telling twice. Then they both went and joined the rest of 4 Platoon.

Pte Tony Barlow

After Lt Bickerdike was shot he was moved to a safer area, and I said to him, 'Sir, would you like me to stay with you, or do you want me to move on?' He replied, 'If you must.' I thought, If that's the way you feel, fuck you, I'm off.

Lt Andrew Bickerdike

I was moved further west to another location, and not long after that, Pte Keith (Taff) Parry, who was in a lot of pain, was carried in over the shoulder of Pte Harry Harrison.

Pte Craig (Harry) Harrison

I saw a group of blokes huddled in the rocks to my front and found Pte Andy Stone and a couple of others treating Dave Kempster, who had been shot in the face and arm, and Taff Parry, who had been shot in the foot and leg. His leg was in a bad way and quite painful, so I picked him up and put him over my shoulder and staggered my way back to a position where Lt Bickerdike was. On the way, we were shot at a number of times. When I reached Lt Bickerdike I accidentally stepped on his injured leg, and I was carrying Taff Parry, so with the weight of two blokes in full kit, he gave a good squeal.

B Company HQ arrive on the western slope at approximately 02.10hrs (zt).

The ground ahead of 4 Platoon running from the base of the First Bowl to the Second Bowl appears to be clear; there is no sign of enemy movement. Cpl McLaughlin has scanned the ground ahead and tells Sgt McKay he thinks the enemy are either dead or have bugged out. Sgt McKay decides to move forward with a small group to the area where Cpl Bailey had been earlier and observed the .50 Cal. It's a movement of approximately 100 metres; he takes with him Cpl Bailey, LCpl Roger James and Pte Tony McLarnon. Radio operator Pte Cullen will also move forward but not with the main group. Once Sgt McKay reaches the rock line he decides to contact B Company HQ and ask for Milan anti-tank support from Wing Forward.

Cpl Ned Kelly

Sgt McKay got all the Section Corporals together, Cpl Stewart McLaughlin, Cpl John Lewis, Cpl John Balmer, Cpl Keith Deslandes and me. He said,

'Cpl Bailey and I are going to move further forward. I think there may be more Argentines around there, so I'll take a couple of blokes and we'll move around and take a look. Scouse, I want your section and Ned's gun team to provide covering fire. Take them over there on the high ground and be prepared to put fire down on anything that moves.' I told my gun team to join up with Scouse McLaughlin's 2 Section. Before Sgt McKay left, he said, 'Ned, you're now in charge.'

LCpl Roger James

I was in the cover of some rocks when I was approached by Sgt McKay. He touched my arm and Tony McLarnon's arm and whispered, 'You and you, follow me now.'

Pte Mick Cullen, 19 yrs – 4 Platoon Commander's Radio Operator

Once it became apparent that the Platoon Commander was out of the game I moved to locate myself with Sgt Ian McKay. When I did locate Sgt McKay, he was with Cpl Bailey and some others. At some point, and I am not sure when, we were asked over the radio to mark our forward positions. Support Company (Anti-Tanks) on Wing Forward wanted to engage targets forward of our position. I went back to Lt Bickerdike to get his Firefly Beacon. He gave it to me, but I had forgotten how to switch it on. Lt Bickerdike turned it on for me and put it in my hand. I am pretty sure that the Firefly Beacon had switched off on the way back to Sgt McKay, but by then it had become irrelevant as when I got back as the situation had changed. [The two Milan missiles had been fired.]

Vernon Steen, 36 yrs, Civilian Guide

I remember the Milan being fired from Wing Forward at the bunkers and sangers about 50 metres forward of the Second Bowl; I guess you could say east of middle. They were attempting to soften up the resistance for our advance beyond the Second Bowl, although I can only remember one missile being fired.

At approximately 02.15hrs (zt), two Milan missiles are fired from Wing Forward by Cpl Keith McCarthy's Milan detachment including Pte Philip West and Pte Pete Hedicker. The missiles impact in the area of the Third Bowl, taking out possibly two of the enemy machine-gun positions. Unfortunately, shortly after, supporting friendly fire from A Company begins to fall extremely close to 4 Platoon. Pte Dave Kempster, who had already been wounded, is now wounded in the leg by a 7.62mm fired from Wing Forward.

Lt Andrew Bickerdike

I got on the radio to Major Argue and asked him, in no uncertain terms, to speak to A Company and tell them to stop firing.

3 PARA operational report dated 1982

A Company was keen to neutralize this threat since already casualties had been taken. IR [infra red] viewing signatures could be seen, and at first it was thought that these targets could be taken on with safety to B Company's forward troops. But despite GPMG fire being brought to bear with great determination from A Company's position, it had to be halted since a number of bursts were falling amongst 4 and 5 Platoon's forward position on the ridge.

Once A Company has ceased fire, Sgt McKay calls Cpl McLaughlin's section forward; they move along the high ground till they reach the rock line at the Second Bowl. Cpl McLaughlin places his men out along the rock line facing east. Also included with this move is Cpl Kelly's gun group. 4 Platoon now have a strong firebase of three GPMGs and several riflemen who immediately begin engaging muzzle flashes to the east and high on the ridge.

LCpl Colin Edwards

I crawled forward with my gun team of Pte Nick Hillier and Pte Stuart (Doc) McAllister. Cpl McLaughlin began using his IWS to direct fire at muzzle flashes coming from further east.

Pte Mark Eisler

Cpl Ned Kelly told me that our gun group consisting of Pte Steve Jelf, LCpl John Hedges and me were to go with Cpl McLaughlin in an attempt to take out some of the Argentine gun teams that were located high up in the rocks.

Pte Grant Grinham

All the machine-gunners were brought together. We put our guns on the rocks and began firing up to the right, two o'clock from our location. There was heavy tracer fire being exchanged in both directions, an amazing sight. I remember Mark Eisler saying to me, 'This is going to be some waffle when we get back.' I said, 'Yeah, if we fucking get back!' [Waffle: war story.]

There is still sporadic small-arms fire coming from high up in the rocks of the eastern end of the Third Bowl, and the .50 Cal is still firing away at Wing Forward. Also Cpl McLaughlin has observed through his IWS a number of built-up trenches running along the base of the Third Bowl. However, there has been no fire from the trenches since his gunline has been established, as they have been raked with fire and are now thought to have possibly been abandoned.

Cpl Ian Bailey

From our position we could see the .50 Cal. Sgt McKay and I had a talk and decided the aim was to get across to the next bit of cover, which was about 30 metres away. We thought there may have been some Argentinian positions between us and the main rock face, but we didn't know the exact location.

The .50 Cal is HMG No. 3; it is manned by Cpl Domingo Lamas, Diego Ernesto Iriarte, Pedro Eliseo Ramón Miranda and Jorge Arturo Pacheco.

LCpl Roger James

I still wasn't aware of what the exact task was; I thought we were going after the snipers who had been firing at us. Just before we set off Sgt McKay called up to the fire-support group to prepare to give us covering fire, and then off we went.

At approximately 02.25hrs (zt), Sgt McKay's group move out of cover.

Pte Mick Cullen

After I returned from getting the Firefly I don't remember the Section Commander's 'O' Group. I saw Cpl Bailey, but I didn't see the other two who I believe were Roger James and Tony McLarnon. I informed Sgt McKay that the Platoon Commander was down and said to him that he was now the boss. He acknowledged this and told me to wait there. After that the four of them moved off. There was heavy automatic fire, followed by a grenade explosion, then silence.

Cpl Ian Bailey

I heard Sgt McKay shout up to Cpl McLaughlin, 'Scouse, prepare to give covering fire.' As we moved out we went into extended line: on the left was Pte Tony McLarnon, LCpl Roger James, myself, then Sgt McKay. We had only gone a short distance when we came under fire from multiple positions. We had no choice but to attack them. We grenaded the first position and went past it without stopping, just firing into it. I got shot from another position, which was about 3 metres away. At first, I thought I had tripped but a round had struck me square in the right hip. It spun me around and I fell to the floor. Sgt McKay was still charging on to the next position but there was no one else with him. I then heard a grenade explosion.

I noticed that the firing had stopped as suddenly as it started, and it was now very quiet. I was lying flat on my back looking up at the starry Falkland night sky. I then heard voices shouting, 'Are you all right, lads?' I was lying on my back and in great pain and decided to roll over onto my stomach. Suddenly there was another burst of fire; one round hit me across the back of my neck, and a green tracer round struck me on the middle finger of my right hand. I decided, Fuck that, I'm not moving again. I lay still and decided it would be a good idea to play dead.

Sgt Ian McKay, on realizing the immediate danger his men are in, shows complete disregard for his own life and continues on alone to attack the Argentine position.

LCpl Roger James

We had only gone a short way when a trench that I had not been aware of began firing at us. Tony McLarnon and I ran to the left, I took cover and began firing at the position. I then heard a grenade explosion followed by a burst of automatic fire, and after that it went quiet. I had lost contact with Tony and I could hear someone groaning in pain. I could hear voices calling out to us, 'Are you all right, lads?'

Pte Mark Eyles-Thomas

From where I was I could hear Cpl McLaughlin saying to Sgt McKay's group, 'Be careful, Ian, there on your left, be careful – you're right on top of them,' when suddenly there was a burst of machine-gun fire, which triggered return fire and then a grenade explosion, then silence. Cpl McLaughlin and others started shouting, 'Ian, Ian, are you okay, lads, are you okay?' There was no reply. They shouted again, but nothing came back. I assumed the worst had happened.

At approximately 02.30hrs (zt), Pte Mick Cullen meets up with Cpl Kelly.

Pte Mick Cullen

I tried to contact Sgt McKay on his radio, but had no response; I was now alone and out on a limb, so I decided to head back west towards the last position where I had seen the Platoon Commander. I was using what seemed to be a track of some description. I met Cpl Ned Kelly and told him that Sgt McKay, Cpl Bailey and the others were now missing, and that I had tried to contact them but there had been no reply.

The Argentine view of the incident:

Cpl Gustavo Pedemonte, 20 yrs – 2 Platoon, B Company 7th Infantry Regiment

They threw everything at us; some rockets or missiles [Milan] exploded near my position and killed two soldiers. The crossfire was very intense. It seemed to stop the attack for a short time, but then we received a new download of fire. We saw a patrol advance and could hear their voices. One had something on his back: a radio, I could see the antenna. I opened fire and they opened fire from no more than 20 metres, a soldier fell down almost immediately, and after a pause somebody screamed and ran to our position. He stood silently for a moment in front of us. Perhaps he had lost his direction for a moment. We could almost reach out and touch him with our hands. We all opened fire and he fell. A grenade exploded outside our position but did not harm us. As I tried to reach over and take some of his equipment, I could see smoke coming out of his body as a result of the bullets. One of my men, Enrique Ronconi, grabbed me by the waist and pulled me back into our position. The soldier lay there dead.

Cpl Ned Kelly

I decided to get on the radio to Major Argue. I said to his radio operator, 'Put Major Argue on.' I asked him, 'You know who's speaking, don't you?' Major Argue replied 'Yes.' I then told him, 'Sunray [Lt Bickerdike] has been shot and Sunray Minor [Sgt McKay] is missing and I'm in charge at the moment. What do you want to do?' Major Argue said, 'I will send someone up.'

Pte Craig (Harry) Harrison

Having dropped off Taff Parry at the Company Aid Post I made my way back to 4 Platoon and after helping with Dave Kempster, I was told that Sgt Ian McKay, Cpl Ian Bailey and some others had gone to recce a position for a forthcoming attack, and as there was shooting going on everywhere, I wasn't sure what became of them.

4.5 'Those of you who haven't fixed a bayonet, fix one now'

A Company tries to inform B Company they have identified a number of machine-gun positions forward of Fly Half, more than likely the Third Bowl, but unfortunately B Company does not acknowledge the message, due to radio communication problems:

02.38hrs (zt): from C/S 19 to C/S 29: 'Have now identified three positions, with one controlling two machine guns.'

At approximately 02.40hrs (zt), Sgt Fuller meets up with Cpl Ned Kelly.

Cpl Ned Kelly

Shortly after my chat with Major Argue, I heard Sgt Des Fuller half shouting, '4 Platoon, 4 Platoon, it's Sgt Fuller coming in.' He was trying to find us, so I called him into us. Des said, 'Ned, what the fuck's happening?' I quickly briefed him about Ian McKay and his group going missing, and that Lt Bickerdike, Dave Kempster and Taff Parry had been wounded. Des said, 'Okay, where's Bickerdike? I'll have a word with him.'

LCpl Roger James is still out in the darkness separated from 4 Platoon.

LCpl Roger James

At first, I didn't want to give my position away, but after a short time I decided to shout, 'I'm over here.' Somebody called out, 'Who the fuck's that?' and I replied, 'It's me, Roger!' The voice shouted back, 'Who the fuck's Roger?' and I said, 'It's Roger James from the Officers Mess.' They then asked me where the enemy was and who else was with me, but I shouted, 'I'm on my own and I don't know where the Argies are.' They then said, 'Make your way back in.' I wanted to move back, but was very wary of being shot by either the Argentines or my own side as both sides could hear me talking, but couldn't see me. Then someone shouted, 'Roger, make your way back in now and we'll give you covering fire.' I rather nervously said, 'Okay, I'm coming in, don't shoot me.' So I counted down Three, Two, One, then dashed back as fast as I could go. I jumped over a line of rocks and landed on somebody. At this stage I didn't know whether Sgt McKay, Cpl Bailey or Tony McLarnon were alive or dead, as it had all happened so fast.*

Cpl Ned Kelly, who under Sgt Des Fuller's instruction has moved 4 Platoon forward, informs Sgt Fuller on his return that LCpl Roger James has made it back. Sgt Fuller asks Roger James about what is forward of their position: Are there any enemy? Has he seen any bunkers? However, Roger reports that he has seen nothing, it was pitch black, and it had all happened very fast. Sgt Des Fuller says, 'Right, let's get the rest of the Section Commanders together.' Cpl Stewart McLaughlin of 2 Section 5 Platoon, and from 4 Platoon Cpl John Lewis of 3 Section, Cpl Ned Kelly of 2 Section and Cpl Keith Deslandes of 1 Section, all huddle together at the side of the embankment. Sgt Des Fuller says, 'Right listen in; I am now taking charge of 4 Platoon. Basically, what Major Argue wants us to do is just keep pushing forward, so that's what we're going to do.'

---

* It is not known how Pte Tony McLarnon made his way back to rejoin 4 Platoon, as after leaving the army, Tony suffered from PTSD and spoke very little of his time in the Falklands. Tony died in 2009.

Sgt Des Fuller takes Cpl Ned Kelly and Cpl John Lewis up to Cpl McLaughlin's firebase up on the high ground. He scans the area in front with Cpl McLaughlin's IWS.

3 PARA operational report dated 1982

Sgt Fuller went forward to Cpl McLaughlin's position which was a bit higher up in the rocks and with an IWS he tried to identify the enemy. The only fire now being brought to bear on them was from Full Back. Cpl McLaughlin's group had been firing continuously at the enemy positions directly to their front and 4 Platoon were in cover at the base of the hill behind rocks.

At this stage, the .50 Cal in the Third Bowl is still firing towards Wing Forward. However, the area immediately below it and to their front looks clear, but there are three Argentine positions belonging to 2 Platoon 7th Infantry Regiment, one with a FN Mag (GPMG), and approximately seven riflemen left from the original nine-man section. 4 Platoon would now move out in single file, under covering fire from Cpl McLaughlin, and then turn right and advance uphill in extended line, moving up towards the main ridge, and attempt another attack on the .50 Cal.

Sgt Des Fuller, 31 yrs – B Company HQ

So I made a plan to carry on going forward. It was as simple as that, really. We actually couldn't see where the enemy were: the guys were saying, 'They're out in front,' 'They're over there,' 'They're there,' but it was pitch black. So I told Scouse McLaughlin to go back and give us covering fire. I told him what I wanted him to do, that we would continue to go forward until such time as we came upon them or they opened fire on us, and Scouse was to give us covering fire all the way through.*

Cpl John Lewis

I climbed up to where Scouse McLaughlin's viewpoint was. And he said, 'Lewi, come and stand in here.' As I climbed in I noticed we were standing on the body of a dead Argentine – Scouse seemed oblivious to the fact. Des Fuller then explained what would be happening next, and told us, 'The Support Group will

---

* From *Green-Eyed Boys* by Christian Jennings and Adrian Weale.

give us covering fire while we move forward and then move back up, into the side of the mountain. I want all the 66s to be given to the fire-support group. Are we all okay with that?'

Cpl Ned Kelly
I whispered to Scouse McLaughlin, 'Make sure your lads keep their fucking fire above our heads,' and Scouse replied, 'All right, Ned, you just watch yourself, mate.'

Pte Paul Hutchinson
I was in the fire-support position and Cpl McLaughlin was constantly telling us what was happening and what he wanted us to do. He warned us to be aware that 4 Platoon would be passing in front of us shortly.

Both Cpl Kelly and Cpl Lewis go back down and explain to their sections what is going to happen next.

Cpl Ned Kelly
When I came back down I gave them a quick brief, explaining that we were going to be moving out in single file, and then we would turn right and move up towards the main rock face. I told them, 'I want you all to put a fresh magazine on, and those of you who haven't fixed a bayonet, fix one now.'

Pte Mark Eyles-Thomas
Pte Jason Burt turned to me and said, 'I'm not fixing mine.'

Cpl Ned Kelly
I then shouted up to the fire-support group, 'Prepare to give covering fire now.'

CO has lost communications with B Company:

02.50hrs (zt): from C/S 9 to C/S 19: 'lost contact with Call Sign 2 [B Coy] no relay through 19 [A Company].'

At approximately 02.50hrs (zt), 4 Platoon move out of cover.

Pte Mark Eyles-Thomas

Sgt Des Fuller gave the order, 'Prepare to move,' followed by, 'Move now.' We all began to feed out in single file. Once we fed out we turned to the right and began to move uphill towards the Third Bowl in extended line.

Cpl Ned Kelly's section lead out in single file, followed by Sgt Des Fuller in the middle, with Cpl John Lewis's section to the rear. They have advanced about 20 yards, then turned right and advanced in extended line uphill towards the main rock face, when suddenly a wall of fire erupts to their front.

Cpl Ned Kelly

It seemed to be coming from everywhere. Jason Burt was shot next to me, and then I was shot. I fell to the ground, the machine gun carried on firing, but it was as if they couldn't angle the gun low enough to hit us. The rest of the lads carried on attacking the enemy positions. I saw the dark shape of a body lying by me, and I said to someone, 'Who's that?' and he replied, 'It's young Jason.' I could also hear Neil Grose – he had a chest wound and was struggling for his breath.

Pte Mark Eyles-Thomas

I could see bullets ricocheting off the rock wall directly in front me. The noise of the machine gun and the muzzle flashes almost transfixed me. I ran blindly towards the gun position and dived into cover at its base. The machine gun was still firing; I crawled slightly backwards and bumped into the bayonet of 21-year-old Pte Dave Wakelin, which made me jump. We were then joined by Pte John Wynne-Jones. Suddenly someone shouted, 'Grenade!' On the opposite side to us were Privates Duggie Field, Simon Ward and Sulle Alhaji; they were firing and throwing grenades at the bunker we were hiding behind. I shouted over the noise of it all to Sulle, 'Don't throw any more grenades; we're over here, you'll fucking kill us.'

The enemy machine gun went quiet. John Wynne-Jones had Jeff Logan's GPMG as Jeff had been wounded. I passed my machine-gun link to Wynne-Jones and then acted as his No. 2 [loader]. He poured a long burst into the Argentine position. As John Wynne-Jones was rattling off his rounds Cpl McLaughlin came up behind us, thumped him on the top of his helmet and shouted, 'Fucking stop firing. We need that ammunition, the position has been taken!' He then passed us a bandolier of ammo for the gun, snarled, 'Take this,' and went off into the darkness. He seemed unperturbed as to what had just happened.

Pte Mick Cullen

After reaching the top of the incline, we could hear that others had been wounded. I crawled down to try to identify and help. I came across Pte Neil Grose, who had been wounded quite badly, and whilst I was trying to remove his webbing and move him into cover I was shot in the mouth. I think it must have knocked me unconscious and thrown me further down the hill. When I regained consciousness, I tried to get back to Neil, but I couldn't find him. I found Sgt Fuller and told him that I had been wounded in the mouth, and that he should use Duggie Field as his signaller as I wasn't sure if my speech would be understood on the radio.

Pte Craig (Harry) Harrison

Everyone was running towards the enemy; I was firing and running, desperate to make the rock wall ahead. As I got closer to the rock wall, something struck my thigh really hard and I thought, I've been hit. I dived for the rocks and checked my leg for a wound. Seventeen-year-old Pte Ian Scrivens had also dived into the same bit of cover. He shone a small torch to check my leg: I only had a slight graze where a round or something had passed through my denims. Despite our desperate situation I could see Scrivs smirking.

I looked back across the ground we had just run across and could make out dark shapes and hear groans. I then saw someone sat in the rocks to our front. I could hear him talking on the radio, but his speech was slurred. It was Mick Cullen, who had been shot through the lips, but he just carried on with his job of platoon radio operator.

Scrivs and I decided that we would try to help the wounded in the open ground to our rear. The first body I came to was Jason Burt, and I could see he had been shot in the head. I felt his neck for a pulse, but he was obviously dead; I think he must have died instantly. The next person I came across was Neil Grose. I helped check him and found that he had a sucking chest wound. He also had an entry wound on his other side. I called Scrivs over and together we patched

Neil Grose up. I told Scrivs to stay with him and keep him on his side. We were going to need more help to move Neil.

The Argentine view of the incident:

Cpl Gustavo Pedemonte

We continued to fire wildly. Alberto Petrucelli was firing away with his FAP 7.62mm [heavy-barrelled automatic rifle]. We were shouting, 'Viva Argentina, come on you sons of bitches, we're going to kill you all.' Then someone threw grenades into our position and killed three of my soldiers (Enrique Ronconi, Alberto Petrucelli and Julio Maidana), shrapnel hit me in the buttocks and head. As I was lying on my side on the floor of my trench they fired into our trench and I was waiting to be shot. After a short time, some of the British soldiers approached and shouted something that I could not understand; I sensed that they lamented the English man who had fallen earlier at the front of our position. Someone said, 'Peik or paic,' but I do not know what it means.

Cpl John Lewis

Cpl Keith Deslandes' section and my section were returning fire. I was calling out to anyone to come and help me, just to keep the momentum going. We all changed magazines and then a group of us crawled forward to an Argentine position. It was built up rather than dug in, and was firing away. We threw a couple of grenades, and almost as soon as they exploded, we all jumped up and began firing into the position. No fire was returned and I shouted, 'Position clear.'

Cpl John Lewis grabs Pte Sulle Alhaji and 17-year-old Pte Mick Southall, who cautiously crawl off into the darkness following Cpl Lewis. Random shots are still being fired as they inch across to where the groaning is coming from, and they find Cpl Ian Bailey.

Cpl John Lewis

We came across Cpl Ian Bailey, who had been shot three times in the hip, neck and hand. Pte Sulle Alhaji applied shell dressings as best he could and gave him morphine. While we were doing this Ian began to scream in pain and I had to tell him, 'Beetle, fucking shut up.' In the end, I was forced to put my hand over

Ian's mouth, as every time he screamed the enemy fired at us. I then whispered to Mick, 'Come with me.' We left Sulle Alhaji with Ian Bailey and went to look for any others. It was then we found Sgt Ian McKay. I checked him and whispered to Mick, 'He's dead, let's get the fuck out of here.' We then crawled back to Sulle and Ian Bailey, and dragged Ian as best as we could back into cover.

Pte Mick Cullen

I found Ned Kelly, who had been wounded. At this point it was apparent that 4 Platoon had a number of seriously wounded, and a number of walking wounded. They needed to be evacuated. However, we were pinned down by very accurate fire coming from further along the feature; I tried to identify who was dead and who was wounded, as I had to get a casualty report back to Company HQ.

Sgt Des Fuller begins organizing all-round defence. He also manages to find 5 Platoon's radio operator Pte Steve Phillips. Sgt Fuller tells him to 'Ask for stretchers and medical assistance.' After B Company HQ has been informed of 4 Platoon's casualties, they contact Support Company and request stretchers:

03.00hrs (zt): from C/S 29 to C/S 59: 'Have taken quite a number of casualties and require a lot of stretchers, caused by heavy firefight.'

Then the CO, who is listening in to the radio traffic, asks Major Argue for a situation report:

03.02hrs (zt): from C/S 9 to C/S 29: 'Send Situation Report.'

Major Argue replies immediately:

03.02hrs (zt): from C/S 29 to C/S 9: 'Roger, Call Sign 21 did splinter assault on enemy position, have taken several casualties and a couple of prisoners.'

Cpl Ned Kelly

Pte Harry Harrison crawled over to me and began looking for my wound. Harry found the entrance hole, but he couldn't find the exit wound. My upper chest and shoulders were covered in blood, so he assumed the exit hole might have been in that area. But he did as much as he could in the situation he was in; he put a shell dressing on me and administered morphine. He did all this while we were still being constantly sniped at.

After a short period of time there is still no sign of medical assistance. Sgt Fuller now decides to leave Cpl McLaughlin in command, while he makes his way back to B Company HQ with Pte Steve Phillips, to see what is causing the delay.

Pte Martyn Clarkson-Kearsley
When Sgt Des Fuller came back to B Company HQ he was a different man from the one I had seen just 40 minutes earlier. His face looked completely different; you could tell something terrible had happened.

Major Mike Argue
Casualties were building up and there were two choices: to press on in the hope that the enemy in the face of attack would break, or to stop and reorganize wherever the casualties were or had been extracted to, and use the artillery to achieve the same aim. I chose the latter; an OP was established from which the Forward Observation Officer concentrated the firepower of two batteries and three ships. I was horrified to learn that in addition to the Platoon Commander being hit his Platoon Sergeant had been killed.

CSM John Weeks
Sgt Fuller came back to give me a situation report, saying, 'Sgt McKay is dead, we have a number of blokes that are very badly wounded that need evacuating urgently, we also need more ammo, and we need more people back up there now.' I turned to Pte Clarkson-Kearsley and [Pte] Clifton Lewis and said, 'Right, lads, we have to go forward and collect casualties.'

Cpl Phil Probets
I heard CSM Johnny Weeks shouting, 'Cpl Probets, Cpl Probets,' and I shouted, 'I am over here, Sir.' He said, 'Right, son, 4 Platoon have been badly shot up. You've got to go forward, and you've got to help the casualties. Go up there, and RV with Des Fuller.' The first person I remember treating was Lt Bickerdike, who was sitting up against a rock; he'd been shot in the thigh. In the same location was Pte Keith [Taff] Parry with a foot and knee wound.

Pte Andy Stone

I was still with Dave Kempster, there were still odd shots ringing out, and now Argentine mortar rounds were beginning to land quite close to us. I remember Cpl Phil Probets turning up and he immediately began treating Dave.

Lt Andrew Bickerdike

I remember CSM Johnny Weeks appeared, and he put me over his shoulder and ran with me to the Company Aid Post, which I found extremely painful.

Pte Martyn Clarkson-Kearsley

Our small Company HQ group now began to make our way east. There were about five of us. We cautiously made our way towards the Third Bowl. There was still a lot of fire coming from further east. We were all crouching as we moved, trying to keep a low profile. We could hear Cpl McLaughlin calling out orders to his section, and to anyone else in the area. When we got to the area of the Third Bowl, we found some members of 4 Platoon lying on the ground.

CSM Johnny Weeks

I told my lads to stay where they were while I went forward and assessed the situation.

Pte Mark Eyles-Thomas

I had crawled across to Neil Grose, to help Ian Scrivens, who was treating him. When I reached Scrivs he was feeling Neil's back and said, 'I think he's been shot in the chest, but I can't find an exit wound.' Scrivs then asked, 'How is Jason?' I decided not to go into detail, slowly shook my head and my face said it all. We began to remove Neil's webbing, trying to be as delicate as possible; Neil was in great pain and was struggling to breathe. I checked that the dressing on Neil's chest was sealed and said to Scrivs, 'We've got to move him onto his injured side to help him breathe.' But Neil begged us not to do it. I turned to Scrivs, put my hand on his shoulder and whispered, 'We can't stay here, we've got to move him.'

At that precise moment a bullet hit Scrivs and he died instantly. Simon Ward, who was also lying by us, said, 'Check his pulse,' but I replied, 'There's no need, he's dead.' I couldn't believe what had just happened. Neil groaned, and

I had one of them moments when you think, What the fuck am I going to do now? I turned to Neil and said, 'You'll be okay, mate, I'll look after you.' Neil then asked, 'Where's the helicopters?' as we had been told a totally unrealistic casualty evacuation time of 20 minutes. I lied and said, 'It's on its way, just stay with me.'

Cpl Ned Kelly
I remember CSM John Weeks and Sgt John Ross appearing and shouting across to me, 'Ned, we're going to get you out.' It was about this time that Ian Scrivens was shot whilst helping with the casualties.

Pte Grant Grinham
I helped carry Ned Kelly. He was lying on his back, and I took his left leg and Mick Swain took his left arm, and on his other side were Mark Eisler and John [Taff] Hedges. Even with the four of us, we were still struggling to pick him up. I said to Mick Swain, 'Let's swap over.' We changed position and within a split second Mick got shot in the leg. I heard the round hit him. It sounded like someone had hit him with a cricket bat or something. It was weird because he didn't even shout out. He just said, 'Oh, I've been shot!' I can't remember who took over from Mick, but we carried on moving.

It was clear that Ned was in great pain, but he never moaned or complained at all. He just let us get on with what we needed to do to move him. Luckily, we didn't have to carry him too far. We put Ned down by some other casualties. Most of them were sitting or lying in the protection of a large wall of rocks along the sheep track. I remember seeing Mick Cullen, who, despite the wound to his mouth, was reluctant to be evacuated. Cpl McLaughlin then said, 'Right, lads, start taking the ammunition off the wounded, we're going to need it.'

4.6   **'We're going to have to move you;**
it's not safe here'

The wounded are moved initially on to the sheep track running between the Second and First Bowls.

Radio operator Pte Mick Cullen, although wounded in the mouth, with his lips split and teeth missing, directs an artillery barrage to cover the withdrawal of the wounded, through FOO Captain Willie McCracken, who is based up on Fly Half.

Pte Mick Cullen

During this period I was on the radio to Company HQ. I was trying to coordinate a casevac by sending our location and the numbers of casualties. I also helped to bring in some artillery support. However, I had no map, I wasn't sure where I was, I had forgotten any code words and had no reference points that I knew of. I was trying to remember the Fly Half and Full Back code words from the briefing. I also had a gunshot wound to the mouth, and we were under fire! And I thought that maybe Captain McCracken should have cut me some slack, as the Argentines were only 50 to 60 metres away.

Captain Willie McCracken, 31 yrs – Forward Observation Officer, Commando Regiment Royal Artillery

I was talking to the forward left platoon by a series of chats, which resembled the 'Golden Shot phone-in' rather than Infantry Artillery Target Indication Procedures. However, it did work. The platoon was able to withdraw under cover of a heavy artillery barrage.*

Captain Willie McCracken also mentions this same incident in the 148 (Meiktila) Commando Battery operational report, saying:

> We ended up having a very, very basic Arty Target Procedure, worked out with the forward platoon, and it was simply, 'How's that?' And they said, 'Fine, that's about 50 metres away.' Or whatever, or, 'You can afford to come a little closer.' And we'd creep it back and creep it back, and I was doing this blind at the time, and it seemed to work very effectively.

Pte Mark Eisler

After we left Ned Kelly in the Company Aid Post I made my way back to help with the rest of the wounded; I came across Mick Swain and helped move him back. I then returned and came across Ian Bailey, who was being carried back,

---

* From *Above All, Courage* by Max Arthur.

and I gave a hand with him. He had multiple gunshot wounds. It was around this time I found out about Sgt McKay's death. I'd noticed that he wasn't around, but I just thought he was elsewhere, as it was dark.

Pte Gordon Ellse
I helped carry Cpl Bailey, but I thought it unlikely that he would survive, due to the amount of blood coming out of him.

CSM Johnny Weeks
I could hear Cpl McLaughlin shouting out orders. He was trying to bring more fire down on enemy positions to the east. I now took charge of the situation and asked, 'Who've you got there?' and Pte Mark Eyles-Thomas replied, 'It's Grose, Sir.' I shouted, 'Not his last name, you knob! What's his first name?' Eyles-Thomas replied, 'It's Neil, Sir, but we call him Grose.' I bent down and whispered, 'Right, Neil, we're going to have to move you; it's not safe here, so just bear with us and we'll get you out of here.' I then turned and said to the rest of the group, 'Right, you lot, get him in a poncho and let's start moving him back.'

Pte Martyn Clarkson-Kearsley
Cpl Ian Bailey was already lying in a poncho when I got to him. I was lying by his head; we were wary about standing up because of the incoming fire. Suddenly in the middle of all this carnage Cpl McLaughlin stood up with a pistol in his hand and screamed at the top of his voice, 'Right, you fuckers, get up – get up – everyone get up now!' He was waving his pistol in the air about three metres in front of me, and I was more scared of him than I was of the Argies shooting at me.

We all stood up in the middle of this intense enemy fire and began to pick up the ponchos with casualties. As we began to move off, I stepped on the sleeve of Cpl Bailey's smock as it was hanging out of the poncho and trailing on the floor. Ian screamed in pain. I said, 'Sorry about that, Beetle.' Every time I took a step with my right foot I seemed to step on it again. In the dark I couldn't see where his sleeve was.

Rounds were flying past on our left and right. I remember hearing Mick Swain say, 'Ugh!' I said, 'What's the matter?' He replied, 'I've just been shot in the leg.' I said, 'Oh, fuck off.' I wasn't quite sure whether to believe him; he didn't cry out or fall over. I then said, 'You're fucking joking?' and he just said, 'No.'

The wounded were placed against a rocky feature slightly out of line of sight of the enemy troops situated further to the east. I remember sitting with my back up against a large rock, next to Jeff Logan, who had lost a finger and was in a slight state of shock. I leaned over in order to hear what he was saying and put my hand down in a heap of shit. It was then that I discovered we were in some type of latrine area. There was shit everywhere.

Pte Mark Eyles-Thomas

Someone appeared with a poncho: as slowly and as gently as possible, we slid Neil onto it. Then Pte Dave Wakelin, Pte Simon Ward, Lt Cox and I each took a corner of the poncho and lifted him. We had barely taken two or three steps when Lt Cox, who had taken the rear left corner, was struggling to hold it and it slipped through his hands. His corner hit the ground, and Neil screamed in pain.

I heard CSM Johnny Weeks tell Lt Cox to go and look after his own platoon. After he went, Mick Southall took his place. While this was going on I took off my webbing and placed my weapon on the ground. Once again we picked Neil up. But we had to stop again as Neil was quite distressed. We now set him down on the ground and then sat him up with his back against the rocks. He seemed to settle, and then he started to make a low groaning noise. All around us were other wounded men.

Pte Mick Southall

Dave Wakelin, Steve Jelf and I took all our heavy kit off, as Johnny Weeks was telling everyone to ditch anything we didn't need. We set off in search of our friends. We found Neil Grose with Mark Eyles-Thomas. Ian Scrivens was dead, but he looked like he was sleeping. It was hard to take in. Neil was in great pain, which made it difficult for us to move quickly, and we had to stop several times. I'm convinced that some of the carriers changed over as we paused. It was quite exhausting work given the conditions and terrain.

The wounded are moved from the sheep track to a position further west into a clump of rocks just below the First Bowl. But they will be moved again and again until they eventually reach an area that is the B Company Aid Post. The distance from the Third Bowl, where the 4 Platoon were wounded, to the location they eventually end up in, is approximately 300 yards, and as this move is done in stages, there will be multiple changes in the carrying order.

Pte Mark Eyles-Thomas

Neil seemed to settle and made a low groaning noise. Cpl Bailey was in extreme pain and was being very vocal. He kept saying he needed more morphine. Cpl Phil Probets appeared, did a quick triage along the line of wounded and announced, 'He [Neil] is number one. We have to get him out of here.'

Cpl Phil Probets

It was chaos; I was calling out in the darkness for Sgt Fuller, and at the same time I was attracting fire. I eventually linked up with Des Fuller and found a group of wounded; Cpl Ned Kelly was in great pain with a stomach wound. Cpl Ian Bailey had various gunshot wounds, there was Pte Jeff Logan with a gunshot wound to his hand and Pte Neil Grose with a gunshot wound to the chest. I did a quick triage and decided that Neil was number one, the highest priority. This young man was in a bad way. I said, 'We need to move him further back.' This area was still under fire, and it was impossible to put a torch on, as the incoming fire was at such close quarters. We loaded him onto a poncho, laying him on his injured side, allowing him to breathe with his good lung. However, with the movement of carrying him, he rolled onto his back and started to panic as he was unable to breathe.

Pte Andy Stone

The next thing I remember was seeing Neil Grose being carried back. I was shocked because he was my trench mate and we were good friends. We had paired up together all the way across, and now he was in great pain, and was being told to lie down, but he protested, saying, 'No, I want to sit up.'

Pte Mark Eyles-Thomas

I was trying my best to reassure Neil: 'The choppers are on their way, try to stay awake or you'll miss them. Come on, keep your eyes open.' But Neil whispered, 'It's all right, Tomo; I know they're not coming.' I spluttered, 'No, no, that's not true, they're just delayed, in a couple of hours you'll have nurses all over you, you lucky sod.'

Lt Andrew Bickerdike

I remember Neil Grose being carried in and placed next to me. He'd been hit in the chest, and his breathing was heavy and laboured.

Pte Mark Eyles-Thomas

Cpl Phil Probets came over to check Neil's condition. Phil tried to open Neil's smock, but there was a problem with the zip. He got his torch out, checked Neil's mouth and began to clear it. As he did this, Neil died. We were all shocked at the suddenness of it.

Cpl Phil Probets

I went over to Neil Grose, and he whispered, 'When's the chopper coming?' I replied, 'They're on their way.' I was just trying to reassure him. I said, 'Keep calm, kid, keep calm.' This seemed to work; and he goes quiet, I then asked him, 'Are you okay, Neil?' and he murmured, 'Yes.' I was trying to keep him calm, so as to not raise his blood pressure. Neil again went quiet, and after a short time I asked again, 'Are you okay, Neil?' He replied, 'Yes.' He once again went quiet, and seemed to settle. Then suddenly he grabbed me, and started asking for his mum. It was then that Neil died. I tried desperately doing CPR, but sadly, I could not save him.

Sgt John Ross

I watched as Phil Probets tried his utmost to save Neil. Eventually I had to tell him, 'Phil, enough, he's gone, leave it.'

Pte Mick Southall:

I didn't realize that Neil was dying. He was still and silent for a moment, and I thought, God, his pain has eased. Then someone said, 'That's it; he's gone.' It took a moment for it to register in my head what had just been said and my heart just sank. We had risked a lot to save him and now it seemed it was all in vain. I felt cheated and angry. I asked Phil Probets, 'Are you sure there's nothing else we can do?' Phil snapped, 'Of course I'm fucking sure.' I stood there for God knows how long, just looking down at my friend who was now lying there, covered over with a poncho. Neil had only celebrated his 18th birthday yesterday.

Cpl Phil Probets

I was shocked at the suddenness of Neil's death. However, I then turned my attention to the rest of the wounded. I gave Ian Bailey and Ned Kelly another Syrette of morphine, but Ian kept asking, 'Have you got any more morphine?' He was in such severe pain. I had to tell him, 'I'm sorry, Beetle, it's all gone.' The situation here was really quite desperate.

We have not been able to put a time on Neil's death, but it is generally thought to be not more than one hour after he was wounded.

Pte Martyn Clarkson-Kearsley

CSM Weeks said he needed some volunteers to retrieve any of the ammunition that had been left behind by the wounded and to remove it from the men who were dead. Our ammunition was getting low to say the least. It had been impossible to recover the ammunition during the evacuation, due to the amount of casualties being moved and the lack of people to move them, and the GPMG ammunition was now in especially short supply.

The group consisted of CSM Weeks, Pte Clifton Lewis, a couple of other guys from B Company and me. We moved down the same route as before, so we knew the general area where the equipment would be. Thankfully, all the kit was where it had been left. We immediately started to take the ammunition out of the discarded webbing, and packed as much of it as we could in our own webbing. The majority of ammo I recovered was stuffed into my windproof smock. I'm not a big guy, but I looked like the Michelin Man. We only took the ammunition that had already been loaded into magazines, plus bandoliers of link ammunition for the GPMGs. As I lay there waiting for the remainder of the group to finish I remember thinking that it was only a matter of time until one of us got shot.

Sgt John Ross

Ned Kelly was in an extremely bad way. I honestly thought he would die, and I just kept talking to him and warned him, 'Ned, don't fall asleep. Listen to me; you've got to stay awake!' I knew if he fell asleep, we might lose him.

Pte Craig (Harry) Harrison

When I came across Pte Pete Hindmarsh, he was lying face down on some rocks. I said, 'What's up, Pete?' He replied 'I've been shot in the arse, Harry.' I gave him my quilted trousers to keep him warm, and I tried to speak to Ned Kelly, but he was in a bad way, and I don't think he recognized me.

It was absolutely freezing. The wounded were feeling the cold more than us and we all started to look for blankets, Argentine sleeping bags or anything that would keep them warm. Pte Sulle Alhaji and I began looking in abandoned or destroyed bunkers. It was while we were doing this we came across Sgt McKay's body. He was slumped against a bunker surrounded by a number of dead Argentines. I knew immediately it was him.

Cpl Phil Probets

I carried out a check on Sgt McKay, he was lying against the edge of a built-up trench. It was quite obvious that he was dead and could not have lived with the wounds that he'd received.

Also during this period, once the wounded reach the shelter of the base of the First Bowl, Sgt Des Fuller sends Cpl McLaughlin's 2 Section back along the sheep track into the Second Bowl.

The time is approximately 03.30hrs (zt).

There have been reports in other books stating how 4 Platoon was forced back, but in fact they establish a defensive area that can be held, and send a section to attack the .50 Cal (No. 3) in the Third Bowl. The only reason they withdraw later is to allow an artillery bombardment of the area: 2 Section 5 Platoon is now approximately 170 metres forward of Fly Half and 6 Platoon, who are up on Fly Half, will be ordered to stop firing as they are endangering 5 Platoon with friendly fire.

3 PARA operational report dated 1982

Cpl McLaughlin's group did, however, manage to obtain a commanding position dominating the .50 HMG Sanger. On their way up they had been temporarily halted by the enemy rolling grenades down the rocks towards them. No casualties resulted. Cpl McLaughlin crawled to within grenade-throwing distance of the gun, but despite several attempts to silence it with grenades and 66mm he was forced to withdraw under heavy small-arms fire. Despite the strong resistance, Sgt Fuller's force was, in fact, in a sound position which could be held if necessary; but as a result of his briefing and the Company Commander's assessment of the situation, it was decided to withdraw 5 Platoon and the remnants of 4 Platoon, to evacuate the casualties, reorganize the company and impose heavier artillery and machine-gun fire on the enemy.

LCpl Colin Edwards

I heard Cpl McLaughlin shouting, '2 Section, on me, on me.' We thought, Oh, fucking hell, we'd better get moving. Paul Hutchinson, Terry Mulgrew and me now rejoined Scouse and the whole section was back together again.

Pte Paul Hutchinson

We heard Cpl McLaughlin shouting, '2 Section, on me.' LCpl Colin Edwards turned to Terry Mulgrew and me, and said, 'Come on, lads, we'd better hurry up or he'll fucking kill us too.' We made our way down from our support position, passed through 4 Platoon, and moved up into the Second Bowl. It had been abandoned; there were collapsed tents and a number of dead bodies lying around. The next bowl [the Third Bowl] was occupied by a group of Argentinians firing a .50 Cal towards A Company. We tried firing 66s at it, and then lobbing grenades over, but we could never get a proper look at its location. Every time we popped our heads up we were shot at. They were really close and shouting insults to us in Spanish. Some of them were even laughing.

This is Heavy Machine Gun No. 3 commanded by Cpl Domingo Lamas, and manned by conscripts CC62 Diego Iriarte, CC62 Pedro Miranda and CC62 Jorge Pacheco, plus four men who have left their position on Heavy Machine Gun No. 6 situated on the south-west corner of Longdon and have now made their way to the Third Bowl (CC62 Avellino Lopez, CC62 Enrique Yegui, CC62 Jorge Maciel and

CC63 Mario Zalazar). This area is a known fallback position. Also in this area are an unknown number of soldiers from the 7th Infantry Regiment.

Pte Grant Grinham

We could hear the Argies shouting over to us, and some were even laughing. I shouted to Tony, 'Do these cunts know who we are?' We began shouting back to them, 'You fucking spick bastards.' Cpl McLaughlin fired a 66mm towards the area of the gun position but it struck one of the large rocks by the bunker and exploded. We immediately came under small-arms fire from the group of riflemen who were protecting the .50 Cal. These men had extremely good night sights, and forced us to keep our heads down with their accurate return fire.

Cpl Domingo Lamas, Argentine Marine in command of HMGs Nos 1, 2 & 3

We detected the presence of enemy troops in the rocks that made up the eastern edge of Sub Lt Baldini's Platoon. We could hear voices in English shouting, 'Come on!' The enemy was leaving the protection of the rocks and was exposed to our guns. On four occasions, members of the group tried to advance, and our fire repulsed them. Harassment on the guns continued, appreciating here that the advance was stopped. Not long after this the artillery came hard on the sector, but despite everything, the situation was controlled and consolidated. The thought of this made me strong, and I thought, No one takes us; this resolution will transmit to my men.[*]

Pte Grant Grinham

Although we couldn't move forward, our section could have held the Second Bowl. Cpl McLaughlin had put us out in various defensive positions and we just waited. CSM Johnny Weeks turned up and said, 'Right, Cpl McLaughlin, you need to get your lads out of here, go back and rejoin 4 Platoon. The CO has decided he wants to flatten the whole fucking place.' I was trying to bury my head in the dirt as I crawled out of the position on my stomach, and Johnny Weeks was just standing there as cool as anything, directing our withdrawal, oblivious to the danger of the incoming rounds.

---

[*] Cpl Lamas was located with HMG No. 3 in the Third Bowl. From *La 2ª Sección en Longdon* 'The 2nd Platoon on Longdon' by Lt Sergio Dachary.

4.7   'I remember thinking, I don't fucking fancy this'

03.50hrs (zt): Cpl McLaughlin's section withdraws, and shortly after at 04.00hrs (zt) a bombardment takes place on the area of the Third Bowl.

LCpl Colin Edwards

I met Pte Jeff Logan, who had been shot through the hand and had lost one finger. Jeff mentioned it was a shame about Brian Milne standing on a mine, and that he was in a bad way. This was news to me, and I said, 'Fuck this, I've got to go and get him,' as he was my best mate. I was held back by other members of my section. I was told that I was needed here, and that Brian would have by now probably been treated by medics and been evacuated, so I sat down in a bit of a daze. We sat and had a smoke and tried to keep warm.

Pte Grant Grinham

We were back with 4 Platoon. Cpl McLaughlin told us to stay here, while he went to find out more information. We began to reorganize ourselves. I remember it was freezing cold, and we went searching in enemy bunkers for warm kit. Then some more naval gunfire came in; it shook the entire mountain, and seemed to go on for quite a while.

LCpl Colin Edwards

Once Scouse McLaughlin had placed everyone out, he came up to me and said, 'Taff, I need a shit, cover me.' So he climbed into an Argentine trench and did his business. When he climbed out he whispered, 'Taff, I think there's a live Argy in there; I want you to come around from that side and when I say so, switch on your torch and we'll see what happens.' So I crept over to the trench and on his command, I switched on my torch and there was an Argy crouching down, pointing his weapon. Scouse shot him dead with his P38 pistol.

At approximately 04.30hrs (zt), 4 and 5 Platoons have now fully withdrawn. They are told to rest and get a brew on and sort themselves out. 4 Platoon are unaware that the Regimental Aid Post with its doctor and medics is only 140 metres away down a pitch-dark gully; the nine wounded members of the platoon will not move to this location until approximately 07.00hrs (zt):

CSM Johnny Weeks

I contacted Major Patton on the radio and said, 'I need more medics and my men need evacuating.' He was trying to reassure me that the vehicle convoy was on its way. I told him in fairly tough terms that I wanted people up here taking my wounded out, but it seemed the Snowcats had been delayed due to the lateness of 45 Commando crossing their Start Line. When the Snowcats finally did arrive, they took 6 Platoon's wounded, and then the stretcher-bearers were tasked to run the ammunition resupplies up the western slope.

At 04.40hrs (zt), after firing 156 rounds HMS Avenger's 4.5in gun goes off line; they have been having problems with the gun's gyroscope.

04.55hrs (zt): HMS Avenger's gun is still not working; HMS Yarmouth now takes over HMS Avenger's targets.

At approximately 05.30hrs (zt), Lt Cox is with Major Argue, Major Collett and the CO in the First Bowl, discussing the battalion's next move.

Vernon Steen, Civilian Guide

I was now up in the First Bowl, and what I remember most is the command and control among 3 PARA – they all seemed to know what they were doing. The naval gunfire that night was absolutely unbelievable, it was so close. I was just so cold, the cold was going right through me. At one stage I thought I would actually freeze to death.

Major Mike Argue:

By now the CO was moving A Company in behind us ready to pass through, but before they arrived, in view of the weight of fire put down, I issued orders for a flanking assault on our final objective which was the eastern end of the ridge.

Lt Mark Cox

Major Argue said he wanted me to make another attack by collecting the remainder of the company, who were able, and forming them up again. I yelled for Sgt Ross and told him, 'We need to find everyone we can and get them formed up for another go.' Captain McCracken asked me if I would like naval gunfire support, I replied, 'Yes, absolutely,' and he set about a plan to bring in gunfire from ships at sea on the southern gunline, south of Port Stanley. It was at the extreme range of these weapons, to within 50 metres of us. He requested a 'Fire for Effect' mission, and I remember hearing the first rounds coming down and thinking of all the ocean and countryside they had passed over, and how the primitive ship-borne computer had held the barrel steady on our coordinates. Above all, how small a margin for error 50 metres was over all that distance. We arranged a signal for him to 'Cease Fire'. It would be then that we would begin the assault. I decided that we would go around to the left flank in file. Then at a given point, stop and face up the slope and sweep up it until we gained the high ground, then swing left again towards Stanley.

CSM Johnny Weeks

We would be once again pushing forward along the sheep track on the northern side of Longdon, in order to try a left-flanking attack, which I thought was bloody ridiculous as that was where we had all been shot at from earlier. I said, 'Who the fuck's thought this up?' I decided 5 Platoon would be the lead platoon as they had taken the least casualties so far.

Pte Grant Grinham

Scouse returned and casually said, 'Right, lads, we've got to go back up to where we were earlier, so sort your kit out and be ready to move.' I remember thinking, I don't fucking fancy this. We'd been up there once, and we'd been lucky to get out of there in one piece the first time.

Captain McCracken has two 105mm Batteries on priority call and HMS Yarmouth on station. He brings artillery fire to bear along the ridge. This fire is very accurate and effective. He continues to bring fire closer and closer, in an attempt to silence the .50 Cal in the Third Bowl that has moved its location slightly and is now firing to the west.

HMS Yarmouth fires a few adjusting rounds:

05.47 hrs (zt) x 2 salvos

05.52hrs (zt) x 2 salvos

05.55hrs (zt) x 2 salvos

05.59hrs (zt) x 43 salvos

Naval gunfire finishes at 06.12hrs (zt). This will be the last of the naval gunfire.

HMS Yarmouth and HMS Glamorgan now beat a hasty retreat to rendezvous with the Carrier Group, leaving HMS Avenger to man the gunline with its 4.5-inch gun (Big Bertha), which is now working again.

The Argentinian position:

At approximately 06.00hrs (zt), 46 men belonging to C Company, 7th IR, under the command of 1st Lt Raul Castaneda, arrive at the Full Back location. These men have come from a position north-east of Mount Longdon, codenamed Rum Punch/ Rough Diamond. Lt Castaneda is now briefed by B Company, 7th IR OC Major Carrizo-Salvadores; he tells them that their mission is to counter-attack along the northern side of Longdon. A guide is instructed to lead Lt Castaneda's men, some of whom are equipped with head-mounted night sights. At approximately 06.15hrs (zt), they begin moving cautiously towards the Second Bowl.

Captain McCracken is told by the Fire Direction Centre that naval gunfire is no longer available:

06.18hrs (zt): from C/S 29 FDC to C/S 41B: '41B reference Sea Shelldrake now not available.'

Lt Mark Cox

I gave Captain McCracken the signal, and we began to move to the east in file. I would lead with my radio operator Pte Phillips.

The order of march is Lt Cox and Pte Steve Phillips, followed by Anti-Tank Detachment, 5 Platoon, B Company HQ, followed by 4 Platoon.

Cpl Phil Skidmore

What I remember most is the chaos and lack of information, and the smell of that mountain. When we first reached the bottom it stank, and as I got further into it, they seemed to have shit everywhere. Then Major Argue said, 'I want the machine guns leading. Put the support element at the front.' I confided to

Jon Crow and Kev Connery, 'Fucking hell, lads, I don't like the sound of this. We've got to lead 5 Platoon.'

Cpl Graham Heaton

As we moved down onto the sheep track Jon Crow touched my arm and asked, 'Graham, where's Phil Skidmore?' I replied, 'He's here, just in front of me.' Jon said politely, 'Do you mind if I jump in front of you?' and I said, 'No, go ahead.' Almost immediately after this, I heard a voice call out from the darkness shouting, 'Hey, hombres!' And in a split second, a burst of automatic fire came hurtling down the sheep track.

06.37hrs (zt): HMS *Glamorgan* is hit, port-side hangar and main galley; HMS *Yarmouth* and HMS *Avenger* are going to assist.

06.40hrs (zt): 5 Platoon begin to advance along the sheep track.

LCpl Lenny Carver

Suddenly the black silhouette of an Argentine stepped out from behind a rock and into the middle of the sheep track, holding his weapon at mid-chest height, and called out, 'Hey, hombres!' and fired a burst of automatic fire down the track. Everybody splits, some to the left, some to the right and some dropped to the ground. Jon Crow, who was in front of me, died immediately, I think. I was just in the process of diving to the left when a round passed through my chest puncturing my lung and exited out of my back. It threw me back about two metres. I landed in some cover and I rolled down a steep incline.

People were shouting fire indications, and someone was shouting to 'fire a 66!' I started to take incoming fire; rounds were landing very close to the left and right of me. I was bleeding badly from my nose and mouth. I heard Chris Masterman and Terry Bowdell shouting out of the darkness, 'Lenny, Lenny are you okay?' and I replied, 'No, I've been fucking hit.' Chris and Terry immediately came flying out, under fire, and grabbed me by my webbing and dragged me into cover. They then dragged me up a steep incline into the First Bowl.

Pte Kevin Connery

I was in front of Jon Crow. Almost straight away we began taking incoming fire. As Jon didn't make a sound, I thought he had taken cover. I dropped onto the ground and started firing; someone fired a 66mm over the top of me, and I began to move forward. It was still dark, and at some stage I remember hearing someone yelling, 'Is everyone okay?' I then heard Phil Skidmore urgently shouting, 'Jon, Jon, are you okay, Jon?' Someone shouted back, 'Jon's dead.' I then moved forward to another position where I fired a 66mm, and moved further along the track.

Pte Ben Gough

When we came under fire, Jon Crow dropped down in the centre of the sheep track. Dominic Gray said calmly, 'Go and check him.' I said, 'Fuck off; I'm not going over yet,' as there was still incoming fire, but Dominic ran over to Jon. He quickly checked him and shouted, 'Ben, he's dead.' He then ran back into cover.

Pte Mark Eisler

I remember seeing Captain McCracken, the NGFO, step out and fire a 66mm. It sailed alongside the whole of the platoon and went into a bunker.

Cpl Phil Skidmore

I'd been hit in the leg, but it was only a flesh wound, and I could hear Major Argue shouting, 'Push on, B Company, push on!' I felt like saying, 'Why don't you fucking push on?' Kev Connery and I were lying on the track. B Company was firing over the top of us, and I was shouting, 'We're still fucking here!' Eventually we crawled over to our left into a bit of cover, and threw some grenades up towards the enemy position.

Pte Paul Hutchinson

I remember Major Argue trying to spur us on by shouting 'On, on, B Company, winkle them out with bayonets and grenades.' I heard a few choice words shouted back at him.

Pte Terry Bowdell

Major Argue shouted, 'I want that rock face sprayed with fire from top to bottom.' Which I did, I put down about 250 rounds. I needed more ammo, and shouted across to Chris Masterman to 'Belt me up, Chris.' He replied, 'You can fuck off! I'll throw them to you.' He tossed me a couple of bandoliers of ammunition; Pte Mark [Boots] Meredith also laughed at my situation.

I shouted loudly to Dom Gray and anyone who was listening to me, 'On my count of three, prepare to give me covering fire.' I put some more fire down and shouted, 'One, two, three.' I jumped up and started running; I got myself in another position and started firing. The lads behind me began moving forward and they assaulted the position.

Pte Ben Gough

We gradually began moving forward. We all seemed to consolidate around a large rock approximately four metres high. I remember our radio operator Steve Phillips was firing away right next to my ear. We eventually skirmished forward to the rocks at the end of the sheep track by the Second Bowl. I remember thinking that if I'm going to get shot, this is the place, since there was lots of incoming fire coming from further east along towards Full Back.

Dominic Gray was shot in the head just in front of me. I looked and saw a hole in the front left side of his helmet and there was blood running down his face. I asked cautiously, 'Are you all right?' Dominic took his helmet off slowly and after a quick check of his head, I ran him back up the track towards the First Bowl. Dominic said, 'Ben, my helmet; I've lost my fucking helmet!' And like a dick, I went back along the sheep track for his helmet. We then received an order to withdraw.

As I ran back I bumped into a couple of blokes who I didn't recognize and said, 'Who the fuck are you?' They replied, 'We're A Company.' I said, 'I'm B Company, we're all up in here.' I took them up and into the First Bowl.

The bullet that hit Dominic cut a groove across the top of his skull.

Pte Tony Barlow

I remember Cpl McLaughlin storming past us with his pistol in one hand and his SLR in the other. He was furious; he had that look in his eye, as if someone's going to get knocked out here. I thought, Fucking hell! There was an Argentine position above us, firing down at 5 Platoon. He single-handedly climbed up into the rocks, threw a grenade into it, then climbed into the position, fired a few rounds and yelled, 'Two dead, one wounded.' And I can only assume the Argentine moved for his weapon as Cpl McLaughlin fired a double tap and added, 'Make that three dead.'

Lt Mark Cox

Somebody at the back of the line-up declared they were throwing a grenade and lobbed it. It landed right next to where Pte Steve Phillips and I were taking cover. There it was fizzing away on the peat; it had been too long in the air to kick away and too close to escape. I just crunched my body against the rocks to escape the worst of it. Luckily, it exploded upwards. We escaped without a scratch. I fumbled for my grenade, but I had bent the pin right back so it was difficult to open. I found the strength to squeeze open the pin of my grenade and lob it. It went right to the spot, and exploded. I moved further forward to another rock overlooking where the Argentines were.

I now had Pte Connery with me. I said I was going to fire my 66mm at the enemy position, and then we would simply overrun it. I fired the 66mm and we ran forwards, but there was no explosion. I believe now that we weren't within arming range of the 66mm. It was simply a fast-moving piece of metal. However, the explosion made by firing it definitely helped us get up and go. Once onto the enemy position there were two enemy who were lying there, and another who was asking in broken English not to be killed, and saying that he believed in God.

I moved forward beyond the position, into the Second Bowl area and almost immediately came under fire; I felt a sting on my shoulder, which was accompanied by my ammunition pouches and water bottle flopping down. The strap on my webbing was separated. I stayed down, firing up at the rocks with my SLR. I shouted out that I'd been hit. I recovered myself and ran back to Connery. He and I then covered each other back to the First Bowl where we had originally started from.

Captain McCracken's signaller reports:

06.53hrs zt): from C/S 41B to C/S 29FDC: '41B under fire taken one casualty.'

07.05hrs (zt): from C/S 41B to C/S 29FDC: '41B under sniper fire one dead.'

07.08hrs (zt): from C/S 41B to C/S 29FDC: '41B with 3 PARA using small-arms fire and 66mm's.'

07.15hrs (zt): from C/S 41B to C/S 29FDC: '41B believes the sniper eliminated sending a section forward to check.'

3 PARA HQ asks the CO what's happening:

07.25hrs (zt): from C/S 0 to C/S 9: 'Send brief situation report for higher formation.'

07.25hrs (zt): from C/S 9 to C/S 0: 'Roger: Call Sign 2 has sustained considerable casualties whilst taking its objective, Call Sign 1 will pass through and hopefully take Full Back by first light. There is fierce resistance on the feature and it is difficult to pinpoint the exact location of the enemy amongst the rocks.'

07.25hrs (zt): from C/S 0 to C/S 9: 'Passed to Brigade.'

Pte Kevin Connery
I went forward with Lt Mark Cox into the Second Bowl, where in the chaos that followed I shot three Argentinians. I remember looking at Lt Cox holding his SLR with his bayonet fixed, and it seemed bigger than him. He was in a bit of shock, we then pepper-potted our way back along the sheep track.

Pte Grant Grinham
All of a sudden Cpl McLaughlin jumped up and ran towards the rocks. I thought, If he thinks it's better over there, I'm going as well, so I jumped up and ran after him. Shortly after Cpl McLaughlin had reached the cover of the rocks, I jumped in beside him. I started talking to him, but he turned to me and said angrily, 'Fucking shut up and watch our backs!' So I did; we only seemed to have been there for a short while and then we received the order to withdraw. We began moving back in pairs and eventually got back to the First Bowl.

Cpl Domingo Lamas, Argentine Marine
I knew that HMG No. 1 was out of service. At some time during a break from fighting, I made my way to find it. The crew was not in place and they had moved the whole gun by hand, but without the M63 gun mount, to the location of gun No. 3. It was put into service, but the mechanism was damaged and made it impossible to use. During this stage of the battle came the two missing conscripts from the HMG No. 6, Jorge Maciel and Mario Zalazar, who crept into my position. The first one had been shot at close range. We had to conduct first aid, I told him to open his jacket. I inspected his back, which was very bad,

he had lost a lot of blood, and it seemed to me that this was a bullet wound not shrapnel. We applied two PCIs [field dressings]; I placed him among the rocks and covered him with blankets. One of the ammunition providers was appointed to look after him. He asked for water, and I think he had some idea of where he was and could recognize me.

The option of evacuation to the PUSO [first-aid post] at this time was not feasible for the situation that we were in; it would have required two men to leave who at that moment were very much needed, and I did not know if they would come back alive. I could hear the voices in English on the northern side. It made me appreciate that the enemy could be surrounding me and was nearby.*

Sgt John Ross

After about an hour there was no choice but to pull back. I started to get the lads to put some covering fire down to allow the guys up front to pass through us. It was clear to me, as it had been for the last hour, that we could not succeed with a direct attack on the position without blitzing it first. Lt Cox eventually returned with Kev Connery. I thought at one stage we had lost him. I heard the CO tell Major Argue that he was pulling B Company back and would be passing A Company through. The planning then started to mount a company attack with fire support on the position. I said to Scouse McLaughlin that we should've done that an hour ago and Scouse agreed.

Cpl Graham Heaton

CSM Johnny Weeks appeared and yelled, 'I want everyone back to the First Bowl; we're going to flatten the fucking place, again!' We now began skirmishing back; I ran a short distance, stopped and turned around to provide covering fire. As I turned and dropped onto one knee, I saw green tracer coming towards me. It was two-, three-round bursts and two rounds of it hit me in my right leg. Pte Frank O'Regan was also shot in the left leg at the same time.

---

* From *La 2ª Sección en Longdon* 'The 2nd Platoon on Longdon' by Lt Sergio Dachary.

Pte Andy Steadman

As we were skirmishing back we suddenly came under fire, again! I managed to dive into an Argy shell scrape, and I noticed Frank O'Regan crawling along the sheep track towards me. I could tell he was in difficulty, so I jumped up and ran down, grabbed him by the collar and dragged him into cover. He told me he'd been hit in the leg, but it was still dark and I couldn't see a thing. He was in pain and I asked him, 'Have you got your morphine?' But he groaned and said it was in his webbing back on the track, so I ran back down the track to retrieve it. I proceeded to give him the morphine jab and dressed his wound as best I could.

4.8 'It's fucking hard, mate; you watch yourself'

The time is now approximately 07.45hrs (zt).

Pte Andy Stone

We were now taking fire from various directions; some came from further along the mountain and some came from the north-east. When John Goreing suddenly opened fire right next to my ear, it stunned me for a moment, but then I also began returning fire at the muzzle flashes. Then an Argentine wire-guided anti-tank missile was fired; it came rushing in and exploded on the rocks near the First Bowl.

Pte Duncan Daly

A guided missile went over our heads and the guidance wire draped over the top of us. We carried on moving back, and consolidated in First Bowl.

A Company starts to arrive at the First Bowl.

Sgt Manny Manfred, 30 yrs – 1 Platoon, A Company

As I was coming from Wing Forward, members of B Company were withdrawing towards the First Bowl. I saw Cpl Graham Heaton, and then a burst of fire hit him in the leg. I helped with others to drag him up into the First Bowl, where someone began to treat him. I remember a medic shouting urgently, 'Has anyone got a knife?' I had an old clasp knife that I had had for years on a lanyard with a spliced knot. I quickly took it off and gave it to the medic. I never saw it again. I watched as one of them began cutting his denims open, to see what damage had been done.

Pte Craig (Harry) Harrison

The cry of 'MEDIC!' rang out and I thought, Not again, is this never going to end? We dragged Cpl Heaton into some cover, I cut his trouser open, and I saw his leg was badly damaged and he was having trouble breathing. I tried to give him morphine, but the top had broken off. I happened to turn, and I noticed a long line of A Company sat against the rock face, awaiting orders to move forward.

[These were A Company 2 Platoon.]

Captain Adrian Logan

I remember the CO saying, 'We'll bring A Company forward shortly; they will pass through your guys, and they will carry on and take the next feature.' There seemed to be a mood of 'Thank fuck for that, let's have a brew and get the wounded sorted.' We were still getting shelled but it was intermittent, and their fire seemed to be hitting further down on the eastern slope.

Pte Andy Stone

We just sat and rested in the darkness. Some of my friends from A Company came over and asked, 'What's it been like?' I said, 'It's fucking hard, mate; you watch yourself.' It was still pitch black and freezing. 2 Platoon, A Company was now given our remaining 66s and grenades. The rattle of machine-gun fire was deafening. I sat in a sort of numb silence just watching as a blur of people went back and forth shouting orders.

CSM John Weeks

During this phase, we now had the assistance of an extra medic, LCpl Chris Lovett from A Company, who came up to me and said in a courteous manner, 'Sir, I understand you've got casualties. I'm a medic from A Company, can I help?' I replied, 'Yes, just get stuck in.' He then attached himself to us, and gave us some much-needed help.

LCpl Colin Edwards

It was decided that artillery would once again flatten the Second and Third Bowl areas, which were only 50 or 60 metres away. The rounds came roaring in like express trains descending from the heavens. They were absolutely terrifying; the ground was shaking and the noise deafening.

I started to get a brew on and discovered that a bullet had passed through my water bottle. It was on the left side of my webbing, and on my right side another bullet had gone through one of my pouches. By now we were all absolutely shattered. Everyone looked tired, conversation was hushed, and we were mostly too tired to talk. People seemed to look older, and I don't mind admitting that for a moment it was all too much.

Pte Tony Barlow

We began to sort ourselves out. I remember saying, 'Fuck this, before I do anything, I'm having a brew.' Someone said, 'Yeah, Tony, that sounds like a fucking good idea, let's have a brew.' I was now down to my last ten rounds of ammunition. I remember watching Tony Bojko firing his GPMG up at the top of the First Bowl. The barrel of his gun was glowing red hot.

Sgt John Ross

Scouse McLaughlin came up to me and announced, 'John, I've found the money.' I grinned and asked, 'What money?' He replied, 'Fucking thousands.' It turned out that he'd been in a Quartermaster-type bunker and found a load of Argentine money. It was probably only 40 or 50 pounds, which we laughed about, and he said, 'Tell you what, John, when we get into Stanley, we'll rob the bank.' I laughed and replied, 'Fuck off, Scouse, who do you think we are? Kelly's fucking Heroes?' Scouse laughed and said, 'John, it will be fucking chaos; they won't have a clue who done it.'

LCpl Lenny Carver

They dragged me up the incline and into the First Bowl – with the size of me, I'm not sure how they got me up there, but that's where I ended up. I remember Phil Probets asking, 'Do you know where you've been hit?' I replied, 'I've been hit in the side, but my back is soaking wet, I think I've got a hole there as well.' Phil said, 'Right, okay.' Then Chris Lovett joined us and said reassuringly, 'All right, mate, don't worry, you're in safe hands now; we'll sort you out; we can't give you any morphine because you might be gut shot.' Chris dealt with the wound to my side, then moved on to my back to deal with the exit wound. He then said, 'Shit, that's quite big.' It felt like he had safety-pinned my back together. There was a wave of pain, which went right through my body, and I passed out.

Sgt John Ross

When A Company were preparing to leave the bowl, I gave the night-vision goggles that I'd found earlier in the .50 Cal bunker [No. 4] to Major Collett. Scouse McLaughlin then asked if he could go with A Company, but he was told to stay with B Company. I said, 'Fucking hell, Scouse, haven't you done enough? Come on, let's sort ourselves out and get a brew on.'

At approximately 09.27hrs (zt), there is an incident involving a 105mm recoilless rifle located 2.8 kilometres away at the western end of Wireless Ridge. It has been suggested that Cpl Manuel Medina fired a single round towards the SF machine-gun line on Fly Half. From its location, the 105mm RCL team had a direct line of sight to 3 PARA's machine-gun line. With the distance involved, they would have to use the weapons-spotter rifle to gauge the distance to the target. The main armament would have then been fired. They would have had to aim high, and the HEAT round would have been descending when it reached its target area of Fly Half.

The round passes through the gunline, just missing the CO and various senior personnel. It then plunges down the western slope impacting in the area of a three-man Milan Detachment, killing all three members. Just over 30 minutes after this incident, at approximately 10.00hrs (zt), there is an explosion in the First Bowl; it impacts on the western wall, killing LCpl Lovett. Shortly after this there is a second explosion, also on the west wall, which kills Cpl Wilson. I think the 105mm RCL may have been remanned as both HEAT rounds/missiles came from an easterly direction.

There have been reports that Cobra missiles may have been fired from Tumbledown, but it seems that these weapons have a guidance wire of two kilometres, and Tumbledown is approximately three kilometres away; the missiles would have gone 'rogue' after two kilometres. Another author has suggested a

Strella missile, but it seems these missiles will not launch unless the weapon has a heat source to lock on to. But I am open to any suggestions.

A Company leaves the First Bowl at approximately 09.40hrs (zt):

09.40hrs (zt): from C/S 19 to C/S 9: 'Call sign 1/2 has cleared and now manning the high ground.'

First light approximately 10.00hrs (zt).

Pte Tony Barlow

A Company had all left. I got a brew on with Simon Ward and Steve Playle, and tried to warm myself up. I cannot describe how bad I smelled; I was covered in shit. We were told to start digging in. Some of 5 Platoon were positioned around the edge of the First Bowl. I was with Pte Craig (Harry) Harrison. We had started to dig a shell scrape, but then Harry said, 'I don't like this position; it doesn't feel right.' So we moved to another location and started digging again. A short while later a shell landed exactly where our old position was going to be. It was now beginning to get light, and we noticed a pile of mortar shells by us, and I decided to move them. I was walking towards Captain Logan, who was standing by Chris Lovett. I was just about to ask him, 'Sir, where do you want me to put these?' when suddenly there was a massive explosion.

CSM John Weeks

There was an explosion in the bowl and the blast blew a lot of people over, including Pte Clarkson-Kearsley, the medics and me. There were quite a few of us that were concussed and deafened.

Cpl Phil Probets

I had just returned from the RAP, where I had picked up more medical supplies, drips, shell dressings, morphine, etc. I then headed towards the First Bowl to help with the wounded. When I entered the bowl I saw Chris Lovett, who was treating the wounded. I went over to assist with Graham Heaton when Chris Lovett asked me for a shell dressing. Then there was a terrific explosion.

Pte Duncan Daly

Chris Lovett was killed by the blast; it blew everyone over, including me. I saw Phil Probets pick himself up and run back over to where Chris Lovett lay, but he was dead. Phil was devastated; I put my arm around Phil and said, 'Come on, mate, there's nothing you can do now.'

Cpl Graham Heaton

I was receiving treatment from Chris Lovett when he said, 'Graham, I'll be back in a minute – I'm just going to get some shell dressings out of my Bergen.' At that moment there was a huge flash, and an explosion. I opened my eyes and for a moment I couldn't see, and I thought, Fucking hell, I'm blind! But as my vision cleared, Chris was gone and Captain Logan was leaning against a rock holding his arm and saying, 'I've been hit.' CSM Johnny Weeks picked himself off the floor and said, 'What the fuck was that?'

Captain Adrian Logan

Something rushed past me; it was on my right side, but I never saw it. It hit the west wall of the First Bowl and there was an almighty explosion. A blast wave was thrown out, but Chris Lovett was standing directly between me and the explosion. My left arm was extended, as I made a gesture. When I woke up, I was lying on my back looking up at the sky and for a moment I seemed to be on my own, within my own thoughts. It was beginning to get light. Then I was back in reality; my head was ringing, and I began to check myself. I could not feel my left arm. I held it up and thought, Well, it's still there, even though I couldn't feel it. I took my glove off, and to my relief, my hand was still there. I was in pain, my head was spinning, and I was still quite groggy. It all seemed to go quiet, and I remember someone saying in a panicky voice, 'Is he okay?' Someone else replied, 'No, he's dead.' I turned and looked at Chris Lovett, who was lying dead next to me.

Pte Tony Barlow

I found myself on my hands and knees; everything had turned red, and I didn't know where I was. I put my hands to my face, but I couldn't feel anything. I started to panic and shouted loudly, 'I'm blind, I'm blind.' Simon Ward and Harry Harrison then grabbed me and took me to one side, and they bathed my eyes. I'm not sure how long it took for my sight to return, but it gradually came back. I then felt a bit better; I got up and walked over to where a body lay covered over with a blanket. I asked Phil Probets, 'Who's that?' He hesitated for a moment, then said quietly, 'It's Chris Lovett.' I said, 'It can't be; I've just been talking to him.'

I made my way back to my trench. When there was another artillery barrage, an Argentine prisoner climbed in with me! I told him to fuck off and I pushed him out. After what had just happened, I was not in the mood to cosy up with an Argy.

Shortly after the explosion that killed Chris Lovett, there is another explosion.

Spr Tommy Trindall, 20 yrs – 9 Sqn RE

I went along to the First Bowl to help with some of the casualties. As I walked in, Cpl Scotty Wilson came over and said, 'Hi, Mark, how's it going? Is everyone okay? Where's the rest of the troop?' Just to my right, Spr Steve Tickle was on his knees in a small hollow treating someone who was wounded. As we were talking, I heard this very high-pitched noise, unlike the artillery that we'd become accustomed to. I dropped to the ground and curled up in a ball.

There was a massive explosion about 15 metres away. I got covered in crap, dirt and rocks; my head was spinning. I uncurled from my position, and as I turned to look to the right, about a foot away from my face was the lifeless body of someone looking straight at me. I looked about for Scotty, then realized it was him; I cleared his airway and tried to give him mouth to mouth. I shouted for a medic. Some 3 PARA bloke came over and said, 'Sorry, mate, he's dead. It's too late for him, but there are other blokes over here that need help.' I had a sickening feeling, but he was right. We started to help carry the rest of the wounded down to the Regimental Aid Post; the ground was tortuous and we were still under artillery bombardment, which resulted in further casualties.

Tommy Trindall's real first name is Mark – Tommy is just a nickname. Scotty Wilson was one of the few who used Mark's real name.

Spr Steve Tickle, 9 Sqn RE

I was trying to calm Captain Logan, when I heard Spr Tommy Trindall, who called out my name and said something like 'Look, it's Scotty.' I went over to where Tommy was kneeling. On the ground in front of him was Scotty Wilson, who was lying face down. We rolled him over onto his back; however, he showed no signs of life. We couldn't find any wounds. Eventually we discovered a small wound to the back of his head. I wasn't sure whether it was this or the concussion from the blast had killed him, but I was certain that his death had been instant.

Pte Grant Grinham

When we moved into the First Bowl I was with Tony Kempster. We were knackered after the long night, so we stuck a shovel in the ground and sat against it back to back and fell asleep. We were woken by Sgt George Duffus's two gun teams firing in A Company. Shortly after this Cpl McLaughlin came up to me and said, 'Here you go, Grant, have this.' He gave me an Argentine folding FN rifle, which I was quite pleased with. He added, 'We've got a bunker over there; John Ross is already in it. Go in and get a brew on.'

I went over and climbed inside and sat with Sgt Ross and Nigel [Lippy] Linton. Cpl McLaughlin climbed in after me, and we sat talking about the night. After a while, Sgt Ross said, 'Right, Scouse, we need to check on the rest of the platoon.' Cpl McLaughlin was nearest to the bunker entrance, so he climbed out first. I then shuffled out behind him, legs first. I was just about to pick myself up when there was an almighty flash. I next remember looking across to Cpl McLaughlin; he was leaning against a large rock, and was shouting, 'I'm sucking, I'm sucking.' I then noticed my right leg was hanging off, and the other one was badly injured.

Steve Phillips was one of the first people I remember reaching me. He was about to use his own morphine, but I warned him, 'No, Steve, you have to use mine.' Within seconds there were a number of blokes helping. I was trying to tell them what to do, but they said, 'Grant, just fucking shut up.' I remember Scouse McLaughlin was saying, 'I can't suck. I've got a christening to go to.' He also yelled at someone, 'Will you fucking shut up.' And then John Ross gave me morphine.

More rounds began exploding above the bowl area; fortunately Steve Phillips lay across me to shield me from the falling debris. It was a very brave act and something I have remembered ever since.

Shortly after this it was decided to move me. Harry Harrison, Colin Edwards, Terry Mulgrew and Paul Hutchinson carried me to a more sheltered bit of cover, lower down in the bowl. I remember Harry Harrison held my hand while Cpl Phil Probets treated me. CSM Johnny Weeks shouted loudly to one of the radio operators, 'Get some fucking stretchers up here now.' I remember Major Argue saying the stretchers would be here in about ten minutes. But it seemed to take ages. I remember shouting to him, 'You said it would take ten fucking minutes, where the fuck are they?'

Sgt John Ross

I said to Scouse, 'We'd better check on the blokes.' So Scouse McLaughlin got out first. It was quite awkward exiting the bunker. But, once he was out, Scouse stood up and Grant was in the process of getting out, and I was following behind him. Suddenly there was a bright flash; I wasn't sure what had happened, whether it was artillery, or what. Grant Grinham turned to me and yelled, 'John, they've blown my fucking leg off and I'm only 19.' I still couldn't see exactly what had gone on, as my eyes had been blinded by the flash. I got out and got my wits back together. I saw Scouse McLaughlin lying on the ground and Grant with his leg blown off. Scouse was saying, 'I'm gonna suck.' I said, 'No, you won't.' He said quietly, 'I will, I've been a bastard tonight.'

It seemed for a moment that no one was helping us; I started shouting, 'Fucking get over here now!' Grant was taken away, but Scouse refused to be casevaced. He really needed treatment, his whole left shoulder was open, and he was having trouble breathing. I was over by the bunker bathing my eyes, which were still sore. Once my eyes had settled down I was told that Scouse had gone to the RAP.

Cpl Phil Probets

Cpl McLaughlin was brought to me and I took off his smock and checked his wound. It was a large wound, but I tried to reassure him, saying, 'You'll be okay; it's only a bit of shrapnel.' Then Pete Higgs appeared from somewhere and said, 'Phil, I'll take him down to the RAP.' And with some relief I said, 'Okay, thanks for that, Pete.' And off they went.

Pte Kevin Connery

I was standing next to Cpl Phil Skidmore when there was a huge explosion behind us; we were both picked up and slammed against the rock wall. I was lying there stunned for a moment; my ears were ringing, and my body felt very hot. I gradually became aware of Phil shouting for a medic. He had been hit in the back and was in great pain. I began feeling his back for a wound. Eventually, I found a small hole in the back of his smock: the shrapnel had gone straight through all his layers of clothing. I then found the wound in his back. He'd also suffered a leg wound which I missed, as I was more concerned with his back.

Cpl Phil Skidmore

I felt like I'd been hit by a sledgehammer. Kev Connery was the first to reach me, and then a medic arrived and began treating me. I remember hearing more incoming fire, and thought, Fuck that, I'm off. I jumped up and left the medic and ran for cover back into the bowl; CMS Johnny Weeks was shouting at everyone to get off the top area. I think Kev Connery took me down to the RAP.

LCpl Roger James

We were receiving sporadic shell fire from the Port Stanley area when there was a massive explosion on my right-hand side. I was facing down the western slope of Longdon with my back to Port Stanley. I could feel the heat from the blast down the right side of my body. It threw me through the air, and somehow I had completely turned around and landed on my stomach facing Port Stanley. I rolled over and began checking myself; I had a severe pain in my leg, so I felt along my leg all the way down to my foot and thought, Well, it's still there, but the pain was terrific. I was amazed to see that Tony McLarnon was still standing there; he was in shock and was just looking at me. I yelled at him, 'Fucking get down!' as artillery rounds were still coming in. I shouted out 'Medic' really loudly, and almost immediately an incoming round landed very close to me. I crawled as fast as I could towards a crevice to get into a bit more cover, followed by Tony.

Along came this big bloke with longish hair, who was rather strange looking – I didn't recognize him from the battalion. He carried out a bit of first aid on me, said, 'Right, I am going to take you down the RAP.' He put me over his shoulder using a fireman's lift and warned, 'Right, listen to the shells, if you think it's going to be a close one, tap me on the back, and we'll hit the deck.' I couldn't believe this guy, he was really strong because I'm not a little bloke. He ran out of the First Bowl, and down the northern side of Longdon. I tapped his back a couple of times, and we took cover. Then he was up and running again, when suddenly without warning he dropped me, and I went flying. I thought he'd been shot, I could hear him groaning, and I called out, 'Are you all right, mate?' And a voice came back, 'I'm okay, just winded.' He had tripped over a couple of dead Argentines who had been killed during the earlier fighting. He picked me up, and we started again to make our way to the RAP. When we got there, he put me down and asked, 'Are you all right now, mate?' He gave me a cigarette and then buggered off.

The man who carries LCpl Roger James is one of the naval gunfire team.

Part of Captain Willie McCracken's operational report dated 1982

RO1 Brian [Stan] Hardy was dispatched to help with casualties while we were still under effective enemy fire. Bdr [Jacko] Jackson and Gnr [Titch] Barfoot had a very lucky escape as they were helping take casualties to the RAP when more shelling began and the two people immediately in front of them were killed.

These two people are Cpl Stewart McLaughlin and LCpl Pete Higgs.

Pte Paul Hutchinson

I was going to have a chat with Pte Andy Steadman, when suddenly there was a massive flash and an explosion. I was thrown through the air and landed in a heap. I sat up and checked myself; my ears were ringing, I was slightly disorientated, and I became aware of people screaming. I picked myself up and ran over to Andy Steadman, who was on the ground rolling about in agony. I helped him up and tried to get him into cover, as incoming artillery was still landing around our position.

I noticed Steve Phillips and Terry Mulgrew attending to Grant Grinham. A medic arrived and began putting a saline drip into him and administered morphine. Grant was in a bad way. His leg was only just hanging on and his other leg was badly damaged. I helped carry him down to the RAP. As

I returned to the bowl, I met Cpl McLaughlin, and it was only now that I discovered that he had also been injured. He was making his way to the RAP helped by Pete Higgs. I said to him, 'Fucking hell, Scouse, are you all right, pal?' Scouse grimaced and said, 'All right Hutch, yeah, this doesn't feel too fucking good, though.' I made my way up into the First Bowl and sat with Colin Edwards and Gordon Ellse. I remember Johnny Weeks coming over and rubbing Gordon Ellse's head and saying in a tired voice, 'How are you, son?' as the strain was now beginning to show on all of us.

4.9   'He had fulfilled his destiny that night'

A Company informs the CO that they have secured the eastern end of Mount Longdon:

10.28hrs (zt): from C/S 19 to C/S 9: 'Now on position, very extensive position with Support Gun at end.'

Pte Duncan Daly

I'm not sure where these prisoners came from; I think that it was possibly A Company that may have brought them in off the eastern slope. I now believe that these men were Argentine Marines. There were about ten of them. I started searching them and took various documents and pieces of equipment over to Major Argue as I thought they may have been of some interest. He had just given his zap numbers of our dead and injured to signaller Pte Mark Harding, and I noticed Major Argue had tears in his eyes.

Sgt John Ross

Tony Kempster, Lippy Linton and I made our way down Route 3 towards the RAP. We crossed onto Route 2 and saw some of the 3 PARA cooks standing over two bodies lying face down. I asked them who they were. They said one is Pete Higgs, but we don't know who the other one is because of his head injuries. We carried on into the RAP where I met CSgt Brian Faulkner. I asked did Scouse McLaughlin get out okay? Brian Faulkner said, 'Scouse hasn't been through here.' I replied, 'Yes, he has; he was hit just before, and he came down here,' and Brian Faulkner said, 'John, I'm telling you, he hasn't been through here.' I said crossly, 'Well, you must have missed him.' Brian replied, 'I've missed nobody; I know everyone who's come in and everyone who's gone out.'

We went back up to where we'd seen the two bodies, but by now the ACC stretcher-bearers had removed them. We went back towards the First Bowl, where I met Johnny Weeks. I said to him, 'I can't find Scouse, he's gone missing, but Pete Higgs is dead and there's somebody with him, but they don't know who he is.' Then Steve Phillips added, 'That might be Scouse, as Pete Higgs took him down to the RAP.' A great shudder ran through my whole body with the realization that Scouse may be dead. I quickly made my way back down to the RAP, where I met Brian Faulkner, who softly said, 'I'm sorry, John; Scouse is over there.'

I went over and paid my last respects. When I finished, I took his webbing, which contained food, water and ammo, an act that Scouse would have fully understood as a professional soldier. He would not have needed them in Valhalla. Scouse McLaughlin was many things; he was a hard man, who would always lead from the front, but he was also a loyal friend and one of the most generous men you could meet. He had fulfilled his destiny that night.

Major Argue would later write of Cpl Stewart McLaughlin:

I have known Cpl McLaughlin since the day he was posted to 2 PARA (1973); he was eventually a member of Patrol Company in my troop. He has basically never changed, an out-and-out rogue with a big heart, but a vicious and physical temper which at times he had difficulty in controlling and which, as we know, got him into trouble on more than one occasion. Cpl McLaughlin, nevertheless, was a first-class soldier who revelled in adversity or in the survival situation. Such was his character that his section were proud to work for him. He took his job very seriously and on our voyage one could often find him sitting in some corner with one or two of his lads where he would be going through an aspect of survival or showing them how to get the best out of an item of kit. You have read my citation. Prior to his death, he led his section like a demon on the rocks of Mount Longdon. This was McLaughlin at his best. He leaves a wife (Ruth) and newly born baby boy Stewart and an elder son called Mark.

Have put in for award.

Spr Tommy Trindall

I was tasked with a number of members of 2 Troop, 9 Squadron to go back up and help with the recovery of the wounded. It was now light. We walked up onto Fly Half, where we came across Cpl (Jock) Ferry, Spr Mark Thomas and Spr Sam Robson. It was probably one of the most difficult things I have ever done, telling them about Scotty Wilson. Particularly as Scotty and Jock Ferry were best mates. I had all sorts of things running through my head, but Jock took it quite calmly.

Spr Martin (Spike) Glover, 19 yrs – 9 Sqn RE attached to 3 PARA

We were tasked to go back up and help look for any more wounded. This time we were sent around the northern side. It was quite sunny and about twelve of us made our way back to the First Bowl. We were coming under sporadic shell fire on the way up. At the entrance to the bowl, a badly wounded Argentine lay on the ground watching intently as we moved past him. As we moved up onto the forward edge of Fly Half, I could see some 3 PARA blokes leading prisoners down into the First Bowl. From up here I could see a group of bodies with grey blankets covering them. One of them, LCpl David Scott, was lying on his back where the memorial stone is now placed. Not far from him were another two 3 PARA fatalities [Stewart Laing and James (Doc) Murdoch]. I didn't know either of them. Then four blokes dealt with Dave Scott and I helped with another fatality [Tony Greenwood]. We placed him in a body bag and zipped him up. The bodies were then placed on stretchers and taken away down through the bowl.

I then went exploring around the summit and after a while I climbed down onto the northern side of Fly Half and spotted a Cobra missile perched upon a ledge. I now met up with another member of 9 Squadron, Scouse 'Lightning'. I took cover with him as a salvo of shells came in. He told me Cpl Scotty Wilson had just been killed. Scotty was my 2ic during my last tour in Northern Ireland

and when I first joined 9 Sqn, he was a sort of older 'mentor' to me. I found it really hard to understand that he could actually be dead.

Pte Andy Stone
It was now daylight, and the full horror of war began to expose itself. Scattered around us were about ten enemy, lying in various horrific death poses. Some were missing limbs and heads. It was strange, looking back, as we sat and drank tea and chatted about what had gone on. We looked awful. People you knew, young lads of 17 and 18, looked different in some way, mainly the eyes. The strain etched in their faces; everyone seemed older in a way. I found myself a small cave as the Argentinian artillery bombardment began to increase. I was joined by Sgt Fuller, and we got another brew on, when suddenly we heard a movement from the back of the cave and found an Argentinian hidden under blankets and rubbish. We dragged him out and gave him to someone who was collecting prisoners.

Pte Craig (Harry) Harrison
I needed to eat so I made a bit of porridge. As I sat eating it, my old Platoon Sergeant George Duffus came by and asked how I was. It all got too much for me. I don't mind admitting it, I shed a few tears. George is a decent bloke and gave me a bit of sympathy when it was very much needed. After this I changed my socks, and I felt a whole lot better.

LCpl Colin Edwards
At some time after first light all the sections were reorganized. Due to losses within 5 Platoon, Cpl Jimmy Morham took over as our Section Commander as Scouse McLaughlin was now confirmed as dead.

The time is now approximately 11.00hrs (zt).

Pte Craig (Harry) Harrison
Pte Dave Wakelin and I were tasked to take prisoners down to the POW cage at the bottom of the mountain. On our way down some Argentines popped up from behind some rocks about 50 metres away. It took us by surprise, and we fired at them. However, it turned out these Argentines were also prisoners taking part in a burial service. Then the blokes who were guarding them

thought they were being shot at by our group of Argentines and fired back. We took cover and shouted back, 'We're 3 PARA, we're 3 PARA!'

CSM Johnny Weeks

It became apparent that we would have to relocate B Company out of the First Bowl. We moved them to the lower end of the western slope where I ordered them to dig shell scrapes and find whatever cover they could.

Pte Andy Stone

We all got moved out of the First Bowl area. We moved about three-quarters of the way down the western slope, and then I went down to the RAP to fill my water bottles up. As I was going to do this, I heard someone shouting, 'Air-raid warning red! Seven Skyhawks and seven waves of Hawkeye [helicopters] are inbound. Stand to! Stand to!' and I thought, Oh, fucking hell. It was now believed the enemy were mounting a counter-attack on Longdon. The battalion rapidly went into all-round defence, covering all the possible approaches with designated arcs of fire. The Battalion HQ personnel urgently ran around issuing extra 66mm's. But to be honest, I think everyone was really up for it and we were quite disappointed that they never turned up. Eventually, we were stood down.

Pte Craig (Tommy) Onions, 19 yrs – ACC
Ammunition-Bearer/Stretcher-Bearer

All the wounded had by now been removed from the First Bowl area, so we were asked to help clear any of the remaining Argentine dead. As the side of the bowl was quite steep and we were still being shelled, we rolled them down to the start of the sheep track and from there they were collected and taken over to the burial area just in front of the Third Bowl.

Cpl John Lewis

I was asked by CSM Johnny Weeks if I would assist Padre Heaver in the searching of 3 PARA's dead for personal effects. He said, 'John, it's not an order – if you feel you're not up to it, it's okay.' So I went to where our bodies had been laid out and began the grim job of going through pockets for letters, photographs, rings and all the personal stuff, putting it all into plastic bags. It was quite a distressing job.

We were then tasked with removing Argentine bodies from the trenches and bunkers that we had fought through only 12 hours previously. The mountain was a hive of activity with prisoners being brought in and casualties being taken out. We found some Argentine food and made a scoff. Myself and Taff Goreing had just made a steaming mug of hot chocolate, when I noticed Sulle Alhaji walking past our trench. He looked knackered and cold, I shouted to him to come over and have a hot brew. At that moment the shout went up, 'Incoming!' Sulle dived into our trench and within a nanosecond, the artillery rounds came crashing in. Earth and debris came into the trench, but we managed to protect the hot chocolate from it. When it was safe, Sulle looked out and noticed that the trench he'd been heading for had taken a direct hit. Who knows what would have happened had he not been offered a hot brew.

CSM Johnny Weeks

I began making a list of the casualties that we had taken. We also had the heartbreaking task of recovering our dead and the collection of their ID discs. It was all very moving and brought a tear to my eyes, especially so when we recovered personal friends like Sgt Ian McKay.

Pte Paul Hutchinson

We rounded up quite a number of Argentine prisoners, a few Marines but mainly conscripts. We were tasked to search then remove the Argentinian dead. We did this together with the Argentine prisoners – we would search the bodies, and then they would carry the Argentinian dead to a central burial area in front of the Third Bowl. The searching of the bodies was a very emotional job. As I looked at their family photographs, personal possessions and rosary beads, etc. it really brought it home to you, as one soldier to another, the madness of it all. One thing I remember was that most of the dead didn't have any ID cards on them. This meant that, sadly, these men were buried without being identified.

Pte Craig (Harry) Harrison

We had the task of collecting some of the Support Company dead, and they (Support Company) had the task of collecting some of B Company's dead. This was so we wouldn't have to see blokes from our own company. We went to the position on the western slope where the Anti-Tanks had received a direct hit. It was a terrible sight. The area was littered with shell dressings and bits of torn clothing, a scene I never want to see again. One of the dead, Pte Philip West [Westy] lay on a stretcher covered by a blanket. A small teddy bear had been placed on the blanket over his chest.

Sgt John Ross

That afternoon Argentine soldiers were trying to surrender, but the Argentine forward artillery observers were calling down fire onto their own people.

CSM Johnny Weeks

All through the day we still had prisoners popping out of tiny holes that had been missed. They were climbing out of crevices where they had hidden all night. They were petrified of us. We searched them and processed them. If they were wounded, they were treated exactly the same as our wounded, with a triage system. I must say the two doctors in the RAP were brilliant.

Pte Craig (Harry) Harrison

We were located just across from the CO's bunker, and he told us to keep under cover. Before it got dark, we had a big meal of looted Argentine corned beef and other goodies. The sentry position was 100 metres to the front of our bunker. But due to our reduced numbers, only one person went on stag [guard duty] at a time. That night I had a great sleep. I was only woken once by an explosion in the RAP area.

Pte Tony Barlow

I didn't sleep at all during Saturday night. I said to Duggie Field, 'I can't sit here; I'm freezing to death. I've got to keep moving.' So I went running up and down the western slope to try to keep warm.

4.10 **'I don't know who to kiss first'**

SUNDAY 13 JUNE 1982

First light approximately 10.00hrs (zt).

Pte Paul Hutchinson

On Sunday morning, there was a light covering of snow upon the ground. At some time after first light, Sgt John Pettinger led a D Company Patrol onto the mountain approaching from the west. As they walked past our position, I stood up to take a piss, when I heard the distant crump of artillery, and I knew I had a few more seconds, when out of nowhere dropped a mortar round. Some pieces of shrapnel hit the rock where I had been pissing and the bloke next to me said, 'You're a jammy bastard!' Almost immediately there were screams of 'Medic!' The D Company Patrol had nearly all been wounded.

Pte Andy Stone

I heard a terrific 'whoosh' overhead. Then, screaming and shouts of 'Medic!' I ran down to the scene of the explosion. Dickie Absolon was on his back with an extremely bad head wound. I immediately assumed it would be fatal, I thought there was nothing I could do for him. On his right was Cpl Mark Brown; he had been hit in the lower leg. Cpl Jerry Phillips was still smouldering and in extreme pain, his arm was hanging off. The doctor [Mike Von Bertele] and a medic, John Kennedy, ran from the nearby RAP, and medic Phil Probets had also been close by, along with Pat Harley, who although not a medic was very capable. I let them take over, as I thought better of standing around in a group, and I made my way back to my bunker. I got a brew on and made some Argy scoff. I stayed in my bunker as it was far too dangerous to be out in the open. That night I half slept and half froze.

MONDAY 14 JUNE 1982

First light approximately 10.00hrs (zt).

Pte Craig (Harry) Harrison

That night snow had fallen. I was sent to the RAP area to collect ammunition, for the push into Port Stanley. I loaded up with grenades and a couple of 66mm's, 7.62mm ammunition and yet more shell dressings. I also got more morphine. We had tons of ammo for the platoon, but in reality there were only twelve of us. During my travels to collect stuff I had spoken to a few blokes, and we exchanged news about friends. I noticed everyone seemed to be a bit subdued, but most of them were positive about the battle we had just fought and the battle that was yet to come.

CO holds a Battalion 'O' Group near the RAP area at 12.00hrs (zt). During the 'O' Group the first reports come in that the situation is changing.

12.10hrs (zt): from C/S 0 to C/S 9: 'Enemy withdrawing from Sapper Hill, unconfirmed report 300 enemy withdrawing.'

AAC R/L = Army Air Corps Radio Log.

12.27hrs (zt): AAC R/L from LO: 'Mount William large numbers of troops moving back to Stanley RA may engage, looks like a number of troops about to surrender, mass withdrawal into Stanley, Moody Brook troops moving back, 300 moving from Sapper Hill.'

12.50hrs (zt): from C/S 0 to All Stations: 'All Stations on 30 minutes to move.'

13.44hrs (zt): from C/S 9 to C/S 3: 'C Company now on 30 minutes, get ready now and close up behind 2 PARA, inform me when you're on the move.'

B Company start moving off Mount Longdon at approximately 15.30hrs (zt).

LCpl Colin Edwards
We loaded up and began our move towards Wireless Ridge, when a message came over the radio, 'Cease fire, cease fire, white flags have been seen flying over Stanley.' I cannot describe the wave of emotion that washed over me at that moment. Then the order was to remove helmets and put red berets on, and after that it was a race into Port Stanley.

15.35hrs (zt): AAC R/L from Brigade: 'Urgent report of white flag flying over Port Stanley.'

Pte Chris Masterman
As we were moving off the northern side of Longdon, a message was passed back along the line to 'Make safe your weapons.' This was followed by 'Helmets off, berets on.' We then moved up and over Wireless Ridge, passing through Moody Brook and along the Ross Road into Stanley. I remember seeing a

wounded Argentine at the side of the road being treated by Pte Harry Gannon. We sat exhausted along the side of the road. I remember seeing Brigadier Julian Thompson come walking down Ross Road, and he said, 'What are you lot doing sitting there?' He pointed at the bungalows and said, 'If the doors are open, go into the houses and get yourselves warm.'

Pte Mark Eisler

As we walked through Moody Brook, we caught up with 2 PARA Mortar Platoon and gave them a hand carrying their mortar base plates into Stanley.

Pte Paul Hutchinson

We had not gone far when the signaller passed a message down the line, 'They've surrendered. White flags are flying in Stanley.' Then it was helmets off, berets on. We tried taking a short cut but received a radio message to 'Go firm, do not move; you're in a minefield.' After a bit of discussion, we carried on straight through it, but with a great deal more caution. We reached the Ross Road and marched down to a position just by the old war memorial. It was here that we were told to halt. We were then told to turn back, there seemed to be confusion over where we were supposed to halt. After that, we just sat at the side of the road and waited for a decision to be made.

I was outside the bungalow having a smoke when down the road came Brigadier Julian Thompson and Robert Fox [BBC reporter]. The Brigadier shouted across to us, 'Good afternoon, boys.' There were a few good-humoured 'airborne' comments shouted back, and we were told to take over two of the bungalows. We took over number 23 Ross Road, which turned out to be the home of Hulda Stewart. She was a schoolteacher in Port Stanley. When she arrived back at her bungalow, she said light-heartedly, 'I don't know who to kiss first.' So she hugged and kissed all of us, and then said, 'This is my home, but please consider it your home.' A few minutes later she produced a tray of cakes that she had kept especially for the occasion. She is fondly remembered by all who met her.

Shortly after this, three Huey helicopters landed on the racecourse to the rear of the bungalows. A tall Argentine Colonel got out. He spoke perfect English and politely said, 'I am going to give you my pistol [Colt 45]; these are my men. I would like you to take them into your care.' He then gave me his pistol, handgrip first. I took him to CSM Thor Caithness.

I heard cheering coming from the front of the bungalows on the Ross Road and went to have a look and watched as the Royal Marines marched rather sheepishly into Stanley. As they passed, members of 2 and 3 PARA were cheering and shouting sarcastically, 'We've been saved,' and 'Thank God you're here.' But it was not appreciated as they were probably feeling gutted that the Parachute Regiment had beaten them into Port Stanley. I also managed to send a telegram from the post office in Port Stanley saying, 'Mother, I am OK. Don't worry. Get the stew on,' which was my way of letting her know I was okay.

Cpl John Lewis:

As we walked in there were still fires burning. We passed fire- and smoke-damaged buildings, and I remember seeing a helicopter heading into Port Stanley with a white flag attached to it.* We also came across a couple of wounded Argentines, one of whom I treated by putting a field dressing on him. As we advanced down the Ross Road West, we bumped into members of our D Company who had arrived with C Company ahead of us. It was great to see my old mate Boyd Smith, who was driving up and down in an Argentine Mercedes Jeep. We were told now to go firm.

We were told to go into the bungalows if the door was open. When we got inside the bungalow, it was absolutely wrecked. We were in a house that belonged to a lady called Hulda Stewart. Her husband worked for the BBC, and they had been taken prisoner by the Argentines because of his knowledge of communications. When she returned I was standing by her gate. She said that she was going to kiss the first soldier she saw. She leaned across the gate and gave me a kiss on the cheek; she then went inside the house and lifted up the floorboards to reveal a cache of food and cakes that she had hidden from the Argentines.

16.20hrs (zt): from C/S 0 to C/S 9: '1: Argies have not yet surrendered, 2: All units to remain on Full Alert.'

---

* The helicopter may have been Lt Col Mike Rose flying in to negotiate a ceasefire.

16.52hrs (zt): from AAC R/L: 'Argy Mercy Bird coming into Stanley escorted by two Harriers don't shoot at it.'

17.00hrs (zt): from C/S 0 to C/S 9: 'From Brigade; No move east of 39 easting.'

Pte Terry Bowdell

I had bought a load of Union Jack bunting to bring with me. I carried it all the way across the Falklands, with the aim of hanging the bunting up in Port Stanley when we eventually reached there. However, when we reached Port Stanley, I didn't have the heart to take it out. We had lost so many good men, both dead and wounded. For me, it wasn't a time for celebrating. I didn't feel it was appropriate. I put it in the bin.

Once in Port Stanley Major Mike Argue asked his two remaining Platoon Commanders to give names of men they consider worthy of mention. From these names he makes a note in the back of his personal notebook of the men to be considered for awards. Although this is not the final list, it will be whittled down and changed accordingly, and even though some of these men do not get any awards, they are nominated, and this is worthy of note.

Lt Mark Cox would write of his men:

> *Persons worthy of mention:*

> *Connery – tremendous energy and drive in front of enemy fire and came forward with myself to secure position.*

> *Bailey – with Sgt McKay and James attempted to take out the machine-gun post with near fatal consequences.*

> *McLaughlin – Exemplary leadership of his section while in contact and an inspiration to his comrades.*

> *Gough – Gray – both showed considerable courage in the face of a .50 Calibre machine gun, which they took out using 66 and grenades, killing the gun crew and capturing the gunner. They had covering fire from LCpl Carver, Juliff. Pte Gough acting as 2ic of his section displayed strong leadership qualities and was a strength within the platoon throughout the engagement.*

> *Mulgrew – Lloyd – in the face of enemy fire, they tended to casualties in an exposed location without regard to their own safety.*

Lt Shaw would later write of 6 Platoon:

> *Throughout the night every individual had performed well, but especially Pte Roe (very cool and capable medical work), Pte Lewis (Initiative, energy and attitude) and Pte Gannon, whose courage, medical expertise and unfailing energy contributed more than anything to the treatment of the wounded. Cpl Steggles and Wilson should be praised for their leadership and thanked for their assistance throughout.*

> *Signed, Shaw 18/06/82*

Major Argue's initial award list from the back of his notebook:

> *Cox – MC*
> *Shaw – MID*
> *McKay – VC*
> *Bailey – MM*
> *Carver – MM*
> *Grey*
> *Gough – MM*
> *Phillips*
> *McGlasson*
> *Gannon – QGM*
> *Eaton*
> *Clark*
> *Weeks*
> *Probets*
> *McLaughlin – MM*
> *Fuller – MM*

CHAPTER FIVE

'KEEP GOING UP BUT WATCH OUT FOR SNIPERS'

SUPPORT COMPANY 3 PARA

'Fire immediately began to erupt from the mountain'

FRIDAY 11 JUNE 1982

At 16.00hrs (zt) on 11 June, the main Support Company group is flown forward to B Company's position in order to marry up with our heavy equipment, which has been moved up by vehicle. The man pack group [on foot] is commanded by OC Support Company Major Peter Dennison, while the vehicle group is commanded by the battalion 2ic Major Roger Patton. As the man pack element of the firebase advances, the vehicle group remains in A Company's location Grid 265767 north of Mount Kent. The man pack group moves off at approximately 20.45hrs (zt).

At the 300m contour line, west of Mount Longdon, the B Company Mortar Detachment are dropped off with two 81mm mortars under the command of Sgt Dave Hallas. They have a .30 Browning machine gun manned by Spr Dave Raes of 9 Squadron RE. This weapon is for local protection against a similar weapon that is known to exist on Two Sisters. Shortly before midnight, Captain Mason and Sgt Colbeck inform Company HQ that they are firm in their allocated positions, due north and south of the main firebase. Captain Mason has one Milan post and two SF gun teams and Sgt Colbeck has one Milan post and one SF gun team. Shortly after that, at 00.31hrs (zt) the remainder of the firebase teams, under Major Dennison, CSM Caithness and CSgt Knights, along with the primary RAP under the RMO Captain Burgess, are also in position. At the same time, A and B Company begin their advance from their respective Start Lines.

Cpl Peter (Tomo) Thompson, 26 yrs – Support Company Medium Machine Gun Platoon

The MMG platoon had re-formed at Estancia House prior to the attack on Mount Longdon; before this, they were split into three detachments, each of seven men. A Company's detachment was commanded by Cpl Jon Cook, B Company's detachment was commanded by me, and C Company's detachment was commanded by the platoon sergeant, Sgt Geoff Deaney. But due to a situation beyond our control, we would only have 6 MMGs in the SF [sustained fire] role for the attack on Mount Longdon.

The whole of Support Company received orders from the OC Major Dennison and CSM Caithness. When this was over the MMG Platoon Commander [Mike Oliver], Platoon Sgt [Geoff Deaney] and I went to a quiet area of Estancia House and discussed in detail exactly how we would achieve our mission.

My SF machine gun was to be the point gun for the attack on Mount Longdon and be under the direct control of the CSM, who had the only NOD [night-observation device] in the company. Guns 1 and 2 were under the command of Cpl Jon Cook; they would also have the Platoon Commander with them, and they were all attached to Captain Mason with his Milan team. Guns 3 and 4 were under the command of LCpl Mark (Rolly) Rawlings and attached to C/Sgt Knights' Milan team and gun number 5 would be in reserve under the command of LCpl Tony Peers and attached to Sgt Colbeck's Milan team. Prior to the attack we issued orders to the platoon and issued the ammunition not only to the gun teams, but also to all the stretcher-bearers and attachments.

On Friday afternoon 11 June we were flown by helicopter from Estancia House to the A Company assembly area. From here we would be moving on foot with the Support Company Group commanded by Major Dennison. When we arrived at the assembly area I did a quick head check, and all 17 members of the platoon were present. The OC then called me over and said, 'Cpl Thompson, these gentlemen are from the Press, and they will be coming with us; I would like you to look after them.' 'These gentlemen' were Les Dowd from Reuters and photographer Tom Smith from the *Daily Express*.

I thought these two men were the last thing I needed. They had no equipment, no food and just one water bottle each. I took both reporters to our platoon area and briefly explained to them the orders and our mission. I also informed them that if they were coming with us, they would have to carry two boxes of ammunition each. Both reporters stated that they were non-combatants. However, I explained to them the situation that we were going into and they picked up their allocation.

We also had 18 stretcher-bearers plus attachments, each carrying between 600 and 800 rounds of link; including the amount of ammunition that was allocated to other groups and what all the gun teams were carrying, this would provide us with at least 36,000 rounds of 7.62mm one in five tracer-linked ammunition. We waited until last light at approximately 20.45hrs (zt). We were then called forward. The other gun teams moved directly to the Milan group they were attached to, and we then all moved off together. Each of the gun teams was carrying at least 2,500 rounds. I kept the reporters directly behind me as we moved off in single file. We made our way across the Murrell River and on towards the Furze Bush stream. We were now running slightly late – we should have been in the position for 00.01hrs (zt).

Pte Chris Parris, 21 yrs – Ammunition-Bearer, HQ Company

When we crossed the river, a member of our section was lagging behind. I waited for him, but when he eventually caught up he was exhausted and said, 'You go on; I will catch you up later.' It was then I noticed that the rest of my section had moved off, so after a few minutes walking in roughly the direction of Mount Longdon, I stopped and tried to work out where I was. I remembered Major Dennison's model, and from that I knew how to get to the main firebase. So I skirted along the hillside, and eventually I could hear people talking, and I then heard the very reassuring voice of CSgt Knights saying, 'Who the fuck is that?' I then joined the main Support Company firebase.

Lt Col Hew Pike, 40 yrs – Commanding Officer, 3 PARA

At approximately 20.15hrs (zt), A Company would move off first, followed by my group Tactical Headquarters, followed by B Company, Support Company and C Company in that order. Our H-Hour was 00.01hrs (zt) and our objective was to capture Mount Longdon. It was approximately 6.5 kilometres away from our assembly area; I estimated a three-hour march. However, we had a few problems crossing the Murrell River, which delayed us slightly. A Company would be in position for 11.45hrs (zt) but unfortunately B Company would not reach their Start Line until 00.30hrs (zt). A Company also began their advance at 00.31hrs (zt). We [3 PARA Tac HQ] had found a rocky outcrop approximately 500 metres north-west of Mount Longdon, where we positioned ourselves. From here I could observe the advance of my two leading companies.

Sgt Graham Colbeck, 33 yrs – Support Company Anti-Tank Platoon

As we began to leave the assembly area I received a radio message from Major Dennison instructing me to check the vehicles to see if they contained any 'special equipment'. I had no idea what the 'special equipment' might be, but I assumed it would be apparent when I saw it. I halted my team and returned to the vehicles, which had not yet begun their advance. I couldn't find anything but ammunition and so reported a 'negative finding' to the Company Commander. It later transpired that the 'special equipment' was a steel girder that was to be used to help bridge the Murrell River.

CSgt Brian Faulkner, 34 yrs – Regimental Aid Post Team

We were attached to the Support Company group commanded by Major Dennison. All the medical team carried substantial Bergens full of essential medical kit, but we were also told to carry as much ammunition as possible. For some reason, we were also asked to carry an extremely heavy steel girder, which was to be used for crossing the Murrell River. The steel girder was slowing us down. Even though we took turns carrying it, it was just too heavy. The medical team were completely exhausted, and in the end, I told the lads to 'Fucking dump it!' We would cross the river by whatever means possible.

SATURDAY 12 JUNE 1982

Support Company inform the CO Hew Pike that they are running approximately 30 minutes late:

00.05hrs (zt): from C/S 59 to C/S 9: 'Now at rear, ETA 30 minutes.'

Support Company now inform the CO they were nearly in position:

00.31hrs (zt): from C/S 59 to C/S 9: 'Going firm (Free Kick) ready in five minutes.'

Cpl Peter (Tomo) Thompson

We set up our guns, and I whispered to CSM Caithness that the guns were ready to fire. He said, 'Await my order.' We then just sat and waited. One of the main problems was the lack of night-observation devices. We were now lined up to fire at night without the benefit of night sights. However, CSM Caithness had managed to obtain one of the few NODs available, and with this, he would direct our fire.

CSgt Derek (Dex) Allen, 38 yrs – Regimental Aid Post Team

I was with Captain Mason's group; we took cover in a ditch facing north-west of Mount Longdon. We waited here until the rest of the battalion reached their various forming-up points. It was absolutely freezing.

Sgt Chris Howard, 33 yrs – Support Company
Anti-Tank Platoon

I was on the Start Line with Support Company Group, it was bitterly cold, and both A and B Companies had begun their advance. I remember there wasn't a sound as both companies moved towards the mountain, but after about 40 minutes there was a small explosion, and the battle began. We now lay shivering up against a peat bank watching the battle unfold.

Pte Pat Harley, 22 yrs – Support Company Anti-Tank Platoon

We were laid up in the Support Company Group position. I was now extremely cold, as I'd fallen in the Murrell River while trying to shuffle across the ladder!

I was soaking wet and my back was aching, as I'd hurt it when I fell in the river. I heard a small explosion which later turned out to be Cpl Milne standing on a mine. Fire immediately began to erupt from the mountain; we could see grenade flashes and bullets ricocheting into the night sky.

Approximately 40 minutes after the advance begins, B Company HQ reports to the CO Hew Pike that they are now in contact with the enemy:

01.07hrs (zt): from C/S 29 to C/S 9: 'Contact wait-out.'

LCpl Denzil Connick, 25yrs – Radio Operator
Anti-Tank Platoon

We sat and waited whilst A and B Companies started their advance. I was now shivering; it was absolutely freezing. The radio operators Pte Steve [Errol] Flynn, LCpl Garry Cripps and I peered over the peat bank and were staring at the black silhouette of the mountain when it suddenly erupted into life with small-arms fire and explosions – there seemed to be lines of tracer flying everywhere.

Lt Col Hew Pike

When the first contact was made at the foot of Mount Longdon, I saw a small explosion followed by muzzle flashes and tracer fire. I immediately contacted Major Dennison, telling him to send the RAP team forward to set up at the base of Longdon. I also told Captain Mason to take his Milan team and two SF teams over to A Company on Wing Forward to assist in the support of B Company.

Padre Derek Heaver, 35 yrs – Army Chaplain, RAP Team

Just after the battle started, Captain Burgess [doctor], CSgt Faulkner, Sgt Bradley, Pte Kennedy and I were despatched by Major Dennison to Mount Longdon. He asked us to take as much ammunition as possible with us. So I grabbed two big metal containers of ammunition and made my way towards the mountain. At that time, I didn't know about the minefield. When we reached Mount Longdon Doctor John Burgess chose a spot for us to set up the RAP. There was a huge amount of noise and tracer fire going overhead.

Captain John (Doc) Burgess, 26 yrs – Regimental Medical Officer

I don't recall the mine explosion, but I do recall the radios coming to life with reports of it. We were despatched with a group of stretcher-bearers, who in addition to their own equipment were also carrying large amounts of ammunition forward to Mount Longdon. We'd been tasked to set up the Regimental Aid Post. We moved across the 800 metres of open ground as fast as we could, passing through what we now knew to be a minefield. When we eventually reached Longdon, I did a quick visual appreciation and decided to set up at the base of the north-west corner, keeping close in to the rocks. The time was now approximately 01.40hrs (zt). We waited for the casualties to be brought to us.

CSgt Steve Knights

The CO came over the radio and asked the RAP Team to go forward. We moved out quickly and in my haste to set off, I left my fur-lined leather gloves, which I never saw again! I would regret this as it was fucking freezing. We made our way as fast as possible in single file to the base of the mountain. While en route, we discovered via the radio that there had been a mine explosion and that we were now possibly moving through a minefield; we then moved with great caution for obvious reasons.

5.2 'I want you to get us to the top of that mountain, and I want you to get us there as quickly as possible'

01.15hrs (zt): from C/S 29 to C/S 9: 'Call Signs 2/1 and 2/2 in contact – northern edge of feature. Sporadic small-arms fire, one casualty, anti-personnel mine, artillery now hitting Full Back hard.'

Pte Pat Harley

CSgt Steve Knights said, 'Get your fucking kit together, we're moving.' I gave a groan, picked up my Milan missiles and set off once more with my heavy load and my aching back. We moved forward in single file, straight through the minefield to the base of Mount Longdon. Once there, we paused for a while near the RAP, which was in the process of being established. It was here we would learn of B Company's first casualties. I looked into the night sky at the tracer flying over the top of the mountain and disappearing into the distance. I was apprehensive about what was coming next.

Captain Tony Mason, 27yrs – Anti-Tank Platoon Commander

I received a radio message from the CO telling me to take my Milan detachment plus Lt Oliver with his two SF teams and move as fast as possible to join A Company on Wing Forward. Once there we were to assist B Company with supporting fire. We made our way around the rear of A Company as fast as possible. En route we came across a medic [Pte Wright], who was attending to Cpl Hope, who had been wounded. I knew and liked Cpl Hope; he was a decent steady hand.

Pte Craig (Tommy) Onions

CSgt Allen, Sgt Hopper and I along with some others were told to go with Captain Mason and the Milan and SF teams to join A Company. We made our way as quickly as possible to A Company's location on Wing Forward, which was about 700 metres away. The pace was very fast, and the ammunition carriers were struggling to keep up. There was a lot of incoming fire from Mount Longdon and also Argentine artillery fire.

Sgt Graham Colbeck

I received a message from Major Dennison telling me to move north and RV at his location. After approximately ten minutes I met up with him. I was told that Captain Mason and CSgt Knights had been tasked to join A Company and B Company respectively, but I was unaware of any difficulties that B Company may have been having at this time. We waited for what only seemed like a short time before we moved off.

CSM Ernie Rustill, 38 yrs – D Company, responsible for security of 3 PARA Tac HQ

My group consisting of Captain Selfridge and LCpl Bentall moved on to a ridge between A and B Companies; from here the CO could observe the proceedings. It was an incredibly clear night with a large full moon. We could see A and

B Companies quite clearly, moving toward Longdon. They were getting closer and closer and yet, still nothing was happening. One thing that impressed me was there wasn't a sound; the whole battalion was moving at night in complete silence. The air was electric with the anticipation of what would happen next. Suddenly there was a flash and a small explosion followed by a terrible scream. Shortly after that our group received the order to prepare to move. My group would now move forward about 100 metres in front of the CO's party, and fanned out, waiting for the next order.

Lt Col Hew Pike

We began moving towards Longdon, with CSM Rustill and Captain Selfridge moving ahead of our group, clearing the way. During this move, Major Osborne, OC C Company, contacted me, asking if we needed assistance, but I felt we did not need to use our reserves at this stage:

01.40hrs (zt): from C/S 9 to C/S 3: 'Stay where you are. You will have some sport later on.'

Captain McCracken (Call Sign 41B) contacts the Fire Direction Centre:

01.43hrs (zt): from C/S 41B to C/S 29FDC: 'Still under small-arms fire and mortar fire "FLOT" [Forward Location Own Troops] still uncertain.'

01.43hrs (zt): from C/S 41B to C/S 29FDC: 'Call Sign 3 finished ZU7920 91 rounds; HE expended Z7920 + ZU7918 now unsafe.'

These are artillery target references: Z7920 Full Back, ZU7918 northern side of Longdon 200 metres east of 4 Platoon.

CSgt Steve Knights

We reached the base of Longdon at approximately 01.45hrs (zt). The RAP team was setting up to receive casualties; the stretcher-bearers dropped off their ammunition. I told my group to go firm here until I sorted out what was happening. I wanted to find out where people were and what areas were secure, as there seemed to be conflicting reports over the radio of who held which piece of ground.

01.50hrs (zt): from C/S 29 to C/S 9: 'Call Sign 2/3 [6 Platoon] has several casualties, enemy still firing from high ground, and still advancing and clearing.'

01.52hrs (zt): from C/S 19 to C/S 9: 'This Call Sign [A Company] has one casualty; we are pinned down by sniper fire and are staying put until cleared by call sign 2.' [Cpl Hope has been wounded.]

Lt Col Hew Pike

A Company informed us that they had taken one casualty and were pinned down by sniper fire. B Company had also taken casualties. We needed to move up the support weapons; the original plan was that the support weapons would be back on Free Kick, and that wasn't really working. I also wanted to speak to Major Argue to try to get a clearer picture of what was happening. As I made my way to Mount Longdon, we came under sporadic small-arms fire and Argentine artillery fire. We eventually arrived at the base of Mount Longdon. We had now lost all radio contact with Major Argue. I wasn't sure where on the mountain he was. The radio signal was very intermittent. At this time the mountain was not safe in any direction. My main aim was to make contact with him; we went firm here, until I had a clearer picture of what was happening.

Major Dennison reports to the CO. He is now moving Support Company towards Longdon:

02.00hrs (zt): from C/S 59 to C/S 9: 'Now moving forward to west end of feature.'

02.00hrs (zt): 42 Commando now cross their Start Line to capture Mount Harriet and Goat Ridge.

Cpl Peter (Tomo) Thompson

CSM Thor Caithness came over to me and said, 'Cpl Thompson, I want you to get us to the top of that mountain, and I want you to get us there as quickly as possible.' I turned to my gun team and just said, 'Right, pack up your kit and prepare to follow me.' We moved as fast as we could across the difficult terrain with all the SF kit and extra ammunition. At first, we moved in 'file', and then I decided it would be safer in 'single file', since we were going through an area that was now known to be mined. At this stage, I didn't know where anyone was on Longdon. I knew my gun team were behind me, but I had no idea of who I would make contact with.

Acting Captain Giles Orpen-Smellie

On arrival on the western slope, we spread out around the CO, so that we were in earshot of what he was saying on the Command Net. It was clear there was a lot of confusion and the CO spent his time trying to understand how far both A and B Companies had got and resolving the suggestion that A Company was firing at B Company.

CSgt Steve Knights

I told everyone to get ready. It was about 02.30hrs (zt), and we now started to make our way up the western slope. During the ascent to Fly Half, we could see both rapid and spasmodic tracer fire coming over Fly Half. I assumed it was coming from the Full Back position. I could see very little, and there was still occasional gunfire, so I stopped the group and decided to contact B Company over the radio and asked, 'Can you confirm that the western slope has been secured?' B Company replied, 'Yes; it has been taken and is secure. Can you bring your gun teams up to Fly Half and set up a firebase.'

On reaching Fly Half I positioned the two gun teams where I thought they would have a good field of fire, and told them to engage any area where enemy tracer fire was coming from. One gun failed to fire; the team dismantled it, I poured a load of oil on it, they readjusted the gas setting, and got the gun working. However, the gunner voiced concerns on the amount of smoke it was producing. I told him not to worry and just keep firing towards the enemy.

Sgt Chris Howard

When we reached the bottom of the western slope, I met CSgt Steve Knights. We both went up to check who was up on the western slope. We all walked up straight up the middle in single file, all carrying our various pieces of specialist equipment, i.e. the Milan and SF kit. When we got to the top someone said, 'Did you clear those bunkers?' and I said, 'What bunkers?'

We then moved up to Fly Half. Just to our front lay the bodies of two members of 6 Platoon and just beyond them, in a sort of no-man's land, lay some more dead and wounded. Some of the wounded were shouting across to us, saying they were lying in a dip and were pinned down. Although we could hear them, we couldn't see them. We shouted back, telling them to throw grenades at an enemy gun position to our front. There was a GPMG gunner by me, and he was having problems with his GPMG. He wanted to change the barrel on the gun. I said to him, 'If you do, I will beat you to death with the fucking barrel; you fire that gun until it fucking melts.'

Cpl Peter (Tomo) Thompson

The enormous amount of kit and ammo that we were carrying was now beginning to take its toll. As we neared the base of Mount Longdon, I had to stop for a moment and I leaned against a large rock to catch my breath. CSM Caithness, who was not far behind me, came up and asked, 'Cpl Thompson, are you all right?' and I said, 'Yes, Sir, I'm just catching my breath.'

The Press detachment of Les Dowd and Tom Smith then came up to me and asked, 'What's happening now?' I said, 'You two have got to stay here; I have too much to do, and I can't be held responsible for your safety. We are now about to go into battle.' Tom Smith replied, 'No; we've got to stay with you.' I said, 'I am not arguing with you two; if you choose to follow us, that's up to you, but I've told you to stay here.'

Then CSM Caithness came up to me and said, 'Cpl Thompson, I want you to go forward [along Route 3]; I will move parallel to you, up here [left-hand side of western slope]; we will keep in verbal contact; we have to find B Company.' I started carefully making my way forward up Route 3, calling out, 'Is anyone here from B Company?' I walked a bit further and shouted, 'B Company, where the fucking hell are you?' CSM Caithness was shouting across to me, 'Cpl Thompson, have you found them yet?' I shouted, 'No, Sir, there's no sign of them.' I passed a large gap in the rocks, stumbled, and slowly picked myself up. It was then that I saw the black outline of a figure coming towards me. I shouted up to CSM Caithness, 'Sir, I've found B Company!' but it turned out to be three Argentines who immediately surrendered.

During this period, both 4 Platoon and 5 Platoon (B) are further east ahead of the First Bowl. A spur of land jutting from the side of Mount Longdon blocks the line of sight so they cannot been seen from the western end.

CSM Ernie Rustill

We had lost all communications with B Company. The CO was frantically trying to find out about the whereabouts of B Company, and Major Argue. We went firm in an area where there were some collapsed tents and ground sheets; we had only been there for a few minutes when some Argentines were discovered hiding under the ground sheets. They were quickly taken prisoner.

The CO asked us to clear a route up to Fly Half, and we then moved forward on to the western slope. We cautiously did fire and manoeuvre up the western slope. I was calling out trying to contact anyone. The first person I spoke to, but never actually saw, was CSM Thor Caithness. He shouted, 'Is that you, Ernie?' I said, 'Yes, we're looking for B Company.' He said, 'Keep going up but watch out for snipers.' We eventually reached Fly Half without encountering any enemy. I reported back to the CO's group that the route up to Fly Half was clear. The CO and his group now followed up.

Cpl Peter (Tomo) Thompson

CSM Caithness called across to me to rejoin him, as he now had made contact with members of B Company. I took hold of the arm of one of my prisoners and said, 'Come on, come on,' and led them back to the gap in the rocks and climbed through on to the western slope. I made direct contact with CSM Caithness and he told me to pass my prisoners to members of D Company, then said, 'Cpl Thompson, the rest of the machine-gun platoon is over there.'

Cpl Phil Heywood appeared out of the darkness. He had just been up on Fly Half and was now talking to Major Dennison. He started telling Major Dennison about snipers pinning 6 Platoon down. I stumbled up over the rocks to where the CSM had indicated the Machine Gun Platoon was. I couldn't actually see them, so I called out as quietly as I could, 'Are there any Machine Gun Platoon over here?' Londoner Pte John Skipper called back, 'Tomo, we're here.' It was so dark you couldn't see anything beyond a couple of feet. I then said, 'Who've we got here?' A number of voices called back: 'Taff McNeilly,' 'Tony Jones,' 'Chris Dexter,' 'Dave Chambers' and 'Rolly Rawlings.' I had three complete gun teams including mine. I said, 'Stay here; I am going up to have a look at the situation on Fly Half.' I then took off my tripod, link ammunition and webbing, and started cautiously moving towards the very top of Fly Half.

Sgt Graham Colbeck

As I moved on to the western slope, I could hear British voices coming out of the darkness and was then passed by a group of Argentine prisoners being escorted off Longdon. I bumped into Pat Harley, who was struggling with his two Milan missiles. I took one off him and carried on moving up. Eventually Major Dennison told us to go firm about 20 metres from the summit in some abandoned bunkers. We unpacked all our Milan kit and prepared everything for a move up to the summit; I was eager to deploy the Milan but Major Dennison told me to wait. I noticed a 'Rasit' ground surveillance radar not far away from where we were. I then decided to check inside one of the bunkers, partly out of curiosity and also in the hope of finding something useful, or at least something warm. I found a control unit for a Cobra missile system and a plastic box containing a brand-new set of head-mounted night-vision goggles.

There are two Rasit ground-radar systems, one located on the western slope facing west, and one on the northern side, located outside the Second Bowl facing north.

RSM Lawrie Ashbridge, 40 yrs – HQ Company 3 PARA

At this time no one knew where was safe and where wasn't safe. We needed to locate Major Argue to get an update on what was happening. I remember LCpl Bunkle and LCpl Begg trying to raise him on the radio. Unfortunately, with the surrounding rock formations, all radio traffic was very intermittent. I found two Argentines hiding in a trench. I pulled them out and passed them on to others. I recall someone saying there were four casualties, and then seeing members of 6 Platoon coming out of the darkness, struggling to carry a wounded man in a poncho. They were stumbling all over the place. I had a quick look and knew he was in a bad way. I said to someone, 'You, get that corner,' grabbed another and said, 'Right, let's get him off here now.'

I then left 3 PARA Tac HQ. I would now leave Lt Col Hew Pike to run the battle, and I would look after my men, basically moving about and just speaking to them and reassuring them, letting them know I was there with them. When we arrived at the RAP I remember handing Pte Dodsworth over to a medic [Pte John Kennedy]. I said, 'Alright, pal, it's the RSM, look after this man, I've got to get back up the mountain.'

LCpl Mark (Rolly) Rawlings, 21 yrs – Support Company, Machine Gun Platoon

Cpl Thompson and I began to move up the western slope, but we had to stop as there were bunkers ahead of us still being cleared, and there were grenades going off everywhere. We then all moved forward to a clump of rocks; all the gun teams now waited here. Cpl Thompson then went forward to do a battle appreciation of where the guns would best be sited.

Cpl Peter (Tomo) Thompson

As I reached the top of Fly Half I saw some dark figures on my left and on my right. I called across in a half-whisper, 'Who the fuck's that?' The reply came back from my left, 'It's Chris Howard, is that you, Tomo?' I said, 'Chris, what's happening?' Chris replied, 'It's fucking chaos, Tomo, there's some wounded to our front, but we can't get to them. Doc Murdoch's been wounded, and he's out there somewhere, and Geordie Laing's just been shot trying to reach him.' I could now see the body of a member of 3 PARA, and I said, 'Chris, there's a dead bloke over here!' Chris said, 'It's Dave Scott.' I called across to my right and Cpl Trev Wilson gave me a brief rundown on the situation. I asked him if there were any of his lads out in front of us; he said there were dead and wounded out there somewhere.

There was sporadic fire coming from along the northern ridge, but the main source of fire was coming from the Full Back position approximately 500 to 600 metres away; there were constant green muzzle flashes. There were also the occasional shots being fired from the right side (southern side) of the eastern slope. There was no effective fire being returned from our location. My battle appreciation probably took only five minutes at the most.

I made my way back down to where I had left the gun teams. I thought, I don't want to order someone to come back up to Fly Half with me, but we have to do something to reclaim fire control and win the firefight. I had to make a decision and make it fast, so I decided to ask for a volunteer.

CSgt Steve Knights

I was on the western slope when B Company OC came over the radio reporting that they had taken casualties and required stretchers. I said, 'Sir, I don't have the stretchers any more; they are at the western end of the feature with Captain

Burgess in the RAP. I suggest you contact him directly.' Shortly after that, the CO Hew Pike shouted across to me and said, 'CSgt Knights, can you tell me what's happening?' I told him, basically, that B Company had taken the western end of the objective and that we were returning fire at the Full Back position, but it would appear we'd slowly ground to a halt because of the heavy return of incoming enemy fire.

03.00hrs (zt): from C/S 29 to C/S 59: 'Have taken quite a number of casualties and require a lot of stretchers, caused by heavy firefight.'

Lt Col Hew Pike
As we made our way up towards Fly Half, I heard Major Argue speaking over the radio asking for stretchers, and I immediately requested a situation report from him. He informed me that 4 Platoon had taken quite a number of wounded and required a lot of stretchers.

5.3   'Where's the fucking missile gone?'

03.02hrs (zt): from C/S 9 to C/S 29: 'Send situation report.'

Major Argue immediately informs the CO:

03.02hrs (zt): from C/S 29 to C/S 9: 'Roger, call sign 21 did splinter assault on enemy position, have taken several casualties and a couple of prisoners.'

Sgt Chris Howard
There was a .50 Cal on the eastern slope that was giving us some problems; Cpl Morham fired at least four 84mm anti-tank rounds at it, but it kept firing. At one stage, we thought we had succeeded in hitting the gunner, but the gun was remanned and carried on firing. The next day we found a body lying nearby it, also the cocking handle of the gun had been removed, in order to disable the gun.

We were now beginning to gain some control over the area to our front. One of the gun teams was now sighting its SF machine-gun position and Graham

Colbeck and I began sighting our Milan post. Captain Willie McCracken and his radio operator Titch Barfoot were now calling in fire missions onto the Full Back position and rolling it back along towards us.

I scanned the area for a target to fire at, using a set of captured night-vision goggles that Graham Colbeck had found. I decided to fire a Milan missile at a particularly annoying Argentine position. But as I fired the missile it exploded with a blinding flash, whilst still on the firing post. The tube blew to bits; the blast came out sideways and blew the blast shield off. The missile flew off at a 45-degree angle, soaring high into the night sky and the camouflage scrim on my helmet ignited. I shouted to Colbeck to cut the missile loose. But Graham had been blown over by the blast. Cpl Bert Oliver cut the guidance wire, and away it went.

CSgt Steve Knights

When Chris Howard fired the Milan, I was behind him and got covered in shit. I said, 'What the fucking hell have you done?' He said, 'I don't know, it just blew up on me.' I said, 'Where's the fucking missile gone?' and he replied, 'I don't fucking know! It's gone down the range somewhere. I think it's heading for Stanley.'

Sgt Chris Howard

We found out later that the first Milan missile landed quite close to Port Stanley, not far from a 105mm artillery piece. I moved back down the western slope where I found Pte Andy Dunn. I borrowed his Milan frame, and we set up again and this time the missile launched, and I tracked it all the way down to Full Back where it impacted with an enormous fireball.

Cpl Peter (Tomo) Thompson

When I asked for a volunteer, all the men of the three gun groups volunteered in unison. I explained I could only take one person with me. Again they all volunteered. I picked the person who was furthest up the slope. I reached out and grabbed his leg and said, 'Who's that?' He replied, 'It's Rolly.' I knew he had a tripod, so I turned to Rick [Westray], my gunner, and said, 'Give me your gun, here's my tripod and rifle.'

I gave the group a very brief set of orders: me and Rolly would set up the gun on the top of Fly Half and begin engaging the enemy; the rest of the group were to supply us with ammunition. Cpl Mick Matthews of the Anti-Tank Platoon whispered, 'Is there anything I can do to help?' I said, 'You go to CSM Caithness and ask him to get all the ammunition-bearers to bring all the ammunition to this location and my lads will ferry it over to us, as we need it.'

Rolly and me moved up to Fly Half. We crawled over the forward slope and began setting up the machine gun in the low mount next to the body of one of our men. We then started to load up the gun and lay the ammunition out. With the machine gun loaded and ready to engage, I now considered which target to engage. I decided on Full Back as this was where the main machine-gun and rifle fire was coming from. I put my hand on Rolly's arm and said, 'I'm about to fire, get ready.' I knew the enemy would throw everything they had back at us once I took hold of the trigger and opened fire.

LCpl Mark (Rolly) Rawlings
We linked up about four or five bandoliers of ammunition and began firing. Initially we had quite a few stoppages due to the ammunition. Cpl Thompson kept recocking the gun and firing it, but once we began using ammunition taken out of ammunition liners we had no problems. We were just aiming at the green flashes. Cpl Thompson would shout, 'UNLOCK!' and I would automatically unlock the cradle-locking lever. Cpl Thompson would roughly align with the next target and shout, 'LOCK!' He would then fine-tune the sight, and shout, 'ON!' Some of the targets were quite close on our left; this would be along the main spine west to east in the area of the Second Bowl. We were basically just firing at whoever fired at us. We knew there were wounded to our front, but we couldn't be sure where they were, or if by now they were still alive or dead.

The next radio message relates to Support Company telling the CO that four of 6 Platoon's wounded have managed to extract themselves, under the covering fire of Cpl Thompson's SF machine gun. LCpl Steve Wright, Pte Stuart Grey and Pte Dennis Dunn are now back on the western slope:

03.20hrs (zt): from C/S 59 to C/S 9: 'Four casualties taken by C/S 59 stretcher party.'

Cpl Peter (Tomo) Thompson

I was aware that if we carried on firing at this rate, we would soon run out of ammunition, so I decided to fire only at targets when they engaged us or I could clearly see the enemy. We were also in contact with the wounded as we were within shouting distance of each other. We kept calling out to reassure them.

All the time we had been firing there had been British and Argentinian artillery falling in a rolling barrage on our position: you couldn't tell the difference. It fell extremely close to our position; the vibrations were shaking the entire mountain and waves of hot air would blow over us. Some artillery rounds were landing as close as 30 metres away to the south of our position; how they never got us I will never know.

At some point while we were firing away a dark figure appeared at the side of me, and I said, 'Who's that?' He said, 'It's Jock Begg' [LCpl Alan Begg is the CO's signaller] and I said, 'What the fuck you doing here?' He replied, 'I'm just having a look.' I said, 'Jock, fuck off, you shouldn't be here.' About thirty minutes later, I received a message: 'The CO is moving over to the left, prepare to give him covering fire.' I said, 'Not a problem, just tell me when.' Shortly after this someone shouted, 'Fire now!' and they ran down into the First Bowl. At that time I thought, What the fuck is the CO doing this far forward? Where are the forward elements of C Company?

We were winning the firefight and slowly controlling the battlefield with this one gun, so I continued to engage targets that presented themselves. At one point, out of the corner of my right eye, I became aware of movement. I couldn't see properly because of the darkness, but I could make out shapes. I shouted to Rolly, 'Unlock the gun and move out of the way!' I swung the gun to the right; they were really close to our position. As I took aim, a flare went up and illuminated the area. I immediately recognized the shape of the helmets and camouflaged uniforms of 3 PARA. I thought, What are they doing out there? I was told that there was nobody in front of us.

The men running back are Pte Phil Simpson, Pte Morgan Slade and Pte Bryn Cowley, making their way back to 6 Platoon. They come incredibly close to being shot.

Lt Col Hew Pike still cannot find Major Argue. Eventually the CO manages to contact him over the radio. Major Argue confirms his location: he is with 6 Platoon. The CO is also with 6 Platoon but in the general confusion, partly due to the darkness and rocky terrain, it is hard to locate anyone:

03.30hrs (zt): from C/S 9 to C/S 29: 'Can you assess the situation?'

03.30hrs (zt): from C/S 29 to C/S 9: 'Roger, I am now with Call Sign 2/3. There are a few well sited automatic weapons, but believe little resistance left, do not think it necessary for Call Sign 3 [C Company] to pass through us yet. We will keep knocking the enemy bit by bit.'

Captain Willie McCracken and his team of naval RO1 Stan Hardy, Bdr (Jacko) Jackson and signaller Gnr (Titch) Barfoot have moved up onto the western slope to grid 326751 in the rocks on Fly Half. Shortly after 5 Platoon clear the First Bowl, he moves his team into the bowl, and from here he calls in salvos of naval gunfire onto the Third Bowl approximately 120 yards away.

Lt Col Hew Pike

I finally made contact with Mike Argue. He made it pretty clear to me that all his attempts to get forward were being thwarted. I also realized that his company had taken quite a few casualties.

Captain Kevin McGimpsey, 30 yrs – Adjutant 3 PARA

We moved up to locate and liaise with Mike Argue. I thought that this was madness; we were running and ducking over exposed areas with sniper fire and tracer. The CO would keep on shouting that we had to get forward. For the first two or three hours after H-Hour, the CO's Tac HQ kept moving back and forth between A and B Companies. The CO was encouraging and cajoling B Company to keep pressing forwards.

At approximately 04.00hrs (zt), Captain Tony Mason, who is located on Wing Forward, is ordered to bring his Milan detachment and two SF teams across to Mount Longdon and up to Fly Half.

3 PARA HQ informs Brigade that 1 x .50 calibre is still causing problems:

04.01hrs (zt): from C/S 0 to C/S 99: 'Situation report, fighting hard, 1 x .50 Browning machine gun, also under mortar fire, number of own casualties and prisoners taken, once .50 Browning taken out should have no problem.'

04.16hrs (zt): from C/S 41B to C/S 29FDC: 'C/S 3 End of mission ZU7920 on add 600 metres 55 rounds expended.'

Cpl Peter (Tomo) Thompson

A flare had gone up from around the Full Back area and I noticed a large group of figures moving forward towards us on the southern side. I said to Rolly, 'I think we have a counter-attack coming in forward right of us. Link up all the ammunition, everything we've got.' I traversed the gun about 30 degrees to the south-east. This was the first time I had seen actual figures to fire at, and I began to engage; we traversed the area and fired about 2,000 rounds. I didn't have time to get other people to help us, as we had not been issued radios, and we had no night sights, so I just continually fired into that area for about 20 minutes. While we were firing we received accurate direct machine-gun/rifle fire from Full Back and the enemy's artillery opened up onto us again. We then had a resupply of ammunition and I told Rolly to go silent and waited to see that if the counter-attack materialized from the right. Fortunately it didn't.

At approximately 04.20hrs (zt), Major Carrizo Salvadores sends 46 men of the 10th Mechanized Engineer Platoon under the command of 2nd Lt Hugo Quiroga along the southern flank to launch a counter-attack on the summit. They come under heavy fire and several are wounded and they withdraw. These may be the men Cpl Thompson fired at. This group of Argentines cause no casualties among the men of 3 PARA, and apart from Cpl Thompson and LCpl Rawlings no one else sees or hears the half-hearted counter-attack.

Acting Captain Giles Orpen-Smellie

I was wounded by a ricochet in the right arm about an hour after Tac HQ arrived on Fly Half. The Argentine defenders were firing GPMGs semi-blindly into the rocks where we were. A round from one of these ricocheted off a nearby rock and then into my arm. I turned and said, in a very calm and measured way, 'I've been hit' to Cpl John Sibley, who thought I was joking and told me to stop taking the piss! It was only when, by the light of a carefully shaded torch, he saw my hand was covered in blood, that he accepted my story and immediately launched into a swift and highly efficient assessment and began dressing my wound. That was the mark of the very professional medic that he was.

At approximately 04.40hrs (zt), Captain Tony Mason has now arrived on the western slope.

RSM Lawrie Ashbridge

I was moving about talking to the younger soldiers. I thought it was vital the soldiers see me up there with them. I remember hearing someone saying, 'Fucking hell, is that the RSM?' I said, 'Yes, it is, are you all right, pal? It's okay, let's just crack on.'

04.40hrs (zt): After firing 121 salvos, HMS Avenger's 4.5-inch gun 'Big Bertha', now has problems with her gyroscope and is unable to fire.

04.45hrs (zt): Lt Col Hew Pike contacts Major David Collett with regards to advancing forward, but is told it is not possible as the .50 Calibre in the Third Bowl and small arms are still dominating the northern approaches.

5.4   'Well, pal, he's still alive, get him fucking out of here!'

Lt Col Hew Pike

It was around this time I thought, Right, we need to get A Company involved, but after speaking to David Collett I was able to establish that A Company was unable to move forward due to heavy machine-gun fire from various gun positions on the northern side of the objective.

04.50hrs (zt): Lt Col Hew Pike contacts Major Collett and tells him to make his way across to Longdon, to discuss the best use of A Company. Major Collett departs Wing Forward with Sgt Mac French and radio operator Pte Terry Kipling.

04.55hrs (zt): HMS Yarmouth takes over HMS Avenger's targets.

3 PARA HQ informs Brigade that HMG No. 3 in the Third Bowl is still causing problems. The gun is no longer firing to the north against A Company; the crew have repositioned it facing west. From its new position, fortunately for 3 PARA, due to rock formations it cannot hit the area from where the SF team are firing:

05.03hrs (zt): from C/S 0 to C/S 99: 'Situation report, no change still trying to take out the 1 x .50 Browning position.'

At approximately 05.10hrs (zt), BV vehicles carrying mortar ammunition begin to arrive at the Mortar Line.*

LCpl Kevin Robison, 20 yrs – Mortar Platoon, B Company Mortar Detachment

The Mortar Platoon moved as part of the vehicle convoy, consisting of a number of BVs and tractors carrying the battalion ammunition. Each of our mortar detachments had about 200 bombs. These were loaded on board the vehicles and the platoon walked alongside, but I think the Mortar Command Post Operators [Sgt Dave Hallas – B Company, Cpl Leuan Bullivant – A Company, Cpl John Mountford – C Company] went ahead with either Support Company or the rifle companies to mark out the Mortar Line. The Mortar Line was shielded by a rocky ridge.

We split into three groups, acting as independent sections at a set distance apart that matched the ground. We were working to fire missions firstly from Cpl Terry McGlasson and Cpl Ronnie Cooper, and then later, Cpl Mark [Geordie] Crowne and Cpl Steve Baxter. We fired smoke-adjusting rounds, at varying rates, but mainly fire for effect, with HE [high explosives]. The MFCs [Mortar Fire Controllers] were having trouble identifying their rounds among all the other explosions from HMS *Avenger* and 79 Kirkee Battery that were landing on and around the mountain. I was listening to the chitchat on the net, that was coming from the MFC describing what was going on, short situation reports. The other detachments were firing at the same time. I would estimate we fired about 150–200 rounds per barrel, mostly on charges six, seven and

---

* It has not been possible to speak to any senior ranks of the Mortar Platoon, consequently there is very little information about the excellent job that 3 PARA Mortars did.

eight. Throughout the night counter-artillery fire constantly landed around the Mortar Line; I remember C Company Detachment having a very close hit, but fortunately they were all okay.

Lt Col Hew Pike

I reported back to Brigade HQ that we were having a tough time, we would get there in the end, but it was taking a hell of a long time. I have no idea of what time it was; I don't remember looking at my watch all night. I mean, we were shelling, and they were shelling; artillery fire was coming down all around us, and we were so mixed up, we didn't know whether it was ours or the enemy's really.

LCpl Denzil Connick

The thing I remember most about this time was the urgency of it all; I looked on as an 'O' Group was held with Lt Col Hew Pike, RSM Lawrie Ashbridge, Major Argue, Major Dennison, Major Collett, WO2 Thor Caithness and CSM Johnny Weeks. All of them were now forcefully discussing our next move.

Major Argue tells the CO that he would like another go, he wants B Company to try a left-flanking attack; this would involve sending 4 and 5 Platoons along the sheep track on the northern side of the mountain.

HMS Avenger is still out of action; Captain Willie McCracken will now direct fire from HMS Yarmouth onto the main ridge with special attention to the Third Bowl area.

05.47hrs (zt): 2 salvos

05.52hrs (zt): 2 salvos

05.55hrs (zt): 2 salvos

05.59hrs (zt): 43 salvos

3 PARA HQ send a situation report to Brigade:

06.10hrs (zt): from C/S 0 to C/S 99: 'At present winning firefight on last known position on eastern end of Mount Longdon, from POWs, there are 6 x 120mm mortars at grid 338748 our call sign investigating.'

06.12hrs (zt): NGS completed: this is the last of the naval gunfire. HMS Yarmouth and HMS Glamorgan head back to the carrier group leaving HMS Avenger, whose gun is now working, manning the gunline:

At approximately 06.15hrs (zt), A Company are given orders to withdraw from Wing Forward. Sgt Mac French of A Company is sent back across to Wing Forward to act as a guide.

06.30hrs (zt) approximately: B Company begin forming up for their left-flanking attack.

06.33hrs (zt): from C/S 29 to C/S 83(MO): 'Approximately 10 casualties Call Sign 2 [B Company] for BV casevac.'

06.37hrs (zt): HMS Glamorgan is hit, port-side hangar and main galley. HMS Yarmouth and HMS Avenger go to assist.

At approximately 07.00hrs (zt) on northern side of mountain:

RSM Lawrie Ashbridge

As I walked across to the north-west corner not far from the RAP, I heard someone groaning and British voices coming from around the other side of some rocks. I found a group of B Company's wounded. They were just sitting there, all huddled together in the dark. I particularly remember Cpl Kelly, Cpl Bailey and Pte Hindmarsh. As it was pitch dark, I happened to stand on someone who said, 'Ahh, who the fucking hell's that?' I said, 'Who's that?' He said, 'It's Cpl Bailey.' I shouted, 'Why the fuck is this man lying here?' I was told by someone in a hushed tone, 'Sir, he's dying, he's not going to make it.' I said, 'Well, pal, he's still alive, get him fucking out of here!'

3 PARA HQ contact the CO and tell him, 'Brigade wants to know what's happening.'

07.25hrs (zt): from C/S 0 to C/S 9: 'Send brief situation report for Higher Formation.'

The CO explains to 3 PARA HQ that B Company has taken considerable casualties, and he will pass A Company through before first light at approximately 09.40hrs (zt):

07.25hrs (zt): from C/S 9 to C/S 0: 'Roger: Call Sign 2 has sustained considerable casualties whilst taking its objective, Call Sign 1 will pass through, and hopefully take Full Back by first light, there is fierce resistance on the feature, and it is difficult to pinpoint the exact location of the enemy amongst the rocks.'

3 PARA HQ then passed the message directly to Brigade:

07.25hrs (zt): from C/S 0 to C/S 99: 'Situation report, Call Sign 2 considerable casualties whilst clearing feature, firefight still going on, once Call Sign 2 has secured saddle Call Sign 1 will pass through them and hopefully secure Full Back by first light.'

Brigade now informs 3 PARA that they intend sending 2 PARA to reinforce 3 PARA:

07.28hrs (zt): from C/S 99 to C/S 0: 'We are going to reinforce you with 2 PARA, but need to know, which flank you want them on and how you will tie up with them.'

07.40hrs (zt): B Company, after advancing up the sheep track, begin to withdraw from the Second Bowl.

A Company are beginning to arrive on Mount Longdon at roughly 07.40hrs (zt). Support Company and HQ Company are now transporting ammunition up to Fly Half from the resupply area/RAP, in readiness for their forthcoming task, which is to fire in A Company:

07.45hrs (zt): from C/S 0 to C/S 9: 'I have vocab message from Call Sign 99, can you take it now?' [Vocab = Battle cipher code used with vocabulary cards.]

The CO is too busy at that precise moment:

07.45hrs (zt): from C/S 9 to C/S 0: 'No, wait-out.'

Cpl Peter (Tomo) Thompson

From our gun position we could see vehicle lights moving about in Stanley; some of them would come down as far as Moody Brook, then they would turn around and go back. We became aware of four vehicles coming towards us heading up the Moody Brook valley (south-east of Full Back) with their headlights on, three large vehicles and one small. I said to Rolly, 'Look, vehicles. Link up all the ammo as quick as you can.' I estimated that the vehicles were maybe two or more kilometres away. I put the gun in the high arc and fired. I tried to estimate the fall of my rounds in the darkness, as the tracer burnt out at 1100 metres; I fired approximately 1,500 rounds in the general area of the vehicles. The vehicles did stop – I'm not sure it was anything to do with us, but the headlights went off.

After that we again turned attention to Full Back, but I kept an eye on the area where we thought the counter-attack had previously come from. Shortly after that incident, one of the Machine Gun Platoon came forward and said, 'Tomo, the OC [Major Dennison] wants to see you.' I asked him what for, and he said he didn't know. I said, 'Well, you'd better go and fucking find out, because I'm not moving from this position!' I then carried on firing. He came back and said, 'Tomo, the OC wants to see you now, it's really important.' I was not happy and I shouted, 'Right, fine. Rolly, start packing the ammunition up, I'll find out what's going on.'

I ran back and went to see the OC. Major Dennison said, 'Cpl Thompson, this is what's going to happen.' In short, the Machine Gun Platoon was to set up a gunline to support A Company. They were going to assault along the eastern slope and hopefully capture Full Back, and we were going to fire them in.

3 PARA HQ tell Brigade they are still awaiting a reply from CO regarding 2 PARA:

07.53hrs (zt): from C/S 0 to C/S 99: 'Reference attachment of 2Q message passed to Sunray awaiting answer!'

08.00hrs (zt): from C/S 9 to C/S 0: 'Reference message: 1, North Flank, 2, liaise with Call Sign 3 on North flank, they have secure communications with the main and insecure High Frequency direct to Sunray.'

08.00hrs (zt): from C/S 0 to C/S 9: 'Passed to Brigade, they also require RV and guide.'

08.15hrs (zt): from C/S 9 to C/S 0: 'Will give grid for rendezvous soon, they will be guided by C/S 4 and it must be stressed that they must take the most covered route, call sign 4 [D Company] will rendezvous with them at GR AZ DLY.'

08.15hrs (zt): from C/S 0 to C/S 9: 'Passed to Brigade grid reference 335765.'

08.18hrs (zt): 45 Commando now go firm on Two Sisters.

08.20hrs (zt): from C/S 0 to C/S 99: 'RV for 2 PARA is grid reference 335765 they will be met by Call Sign 4, and guided to position by sub unit C/S 3, it must be stressed that the most covered route must be taken.'

Although 3 PARA get on famously with 2 PARA, this is the last thing 3 PARA want!

08.30hrs (zt): from C/S 0 to C/S 99: 'Sunray to contact you on other means very shortly.'

CO's signaller tells 3 PARA HQ the CO cannot speak to them at the moment!

08.30hrs (zt): from C/S 9 to C/S 0: 'Reference 99 talking to Sunray, he is separated from the set and will call 99 when it joins him.'

Mortar Platoon now inform 3 PARA HQ they have run out of ammunition:

08.30hrs (zt): from C/S 50B to C/S 0: 'We have no mortar ammo.'

08.30hrs (zt): from C/S 0 to C/S 50: 'Roger, stacks of it with 9A.' [9A = RAP.]

Brigade request another situation report:

08.37hrs (zt): from C/S 99 to C/S 0: 'Request number of casualties and prisoners soonest.'

At approximately 08.45hrs (zt), the SF teams begin setting up on Fly Half. 3 PARA HQ were still trying to sort the link-up with 2 PARA:

08.55hrs (zt): from C/S 0 to C/S 99: 'Send approximate time for ETA of 2 PARA at the RV given [335765].'

08.55hrs (zt): from C/S 99 to C/S 0: '1½ hours [= 10.30hrs (zt)].'

Cpl Peter (Tomo) Thompson

I then said to Pte Rick Westray, 'Rick, I want you to come with me, now.' We went back to my gun position on top of Full Back, where Rolly was preparing the machine gun for removal. I told him to stop what he was doing, leave everything where it is, and that he was to move down to where the rest of our machine-gun platoon were. I said to Rick, 'Stay here, I am going to get the other gun teams and place them out. When I've done that, I will come back here.'

I made my way back over Fly Half with Rolly and located the Machine Gun Platoon. I told them to try and get under cover, as we were expecting an artillery barrage. I then heard Captain Mason's voice and said, 'Sir, Major Dennison has told me to take the guns and put them in position up on the top.' I spotted a group of blokes and shouted, 'Who's that?' A voice shouted back, 'It's Johnny Cook.' I said, 'Johnny, how much ammunition have you got?' and he replied, 'I've still got all my ammunition; both of my guns haven't fired yet.' I said, 'Right, you follow me, your other gun team is to stay here and I'll come back for them once I've placed you out.'

I took Johnny out to his position which was on the left of my gun position. I said, 'Do you see the pinnacle in the distance? It's approximately 600m, that will be your "centre of axis". Be ready to fire on my order.' I then went back down to collect his other gun team [LCpl Bramley] and put him on the right-hand side of where my gun was located. I explained to the controller that between him and me was CSM Caithness using his NOD. He would indicate targets to me; once I was on the target I would order him to fire on my strike. At the time I believed there were only three guns about to fire, I didn't know that one of my gun teams, LCpl Tony Peers' detachment under the command of Sgt Graham Colbeck, had been taken away and moved further forward and to the right [southern side].

CSM Caithness shouted, 'Guns standby, Cpl Thompson, you fire first.' I then fired a long burst directly at the pinnacle. He then shouted, 'Guns one and two, fire.' Gun number one fired a short burst and stopped; I then heard them shout, 'Stoppage!' Cpl Cook and Pte Ratchford desperately tried to clear the gun. My gun and guns 2 and 5 were now putting heavy continuous fire down around the Full Back area.

A Company's Support Group is based on the forward lip of the First Bowl; they are also putting heavy fire onto Full Back.

Sgt Graham Colbeck

We now formed a gunline with four SF machine guns and a number of GPMGs in the light role, one LMG and one Milan post. CSM Thor Caithness was adjusting fire through his NOD, we were all firing away when instructed to, rounds were continually going towards Full Back, and we were all taking his direction towards similar targets. Major Dennison then said to me, 'A Company wants some more direct fire, can you move forward?'

I thought it was a strange request but said, 'Yes, I can.' He then said, 'Is there a covered way forward for you?' I said, 'Not really, but I can get forward.' He replied, 'That will do.' We picked up the gun and moved forward about 100 metres on the southern side of the eastern slope. We continued to fire at targets when told to. I saw the flash signature from what I thought was an Argentine 105mm rocket being fired from the direction of Full Back. It came flying up the eastern slope hitting the rocks and then exploding on the western side of Fly Half not far from where I had left my Milan team. There was a terrific explosion, and I did fear the worst for my team.

This is a 105mm heat round fired by Corporal Manuel Medina of Lt Castaneda's platoon, from a Czekalski recoilless rifle situated at the western end of Wireless Ridge. It is an extremely lucky shot, firing in the dark, aiming at muzzle flashes approximately 2.5 kilometres away. He opens fire at the gunline. The round is fired high, travels in a gentle arc descending as it approaches the gunline on Fly Half, clips a rock and plunges down the western slope, impacting with deadly effect among a Milan crew.

Pte Andy (Stretch) Dunn

My Milan post had been positioned by Sgt Chris Howard, over on the right-hand side of Fly Half. We had a good view of Full Back, but I felt really exposed as we were extreme right, on the very end. We were looking at the green muzzle flashes and asked permission to open fire, but it was refused. Suddenly there was a massive explosion. I think it was a 105mm coming up from the direction of Full Back.

Acting Captain Giles Orpen-Smellie

The 105mm round skimmed a rock on the crest, throwing up sparks, and then plunged downwards on our side of the crest. There was an intense flash, and the next thing I remember was hearing Pte Pat Harley shouting urgently for help with casualties; I was one of those who rushed across, but it was clear that there was nothing we could do.

LCpl Mark (Rolly) Rawlings

I heard a massive whoosh followed by an enormous explosion. It was absolutely deafening. I wasn't quite sure what had hit us. Pte Chris Dexter was stood in front of me and had his back to the blast; a piece of shrapnel hit him in the back of his thigh, which would have hit me at head height if he hadn't been standing there. A couple of us did some first aid on Chris, who was in great pain, then the stretcher-bearers arrived and Chris was taken away.

Pte Quintin (Q) Wright

Pte Craig [Jonah] Jones and I took our Bren gun and formed up on top of Fly Half with the SF machine guns to act as fire support for A Company's assault. Suddenly there was something that passed right between our gun and the next, it sounded like a Wombat anti-tank gun [rushing train type], followed by a huge explosion to our rear right. At the time I had no idea what it was, then someone started screaming and there were shouts for a medic. I made my way across, and I remember seeing a very calm Pat Harley asking for more morphine.

Lt Col Hew Pike

One thing I do remember was when Ginge McCarthy's crew were killed, a shell from a 105mm recoilless rifle passed over my right shoulder between myself and Major Peter Dennison. There was a massive explosion just behind us, killing the entire Milan crew.

09.27hrs (zt): from C/S 0 to C/S 9B: '4 x casualties from 59, exact number not known.'

L–R: James O'Connell (author), Cpl Alan Burton, Cpl Martin Richardson, LCpl Geordie Rowel and Pte Karl Oxbury on Mount Estancia before the battle, 11 June 1982. © James O'Connell

Members of the Milan platoon – three were later killed in action (KIA). Back row, L–R: Pte Pat Harley, Cpl Tim Whittle, Pte Ian Whitehead, Pte Chris Hamill, Cpl Keith McCarthy (KIA), Pte Peter Hedicker (KIA) and Pte Brett Easter. Front row L–R: Pte Tony Hornett, Pte Phillip West (KIA) and Pte Brendan Madden.

Major Peter Dennison (pointing) giving the Support Company orders with
CSM Thor Caithness, who has his back to the camera. © Tom Smith

Cpl Oscar Carrizo is led to the Regimental Aid Post by his colleagues Cpl Casio (left) and Pte
Angel Luis Leiva (right). To the right of them a wounded soldier is being carried by Cpl Pablo
Zeballos Marra (with beard), Pte Roberto Raul Baez (carrying the left leg), Pte Eduardo A
Gonzalez and Pte Ruben Elpidio Linares (carrying the right leg). © Tom Smith

The Regimental Aid Post.
L–R: Sgt Bob Whitehill, Sgt Keith Hopper, an unknown soldier and Cpl Oscar Carrizo after being treated. Pte John Kennedy and Captain Mike Von Bertele are sitting in the background. © Tom Smith

Pte Julian Barrett is carried to a helicopter by Pte Ashley Wright (far left), Cpl Neil Parkin, Captain John Burgess and Pte John Kennedy. © Tom Smith

Pte Chris Dexter being carried by Pte Ashley Wright and an unknown helper to a Gazelle helicopter for evacuation. © Tom Smith

The Regimental Aid Post where the wounded and medical staff keep close to the cover of the rocks. Looking west across the minefield, a 3 PARA helicopter marshal with yellow flags stands at the ready. © Derek Broadbent

The Regimental Aid Post in full flow: Pte Simon Clark is helped into Sgt Dick Kalinski's helicopter while Captain Von Bertele is carried on a stretcher. A drip hangs from the roof of the Snowcat. © Tom Smith

LCpl Roger James is helped into a waiting Gazelle helicopter. © Tom Smith

Aircrewman Cpl Ian Mousette stands at the side of his Scout
helicopter ready to load a wounded man on to the externally-
mounted casualty pod. Sgt Dick Kalinski sits at the controls
looking over his shoulder at the ready. © Barry Stolton

Argentine prisoners being searched. © Derek Broadbent

Seventeen-year-old Pte Mick Southall stands guard over Argentine prisoners.

© Derek Broadbent

The Argentine prisoners, after being searched, will be centralized in a holding area just to the left of the rocks in the photo, fifty metres from the Regimental Aid Post. © Tom Smith

A medic escorting Argentine prisoners to the containment area. © Tom Smith

Cpl Harry Heap (right) escorting a wounded Argentine to the Regimental Aid Post. © Tom Smith

Wounded Pte Pablo Di Meglio stares directly at the camera. © Tom Smith

Argentine prisoners sit huddled in the containment area.
The look in the eyes of Pte Jorge Suárez (centre) reflects the
night he has endured. © Tom Smith

Sgt Chris Howard checks HMG number 3; this is the gun that Sgt McKay had
been trying to silence. In this photo, it has been moved from its original position
facing north to facing east – a move made by A Company during their advance
to capture Full Back. © Graham Colbeck

Argentine soldiers remove their dead colleagues from the First Bowl.
The bodies will be centralized in shell holes on the northern side
of the mountain by the Third Bowl. © Graham Colbeck

After the battle, Sgt Chris Howard surveys the scene where a Milan Detachment took a direct hit from a 105mm HEAT round, killing three men. © Graham Colbeck

3 PARA battle group graves at Teal Inlet. © Graham Colbeck

Monday 14 June 1982: A Company begin moving from their position on Full Back. Smoke is seen drifting from the burning Moody Brook barracks.

3 PARA battle group begin to move off Mount Longdon. Support Company are seen moving along the low ground on the northern side. © Graham Colbeck

Pte Steve Richards loaded up, ready for the move into Port Stanley. © Tom Smith

As C Company reach the outskirts of Port Stanley, Ross Road is deserted – this was supposed to be the stopping point. The road seen to the right has since been named Holdfast Road.

Cpl Boyd Smith stands on Ross Road. His patrol guided C Company 3 PARA to the outskirts of Port Stanley, following behind A and B Company 2 PARA who were first to enter.

A Company Support Group on Ross Road.
Back row L–R: Pte Ilija Lazic, LCpl Graham Tolson, Pte Len Baines, Sgt Chris Phelan,
Pte Kev Darke, Sgt George Duffus, WO2 Sammy Dougherty, Sgt Manny Manfred
and Pte Tim Sidaway. Front row L–R: Pte Pete Maddocks, Pte Terry Martin,
Pte Tony Bojko and Pte Steve Fitton. © Adrian Freer

C Company advancing into Port Stanley towards Government House.

Support Company 3 PARA arrive in Port Stanley. © Graham Colbeck

One of the 105mm pack howitzer guns that pounded Mount Longdon.
Ironically, howitzers were sold by Britain to the Argentine army and a number
of them were used against airborne forces during the Falklands conflict.

Support Company 3 PARA raise the Union Jack in Port Stanley.
L–R: Cpl Bert Oliver, Cpl Tim Whittle, Sgt Graham Colbeck and LCpl Geordie Rowell.

L–R: Cpl Graham Heaton, Sgt John Ross, Cpl Stewart McLaughlin (KIA), Lt Mark Cox
with young boy Gavin Hutchinson.

L–R: Major John Crosland, Major David Collett, CSM Alec Munro
and Captain Adrian Freer. © Adrian Freer

Pte Andrew Williams meets some Argentines who seem glad the war is over. © Andrew Williams

Pte Gustavo Osvaldo Pedemonte.

Cpl Carlos Colemil, Argentine Marine.

Lt Juan Domingo Baldini (KIA),
7th Infantry Regiment.

Cpl Domingo Lamas, Argentine Marine.

Naval Lt Sergio Andres Dachary, Marine.

L–R: Pte Tim Jenkins (KIA), Pte Ged Bull (KIA) and Pte Dave Herbert.

Pte Grant Grinham (left) and Pte Ben Gough.

Brothers Pte Tony Kempster (left) and
Pte Dave Kempster.

Cpl Phil Skidmore (left) and Cpl James Morham. © Phil Skidmore

Sapper Paul Moore (left) and Sapper Tommy Trindall, 2 Troop, 9 Squadron RE.

Pte Mark Dodsworth (left) and LCpl Chris Lovett – both were killed in action.

Pte Pat Harley

Cpl Keith McCarthy had asked me would I like to join his detachment (Philip West and Peter Hedicker) for a brew, but not being a tea drinker, I said, 'Thanks, Ginge, but I'm going to look for some warm kit, and change my socks.' I walked down to a group of tents situated in roughly the centre of the western slope. I crawled in and noticed a couple of kit bags, so I rummaged through them and found three or four pairs of white socks. I changed my socks and stuffed the others into my smock pockets. I also picked up a bayonet. I then crawled back out of the tent and spotted a stone bunker, so decided to investigate. Inside there were lots of bottles filled with petrol, with wicks in the top. I also found a Cobra missile control box.

I was leaving the bunker when there was an almighty explosion outside. I thought the bunker was going to collapse; dust filled the air. I quickly scrambled outside and shouted, 'Has anyone been hurt!' I didn't hear anyone reply, because I had been deafened by the explosion. I made my way towards the sound and found Cpl Keith McCarthy and Pte Philip West. Both were severely injured and I knew I must get help. I went up to Fly Half (about 30 metres away) to ask for medical assistance, but I was in shock and could barely speak, so at first when I spoke it was gibberish, and CSM Thor Caithness told me to calm down and say it again. The second time I managed to tell them. Thor said, 'Right, you go and deal with it, and I'll get on the radio for medics and stretcher-bearers.' Captain Mason said, 'I'll come with you.'

It was extremely distressing. It was clear that newlywed Keith McCarthy would not survive, it would only be a matter of time. I turned my attention to Phil West who was unconscious and had a leg wound; I bandaged his leg and checked his body for other wounds. He had a sucking puncture wound to his chest which I treated, and then rolled him onto his side, to help him breathe.

I went to help LCpl Garry Cripps [Royal Corps of Signals signaller attached to 3 PARA]. He had a cut on his head, an injury to his knee and was very concussed. I found Cfn Clive Sinclair [REME attached to 3 PARA] had received a head wound, which at the time didn't look that bad, as there wasn't much blood, but I have since found out it was very serious. I put a shell dressing on him.

John Kennedy, the medic, had now arrived and he quickly started dealing with the more seriously wounded. I remember everyone was shouting for blankets to keep the wounded warm. During all this time I never gave one thought to Peter Hedicker; I thought he may have gone off somewhere. I helped load Garry Cripps onto a stretcher, and with the help of others, we made our way down the hill with the stretcher. I met Pte Tony Bennett who took my place carrying the stretcher. I then made my way back up the hill to Captain Mason, who told me that Phil West was dead. Captain Mason was visibly upset, and, it must be said, he wasn't the only one.

Pte Pete Hedicker has taken the full brunt of the explosion.

Pte Chris Parris

The gun teams were running low on ammunition, and I was re-linking Argy ammo with our link when I heard a whoosh as something went past me, then a flash. I was deafened for a few seconds and couldn't see anything either. I went over to where the Milan team were and found Cfn Clive Sinclair and Pte Phil West. Then Pat Harley appeared and told me to hold his torch while he treated Phil West. Once Pat had dressed Westy, we turned him on his side, but there was a Bergen frame by his legs. Pat moved the frame to one side, and we heard a moan. Pat shone his torch and it was Cpl Ginge McCarthy, who had been terribly injured. Pat went to assist him. I remember others turning up, particularly Captain Tony Mason, who was visibly shocked by the whole thing, as we all were.

This is the one incident that has haunted me for 40 years. Even though I saw more of our dead and injured later, this is the event that has always remained with me. Pat Harley did an amazing job in a very difficult situation: he remained methodical and gave me instructions, otherwise I may have found the whole situation completely overwhelming.

Cpl Peter (Tomo) Thomson

We had now been firing for approximately 30 minutes, directed by CSM Caithness with commands of 'Switch right, switch right' etc., and were nearing the end. The gun on my right packed in; my gun continued to fire, but the ammunition was now running low. A Company had begun to leave the First

Bowl at 09.40hrs (zt). I was now firing for all I was worth; as they progressed further forward we began to switch our fire, and then CSM Caithness shouted, 'Cease Fire!'

2 Platoon of A Company are now on the eastern slope:

09.40hrs (zt): from C/S 1 to C/S 9: 'Call Sign 1/2 (2 Platoon) has cleared and now manning high ground.'

09.40hrs (zt): from C/S 70 to C/S 9B: '1 Dead plus 1 VSI trying to get him to you.'

3 PARA HQ located at Estancia House update Brigade Headquarters on our total known casualties:

09.40hrs (zt): from C/S 0 to C/S 99: 'Reference number of casualties, approximately possibly two dead and 20 injured.'

Quick situation report from 3 PARA HQ to Brigade telling them B Company has gone firm, and A Company has exploited east supported by Support Company:

09.50hrs (zt): from C/S 0 to C/S 99: 'Situation report, Call Sign 2 has gone firm, Call Sign 1 exploited East, Supported by 59.'

First light approximately 10.00hrs (zt).

At 10.00hrs (zt), A Company MFC orders check [stop] firing.

RSM Lawrie Ashbridge
Not long after this there were two more explosions in the First Bowl. I knew LCpl Chris Lovett was working in the area of the first explosion, and shortly after I heard someone say that Chris Lovett had been killed. I thought, You bastards. I knew Chris Lovett quite well, and he, like all the medics, had worked tirelessly throughout the night.

Cpl Peter (Tomo) Thomson
When we stopped firing it was still dark, although the light was starting to break through. CSM Caithness said to us, 'A Company is now in position, dismount the guns and tripods and get down into cover now!' I quickly said to the lads, 'Right, move back down to there, and get yourselves into cover [indicating the

rocky western slope].' I stayed in my gun position until all the wounded had been recovered. There was a light mist: somebody had thrown a couple of white phosphorus grenades for instant smoke, which gave the stretcher-bearers good cover. Rick and I then dismounted our gun and tripod, picked up what little ammunition we had left [one box of 200 rounds] and moved back down onto the western slope.

Sgt Graham Colbeck

Our gun team pulled back up to Fly Half. I was anxious to see if Stretch Dunn and Steve Wake were okay. I looked about and shouted and eventually found them sitting in an Argentine two-man tent, none the worse for the 105mm recoilless explosion. I gave them a bit of a bollocking but was just glad that they were okay. Over at the Support Company HQ I was shocked to find Cpl Keith McCarthy and his crew had been killed. It was a terrible sight. We now began to take a lot of artillery fire and pulled further down the western slope.

Chris Howard and I were making a brew when we saw some 3 PARA wounded being brought down towards us. Pte Bryn Cowley was carrying Pte Simon Clark over his shoulder; Simon had been shot in the back of his calf. We went over to help and as Bryn sat Simon down, I put a shell dressing on his wound as it hadn't been dressed. We put Simon in a sleeping bag as he was shivering, and we gave him some of our brew. Shortly after this he was taken away by the stretcher-bearers.

Major Dennison said, 'Right, we're moving forward away from this area, it's attracting too much fire.' We now moved towards the First Bowl, the CO, RSM and Tac HQ appeared. The CO looked quite saddened by it all and said, 'Sgt Colbeck, I am sorry about Cpl McCarthy and his crew, very sorry indeed.' I just said glumly, 'Yes, Sir,' as I couldn't think of anything else to say.

There were bodies still lying all over the place. Support Company HQ would now stay in the First Bowl; the SF teams were also here. Argentines were now being found in all sorts of hiding places, many looking extremely scared, and clutching rosary beads.

5.5 'And then of course the shelling started again'

Major Collett now informs the CO that A Company has taken Full Back:

10.28hrs (zt): from C/S 1 to C/S 9: 'Now on position, very extensive position with Sp Gun (Support gun) at end.'

10.30hrs (zt): 42 Commando report their objective Mount Harriet is now also secure.

Lt Col Hew Pike

Once the mountain was ours we started taking stock of the terrible price of success. I do remember very clearly, talking to members of B Company as they reorganized on the lower part of the western slope. I was trying to tell them that although we had had all these terrible losses, we'd achieved the mission and achieved the objective; it had been a huge success, despite the terrible cost of it. I wondered, could these young men come to terms with the fact: was this lump of rock worth a single life, let alone 17 of our own?*

I have this clear memory of watching Lt Ian Moore; having gotten to the far end, he then came back to reorganize. I just remember seeing his group of guys coming back through a thick mist, with bayonets fixed, looking as if they had fought and won a battle. It was an extraordinary sight, of tired but triumphant men.

The shambles of the battlefield was beyond all imagination – corpses scattered about, starting to give off that distinctive odour of death; clothing, bloody shell dressings, discarded boots, belts of ammunition; life's detritus spread all over the hillside. And then of course the shelling started again.

CSgt Steve Knights

Cpl Mick Matthews and I moved back on to the western slope and met up with Major Dennison and Thor Caithness. We then discussed any casualties. At this

---

* Seventeen known dead at that moment.

stage Pete Hedicker was still missing, and it had been assumed he might have been elsewhere helping with casualties.

LCpl Kevin Robison

Later in the morning, after first light, the Mortar Line relocated to the area occupied by C Company 3 PARA, who were north of Longdon. Each section was spread out maybe 100 or 200 metres between each section. B Company detachment was on the right side of the line. Shortly after we bedded in, I recall Cpl Mark [Geordie] Crowne calling in fire missions and giving short sit reps on how he was chasing enemy off the mountain towards Moody Brook, like herding sheep, which I relayed to the blokes. We continued firing through the day, and in return the Mortar Line attracted a lot of artillery fire, which landed quite close to the mortar detachments and also to C Company, causing casualties.

CSM Ernie Rustill

Shortly after first light our group, under Captain Pat Butler, left the CO's Tac HQ and were then sent to link up with 2 PARA.

Cpl Peter (Tomo) Thomson

We began being shelled with heavy enemy artillery. CSM Caithness said to me, 'Cpl Thompson, take the Machine Gun Platoon further down the western slope and get into the rocks and get a brew on, you deserve it.' I turned to the entire platoon and told them, 'Pick up everything, follow me.' I moved as fast as possible to a position halfway down the western slope.

Once the brew was on I moved around each team checking on our ammunition and equipment status. I discovered Chris Dexter from number three gun had been wounded, the Platoon Commander was missing and we had approximately 2,000 rounds left between the six gun teams. I thought, We must have more ammunition left than this. I went back round the gun teams telling them to check their ammunition again, as we'd had 36,000 rounds when we left Estancia House. Our gun had been in position on the top of Mount Longdon for over seven hours and with being in constant contact with the enemy, John Skipper said, 'Including the Argentinian ammunition that everybody had been linking up, you fired well over 30,000 rounds through your gun last night, so it will need some cleaning.'

I went back up to CSM Caithness and explained we needed to get more ammunition quickly. CSM Caithness said to me, 'Right, Cpl Thompson, tell your men to be prepared to move.' After a short time the Platoon Commander, Lt Oliver, came over and said, 'Cpl Thompson, we need to split into three groups, we are moving to another position.' I said, 'Okay, Sir.' I shouted to the platoon, 'Prepare to move. Johnny, your two gun teams will go first with the Platoon Commander followed by Rolly's gun team and I will bring up the rear with Tony Peers' gun.' We then moved back to the top of Mount Longdon.

Pte Mark (Zip) Hunt

Just after first light, Sgt John Pettinger reappeared and said, 'Right, you lot [Dickie Absolon, John [Jock] Wilson and Zip], follow me.' He also grabbed two SF machine-gun teams and said, 'Pick up your kit, we're going to give fire support to A Company.' We went into the First Bowl and grabbed some members of the Anti-Tank [Milan] Platoon. The Milan teams quickly loaded up and followed us out of the First Bowl, moving up through a gap and running into the Second Bowl.

As we were passing a group of rocks that divide the First and Second Bowl there was movement to our left-hand side. An Argentine [Cpl Oscar Carrizo] appeared out of the rocks holding a weapon and began to raise it. Sgt Pettinger fired. Shortly after this incident, we arrived at the bottom of the Second Bowl. I received a message over the radio that our task had been cancelled, and we would not be needed.

The time is now approximately 11.15hrs (zt).

Pte Pat Harley

Sgt Pettinger fired what is known in military terminology as a snapshoot, i.e. he fired on the run, and we carried on, in fact, I don't think we paused at all, it happened that quickly. Shortly after this incident, we arrived at the bottom of the Second Bowl. Sgt Pettinger then received a message over the radio that we would not be needed, so we made our way back, passing the Argentinian who had just been shot, and who I believed was dead. We entered the First Bowl to find our comfortable stone bunker had now been reoccupied by someone else.

Pte Mark (Zip) Hunt

For some reason we [Sgt Pettinger's patrol] made our way across to Full Back. The scene of carnage was awful, with bodies and body parts scattered about. We met up with CSM Alec Munro and Major David Collett, who were now firm on the Full Back, and were busily consolidating and preparing their defences for a possible counter-attack. After Sgt Pettinger had spoken to various people, we came across a .50 Cal, the back plate had been removed in order to disable the gun. Just by chance, I found the back plate lying in the grass. I refitted it and we decided to have a fire of the .50 Cal.

At that moment an Argentine Huey helicopter appeared, flying across our front, heading in the direction of Port Stanley, so we opened up. You could see the large green tracer arcing across the valley towards the helicopter, but then the gun jammed, and we thought, Shit. CSM Ernie Rustill was shouting, 'What the fucking hell are you lot doing?' I said, 'Sir, trying to hit that helicopter.' He replied, 'Right; this is what you do.' He quickly cleared it, and fired a few more rounds, but it jammed again. By now the novelty had worn off as the helicopter had long gone.

We were tasked to go and clear some trenches and tented positions on the northern side of Longdon, roughly opposite the Second Bowl. We approached them cautiously, calling out for anyone in the tents to come out and surrender. We fired into the first tent, which proved to be empty. We then moved on to a second tent, and two very scared occupants climbed out; they looked like Argentine military policemen. We indicated that they should lie down while we searched them. I remember Sgt Pettinger gave me one of their watches.

Sgt Pettinger now decided to take our D Company element off the mountain as we had been awake for over 36 hours [because of reconnaissance patrols] and we badly needed sleep, as we would be needed for further reconnaissance patrols planned for the next day on Wireless Ridge. We made our way through the RAP area, where we spotted our Colour Sergeant, Terry Carroll, and Cpl Neil [Geordie] Moffett, who, for some reason, had a large box of Mars bars. We then made our way to an OP position which was about half a mile away to the west of Longdon. Here we did our personal admin, cleaned our weapons, got something to eat and slept.

LCpl Mark (Rolly) Rawlings

In daylight the mountain looked totally different from the way I had imagined it in the dark. The Argentine artillery had intensified and we were all told to move into the First Bowl. In one of the bunkers Pte Dave Chambers found an Argentine, who had sat there hidden in a corner with blankets covering him. This was after the bowl had been occupied by 3 PARA for at least 9 hours. After a short while we moved to another location, to the front of the First Bowl on the northern side. My gun team [No.3] was now Pte Nigel McNeilly and Pte David Chambers and me. We had been told to have a look around the forward area for any British dead or wounded that may have been missed. I walked around Route 2 and found two blokes lying face down. As I got closer I recognized one from the back as my friend Pete Higgs who I had just done a Tactics Cadre with. Both men had been killed by an artillery round that had buried itself in the peat, but the blast and shockwave had killed them instantly.

3 PARA HQ send Brigade casualty updates: X = Dead, Y = Wounded, Z =Missing:

12.41hrs (zt): from C/S 0 to C/S 99: 'Casualty report, X12 / Y41 / Z=Unknown.'

Sgt Graham Colbeck

An Argentine came staggering down into the bowl, and someone said, 'Look at that Argy!' so I walked over with Rob Jefferies and Steve Knights and I shouted, 'Put your hands up!' There was blood all over his face, and his helmet was lopsided. He then just toppled over, hit a large rock and slid down. I thought, Oh, he's dead, as he did look as if he had just died, so we left him there.

Pte Pat Harley

Somebody nudged me and said, 'Look at him.' An Argentine had come staggering into the First Bowl area; he had a terrible head wound and looked as if he was about to drop dead at any moment. I thought, That's the bloke that John Pettinger shot. He looked like a zombie. He collapsed and I thought he had died; he lay there for quite a while. When suddenly he surprised everyone by getting up, I went over to him and told him to sit down. I spoke slowly and clearly to him, saying, 'Stay there, I will get someone to treat you.' His head wound looked really bad.

I turned my back for a moment, and he picked up an M3 sub-machine gun [grease gun]. I don't think he knew what he was doing, I think he was just confused, but CSM Thor Caithness had seen this, and shouted, 'Someone disarm that man.' LCpl Tony Peers ran across and grabbed the gun off him – he never struggled., Shortly after that he was taken away by a group of Argentinian prisoners to the RAP with another wounded Argentinian who had facial injuries and was bleeding from the mouth and nose. For some reason, in the bitter cold, he was only wearing his trousers! There were many strange sights on that mountain that made you think, What the fuck's happened here?

Sgt Graham Colbeck

Someone shouted, 'There's more over here!' We found several Argentines hiding in and around the First Bowl – we eventually found about eight altogether. We searched them and then gave them some water. Thor Caithness said, 'Right, let's get them down to the RAP area,' as a prisoner holding-area had been established there.

Pte Quintin (Q) Wright

Sometime after first light, our group finally moved over Fly Half. As we walked past members of 4 and 5 Platoons I noticed that they all had wide staring eyes. With fading cam cream on their faces, they looked quite a sight, but I can only guess we all looked the same. Craig [Jonah] Jones and I set up a shelter down on a track [Route 3] leading down to what became the Battalion Tac HQ position. We dug a large trench under an overhanging rock, which provided good protection: before long we heard some 105mm coming our way. Initially they were aimed at the Mortar Line which had set up on Wing Forward – a couple of volleys came in, then it was switched our way. I smoked a load of tobacco while this barrage went on. Quite a few rounds landed in amongst us. Eventually we reappeared out of these bunkers like weevils out of the woodwork.

Lt Col Hew Pike

We wanted our casualties taken off as quickly as possible and I also wanted Argentine prisoners removed. The remainder of that day was spent taking stock of where we were, who was killed and who was wounded. During the daytime the heavy mortar fire was a particularly nasty threat, as there was an observation post on Mount Tumbledown watching us, and it was calling down extremely accurate fire from heavy mortars and artillery from bases around Port Stanley. The terrible thing about the heavy mortar was you couldn't hear the whistle. Suddenly there was just this great thump as it hit the ground. Furthermore, every time helicopters appeared in the RAP area, they were immediately shelled.

The CO contacts 3 PARA HQ. He wants 3 PARA fatalities to be removed from Longdon:

13.55hrs (zt): from C/S 9 to C/S 0: 'Collection of fatalities from position: to be taken to a suitable place for temporary burial, or to a place Brigade suggest.'

3 PARA HQ request a helicopter lift from Brigade:

14.00hrs (zt): from C/S 0 to C/S 99: 'Reference our DEAD we would like to remove them off the mountain, could we do a lift to Teal OKAY.'

Brigade wants more information, 3 PARA Company locations, enemy strength, etc:

15.05hrs (zt): from C/S 99 to C/S 0: 'In order that Command can see strength Seagull are to submit "A" return to Brigade by Seagull by 17.00hrs (zt) today.'

The CO Hew Pike is not happy and contacts 3 PARA HQ asking them to tell Brigade about the reality of the situation on Mount Longdon:

15.15hrs (zt): from C/S 9 to C/S 0: 'Mount Longdon under continual heavy shell fire and we are sustaining further casualties, <u>Sunray Higher Form to be informed.</u>'

[This message was underlined in the radio log.]

15.15hrs (zt): from C/S 99 to C/S 0: 'Send position of Tac HQ.'

15.16hrs (zt): from C/S 0 to C/S 99: 'Western end of Fly Half, grid 322752.'

Pte Pat Harley

Not long after the incident with Oscar Carrizo, I was in the area by the Second Bowl. There were two dead Argentines, one lying on top of another. As we rolled the top one off, the bottom one was alive and had been lying there using his dead colleague for cover. He had been badly wounded in his legs; they were peppered with shrapnel. He was about 19 or 20 years old and looked absolutely petrified. I said in my best Argentinian, 'No, I, Medico.' I tried to administer morphine, but he thought we were trying to poison him, and I kept saying, 'It will stop the pain.'

We found a stretcher from somewhere, then secured him to it, to prevent him falling off while we carried him further down the sheep track. Unfortunately an Argentinian spotter had seen us and called in a fire mission onto us – we all took cover, but the Argentine who we'd placed on the stretcher was strapped down and couldn't take cover from the incoming fire. How he wasn't killed I don't know, but he was laughing like a madman while explosions went off all around him.

Cpl Peter (Tomo) Thompson

I positioned my gun teams in sheltered positions along the northern side between the First and Second Bowls. I now found out that supplies were beginning to get through, and I sent some of my lads to go down and pick up more ammunition and rations. All through this period we were under artillery fire. I was detailed to go and temporarily disable the .50 Calibre machine guns, as members of 3 PARA were playing around with them, and firing at various locations, i.e. Wireless Ridge and Mount Tumbledown, and this was bringing unwanted attention to us in the shape of artillery fire.

LCpl Denzil Connick

One of the worst memories I have of Saturday afternoon was helping to recover the body of James [Doc] Murdoch. He was a battalion character, known and liked by all ranks. His laughter was infectious – when he laughed, we all laughed. He was a good friend, and it was incredibly saddening, but none the less an absolute honour, to carry Doc and Stewart Laing's bodies off the mountain down to the RAP.

Sgt Graham Colbeck

At some stage Chris Howard, Denzil Connick and I helped in the recovery of the bodies of Stewart Laing and Doc Murdoch. We lifted them onto the stretchers and they were taken away. Chris and I then walked back onto the western slope, down by the 81mm mortar. The incoming shell fire was dropping more frequently now.

We decided to have a look at the Argentine 105mm recoilless facing Tumbledown, to see if we could fire it at Tumbledown. We climbed into the gun pit, but there was no ammunition. We then had a wander about the place looking at the various gun positions; we walked up to Full Back and started looking at the .50 Calibre, when Captain Willie McCracken said, 'You're not going to fire that, are you?' Chris Howard said, 'Fucking right I am!' Chris then began firing the .50 Cal across the valley at Mount Tumbledown. Eventually he ran out of ammunition. We then went across to the Third Bowl as Chris knew that there was a pile of ammunition there, which we brought back to the gun on Full Back and fired it until the gun jammed solid.

Pte Quintin (Q) Wright

I went over to 3 PARA Tac HQ and met up with Sgt Graham Pearson, our Intelligence Sergeant, and Cpl Gordon Goldsmith, and we went down to the resupply area for some rations and cigarettes. I then made my way back to my bunker and made a scoff. Cpl Phil Heywood, the HQ Company sniper, walked the entire length of Longdon to ask me for some cigarette papers as he knew I had the liquorice ones that he liked.

Pte Pat Harley

I was back on the western slope, around the area where the Milan team had been killed, when I found some identifiable British human remains. I wrapped them in a blanket, and asked CSgt Steve Knights what I should do with them. He told me to take them down to the bottom, as everything was being centralized down there. So LCpl Mark Hamill and I made our way down. It was then I first noticed Stewart McLaughlin was dead. I saw his name on one of the body bags and I said, 'Oh look, Scouse McLaughlin's been killed.' Padre Heaver came up behind us. He was clearly upset, and said quite loudly, 'His name is Cpl Stewart McLaughlin, and what are you doing here with the bodies?' I said,

'Padre, we've found a piece of Soldier X and we thought it best to bring it down here.' After that I went back to my bunker and sat miserably contemplating what I had just done.

The CO updates his casualty reports to 3 PARA HQ:

17.12hrs (zt): from C/S 9 to C/S 0: 'Casualty report: X 18/Y 39 including 3 officers Captain Logan/Captain Orpen-Smellie/Lt Bickerdike.

> X details:
> HQ 5: Pte Greenwood.
> B 48: Sgt McKay.
> B 05: Pte Burt.
> B 24: Pte Scrivens.
> B 94: LCpl Murdoch.
> B 07: Pte Grose.
> D 30: LCpl Higgs.
> SP 112: Pte Crow.
> HQ 95: LCpl Lovett.
> E 9223: Cpl Wilson.
> A 102: Pte Jenkins.
> SP 200: Cpl McCarthy.
> SP 215: Pte West.
> SP 218: Pte Hedicker.
> HQ 18: Pte Dodsworth.
> HQ 16: LCpl Scott.
> SP 119: Pte Laing.
> B 43: missing/dead Cpl McLaughlin.'

A situation report is sent from 3 PARA HQ to Brigade (Intelligence Summary 27: dated 11 June 18.00hrs / 12 June 18.00hrs). It gives the locations of all the 3 PARA rifle companies. Unfortunately the grid reference given for C Company's location is wrong: they are located at 335753, not at the grid reference given 345753 (Rum Punch). One figure is wrong, a distance of 1 kilometre.

18.00hrs (zt): from C/S 0 to C/S 99: 'Require estimated time of arrival of Watchdog this location reference movement of POWs.'

18.00hrs (zt): from C/S 99 to C/S 0: 'No chance of helicopter for lift of POWs, take to grid 290703 and hand over to 1 Welsh Guards.'

Brigade informs all stations that helicopter supply is very limited:

18.30hrs (zt): from C/S 99 to All Stations: 'Support helicopter in limited supply. Priority one, shells for gun batteries only. Priority two, Bergens, supplies, other units to make alternative arrangements.'

18.50hrs (zt): from C/S 99 to C/S 0: 'Reference POWs, we are to escort them to grid 290703, where a Company of 1 Welsh Guards will take them and escort them to Fitzroy.'

18.55hrs (zt): from C/S 99 to C/S 0: 'Reference Bergens, Where are they, are they netted and where do you want them taken to?'

19.20hrs (zt): from C/S 0 to C/S 99: 'We have moved figures 10 POWs by Wessex C/S and have 29 POWs left to move, also 18 of our own dead for movement to Teal, POWs Priority one: Dead may not be moved till tomorrow.'

20.00hrs (zt): from C/S 9A to C/S 0: 'We would like our Bergens tomorrow if possible, but do not worry if it cannot be done – dubious of helicopters flying into our area.'

20.10hrs (zt): from C/S 50B to C/S 0: 'A, 500 HE [high explosive] plus bipod / B, 300 WP [white phosphorus munition] / C, 100 Illumination [illumination rounds].'

20.15hrs (zt): from C/S 1 to C/S 9A: 'Another fatality No. A 107 [Pte Bull].'

Pte Quintin (Q) Wright

Shortly before last light I had walked across to see a mate in A Company, Tony Hornett, who was based over on the north-eastern side of Longdon on Full Back. After I'd had a chat it seemed to get dark really quickly, and I didn't fancy making my way back across the eastern slope in the dark as there were still some uncollected bodies. So I decided I would spend the night there. I looked around and found a fantastic rug. I rolled myself up in it and slept like someone had belted me over the head.

Pte Pat Harley

Once it started going dark, I spent the rest of the night in my bunker listening to air bursts exploding outside. I heard moaning and groaning, and I called out, 'Has anyone been hit?' A few voices called back, 'No, I'm okay,' and 'Same here,' and 'We're okay.' But still the moaning continued, so I went out to investigate just in case someone needed help. It turned out to be Cpl Mick Matthews moaning and groaning in his sleep.

Cpl Michael Matthews was later murdered by the IRA in a landmine explosion near the village of Cullyhanna in Northern Ireland on 28 July 1988.

With the exception of incoming artillery, the night is fairly quiet, with the following radio transmissions:

20.35hrs (zt): from C/S 99 to C/S 0: 'Why is helicopter being sent away from your area?'

20.35hrs (zt): from C/S 0 to C/S 99: 'Position under fire, helicopter unable to land.'

20.35hrs (zt): from C/S 9 to C/S 0: 'Information from today's activities: Enemy dead – counted so far 50 / Enemy wounded – 8–10 / Enemy prisoners 40, Equipment includes – 2 x 120mm mortars / 50 x FN rifles / Numerous GPMGs and machine guns/ Several rocket launchers / 1 x recoilless rifle, Ancillary equipment – laser range finder / passive binoculars / single point sights.'

20.50hrs (zt): from C/S 9A to C/S 0: 'One minor casualty: B 44 [Pte Mark (Boots) Meredith], graze to abdomen by shrapnel casevac to Teal.'

21.00hrs (zt): from C/S 0 to C/S 9: 'Any indications what unit was on Longdon?'

21.00hrs (zt): from C/S 9 to C/S 0: 'From Acorn minor: Unit on initial 1 Company of 7th, Infantry Regt, small amount marine back-up, they moved back to take up anti-aircraft defences, supposed to be eight pieces of AA defences, between here and Stanley, the Company of 7th Infantry numbers 60, captured 40, 5 wounded, 11 dead, 4 missing.'

21.05hrs (zt): from C/S 9 to C/S 0: 'Acorn underestimated, 50+ dead, position and length suggest more than one company, I estimate 200 men.'

['Acorn' is the code name for Intelligence Officer.]

21.24hrs (zt): from C/S 0 to C/S 99: 'Your Call Sign 98 has arrived at our location and intends moving into position at first light.'

21.33hrs (zt): from C/S 99 to C/S 0: 'Tell your Tac to contact us ASAP send your "A" return again.'

21.33hrs (zt): from C/S 1 to C/S 0: 'Sighting of vehicle lights moving through Stanley from airport to Moody Brook to Sapper Hill.'

Cpl Peter (Tomo) Thompson

As it neared last light we all took to our individual bunkers for a scoff. I managed to get round all the gun teams to make sure they were all okay and gave them a quick update on the situation. A Company was still running a resupply chain. Pte Ged Bull was killed not far from our location, but we had no dealings with it. We now settled down for another cold night. A member of our platoon, Pte Rick Westray (my gunner), while answering a 'call of nature' slipped on icy rocks and had an extremely bad fall. Such was his pain, he was suspected to have broken his neck. Stretcher-bearers were called which took some time and Rick was taken to the RAP. We spent the rest of the night in freezing conditions. None of us got much sleep.

21.40hrs (zt): from C/S 59 to C/S 83B: 'Suspected broken neck at my location [SP 206 Pte Rick Westray].'

21.40hrs (zt): from C/S 0 to C/S 99: 'My C/S 1 reports several vehicle lights moving from the airport to Stanley and then up to Moody Brook and Sapper Hill.'

3 PARA HQ asks Brigade:

21.50hrs (zt): from C/S 0 to C/S 99: 'Is 2 PARA task still on tonight?'

21.50hrs (zt): from C/S 99 to C/S 0: 'No.'

22.12hrs (zt): from C/S 0 to C/S 99: 'Heliquest MQ/01/122205Z.'

22.12hrs (zt): from C/S 99 to C/S 0: 'Sent.'

22.12hrs (zt): from C/S 99 to C/S 0: 'Require new location for POW collection.'

22.35hrs (zt): from C/S 0 to C/S 9A: 'Are you moving the prisoners tomorrow?'

22.35hrs (zt): from C/S 9A to C/S 0: 'First light.'

22.35hrs (zt): from C/S 9A to C/S 0: 'Is Padre moving with bodies?'

22.35hrs (zt): from C/S 0 to C/S 9A: 'Tell you later.'

22.45hrs (zt): from C/S 0 to C/S 4: 'Is Civvy guide that has been with us since first location safe [Terry Peck]?'

22.45hrs (zt): from C/S 4 to C/S 0: 'Yes, with A Company.'

5.6   **'It's my foot, mate, it's on fire!'**

SUNDAY 13 JUNE 1982

00.35hrs (zt): from C/S 85B to C/S 0: '19.00hrs (zt) service, Dogfish [Teal Inlet], 9 to inform Brimstone [Padre], Sunray Higher Formation will attend.'

01.40hrs (zt): from C/S 99 to C/S 0: 'For Acorn, requires intelligence report giving detailed locations stated on all enemy positions seen from your present position, this intelligence report is to be with Acorn by 13.30hrs (zt) today.'

['Acorn' is the code name for Intelligence Officer.]

01.45hrs (zt): from C/S 99: to All Stations: 'Large helicopter believed to be enemy sighted around Teal Inlet.'

04.00hrs (zt): from C/S 99 to All Stations: 'Situation Report.'

05.45hrs (zt): from C/S 99 to All Stations: 'Burial, it is intended to bring all the men who died in action on 12th June to either Teal / Ajax Bay, 13th 19.00hrs (zt) June, Ajax Bay for 42 Commando / Teal for 3 PARA, 59 Commando,

9 PARA RE and 45 Commando, 2 Padres, 3 PARA / 45 Commando will give short service.'

08.10hrs (zt): from C/S 0 to C/S 9A: 'For Acorn minor; detailed intelligence report required giving details of all enemy positions seen from your present location, details to be at this location by radio or memo via Hawkeye no later than 13.00hrs (zt).'

08.10hrs (zt): from C/S 9A to C/S 0: 'Roger, might be pressed to get it to you by 13.00hrs (zt) but will try.'

Captain McCracken C/S 41B reports aircraft:

09.06hrs (zt): from C/S 41B to C/S 0: 'What sounds like a C130 has just landed at Stanley airfield.'

09.06hrs (zt): from C/S 0 to C/S 41B: 'Roger, passed to Brigade for action if necessary.'

09.06hrs (zt): from C/S 0 to C/S 99: 'What sounded like a C130 Hercules has just landed at Stanley airfield.'

09.08hrs (zt): from C/S 41B to C/S 0: 'Can hear a definite C130 taxiing at Stanley airfield.'

09.08hrs (zt): from C/S 0 to C/S 41B: 'Brigade informed.'

09.10hrs (zt): from C/S 0 to C/S 99: 'Confirmed C130 Hercules now taxiing, from Call Sign 4.'

09.35hrs (zt): from C/S 0 to C/S 49: 'Tell CO 2 PARA my Call Sign 3 is available for any task he wishes, and can be used as part of his plan.'

First light approximately 10.00hrs (zt).

10.00hrs (zt): from C/S 41B to C/S 0: 'Aircraft noise stopped, heavy mist down, can no longer hear or see anything.'

10.00hrs (zt): from C/S 0 to C/S 41B: 'Brigade informed.'

10.12hrs (zt): from C/S 0 to C/S 41B: 'Shelldrake [code name for artillery] will have a go at the airport on max elevation.'

10.25hrs (zt): from C/S 41B to C/S 0: 'Aircraft engines started.'

10.25hrs (zt): from C/S 0 to C/S 41B: '9 acknowledged Brigade informed.'

11.04hrs (zt): from C/S 0 to C/S 9A:'Have you any immediate casevac in your location?'

11.04hrs (zt): from C/S 9A to C/S 0: '1 immediate casualty.'

11.30hrs (zt): from C/S 9 to C/S 9A: 'One person [A 120 Cpl Sturge] from C/S 1 transfer to Teal from 9A.'

11.55hrs (zt): from C/S 1 to C/S 0: 'With re-supply extra: 6 x 351 batteries / 8 x 349 batteries / 4 x 350 batteries.'

11.56hrs (zt): from C/S 9A to C/S 0: 'Need foam-filled tension wheel, need more body bags as well.'

3 PARA HQ informs the CO that Captain McCracken will be attached to 2 PARA:

12.55hrs (zt): from C/S 0 to C/S 9: 'Our latest Shelldrake representative is to be attached to 2 PARA.'

13.05hrs (zt): C/S 9 to C/S 0: 'Situation determines that no 3 PARA personnel on forward positions to attend funeral, representation from 85B.'

13.05hrs (zt): C/S 0 to C/S 9: 'Passed to echelon.'

13.10hrs (zt): C/S 9B to C/S 0: 'All 6 POWs taken back.'

13.10hrs (zt): C/S 0 to C/S 99: 'What time will we get our Scout for casevac?'

Pte Mark (Zip) Hunt

We were all now feeling much better, after having something to eat and a good night's sleep in our lay-up position. I received a message over the radio saying the Boss [Hew Pike] wanted us back on Longdon for a briefing. So we packed our kit and made our way back to Longdon. As we approached, we walked in the BV tracks leading to the RAP area. Once on Longdon we made our way up towards the rocks that divide Routes 2 and 3. The CO had a bunker on the right-hand side of Route 3, and we stopped just before the rock divide where we met Cpl Mark Brown and Pte Jock Wilson. Sgt Pettinger said, 'Stay here while I go and speak to the Boss.' He then left us while he went to speak to the CO.

Johnny Pettinger had only walked about 10 metres away from our group when a 120mm mortar round landed amongst us. There was a terrific explosion. I next remember I was lying face down on the floor, the air had been knocked out of me, my ears were ringing, but I could hear someone screaming. I picked myself up and made my way over to Dickie Absolon, to try and help hold him while Pat Harley tried to put shell dressings on his head. Then with help of others we carried Dickie to the RAP.

RSM Laurie Ashbridge

I was walking to my bunker, following just behind Sgt Pettinger who'd stopped to chat with the CO, when there was an explosion behind us, followed by someone screaming in terrible pain. I turned, and I remember seeing Pte Harley and others running over to assist. I then heard someone shouting, 'There's more incoming, take cover!', then another round exploded just behind us on the western slope. I shouted at soldiers who had gathered, 'You lot, there's enough people helping, get yourselves into cover now!', as I didn't want us taking any more casualties.

Cpl Mark Brown, 22 yrs – D Company Guide

I'd just climbed out of my shelter and was trying to warm my body up when I spotted Sgt Pettinger leading a patrol towards my position. John Pettinger said, 'What's it like now?' and I replied, 'It's not too bad, it's quite quiet at the moment.' John then told his patrol to wait by us, while he went across to speak to the CO. We had just begun to chat when in a fraction of a second, I saw the shell go in the ground. There was no noise, then the ground just seemed to open up on my right-hand side.

The next thing I remember, I was on my knees, totally confused. My trousers were all shredded and my right side was covered in fine mud. I looked across to my left and saw Jerry Phillips topple over from his knees to lying face down and begin screaming. All the back of his smock was ripped to pieces, there was blood, gore and mess everywhere, his body was smoking, and the screams from him were bloodcurdling. I tried to stand up and for some reason I couldn't.

I looked at my left leg and it was smoking. Then somebody came up behind me and began to treat me.

Someone shouted, 'It could be the first of a salvo!' and then they all began to take cover. To this day, I remember Captain Julian James shouting, 'Get fucking back here now, and help those men!' People started pulling my kit off. A member of 9 Squadron started treating my leg, and I said, 'It's my foot, mate, it's on fire!' I had shrapnel in my leg, but I had a hot piece of shrapnel lodged in my heel. At this stage I was not aware of Dickie Absolon as he had fallen behind me. I didn't want morphine, I said. 'Give mine to Jerry,' as we were best friends, but the 9 Squadron bloke just stuck the morphine into my left leg. Someone was trying to take my boot off and I said, 'Don't take my boot off.' Doctor Mike Von Bertele appeared from behind me and stuck a syringe of morphine in my left leg. Then two blokes picked me up using a two-handed seat carry, and carried me to the RAP.

Pte Pat Harley

I was probably not more than 20 yards away when an incoming round exploded amongst the patrol. I ran across, and the first person I reached was Dickie Absolon. He'd received a very severe shrapnel wound to the forehead, and I immediately thought to myself that this was likely to be a non-survivable wound. I tried to configure a donut type of dressing to the wound. While I was doing this another shell landed quite close by. With help of others, we carried him to the Regimental Aid Post which was only a short distance away.

All this time, in the background, I could hear the constant screaming of Cpl Jerry Phillips. He was in an extremely bad way, having nearly lost his left arm. He had tried biting down on his old-style canvas and leather chin strap, but such was his pain he'd bitten it in two. At some time later, I became aware of Pte John [Jock] Wilson. He had been knocked unconscious by the blast and his body blown into a rock crevice; he was physically okay, but he'd received a blow to the jaw and was very concussed.

I think I was in shock after all that had just gone on. I was walking because at this stage, I was fed up running everywhere, and now thought, If they get me, they get me. I met Captain McGimpsey, who was collecting casualty numbers, and I said to him, 'There's four more casualties down there, and I am fairly sure one will be a fatal, as I can't see Dickie Absolon making it.' He said, 'Right, now fuck off, Harley; I'm sick of seeing you.' [But this was not said in a bad way.] I eventually reached the Second Bowl and the story of our four most recent casualties had already reached the bowl ahead of me. CSgt Steve Knights said, 'What the fuck are you doing here, Harley? I've got you down as dead, fucking hell! I'll have to change the fucking list now.'

Steve was known throughout the battalion as 'Shakespeare' because of his use of colourful language.

Sgt John Pettinger

After my patrol had been hit, I still had to continue with the original task, which was to locate and destroy a 120mm mortar that had been firing onto Longdon, and had probably just taken out my patrol. I spoke to Sgt Dave Robson of the Mortar platoon. He said, 'Get me some coordinates of the area that it's firing from, the tighter the area the better, then we [the Mortars] will do a search and destroy.' So I went out with Cpl John Graham, Cpl Pete Haddon and LCpl Derek [Del] Jones, Pte John [Jock] Wilson and Pte Mark [Zip] Hunt. We made our way to the forward edge of Wireless Ridge to try and locate the 120mm mortar. We called a number of fire missions in on a couple of likely locations and at about 15.00hrs (zt) from our OP, we could see three of the 155mm artillery pieces plus all the 105s on the racecourse on the edge of Stanley. It took hours for our guns to be allocated, as they were adjusting fire for 2 PARA's attack later that night. But eventually when we got them, just before last light about 20.00hrs (zt), after adjusting, we got a mega 'Fire for effect'.

Pte Mark (Zip) Hunt

We were scanning the area looking for anything that would possibly give away the location of the 120mm mortar, possibly the signature [flash] as it was fired. We called a number of fire missions, on various locations on Wireless Ridge, and also on the racecourse in Stanley, where we could see artillery pieces firing onto Longdon. But while we were observing, a fire mission was also called on the Argentine position just to our front, and it very nearly took us out – Sgt Johnny Pettinger was absolutely furious!

Cpl Mark (Tomo) Thompson

About midday, I was told that my Detachment Commanders and I would be going to recce a position that we'd be using later that night to support D Company 2 PARA during their attack on Wireless Ridge. We set off with Captain Mason leading. Also with us were the Milan Detachment Commanders. As we neared the position we came under artillery fire, but I managed to have a good look at the ground and put a fire plan together for my gun locations, my routes in and out, also RV and FRVs [Rendezvous and Final Rendezvous], then made our way back.

I reported to the OC and CSM Caithness, who was happy with my plan for the machine guns, the Anti-Tanks would be in reserve. I went back down to my position at the end of the sheep track, and told Pte Billy Knights, who was now my gunner as Rick had been medically evacuated, to go and collect some more resupplies, which he was not happy with and we exchanged a few harsh words.

An artillery round came in and for some reason I didn't hear it. I was told it blew me through the air. I woke to find Major Dennison and CSM Caithness looking down at me. I picked myself up, dusted myself down as I was full of mud and dirt, and I said, 'What the fuck was that?' CSM Caithness said, 'Cpl Thompson, are you all right?' and I said, 'Yeah.' Billy Knights shouted 'Tomo, look over there,' and he pointed to a large smoking shell hole approximately 3 metres from where I was sat. CSM Caithness then said, 'Cpl Thompson, are you sure you're okay?' I said, 'Yes.' He then told me to, 'Go and have a brew and get some rest as we will be moving out at last light.'

Lt Col Hew Pike

I was stood somewhere on Longdon and watched seven Argentine Skyhawks fly past, coming from the direction of Port Stanley heading west. Shortly after this they attacked Brigade HQ but fortunately there were no casualties. Soon after this, I would go to a Brigade 'O' Group where the divisional plan for the capture of Port Stanley on the 14th/15th was to be discussed.

15.10hrs (zt): from C/S 1 to All Stations: 'Air-raid warning RED.'

CO's helicopter is confirmed for rescheduled 'O' Group:

15.16hrs (zt): from C/S 9 to C/S 0: '16.30hrs (zt) for pick up from 9A location.'

Seven A4 Skyhawks attack Brigade Headquarters:

15.17hrs (zt): from C/S 0 to C/S 9: 'Airstrike thought to be on Brigade HQ – now confirmed.'

15.22hrs (zt): from C/S 98 to C/S 0: '1 x Skyhawk hit trailing smoke heading north.'

15.22hrs (zt): from C/S 0 to C/S 98: 'Passed to Brigade.'

15.40hrs (zt): Note: 'No casualties suffered by Brigade, but 1 x Sea King with shrapnel through rotor blade.'

15.43hrs (zt): from C/S 9A to C/S 0: 'Put on Helicopter going to 9B the following: *15 x 350 batteries / 15 x 351 batteries / 3 x 350 headsets / + other spares.*'

15.43hrs (zt): from C/S 0 to C/S 9A: 'Passed to echelon.'

15.45hrs (zt): from C/S 99 to C/S 0: 'Air-raid YELLOW.'

16.15hrs (zt): from C/S 9A to C/S 0: 'Did we get any extra 66mm and what happened to the ammo we were going to get sent forward? We need 50 x 66mm.'

16.30hrs (zt): C/S 9A to C/S 0: '50 x L2 Grenades / 50 WP Grenades to go to 9B.'

16.30hrs (zt): C/S 0 to C/S 9A: 'Passed to echelon.'

16.40hrs (zt): C/S 3 to C/S 0: 'One of 43B personnel used his sleeping bag on casualty, can it be replaced?'

16.40hrs (zt): C/S 0 to C/S 3: 'Passed to echelon, to take bag from one of the dead Bergens.'

The next message would bring REME Cfn Alex Shaw to Mount Longdon:

16.45hrs (zt): C/S 50B to C/S 0: 'We require as many charge seven and eight augmenting cartridges asp + bluebell [Bluebell = REME] this location, three containers.'

16.50hrs (zt): from C/S 9B to C/S 0: 'Only five bodies now to go back there.'

17.15hrs (zt): from C/S 99 to C/S 0: 'Funerals will now not take place – new date and time ASAP.'

17.15hrs (zt): from C/S 0 to C/S 99: 'Kestrel informed.'

17.30hrs (zt): from C/S 1 to C/S 0: 'For Seagull your location: add 1 x Grail SAM7 to enemy weapons found.'

17.30hrs (zt): from C/S 0 to C/S 1: 'Passed to ops officer.'

18.00hrs (zt): from C/S 99 to C/S 0: 'Reference funerals – will now take place as planned at 19.00hrs (zt).'

18.00hrs (zt): from C/S 0 to C/S 99: 'Ops officer informed.'

18.15hrs (zt): from C/S 85 to C/S 0: 'Can A 120's Bergen be sent back to Teal?' [A 120 = Cpl Sturge.]

The Echelon area has been under adjusting artillery fire and, with more supplies coming in, for the safety of troops in this area it is decided to stop helicopter supplies for the evening:

18.25hrs (zt): from C/S 9B to C/S 0: 'Coming under adjusting artillery fire, no more re-supply to this location, all further re-supply to go to Murrell Bridge.'

18.25hrs (zt): from C/S 0 to C/S 9B: 'Passed to echelon 9B asked to supply GR at Broken Arrow [i.e. Murrell Bridge].'

18.53hrs (zt): from C/S 9B to C/S 0: 'Will be establishing alternative landing site tonight.'

19.15hrs (zt): from C/S 99 to C/S 0: 'Six waves of helicopters landing to the north of CF (?) No further information.'

19.30hrs (zt): from C/S 5 to 0: 'It is confirmed that Support Company number 200 [Cpl McCarthy] died yesterday.'

19.45hrs (zt): from C/S QR to C/S 0: 'How much ammunition at your location?'

19.45hrs (zt): from C/S 0 to C/S QR [i.e. 2 PARA]: '30mm x 699 / 76mm AP x 28 / 76mm HESH x 79/ 4 x WP, the bulk was on Samson [an armoured recovery vehicle] which overturned.'

19.55hrs (zt): from C/S Z9 to C/S 9A 'We have just taken one casualty [Craftsman Alex Shaw].'

19.55hrs (zt): from C/S 9A to C/S Z9: 'Roger.'

20.00hrs (zt): from C/S Z9 to C/S 9A: 'We need two more stretchers; more casualties [LCpl Denzil Connick and Pte Craig Jones].'

20.00hrs (zt): from C/S 9A to C/S Z9: 'Roger.'

Cfn Michael Hall, 20 yrs – REME

On Friday 11 June, Cfn Alex Shaw and I had been flown by helicopter from Teal Inlet to Estancia House. As we arrived there the main body of 3 PARA had just left, to attack Mount Longdon. Later on we watched as the sky lit up, as the battle raged. The following day, Saturday 12 June, a continuous stream of helicopters arrived, and we loaded them up with ammunition and primed grenades which they ferried back to Longdon. In the 3 PARA HQ, which was a large wriggly tin shed, you could hear the battalion clerk, who was in radio contact with the troops on Longdon. We could hear him repeating the names of soldiers who had been killed or wounded. I thought I had missed my chance of fulfilling my desire to be in a battle, and perhaps be a hero.

But on the following day, Sunday 13 June, a request was sent from 3 PARA Mortars to 3 PARA HQ requesting a Bluebell [REME] to be brought forward to Longdon. Later on Captain Brown, the QM Tech, asked me, as the REME armourer, if I had any mortar spares. I told him that I did, and he said, 'A mortar bipod has broken on Mount Longdon; a helicopter will be picking you up in 30 minutes to take you there to fix it.' I asked Alex Shaw if he wanted to come with me, and Alex agreed.

Our flight to Mount Longdon was fast and low. We stopped about a mile short at 3 PARA's Echelon area, which was in a small rocky outcrop. No sooner had we landed when a couple of spotting rounds landed close to the helicopter, and the Loadmaster was extremely nervous and wanted to get us off as quickly as possible. We took cover in the rocks as a couple of rounds came in. Alex seemed apprehensive – I put it down to him being older than me. However, in hindsight he may have had a clearer understanding of the danger that we were in.

A BV picked us up and took us to the resupply area at the base of Mount Longdon. One of the first people we saw was Cpl Ross Noble [REME] who we had gotten to know on the journey south. Ross had been very gung ho and had been really looking forward to seeing some action, but now he looked totally different, he looked as if he'd aged. Ross began reeling off the names of blokes from the MT platoon who had been killed or wounded during the battle, Tony [Fester] Greenwood and David [Scotty] Scott had both been killed and Roy [Shirley] Bassey wounded. I was shocked: these were people I knew.

Suddenly there was a commotion; apparently several Argentine Chinooks had been seen taking off from Stanley and a counter-attack on Longdon was expected. We were hurriedly given 66mm anti-tank weapons and lined up facing the flat ground to the north. We were then briefed to wait until the Chinooks were about 50 feet off the ground and then let rip. However, the eagerly awaited Argentine Chinooks never arrived, and we were stood down about half an hour later.

We made our way up along the side of Longdon to just below Fly Half and climbed into the rocks, where some REME lads had begun making a brew. I climbed into a crevice with Ross Noble and LCpl Geoff Hamilton, while Alex Shaw, LCpl Simon Melton and LCpl Steve Lint climbed into another crevice. Both groups were not far apart, maybe 20 feet away from each other. I was standing up viewing Longdon while Geoff Hamilton made the brew. Then Geoff heard the distant crump of artillery being fired and shouted to me, 'Get your fucking head down.'

About three shells came in at once. I watched mesmerized as one landed about 50 feet away. I then became aware of someone screaming, 'Medic!' He sounded terrified. He then started screaming, 'I've been hit, I've been hit.' Then it slowed to a low moaning, 'I've been hit.' My illusions about war were instantly shattered: this was no adventure and I was terrified. Geoff Hamilton verbally dragged us from our shelter: 'Fucking come on, somebody's just been hit.' We went into the next crevice and there was Alex, unconscious. He had blood spattered on his face and Steve Lint was applying a shell dressing to his leg. Now I was totally shitting myself with fear, I was just waiting for the next salvo to come in.

Spr Tommy Trindall

Just as we were getting some scoff, we got shelled again and an incoming round landed extremely close to the rock face, wounding Cfn Alex Shaw with either shrapnel or secondary fragmentation. I heard someone shouting for a medic and ran over to help. He was bleeding heavily and we applied five or six shell dressings on him. The medic John Kennedy turned up and he began trying to get a drip into him. A stretcher arrived and we carried him down to the RAP as fast as we could.

Cpl Peter (Tomo) Thompson

At approximately 19.30hrs (zt), I was doing my last checks of the gun teams, when two young 3 PARA lads turned up and said, 'We're looking for Cpl Thompson.' I said, 'Yeah, it's me, what do you want?' Unbeknown to me, one was Pte Craig Jones. He said, 'We've been sent here to help the machine guns.' At the same time, I heard Denzil Connick being told to go down to Tac HQ and pick up some things from the resupply area. I was just about to issue my final orders to support 2 PARA's attack on Wireless Ridge, so I said, go with him and do something, that to this day, I cannot remember what it was, and off they went. The next thing I heard was artillery rounds landing all around our area, I took cover and waited. In a matter of maybe 10 seconds, I heard someone shout, 'Fucking hell, Denzil's been hit.'

Pte Chris Parris

Craig Jones and I had been going up and down the mountain bringing link ammunition forward for our machine guns. We were carrying about 800 rounds each and I was knackered; we were only managing to run about 20 or 30 metres, then taking cover in between salvos of incoming rounds. It was very mentally and physically tiring. We had only just dropped off our ammunition when someone came to our group and said, 'One of you needs to go down and let the other fire-support team know that we are moving out at 20.30hrs (zt), and not 20.00hrs (zt) as per the previous orders.' I said, 'For fuck's sake!' but Craig said, 'I'll do it; I want to go and see a few people anyway.' So Craig set off with Denzil down the mountain.

CSgt Steve Knights

On Sunday, late afternoon, Captain Tony Mason, Sgt Chris Howard, Sgt Graham Colbeck, Cpl Thompson plus various personnel and I, had returned from our reconnaissance patrol. Our task had been to recce a position where we would set up a firebase for later that night in support of 2 PARA, who were attacking Wireless Ridge. During the debriefing with Major Dennison, we were confirming where everyone in the battalion was deployed. This led to some confusion as I disagreed with where he thought C Company was located. I said, 'I thought they were still in the valley bottom to the north of Mount Longdon.' He said, 'Well, there seems to be some confusion, as that's not where Battalion HQ think they are; they think they're much further forward.' He then asked me to go down to the Battalion HQ and update them with this info. I said, 'Okay, Sir.' However, at the same time I thought to myself, Not yet, as I had been out all day doing a recce for the task tonight, and I thought, I'm having a brew and scoff first! LCpl Denzil Connick was listening to our conversation, and as he had not taken part in the recce, offered to take my map down and brief the CO. He had an ulterior motive because he told me that a supply of cigarettes had arrived at the resupply area. Selfishly, I agreed and told him to make sure he got me a packet of cigarettes as well. It was sometime later that I found out that on his way to the Battalion HQ, he'd been wounded by artillery fire.

Pte Andy (Stretch) Dunn

I heard the crump of a number of rounds being fired and knew I had to get myself into a bit of cover. I crawled into a fissure in the rocks, and I could tell from the whistle of the shells these were going to land really close. I watched as Craig Jones and Denzil Connick walked past. I shouted to them, but I'm not sure if they heard me. I braced, closed my eyes, and thought, These are going to land on top of me. There was a terrific explosion, followed by bits of shrapnel, rock, earth and various bits of stuff flying through the air. There was a moment of silence, and after that the most awful screaming.

I ran to help. I knelt down by Craig Jones, who was lying face down and was trying to get up, and for a moment I thought he looked fine. I said, 'Are you all right?' He said, 'I can't breathe.' We lifted the back of his smock up to check him for wounds; he was peppered with lots of small holes, but they weren't bleeding. Sadly, he died shortly after the medics arrived despite their best efforts. While we were dealing with Craig, Denzil Connick was lying next to us and was screaming. I went over to help put a tourniquet on what was left of his leg. There was a red beret lying close by and this was also pushed on top of a shell dressing, and yet another shell dressing put on, anything available to try to stop the blood loss.

I remember the medic Pte John Kennedy arriving. He had an air of 'don't worry, I'm here now' with his calmness. He tried to get a line into Denzil's arm but he couldn't find a vein. He said to Denzil, 'You're fine now, Denzil, I've got it in, you're going to be okay.' However, he still hadn't got it in, but he did eventually. He gave me a bag of saline and said to me, 'Hold this up.' After I'm not sure how long, Denzil was stabilized, and we put him on a stretcher.

LCpl Mark (Rolly) Rawlings
We were waiting for last light when the first of four or five salvos came thundering in with a massive whoosh. A warm blast wave blew me over and blew my helmet off. I picked myself up and waited for a moment in case any more rounds were incoming. I decided to go and retrieve my helmet from where it had rolled. While I was doing this I noticed Vince Bramley and Tony Peers dealing with someone, I wasn't sure who, but there was a group of them beginning to form, so I decided to go back to my shelter as it wasn't a good thing to have so many people in one place, as it could become a target of opportunity for an Argentine spotter.

LCpl Denzil Connick
CSgt Steve Knights had a very detailed Argentine map and Major Dennison said, 'The CO should see it.' But Steve Knights was knackered and I said, 'Give it to me, I'll take it,' as I'd heard a rumour about cigarettes in the resupply area! I set off along the sheep track, when I saw Craig Jones. He stopped to ask for directions or something, and then there was an almighty whoosh.

The next thing I remember is, I was lying on my stomach, my ears were ringing, and I was coughing. I was trying to get my breath, and I thought, Jesus! That was close. I watched as my helmet went rolling down the hill and I thought, Bastard! I'll have to go down there and get that. I then had an overwhelming feeling of heat on my body, and noticed smoke coming out of the cuffs of my smock. When I tried to get up on my knees, nothing was happening. I could hear someone else groaning, so I rolled onto my back and sat up. It was then that I saw the full extent of my injuries: my left leg was more or less hanging off and my right leg was a tattered mess, with a compound femur fracture and a lot more. I started screaming. I knew I was in a bad way but the blokes were trying to reassure me, saying, 'You'll be all right, Denzil, don't worry,' but I knew that I was not going to last long like this.

Pte Pat Harley

Denzil Connick had no sooner left us when the sound of incoming shells filled the air, followed by the sound of explosions and, shortly after, cries of 'Medic!' I picked up my bag of medical kit and raced to the scene; Denzil Connick had been extremely badly injured. He was being attended to by LCpl Tony Peers and medic Pte John Kennedy. I remember looking at Denzil; he was biting the grass, he was in so much pain.

I immediately tried to get a tourniquet on the leg that was most seriously injured. I slipped part of an improvised tourniquet underneath his leg, and with my other hand reached around the other side to pull it back around, but with all the blood and gore I had inadvertently grabbed a piece of muscle and was trying to pull it over, much to Denzil's distress. I eventually tied the tourniquet tightly, and then Denzil remembered about his mission to deliver the map, and started saying, 'Take the map, they must get the map!' and I replied, 'Fuck the map!' to which Denzil said, 'No, they must get the map!' Finally, after this ridiculous conversation ended, we got him on a stretcher and started running towards the RAP. Denzil was saying, 'I'm tired, I want to sleep.' I had to tell him bluntly, 'If you go to sleep you'll fucking die, now don't fucking go asleep.' We arrived at the RAP and it was quite a relief to hand him over.

I made my way back to the Second Bowl, and as I entered a member of the Anti-Tanks said, 'Here's Doctor Harley!' I blew my top, and said, 'You with the fucking mouth, that's Denzil! And I think he's lost both his fucking legs, and that's your friend.' It really made me despair; some people just don't think before they open their mouths. For the next hour, I sulked and refused to talk to anyone.

20.10hrs (zt): from C/S 9A to C/S 0: 'Two stretcher and one walking wounded need casevac very urgent.'

20.15hrs (zt): from C/S 0 to C/S 99: 'Request casevac from my 9A of two VSI and one walking wounded.'

20.19hrs (zt): from C/S 0 to C/S 9A: 'Charlie [Gazelle helicopter] Call Sign, 2 minutes, Delta [Scout helicopter] Call Sign 10 minutes, confirm now three stretcher cases.'

20.25hrs (zt): from C/S 0 to C/S 99: 'Troops for casevac now 3 x stretcher cases, no walking wounded.'

Enemy troops are spotted moving down from Mount Tumbledown to a mortar position used the during the battle. They are extremely close to Support Company, who are also moving towards their firebase position in roughly the same area:

20.25hrs (zt): from C/S 0 to C/S 9A: 'Enemy troop movements grid 338742 possible mortar position from neighbours to south.'

The incoming rounds fall approximately 300 metres from Support Company:

20.25hrs (zt): from C/S 9A to C/S 0: 'Engaging by G72, ensure target is recorded.'

45 Commando reports enemy moving towards Support Company Firebase:

20.30hrs (zt): from C/S 45 Cdo to C/S 0: '56A reports troops carrying mortars in grid 338742 possible enemy troops.'

20.40hrs (zt): from C/S 9A to C/S 0: 'Reference casevac: 3rd helicopter not required; casualty is now a fatality.'

20.40hrs (zt): from C/S 0 to C/S 9A: 'Passed to brigade.'

20.50hrs (zt): from C/S 99 to C/S 0: 'Do you have troops in grid 338742?'

Fire mission call in on the enemy location which is very close to Support Company:

20.52hrs (zt): from C/S 0 to C/S 99: 'We are now engaging 338742.'

21.08hrs (zt): from C/S 0 to C/S 99: 'Reference casualty request Aircraft: Please ensure Aircraft have pods as with the long journey, a wounded man in the open will suffer, also helicopter must go onto VCN frequency.'

21.25hrs (zt): from C/S 9A to C/S 0: 'One of the wounded: HQ 172 Pte Jones 627 Died, HQ 171 Cfn Shaw Died, SP 104 LCpl Connick wounded.'

Pte Chris Parris

We moved out that night with the SF teams to give fire support to 2 PARA. As we moved through A Company's area, I remember passing Pte Phil [Taff] Adkins, who was standing guard by a mortar round that had not detonated, and he warned us about it. We then went beyond A Company's location to set up a firebase. 105mm artillery rounds were being fired at us, screaming overhead like express trains – a few hit the rocks to our right but fortunately none landed by us. I met up with Cpl Ross Noble, and we squeezed in between the rocks, chatted and half froze while we waited for the order to fire in 2 PARA, but it never came.

Cpl Peter (Tomo) Thompson

I called in all the gun-team commanders. I said, 'We will be going out shortly and we will be following a similar route to the one we took today. When we leave A Company's forward position that will be the first RV, and further on I will indicate the FRV [final rendezvous]. I will go forward with Billy Knights and set up my gun first and leave Billy to man it, and then I will come back to you at the FRV and then lead you into the gunline and I will place you out one at a time.'

I set off with all the machine-gun teams behind me, followed by the HQ element of the company and then the Anti-Tanks, finally bringing up the rear were the ammunition-bearers. We headed towards the far end of Full Back and as we moved through A Company's area, I remember passing Cpl Laurie Bland, who shouted over to me, 'Come on the machine guns, go and get them!'

We reached the FRV. I called to Billy, my gunner, and we both moved forward to our intended gunline. Unfortunately, we had no night sights, no maps and no radios, we were in the middle of no-man's land, and I couldn't see a thing. We crawled across to our gun position and mounted the gun. I locked it on target, sorted the ammunition out, then said, 'Right, Billy, stay here, do not fucking move; I'll be back shortly.' I then went to get the next gun team and placed them out. I kept the gun teams quite close together, so I could control the fire.

It was absolutely freezing. I'm not sure how long we waited but suddenly CSM Caithness, who had a night observation device, whispered to me, 'Cpl Thompson, have a look at this!' I looked through the NOD, and saw D Company 2 PARA advancing towards the gunline. I thought, 'What the fuck do we do?' This could be a possible blue on blue; I quickly crawled across to the gun teams and whispered, '2 PARA will be passing right in front our gunline in about 5 minutes' time. I quickly briefed the gun teams and said, 'Lay down, don't move, don't make any noise, don't fart, don't do anything.' We lay there, as the end section of D Company 2 PARA walked no further than 20 metres from our guns. Luckily, it passed off without incident.

Through the darkness I tried to watch D Company 2 PARA moving up to their intended Start Line. I asked CSM Caithness if I could use the NOD to check something. My fears were confirmed, D Company were now in our arc of fire, and there was no way we could open fire on the enemy positions on Wireless Ridge without firstly firing into D Company. We were in a useless position: our only other option was to dismount the guns and tripods and move approximately 600 metres south to the D Company Start Line, and hope to be able to support them from there. The problem with this option was the time constraint: I could see through the NOD that D Company were advancing on Wireless Ridge. I moved back to where the OC and CSM were and explained the situation. A message was now passed to 2 PARA: 'We cannot help you any more, happy hunting.' Shortly after this we dismounted the guns and tripods, and made our way back to Mount Longdon, using the same route in which we had approached the gunline.

Captain Kevin McGimpsey
After the CO returned from his Brigade briefing, he and I had found a sheltered position that had a degree of overhead protection. I was quite in awe of the way the CO managed to control his emotions; the weight of command can be a heavy burden. I held a torch as he studied his maps and aerial photographs. He even had a cigarette or two, although he didn't normally smoke. I brewed up some coffee, and he asked me the odd question and spent the next six or seven hours formulating the plan to take out the Moody Brook Barracks and the racecourse area, which would take place over the following night of 14/15 June.

Pte Mark (Zip) Hunt

Sunday night we watched 2 PARA attack Wireless Ridge. It was a fantastic sight, and I remember thinking I am witnessing regimental history being made.

5.7   'From that moment it was time to rock & roll'

MONDAY 14 JUNE 1982

First light approximately 10.00hrs (zt).

Pte Pat Harley

Just before first light as we moved back to Mount Longdon, sleet began to fall. My feet were numb, my back was killing me, I just seem to be aching all over. We received a briefing telling us that we would now be advancing to Moody Brook and then into Port Stanley. At this stage the war was very much still on. I don't remember being afraid, I was just thinking, I will be glad when this is over, and if it means fighting in Stanley then so be it.

Cfn Michael Hall

As morning came I was starting to get used to shells – the longer the whine, the further away they were going to land. I was going somewhere, but I'm not sure where, when I met a cook who had been acting as a stretcher-bearer the night before, and he said, 'It was a shame about Alex Shaw.' I wondered why, as I thought Alex's wound hadn't looked that bad, and replied, 'Well, at least he'll be on a hospital ship by now and out of this crap.' But he said, 'I'm sorry, mate, Alex died last night.'

Sgt Graham Colbeck

On Monday morning, there was a thin layer of snow covering Longdon. I noticed there was an unusual silence; we had not been shelled since 2 PARA had attacked Wireless Ridge. We were now waiting for further orders for our next objective.

10.50hrs (zt): from C/S 3 to C/S 9: 'Area of O Group?'

10.50hrs (zt): from C/S 9 to C/S 3: '9A location.'

Lt Col Hew Pike

That morning I remember it was bitterly cold, and a mixture of sleet and freezing rain began to fall. We were at the bottom of the mountain and I was giving the orders for the attacks to take place that night; and I was thinking, Well, we can sustain this for some time yet, but we all have our limits, both physical and mental. C Company was going to lead this time. Shortly after I had begun giving my orders, a signaller, either Jock Begg or Harry Wilkie, and I always feel rather bad about this, because I was quite rude to him, he said, 'Excuse me, Sir, there's a message for you.' And quite out of character, I hissed, 'Fuck off! I'm in the middle of Orders.' And he said, 'But Sir, it really is important.' The message was that we were to be prepared to move, but not until further orders, so clearly there was something afoot. At this stage we had no idea what was happening – we were completely unaware that the collapse had begun.

A brief outline of orders for 14/15 June:

H Hour 04.00hrs (zt): C Company 3 PARA will capture Moody Brook including water-pumping station, A Company will pass through C Company and capture ESRO building complex, D Company will combine with B Company and will exploit to the western edge of racecourse.

Orders subject to change.

3 PARA HQ inform the CO that the situation is changing!

12.10hrs (zt): from C/S 0 to C/S 9: 'Enemy withdrawing from Sapper Hill, unconfirmed report 300 enemy withdrawing.'

12.50hrs (zt): from C/S 0 to All Stations: 'All Stations on 30 minutes to move.'

13.44hrs (zt): from C/S 9 to C/S 3: 'C Company now on 30 minutes, get ready now and close up behind 2 PARA, inform me when you're on the move.'

Spr Tommy Trindall

We were clearing a path through a minefield on the northern side of Longdon when we first heard of the ceasefire. We were moving in single file and could see anti-personnel mines to our left and right with all their tops exposed. The Troop Commander, Captain Burns, put his hand up and stopped, then the signaller Spr Willie MacDonald told Captain Burns, 'Sir, there's reports that the Argies are surrendering.'

Pte Quintin (Q) Wright

After we'd returned from our mission to support 2 PARA, I was shivering with cold and frozen to the core. We seemed to have only gotten back when we were once again on the move. I remember we heard a call sign on the battalion net saying, 'There's no one here, it's empty [referring to Moody Brook], can you support us.' From that moment it was time to rock & roll, various call signs came up saying 'We're with you,' 'Us too,' etc. Suddenly we were all shaken out, tabbing down the side of the hill heading towards Wireless Ridge.

Major Osborne, who is now in Moody Brook, informs the CO the situation has changed and it is time for the battalion to move:

15.25hrs (zt): from C/S 3 to C/S 9: 'From Blue 2: the enemy appear to be surrendering, move down at best speed to Moody Brook.'

3 PARA HQ receive no order from Brigade to leave Mount Longdon. Lt Col Hew Pike knows that regimental pride is at stake and takes it on himself to order the battalion to follow 2 PARA into Port Stanley.

Lt Col Hew Pike

When we found out that the Argentines were collapsing, it was with some considerable pleasure and relief, but what one still could not get away from was the terrible cost of capturing that mountain. We then abandoned our orders and hitched up for the move into Port Stanley. The weather had changed. In fact, by the time we reached Wireless Ridge, it was quite nice. We were advancing across Wireless Ridge heading towards Port Stanley. We had got a bit ahead of ourselves as we hadn't actually been told to move, but we set off anyway. In fact, I met the Brigadier on Wireless Ridge, and we had a slightly awkward discussion on whether 3 PARA should be advancing, but he realized we would not be stopping. We now moved down to the Ross Road and into Port Stanley.

RSM Lawrie Ashbridge

We had just moved on to the ridge when a helicopter came in on our left and landed about 200 metres away. Out stepped Brigadier Julian Thompson with his marine close-protection party, gesturing to us to stop. I said to the CO, 'He wants us to stop.' The CO said, 'Keep going, keep going.' A corporal from the Brigadier's protection party came across and said, 'The Brigadier would like to speak to the CO.' The CO whispered, 'Don't stop, keep going.' He then went across to speak to the Brigadier, and after a short time, the CO caught up with us. When we entered Port Stanley, I have never seen so much crap in my life. The Argentines had left Port Stanley looking like an absolute shit hole.

Major John Patrick

As Battalion HQ moved over Wireless Ridge, we met the Brigade Commander ,who had been flown forward by helicopter, and the CO got a mild bollocking, whilst the Battery Commander tactfully moved to one side. But we did not actually stop until we got to the edge of Port Stanley, and the real negotiations for the armistice did not take place for several hours after we were in Port Stanley. We now began sorting ourselves out and setting up defensive positions.*

Pte Pat Harley

We set off from Mount Longdon towards Wireless Ridge, and I received a message saying, 'Be aware, you are in a minefield, proceed with extreme caution.' I stood still for a moment thinking, Oh no, when we received another message, which said, 'Reference, my last message, disregard, you are not in a minefield.' This was followed by: 'A white flag has been seen flying over Stanley, they have surrendered, make safe your weapons.' I gave a rather tired 'Roger' and passed on the news, and a large cheer went up. Now it was helmets off and berets on. As we continued, we came across the body of one of 2 PARA's dead (19-year-old David Parr). He was lying covered over with a camouflage waterproof jacket.

---

* From a tape-recorded debrief in 1982 by General Sir Anthony Farrar-Hockley with Major John Patrick RA.

Sgt Graham Colbeck

We were told that 2 PARA had reported signs of collapse in the Argentine forces, and we quickly abandoned Mount Longdon and began advancing towards Wireless Ridge. As I led my fire team out of the boggy low ground up towards Wireless Ridge, I received a radio message: 'The enemy are running away, take off your helmets and put your berets on.' A rifle stood with its muzzle stuck in the ground-marking where the body of a member of 2 PARA lay. I noticed a waterproof jacket that had been used to cover his face had been blown to one side and was flapping in the wind; I walked over and replaced it. We now passed through the rocks and descended towards Moody Brook. I could see long lines of maroon berets stretching ahead of me all the way into Port Stanley.

3 PARA HQ inform CO of message from Brigade: no move forward of 39th easting:

17.00hrs (zt): from C/S 0 to C/S 9: 'From Brigade; No move east of 39 easting.'

Captain Kevin McGimpsey

As we walked into Port Stanley, I remember a look of devastation, smoking, damaged buildings. It did look like an actual war zone; kit scattered all over the place, weapons, clothing. At first it was deserted, like a ghost town, smoke from burning buildings, the smell of smoke and cordite from the Argentine gunline, but as we got further in, we saw Argentine soldiers who stared at us looking bewildered. I don't think they knew what was happening.

Pte Colin Charlton, D Company Guide

I think we were halfway to Wireless Ridge when someone said, 'Red berets on, there's white flags flying in Stanley.' We carried on, but obviously with a great deal of caution. As we moved through Moody Brook we met up with 2 PARA Machine Guns and Mortars, I remember seeing a bloke from 2 PARA sitting on his Bergen rubbing his hands, and I asked, 'Are you all right, mate?', and he replied, 'No, I'm fuckin' freezing.' I said, 'Haven't you got any gloves?' And he answered, 'No, I've lost them somewhere.' So I said, 'There you go, mate' and I gave him my spare pair.

Pte Paul Bachurzewski, 19 yrs – D Company

The Ross Road was deserted. There was kit everywhere, an absolute mess. The Argentines seemed to have vanished. There were some buildings smouldering, the heavy smell of cordite – it was like what you can imagine a war zone to look like. We proceeded along the road till we reached the old war memorial not far from Government House, and then were ordered to pull back and go firm. We sat at the edge of the Ross Road and brewed up.

CSgt Steve Knights

I can remember looking up at the Governor's house and thinking, what happened to the big battle around Government House? There was fuck all wrong with the place, not a pane of glass was broken. Shortly after this we were told to move back about 600 metres to the 39th easting line, which was back towards the racecourse. We were given a bungalow, and I organized with my platoon NCOs the weapons checks, ammunition checks. A couple of Argentine Huey helicopters landed at the back of the bungalows and surrendered.

Pte Andy (Stretch) Dunn

A haze hung over Stanley, the 'fog of war', the smell of cordite, burning houses, discarded clothing and weapons. We [the Anti-Tank Platoon] took over a bungalow, and we began sorting our kit out and cleaning our weapons. I remember sitting cleaning one of the Milan frames in the bathroom, scrubbing all the blood off it.

Pte Quintin (Q) Wright

We put on our maroon berets and moved off Wireless Ridge. As we moved through Moody Brook there was debris and smoke drifting from the various fires; the area had been completely devastated. We continued on along the Ross Road and we eventually arrived at the outskirts of Stanley. We'd been in town for a short while when I met LCpl Glynn Jones from the Int Cell. It was then he told me that Craig [Jonah] Jones was dead. I cannot describe in words how upset I was.

CHAPTER SIX

'WHO'S WITH ME?'

A COMPANY 3 PARA

**'It felt like only a matter of time
before one would hit me'**

FRIDAY 11 JUNE 1982

The Officer Commanding A Company, Major David Collett, holds his Platoon Commanders' 'O' Group at approximately 16.00 hours (zt). The briefing is interrupted by artillery fire, wounding Pte Lee Fisher of D Company:

16.15hrs (zt): from C/S 1 to C/S 0: 'Casualty report: D Company No 37, shrapnel wound to small of back, but walking, Location Call Sign 1.'

Pte Fisher is evacuated:

17.45hrs (zt): from C/S 83A to C/S 0: 'Casualty from Call Sign 1 now back at Teal.'

Shortly after last light the battalion begin to move out at approximately 20.15hrs (zt). A Company lead, followed by the Battalion Tac HQ, then B Company. Support Company and C Company bring up the rear. Once A Company reach the Battalion Start Line they then wait for the rest of the battalion to arrive.

A Company are now in position on the Battalion Start Line:

23.46hrs (zt): from C/S 19 to C/S 9: 'Now at Jungle Boot.'

Cpl Mark Brown, 22 yrs – D Company Guide

I attended the A Company Platoon Commander's 'O' Group, and whilst the orders were being given out, a salvo of about three or four Argentine artillery rounds came in. A member of my patrol, Pte Lee Fisher, was wounded. During the orders I was told that I would have a civilian guide attached to my patrol. His name was Terry Peck; he was a Falkland Islands policeman and had local knowledge of the area. My patrol was tasked to lead A Company to the Battalion Start Line. I hadn't been over the route that I had been instructed to take them on, due to other D Company patrol commitments, and I was advised not to mention that to Major Collett.

We moved out just after last light at approximately 20.15hrs (zt). Our civilian guide was moving too fast as he was only carrying a rifle. I said, 'Terry, the blokes are carrying a lot of weight; you will have to slow down so we can keep everyone together.' With that he got in a huff, and went off ahead of us. I stayed with A Company. We met up again at the Murrell River where some 9 Squadron Royal Engineers had arranged for a ladder to help the battalion to cross over the river. About two hours after we crossed the Murrell River, Terry Peck came up to me and said, 'This is it; this is the Furze Bush Stream. It's the Battalion Start Line.' I thought, No, he's wrong, but I only had him, with his local knowledge, to go by and after all he was the guide. He told me that he took children camping here in the summer, so I assumed he must know! I went back to Major Collett and told him, 'The civilian guide says this is it, and he knows this place better than me, but I don't think it is.' Major Collett agreed with me and we moved off. I was thinking, I hope I'm right! Terry Peck had gone off somewhere, and I was hoping I hadn't taken them over the Start Line early. Then Terry appeared and said, 'Mark, you're right, it's over here, I was wrong.' I thought, Thank fuck for that, you twat.'

The moon was just coming out and I said to Major Collett, 'This is it, this is the middle of the Battalion Start Line, there's your left and there's your right.' He looked at me and said, 'Where is everyone?' as I think Major Collett was expecting the Start Line to be marked by D Company. I said, 'I don't know, Sir.'

Pte Len Baines, 25 yrs – Signaller, Support Group

Once we reached the Start Line, we waited for the rest of the battalion. I was with LCpl Chris Lovett and LCpl Phil Jones. I whispered to Phil and Chris, 'If

I get killed tonight, tell my parents I didn't suffer.' Phil Jones whispered to me, 'Yeah, same here, if I get killed, let my wife know I didn't suffer either.' Chris Lovett said, 'Don't be daft, we'll all be okay.'

SATURDAY 12 JUNE 1982

B Company have started their advance towards Mount Longdon:

00.30hrs (zt): from C/S 29 to C/S 9: 'Now across Jungle Boot.'

Almost immediately the CO orders A Company to move to their form-up area north of Wing Forward:

00.30hrs (zt): from C/S 9 to C/S 19: 'Call Sign 1 move now.'

A Company now advance in a north-easterly direction into the Furze Bush Pass. When they reach the area of grid 332764 they will shake out into assault formation facing south.

Major Collett now informs the CO that A Company is in position, in Furze Bush Pass:

01.00hrs (zt): from C/S 19 to C/S 9: 'Now static.'

Cpl Louie Sturge, 28 yrs – Section Commander, 2 Section, 2 Platoon

2 Platoon was forward right with 2 Section forward left, and Cpl Laurie Bland's 1 Section were forward right with Platoon HQ in the middle, and Cpl Mick Ferguson was about 30 metres to the rear with 3 Section. We were weapons ready, bayonets fixed, grenades primed, teeth bared and arseholes twitching. We began our advance to Wing Forward. The moon was full and the area to our rear bathed in moonlight, I scanned the area but couldn't see anyone! I thought, Christ, where the fuck is Mick Ferguson and 3 Section? I felt a mild panic starting to break out.

Pte Trevor Bradshaw, 21 yrs – 3 Section, 2 Platoon

It was a bright moonlit night, but we got to a point where we couldn't see anyone else other than ourselves, and there was a lot of whispering while trying to identify where we were. Someone came on the radio and was obviously trying to point out features, and I remember someone saying, 'Can you see the big feature right up towards the top?' It turned out we were actually on it! We had gone way too far ahead and had to turn around and go back and rejoin A Company.

Approximately 40 minutes after B Company begin their advance comes the first contact report:

01.07hrs (zt): from C/S 29 to C/S 9: 'Contact wait-out.'

As soon as the first contact is made at 01.07hrs (zt), Captain Mason of Support Company receives orders from the CO to move from his location at grid 320760. He is to take his Milan detachment (Cpl McCarthy) plus two SF teams under Lt Mike Oliver (Cpl Cook and LCpl Bramley's detachments) along with ammunition-bearers and move as fast as possible across to Wing Forward.

Captain Tony Mason

I'm not sure if it was the CO or Major Dennison who told me to take my group and move as fast as possible around to Wing Forward, and from there we were to provide support for B Company.

Pte Craig (Tommy) Onions

We were told to make our way as fast as possible across to A Company. I found the move very hard going due to the weight of ammunition I was carrying, as it was an extremely fast pace.

Major Collett now informs the CO that although under indirect fire, they have not encountered any direct opposition:

01.25hrs (zt): from C/S 19 to C/S 9: 'We have not encountered any opposition.'

Pte Trevor Bradshaw

It was all very quiet during this stage. Then there was an explosion to our forward right, which turned out to be Cpl Milne standing on a mine. I heard him scream. It was then we started to take incoming fire. I had only been in 3 PARA about four months and was not what you would call an experienced soldier. I was waiting for someone to say, 'We are now taking effective enemy fire, take cover!' and that didn't seem to be happening. We were just walking towards this incoming fire; it was coming down all around us. I felt incredibly vulnerable. There were rounds fizzing by me and it felt like only a matter of time before one would hit me. My chin was touching my chest as I tried to crouch lower and walk at the same time.

The CO contacts Major Collett to confirm his company location as he is about to call in artillery support:

01.30hrs (zt): from C/S 9 to C/S 19: 'Are you too far forward for us to call down artillery fire on Rum Punch?'

'Rum Punch' is the Argentine C Company 7th Infantry Regiment position. This area would also be later known by 2 PARA as Rough Diamond:

01.30hrs (zt): from C/S 19 to C/S 9: 'No, we are clear.'

Cpl Louie Sturge

We started to come under fire. A couple of my blokes went to ground and I said, 'Fucking get up and keep walking, you don't take cover till I tell you to.' However, I thought to myself, There's no fucking way we're all going to get to this mountain in one piece because the ground is too open, we're all going to get nailed.

As A Company begin to emerge from the dead ground the enemy fire becomes more effective and Cpl Hope is wounded.

Pte Ashley Wright, 22 yrs – A Company Medic

As we began to advance towards Mount Longdon I remember illumination flares being fired overhead. We could see the silhouettes of our blokes moving forward ahead of us, and I thought, Why haven't they gone to ground? Then we began to take a lot of incoming fire. The company advance stopped for a moment, while the flares burnt out. Once in the cover of darkness they all got up and began advancing again towards Longdon. The tracer fire was still mainly going over our heads, but as we began to get closer it was becoming more accurate.

Sgt George Duffus, 27 yrs – Anti-Tank Platoon attached to A Company

Flares went up, we stopped; then started, then stopped again. I said, 'Fuck it! Let's just keep moving.' We were all moving in extended line apart from Company HQ who advanced in arrowhead formation. At one stage our group was lost and Major Collett came over the radio and said, 'Where the fuck are you?' He then said, 'Look left and look right, I am going to switch my torch on.' We saw it and that was that, we continued moving forward. The incoming fire was now getting more accurate as we were getting more exposed.

Sgt Manny Manfred

The Argentine fire began almost immediately, coming from locations all along the mountain. At this stage the fire was not effective and was going high, passing over our heads, but as we advanced it began to get more effective, until eventually we ran for the cover of a peat bank to our front. I made contact with Lt Moore of 2 Platoon. I heard his Australian accent in the darkness and I shouted, 'Mr Moore, 1 Platoon are just over here. I'm just letting you know where we are, as I'm more afraid of you than I am of the Argies!' I heard someone yell, 'Fucking hell.' Someone shouted, 'It's John Grant, he's been hit.' At first I thought he had been shot in the head, but it turned out that a bullet had hit his helmet. In fact, it looked like a chainsaw had cut a path across the top of his fibreglass helmet. I shouted to the rest of the platoon, 'Listen in, you lot, keep your fucking heads down.'

CSM Alec Munro

We continued moving forward till we came under increasingly heavy fire. Each time an illumination popped we dropped to the ground; I could see bullet strikes kicking up the peat around us. It wasn't an ideal position to be in. I could make out the dark outline of a peat bank to our front – we needed some form of cover and I mentioned this to Major Collett and we agreed to move forward with the HQ Group. As soon as the illumination round burnt out, we would make our move.

When the illumination expired Dave Collett gave the order to move; we ran forward to the cover of the peat bank. We continued to receive heavy fire. I noticed that Stevie Hope wasn't with us; I sent a couple of lads back to our previous position to find him, as it was vital we had communications to the battalion and to the platoons. One of them came back and told us that he had found Cpl Hope and that he had been wounded. I then told him to go back, get his radio and get a medic for him.

Pte Bill Metcalfe, 29 yrs – D Company Guide
As we were moving through the darkness, I saw a black shape on the floor in front of me; and to be honest I thought it may have been a dead sheep. As I got nearer I realized it was a body. I now know it was Cpl Stephen Hope, I rolled him over and shouted to our patrol medic, LCpl Pete Higgs, 'Pete, there's a guy here.' Cpl Hope was groaning and had very little pulse. I knew from my time in the Rhodesian army that this man would not recover.

Cpl Mark Brown
I noticed the signaller Cpl Stevie Hope, who was in front of me, he just seemed to sit straight down. Cpl John (Jock) Ferry of 9 Squadron RE went over to him and touched him and said, 'Come on, mate.' But Cpl Hope just rolled over onto his side, and started snoring loudly. I heard someone say, 'Shit, he's been shot in the head.'

In the initial flap someone had cut the straps off his Bergen in order to treat him. So now his Bergen that was carrying the radio had no straps. Major Collett shouted, 'I need someone to take over the radio now!' And I thought, Not me, I've got a patrol to look after. Someone stepped forward and I heard him say, 'Fucking hell, who's cut the fucking straps?' I don't know how he carried that radio but it was vital.

Pte Clint McMillon, 22 yrs – D Company Guide
Cpl Mark Brown asked me and Terry Peck to help treat Cpl Hope. He was lying on his back facing up. Terry Peck and I were kneeling over him looking

for his injuries and at first, in the darkness, and with his difficulty breathing, I thought he'd been hit in the chest, but he'd been hit in the head. I could hear and feel the closeness of the rounds whizzing just over us.

Pte Ashley Wright

I began making my way towards the sound of a voice urgently shouting, 'Medic, medic.' Then out of the dark someone else shouted out, 'Don't bother, he's dead.' So I stopped and took cover. After a short while someone shouted, 'Where's that fucking medic?' I jumped up and ran forward shouting, 'Where the fuck are you? It's the medic.' Someone shouted, 'Just keep going forward.' I thought, Yeah, you just keep going fucking forward.

I eventually arrived at Cpl Hope and immediately began checking him. He was snoring heavily, so I knew he was still alive. I took my gloves off and gently ran my hands over his head, and discovered he had a gunshot wound to his head. I said, 'We've got to get him out of here; we've got to get him to somewhere safe so I can treat him.' I reached down to pick up my gloves and couldn't find them. It was fucking freezing. I was shivering and I thought, I won't be able to function properly without them. I was patting the ground when we began to receive more incoming fire. I lay flat, but tried to make myself even flatter as I could hear the rounds cracking just above me. I thought, This is it; I am going to die here.

Pte Clint McMillon

We then tried to move Cpl Hope back down the slope but we found it difficult, because Steve was a huge bear of a man and it was not possible to stand due to the amount of incoming fire. Fortunately I was carrying a sleeping bag strapped to my webbing. I unrolled my sleeping bag and somehow we managed to get Cpl Hope into it; we now half dragged and half carried him down the slope into cover.

Pte Len Baines

We eventually took cover behind some peat banks. It was here I found out that Cpl Stevie Hope had been wounded. Phil Jones was now told to make his way across and take over Cpl Hope's role as radio operator. I quickly took all the stuff that Phil Jones had been carrying. I really wanted to ditch his kit, but the OC wouldn't let me, so now my Bergen was twice as heavy.

Pte Mike Carr, 19 yrs – 3 Platoon

Sgt Jim McCallum shouted, 'I need two big lads to help move a wounded man.' Immediately Pte Pete Lygo and Pte Larry (Doc) Halliday volunteered – although there were bullets flying everywhere they both ran back to help Cpl Hope. The remainder of us waited there, keeping as low as possible.

Captain Willy McCracken Call Sign 41B informs the Fire Direction Centre he is unsure of the position of forward troops:

01.44hrs (zt): from C/S 41B to C/S 29FDC: 'Call sign 3 [HMS *Avenger*] finished ZU7920 91 rounds; HE expended Z7920 + ZU7918 now unsafe.'

01.50hrs (zt): from C/S 41B to C/S 29FDC: 'ZU7910 unsafe for GA.'

Major Collett informs the CO Hew Pike that they have taken one casualty:

01.52hrs (zt): from C/S 19 to C/S 9: 'This call sign has one casualty, we are pinned down by sniper fire and are staying put until (*objective*) cleared by Call Sign 2 [Cpl Hope].'

01.52hrs (zt): from C/S 9 to C/S 19: 'Roger.'

Pte Steve Gaines, 25 yrs – Support Company, Machine Gun Platoon

As we moved around the back of A Company we came across Cpl Hope. There was someone with him, and I remember he was still breathing, I could see his breath on the cold night air. We paused for a moment while Captain Mason spoke to someone; we then carried on and eventually took cover in some peat banks with members of A Company.

Shortly after Captain Mason leaves Cpl Hope, C Company, who are now in their 'Reserve Position', about 100 metres to the rear of A Company, send a section forward to help recover Cpl Hope back into C Company's aid post.

Captain Mason arrives at Wing Forward at approximately 02.00hrs (zt). From this new location he will support B Company. On arrival, he makes contact over the radio with Major Collett and Captain Adrian Freer. He is told to go firm and await further instructions.

Pte Dean (Jasper) Coady, 18 yrs – 2 Section, 2 Platoon
We took cover behind a small peat bank that ran across our front. The bank was higher in some places than others depending on your luck; the part that Tim Jenkins and I found ourselves taking cover behind was about two feet high. The Argentine fire from Longdon was really heavy. Some of it was going just above our heads and some was hitting the top of the peat bank, throwing dust and dirt everywhere. The sight of tracer passing over and around us, and the noise of the rounds zipping through the air, is something I will never forget.

Pte Trevor Bradshaw
The majority of 2 Platoon had managed to run to a small peat bank, but a few of us, including Privates Stuart Dover, Jez Dillon, Eddie Cookson, Paul Johnstone and myself, were pinned down in a small depression. We were probably about ten metres behind everyone else. At this stage there was a lot of incoming fire. Stuart Dover shouted that he'd been hit by a piece of shrapnel. It was decided that 2 Platoon was going to give us covering fire to enable us to run for cover. As we ran across, Eddie Cookson disappeared up to his chest in the bog water. We all managed to reach the peat bank apart from Eddie, whose boots were stuck deep into the bog, cursing and swearing at us to come back and give him a hand. We all ran back and pulled him out. Strange as it may seem, it was extremely funny at the time.

Pte Jeremy (Jez) Dillon, 23 yrs – 2 Section, 2 Platoon
At some point we reached the peat bank and were told to set up our GPMGs up on the embankment. Cpl Sturge came over to me, he took over my gun and he said to me, 'Watch my tracer.' He opened up on a position he had identified. He then said to me, 'Are you watching where this is landing?' I said, 'Yeah.' He stopped and I took over and began firing. Cpl Sturge then went across to Pte Dave Herbert, who was the other GPMG gunner, and did the exact same thing with his gun.

Pte Stuart Dover, 21 yrs – 3 Section, 2 Platoon

Our machine guns were told to engage Longdon, but as soon as they opened up we attracted even more direct fire. The Argentine artillery was firing on pre-registered targets, dropping rounds all around us. I got hit in the leg and let out a yell. We were in fairly open ground at that stage. I shouted, 'I've been hit.' Jez Dillon said, 'Fucking hell, I knew something like this would happen to one of us.' Trev Bradshaw, who was with us, began shouting, 'Medic!'

After a short while, one of our medics, Chris Lovett, crawled quite some distance to reach me. He slid in beside me and asked, 'Where've you been hit?' I said, 'It's my leg.' He cut open my trousers from hip to ankle and began feeling my leg for the wound. He said, 'You twat, it's barely broken the skin!' I had been hit by a piece of shrapnel on the tail end of its journey, and although it was painful, my leg was okay. My mates then started to take the piss. The flapping tear in my windproof trousers proved to be a chilly reminder for the rest of the night.

Cpl Louie Sturge

I could see green muzzle flashes coming from the top of the mountain which I knew to be Argy, and I said, '2 Section, on my command, rapid fire.' What a mistake that was! After we fired, 2 Platoon got a wallop load of shit, as it seemed like every Argentine locked on to us, from what seemed like every gun position along the mountain. But all the fire was going just over the top of us. I had Pte Tim Jenkins with his mate Pte Dean Coady along with my gun team on my left. We were pinned down there for a good 40 minutes to an hour.

Pte Davie Barclay, 23 yrs – 2 Section, 2 Platoon

I vividly remember watching the tracer rounds streaking towards the mountain; they bounced off the rocks in all directions. Schermuly flares were being fired. It was scary and exciting at the same time. We had a Forward Observation Officer, Lt John Lee, with us and he was trying to call in artillery fire in support of B Company, but at this stage we weren't sure where B Company was. Eventually the GPMG gunners were told to stop firing for the same reason.

Cpl Louie Sturge

I was using an IWS [night sight]. I looked up at the mountain and could see all the gunfire coming from B Company, then I scanned back along to the east, where I could see a cluster of active night sights. They were giving off scope signatures, about four of them. I decided to take them on with the two machine guns that I had in my section. I told my lads to put their guns on the peat bank, and I was directing fire using target indication.

Pte Dean (Jasper) Coady

There was a lull. The incoming fire seemed to have paused for a moment. Tim Jenkins and I peered over the top of the peat bank to watch the battle taking place on Mount Longdon. As we were watching I sort of felt the rounds come in. They made me jump; they were really close, zipping right past me. I ducked down and immediately noticed a burning smell. I looked over to Tim, he had not moved from his position, but his head had slumped forward onto the peat bank and I knew he'd been hit. I reached over and pulled him down and shouted to Cpl Sturge, 'Tim's been hit!' I started shouting for a medic, but by the time LCpl Lovett eventually reached us, Tim had died.

Only the day before we had been celebrating Tim's 19th birthday and mine the week before. I thought, What the fuck am I doing here? Tim's dead, I'm 8,000 miles away from home, I'm being shot at and my mate is lying dead next to me. I felt numb. I lay by Tim's body for some time after he had died, and then someone gave me a mug of tea.

Pte Jeremy (Jez) Dillon

The next thing I remember is Cpl Louie Sturge shouting across to Lt Ian Moore, 'Sir, we've taken a casualty.' Ian Moore shouted back, 'Who is it?' Louie said, 'It's Tim Jenkins, he's dead.' Ian Moore shouted back, 'Are you sure he's dead?' and Louie said, 'Yes, I'm sure.' It sounds daft now, but it suddenly dawned on me, that this was the real thing, and I thought, Fucking hell, this is happening.

Captain Adrian Freer, 29 yrs – 2ic A Company/Support Group Commander

There was a certain amount of confusion and the company became split. We had an uncertain 45 minutes till we finally linked up with Company HQ. At that stage we were taking cover behind the peat bank and folds in the ground as the enemy had our assault route well covered with defensive fire. The rounds were landing very close indeed. I met up with David Collett who told me that Cpl Hope, one of the company signallers, had been shot in the head, and Pte Tim Jenkins was dead, also that both 1 and 2 Platoons were pinned down.

LCpl Graham Tolson, 23 yrs – Anti-Tank Platoon attached to A Company

WO2 Sammy Dougherty's radio was turned up to full volume. I could hear it broadcasting clearly over the battle noises. It was choked with chatter from the B Company call signs. The Section Commanders in B Company were obviously under extreme duress, one in particular, Cpl McLaughlin, had come on the air several times. It seemed his section was pinned down by fire coming from two bunkers at the top of a gully. Another call sign, this time from A Company 2 Platoon, reported he had taken a casualty. To my left Tony Bojko said, 'I know him, he's a young lad with blond hair.' But he was cut short by the whoosh of a 105mm artillery salvo that landed close by. There was a flash and a huge explosion, the ground vibrated; the soft peat soil was thrown high in the air before dropping down around us with a splat. As each shell exploded I thought to myself, Please don't let me die.

Pte Bill Metcalfe

I particularly remember hearing someone screaming out in agony, and then I heard a voice shouting, 'Will someone shut that fucker up!' We were here for quite some time, it was bitterly cold but the artillery kept us on our toes. If it hadn't been for the cover of the peat banks, we would have taken a lot more wounded.

Pte Davie Barclay

We were extremely lucky not to take more casualties. I was listening to the whistle of the shells as they approached and then the roar as it rushed in to impact. I curled up into a ball and hoped for the best. Some landed only yards away, exploding and throwing huge piles of earth and bog water into the air. Twenty-year-old Pte James [Jock] Brebner, who was wounded in the leg, was given morphine to ease the pain, but when the morphine kicked in he started singing at the top of his voice, 'Oh, flower of Scotland…' CSM Alec Munro shouted, 'Who the fuck's that? For fuck's sake, someone shut him up!'

CSM Alec Munro

While we were in the cover of the peat bank, Major Dave Collett was on the radio giving a situation report to the battalion. There was heavy fire being returned from 1 Platoon to our left. We were busy trying to establish how far B Company had advanced without getting our heads shot off and the only indication to go by was the flashes of grenade explosions, which we knew indicated close-quarter engagements. There was a real danger that our fire could be too close to B Company.

Pte Craig (Tommy) Onions

As we reached A Company there was a lot of incoming fire from the mountain, also there was quite a bit of incoming artillery fire. A Company were sheltering under the cover of some peat banks to the north of Mount Longdon. Shortly after we arrived, Cpl McCarthy's Milan team was sent forward to set up and fire two Milan missiles at positions on the north face of Longdon. After that we then just sat and waited; it was bitterly cold.

6.2 'I was fucked if I was going to take A Company through a minefield'

At approximately 02.15hrs (zt), the Milan team fire two Milan missiles at the enemy .50 Cal machine-gun position in the Third Bowl on the northern side of Longdon.

Captain Tony Mason

I made contact with Captain Adrian Freer, who gave me the coordinates for a target. It was a .50 Calibre machine gun, which was firing in our direction. The rounds from it were passing just over our heads. We were located in a small defile which gave us some decent cover. We waited as 4 Platoon confirmed their position. Then Cpl Ginge McCarthy, Pte Phil West, Pte Pete Hedicker and I moved forward and set up the Milan. We opened fire and put two missiles into the target area. This was good for morale as the lads felt at last they had done something. I also recall a mug of tea materializing from thin air – how they managed to brew up without me seeing them or even smelling the hexamine was an absolute mystery.

Pte Steve Gaines
Cpl McCarthy's group crawled forward and began setting up their Milan post. We were approximately 600 metres from Longdon and they were trying to take out a gun position. They fired the first missile, it impacted in the target area, and then they quickly withdrew, as the launch signature drew a huge amount of return fire. Not long after, they crawled back out and fired a second missile, but I think this one went high. They quickly withdrew and came back to us, and we now all sat and waited till we received orders to move around to Mount Longdon.

LCpl Graham Tolson
I remember hearing the two Milan missiles being fired from behind us. I distinctly remember the popping noise and then the whoosh as each missile passed over our heads, travelling towards Longdon.

1 Platoon have established themselves in a good covered position along a peat bank and they have initially identified some of the sniper positions using their IWS night sights: Pte Stephen Evans engages initially, and then Pte Edward Dennis engages using his GPMG. The fire has to be carefully controlled due to the danger of hitting B Company and in the end has to be stopped; the risk is too great:

02.18hrs (zt): from C/S 19 to C/S 9: 'Picked up a sniper using infrared: we will try and take him out.'

02.18hrs (zt): from C/S 9 to C/S 19: 'Roger.'

Lt John Lee, the Forward Observation Officer, and his party move forward to 2 Platoon's location. He needed to get a better view of the targets to bring fire down on. However, both direct and indirect fire have to be stopped due to the proximity of B Company. While occupying Wing Forward the company begin to come under increasingly accurate artillery fire. Initially the enemy concentrates its fire on planned DFs. They then begin to adjust their fire onto A Company and

C Company positions, with some accuracy. The company is unable to advance any further over such open ground without risking heavy casualties. There is accurate and sustained heavy machine-gun and sniper fire from the high ground. A Company tries to contact B Company regarding three gun positions around the Third Bowl including one .50 Calibre, but it seems B Company is uncontactable at the time:

02.38hrs (zt): from C/S 19 to C/S 29: 'Have now identified three positions, with one controlling two machine guns.'

02.50hrs (zt): from C/S 9 to C/S 19: 'Lost contact with Call Sign 2.'

02.50hrs (zt): from C/S 19 to C/S 9: 'Roger.'

At some stage the wounded Pte James (Jock) Brebner is passed back to C Company, located approximately 100 metres to A Company's rear.

Cpl Mark Brown

I heard an order being given over the radio for people with night scopes to engage targets, if they could identify them. But lots of people were opening up, and then an order was given to 'check firing'. From our position we could hear shouting and screaming from B Company as they fought through positions.

Shortly before 05.00hrs (zt), I heard a radio transmission: it was the CO, Hew Pike, talking to Major Collett. He said, 'I want you to advance directly forward.' I thought, Shit. You could see from the amount of gunfire coming from the mountain that we would get hammered. Major Collett replied, 'No, the company will be going right-flanking and we are going to come up behind B Company.' I could have kissed David Collett when he said that.

CSM Alec Munro

Dave Collett's opinion was that there was no way he was going to advance A Company across that ground. Without doubt we would have suffered heavy casualties. He said to me, 'It's not going to happen.' I thought that was pretty ballsy, but he was dead right. After a short conversation with the CO, Dave Collett turned to me and said, 'Sgt Major, I want you to hold the position, I'm going across for an "O" Group with the CO.' It seemed to me that the CO was trying to maintain the momentum of the attack, but didn't quite grasp the situation we were in. It was going to be an interesting conversation.

Major David Collett, 36 yrs – Officer Commanding A Company
Hew Pike suggested, 'I want you to advance directly forward and attack the northern side.' I refused to attack uphill, over open ground, as A Company would have been wiped out. There was a minefield in front of us. Hew Pike was insistent because he was bogged down; however, I was fucked if I was going to take A Company through a minefield. I said, 'The Company will be going right-flanking and we are going to come up behind B Company.' That was followed by a short period of silence. Then the CO said, 'David, come over and see me now.'

I skirted around the minefield, went past the RAP and somehow made my way into the First Bowl. It was here that I met up with the CO. There were bodies lying everywhere. B Company looked absolutely shattered – it was chaos. I could hear captured Argentines crying and praying. I didn't want my men to see this; I decided that I would get them in and out as quickly as possible. We tried to work out what we were going to do since we were in a very vulnerable position at that moment.

Once we had come to an agreement on how best to use A Company, I called them over, but instructed them to come forward one platoon at a time. The time then was approximately 06.00hrs (zt). Captain Willie McCracken brought down a tremendous artillery barrage; the rounds were falling within 50 metres of the First Bowl. He really stonked that whole position – the way he put it down was amazing. The 6 Platoon wounded were extremely lucky that they weren't killed in their exposed position on the eastern slope.

A Company would now pass back another casualty to C Company, a shell-shocked member of HQ Company, and then prepared to withdraw from Wing Forward. During this move they would simply move backwards and then pass in front of C Company, although many members of A Company were completely unaware that C Company was immediately behind them

CSM Alec Munro
Due to the efforts of B Company, the firing at this stage seemed to be easing, with just the odd burst of machine-gun fire. The orders were to ease back into the dead ground behind us, and then move the company around to the base of Mount Longdon. We were then to move up the slope and move through

B Company to assault along the ridge line. During the move round we passed in front of C Company who were located to our rear. I recall speaking with Sgt Martin Bird of C Company. I asked about the condition of Cpl Hope, and he reckoned at that stage he would be okay. He was with the other casualties waiting for casevac. He seemed to be asleep and snoring his head off. I didn't realize it at the time, but that was a classic symptom of a bad head injury.

At approximately 06.37hrs (zt), HMS Glamorgan *is hit by an Exocet Missile. This is the end of naval gunfire support for 3 PARA.*

Pte Dean Coady
Suddenly Cpl Sturge said, 'Right, we're moving, get your kit and follow me.' That brought me back to the job in hand. We retraced our steps and proceeded in single file with 2 Platoon leading.

Pte Jeremy (Jez) Dillon
I remember Sgt Gerry Carr telling us, 'Right, lads, we are now going to move to Longdon. When we get there we will be passing through B Company.' It seemed to take a long time, but I was that weighed down with ammunition, I couldn't carry any more than I already had. My smock was full of it; I had bandoliers over both shoulders and a GPMG to carry. My back was killing me. As we reached the base of the mountain we could hear screams in the distance, and gunfire.

Cpl Joe Black, 33 yrs – Anti-Tank Platoon attached to A Company
We moved off, heading for the western end of Mount Longdon. As we passed a large peat cutting, a red torchlight was spotted to our left. WO2 Sammy Dougherty called out, 'Who the fuck's that?' A broad Scottish accent replied, 'It's Ron.' Sammy shouted back, 'And who the fuck is Ron?' Ron replied, 'It's Ron Duffy from B Company, I'm here with Cpl Milne, he's stood on a mine and has injured his leg.' It was only then I realized we were in a minefield!

George Duffus came over and asked if anyone would like to go and help Ron and Chris Lovett. It wasn't an order, but help was needed. Pte Kevin Darke and I volunteered to go. At this stage Brian Milne had been lying in the minefield for six hours, with Ron Duffy lying across him trying to keep him warm. This was the first time I knew Brian had been injured and I wasn't even sure what his injuries were. We cautiously made our way towards LCpl Chris Lovett. I remember thinking, Maybe he's broken his leg. I knelt down and leaned into Brian, he was trying to talk, saying, 'Joe, Joe, fucking Joe.' I couldn't make out what he was saying, so trying to cheer him up, I said, 'All right, Brian, give us a song' [Brian was a big Dean Martin fan and had sung a lot on-board the SS *Canberra*]. Brian groaned, 'Fuck off, Joe.'

Pte Kevin Darke, 23 yrs – Anti-Tank Platoon attached to A Company

Chris Lovett took a tobacco tin out of his smock which contained morphine Syrettes and administered one to Brian. Eventually we could see a Snowcat vehicle coming through the light of the Argentine flares. As it pulled up, LCpl Roy Bassey climbed out to help load Brian. He walked towards us and got within a couple of feet of us, when he stood on a mine blowing part of his foot off. I was hit in the hand by a small piece of shrapnel from the explosion. Cpl Black and Cpl Paul Roberts both received a load of debris in the face, temporarily blinding them. Roy Bassey was in severe pain with the injury to his foot, and Chris Lovett set about treating all of us.

Once everyone had been treated, we began to load Brian Milne, Roy Bassey and Paul Roberts into the vehicle, which was quite a difficult task. LCpl David [Titch] Bowdler, the BV driver, drove them directly to helicopter LS [1 kiometre west of Murrell Bridge]. Both Brian and Roy were beginning to feel the effects of the morphine. As the vehicle trundled away, Cpl Milne could be heard shouting, 'Darky, you bastard, I've lost my leg!' And Roy Bassey shouted, 'Yeah, and I've lost my foot, you fucking good bloke!'

Pte Trevor Bradshaw

I remember hearing Lt Ian Moore on the radio – I think he was talking to Major Collett about the fact that we may be crossing the minefield and he was concerned about moving through it. The language being used by both was very forceful, and the reply was very blunt, saying, 'Just fucking do it, now!' I was then aware we were about to walk through a possible minefield.

Pte Stu Dover

I was quite close to Platoon HQ and could hear the whole conversation between Lt Moore and Major Collett, who just wanted us up on the hill as soon as possible. Having heard all this, I slid in behind the platoon signaller Pte Mick Newbold, carefully treading in the footprints he left in the frost-covered ground. Then I heard Sgt Gerry Carr's voice behind me: 'Get back in line, Dover – and watch where you're walking, remember I'm behind you.'

6.3   'Someone better tell them it's creeping the wrong fucking way!'

Brigade asks 3 PARA HQ to find out what is happening on Longdon:

07.25hrs (zt): from C/S 0 to C/S 9: 'Send brief situation report for higher formation.'

07.25hrs (zt): from C/S 9 to C/S 0: 'Roger: Call Sign 2 has sustained considerable casualties whilst taking its objective, Call Sign 1 will pass through and hopefully take Full Back by first light there is fierce resistance on the feature and it is difficult to pinpoint the exact location of the enemy amongst the rocks.'

07.25hrs (zt): from C/S 0 to C/S 9: 'Passed to Brigade.'

CSM Alec Munro

As soon as we reached Mount Longdon I moved to where the B Company OC, Major Argue, was located. He was in the First Bowl with Major Collett, and they had just attended a briefing with the CO, Hew Pike. Major Collett then briefed me on what our task would be and what ammunition scales were required. I decided that I needed to get hold of my counterpart from B Company, CSM Johnny Weeks. Firstly, to get a handle on the situation that B Company had had to deal with, and secondly, to get hold of any surplus ammo for the next phase of the assault.

John Weeks was as stoical as ever. He gave me a quick rundown on the situation and the difficulties they had been confronted with. They'd had a hard time of it and it showed, but thankfully their efforts weren't in vain and they had made our task easier. I mentioned that I would take any surplus ammo they could afford, particularly grenades, 66mm's and belted link. Without hesitation, he immediately tasked Cpl Stewart McLaughlin to get round B Company and collect all the surplus ammo of the types we needed.

Cpl Louie Sturge

We began moving up towards the First Bowl. Bodies still lay all over the place. Wounded were being attended to, and the B Company walking wounded were making their way to the RAP. I remember seeing Cpl Laurie Bland speaking to Cpl Ned Kelly, who was in great pain and was being helped down to the RAP. We moved in single file. I exchanged a few words and smiles with friends in B Company, including Cpl Stewart McLaughlin, whom I had served with in D Company (Patrols). We paused for a short while, and then Lt Moore reappeared and called us forward into the First Bowl with the remnants of B Company's 4 and 5 Platoons, who were now sitting resting. They all looked extremely tired and had a look of shock on their faces.

Pte Stu Dover

A lot of the lads from B Company had a strange look on their faces. They didn't look like they usually looked, they looked somehow older, but they still offered us encouragement as we passed them. We moved slowly up into the bowl area; the ground was shaking as shells were slamming into the mountain. Pte Paul [Johno] Johnstone said to me that the shelling was getting worse. I told him it was okay, as it was 'friendly' fire, but his reply was that 'It doesn't sound very fucking friendly; it's likely to get us fucking killed.' I told him I'd heard it was a creeping barrage to provide us with cover as we moved forward. He said, 'Well, someone better tell them it's creeping the wrong fucking way!' I watched as streams of incoming tracer hit a large rock, then ricocheted off in all directions like a firework display.

A Company seem to have taken various routes into the First Bowl: A Company HQ, guided by Sgt Mac French, skirt along the northern edge of Mount Longdon, till they reach the large rocky outcrop opposite the First Bowl; they then go directly into the First Bowl. 2 Platoon, Support Group and 3 Platoon, who are following Company HQ in a company snake, somehow become detached, 2 and 3 Platoons come through the RAP, then up along Route 3, but Support Group make their way up the western slope. 1 Platoon take a direct route, moving straight across from Wing Forward to the First Bowl.

Sgt Manny Manfred

As we neared the northern side of Longdon I could see some members of B Company withdrawing back down the sheep track towards us. I saw Cpl Graham Heaton turn and face east to give covering fire, when suddenly there was a burst of fire and he was shot in the legs. I went across to him and with the help of others we managed to drag him up the incline and into the First Bowl.

Cpl Mark Brown

We left Wing Forward and made our way straight across towards the First Bowl. As we approached, a member of B Company shouted, 'There's more Argies,' and threw a white phosphorus grenade! I shouted, 'Fuck off, it's us, A Company!' Fortunately, no one was injured. As we reached the area of the sheep track, I remember passing a Cobra missile which had been mounted just to the right of a prominent large lone rock. I moved past it and on to the sheep track and turned right and made my way towards the First Bowl.

Sgt Manny Manfred

After helping with Cpl Heaton I searched about in the darkness, trying to locate my platoon. I called out, '1 Platoon, 1 Platoon,' and the voice of Pte Bob Taylor called back, 'We're over here, Sarge. Come over here with me, there's a nice wee spot over here, get in here.' I moved over by Bob and I noticed a terrible smell. I could hear people laughing, and I realized I was in a shit pit. I said, 'Bob, this is a fucking shit pit!' He replied, 'Yeah, I know, what a bastard.'

Captain Willie McCracken now hands over to Major John Patrick RA:

07.50hrs (zt): from C/S 41B to C/S 29FDC: '41B going firm – C/S 79 going through to continue mission with C/S 1.'

Cpl Joe Black

It was approximately 08.00hrs (zt) and still pitch black. We would now have to get ourselves out of the minefield. We formed up in single file. My eyes were still quite sore, so Kev Darke would lead, Dex Allen, Chris Lovett and I would follow. Kev would drop his rifle in front of him, then walk forward whilst holding my hand. As we made our way back to the peat cutting we called out to Sgt George Duffus, 'George, George, we're coming back in.' But when we got there they had all gone, so we followed the boot prints that A Company had left as they moved to Longdon.

Pte Len Baines – Signaller, Support Group
We began to move up the western slope. As I was moving up, a member of 3 PARA came running down and ran into me. My bayonet stuck in his leg quite deeply. I pulled it out, and he just laughed and continued on his way to wherever he was going. We moved up to an area just below Fly Half, where we met Cpl Tam Noble and he told us to wait there.

Pte Mark (Chuck) Berry , 21 yrs – 1 Platoon
We finally arrived in the First Bowl, and I remember hearing Cpl Terry McGlasson, the MFC with his unmistakable Glaswegian accent, giving fire-control orders. We waited to be called forward. I remember watching a group of Argentine prisoners who were crying and praying. There was a badly wounded Argentine moaning and groaning asking for his mama: he died after a short while, it was quite a distressing scene. The B Company lads looked absolutely shattered. The noise was tremendous, the mountain was vibrating. The amount of tracer was incredible.

Pte Jeremy (Jez) Dillon
It was pitch dark. I could hear the artillery FOO up in the rocks calling in fire missions. There were Argentine bodies lying about. I found a place to sit among the rocks, and I was thinking, What the fuck am I doing here? We sat there for maybe an hour listening to the noise of the incoming artillery, it was absolutely nerve-racking.

Pte Len Baines
I saw two bodies that were both covered over with ponchos, and I was told they were Dave Scott and Tony Greenwood. Then Tam Noble came over and told us we were going to move down into the First Bowl. He said, 'When I say go, keep your head down and run as fast as you can down there,' which I did.

CSM Alec Munro

After the 'O' Group I was asked by one of the Platoon Sergeants, 'What about prisoners?' I reminded him that it was a linear feature attack – the momentum had to be maintained. The enemy had to be kept on the back foot and rolled up. We didn't want to give them any chance to reorganize, and in the back of my mind was that I had just spoken to CSM Johnny Weeks and he had told me, 'Alec, tell your guys to watch out, there are Argies everywhere.'

The incident at Port San Carlos was still fresh in my mind, when two members of a Royal Marine helicopter crew were machine-gunned in the water, after their Gazelle had been shot down. I was the first to reach them. One of them died as I tried to cut through his immersion suit to treat his wounds. I also thought about the Lt Barry incident at Goose Green: he had been shot in the back under a white flag. This was an enemy who was not going to give up without a fight. I said, 'If you see anyone with a weapon in his hand, shoot first, don't even think about it, I don't want any of our lads being shot in the back.'

Pte Len Baines

There were a lot of key people in the First Bowl, the CO's group, B Company HQ, Major Pat Butler and A Company HQ. I thought that there were too many key personalities in one place. I decided to get a brew on, there were still dead bodies scattered about and I saw a prisoner wearing a white jumper lying face down on the floor; I think he may have been an Argy marine. I then overheard the CO, Hew Pike, telling Major Collett, 'If this doesn't work with A Company, I'm going to get the entire battalion together and we're all going over,' and I thought, Oh shit.

Pte Jeremy (Jez) Dillon

I remember watching Sgt Mac French, who was a great cross-country runner and very health conscious, but he was puffing away on a cigarette. He was just one of many of us who took to smoking that night.

Pte Mick Carr, 19 yrs – 3 Platoon

Someone said to me, 'Mick, I've heard that your brother Jerry's dead.' I made my way across to 2 Platoon and I could hear my brother's voice [Sgt Jerry Carr], he was giving orders to his platoon for the forthcoming attack. I shouted, 'Jerry, are you okay? Someone told me you were dead!' He shouted, 'Fuck off, Mick, I'm giving battle orders!'

Sgt Manny Manfred

I met up with Sgt Jerry Carr and Sgt Jim McCallum, the other two A Company Sergeants. I said, 'Jim, give me a fag.' He went to give me a roll-up cigarette, and I said, 'Jim, none of that shit, haven't you got any proper smokes?' He said, 'Yeah, but I've only got four left.' I shot back, 'Well, Jim, this is the time to smoke them.' And he said, 'Yeah, fair enough, I see what you mean.'

At approximately 09.15hrs (zt), Captain Adrian Freer is tasked by Major Collett to take his two gun teams up to the lip of the First Bowl, facing down the eastern slope towards Full Back, and begin putting down suppressive fire.

Captain Adrian Freer

When I met up with David Collett it was apparent that B Company had come to a halt. They had done well but had taken heavy casualties. The CO, Hew Pike, tasked A Company to clear the remaining ridge line to the eastern end. My group would consist of WO2 Sammy Dougherty, Sgt Chris Phelan, Sgt George Duffus and the Anti-Tank section. We were to set up a firebase at the lip of the First Bowl. Our task was to cover A Company as they began their assault. I crawled out into a slight dip in the ground. We had a line of two gun teams, firing at targets of opportunity. 2 Platoon would move first, followed by 1 Platoon. We, along with the artillery, put down a great deal of fire to try and neutralize the enemy positions.

Cpl Graham Tolson

I remember seeing the CO, Hew Pike, with Major Collett in heated conversation. We had been here for about two hours. Some of the sections had been reorganized, the wounded from B Company were being treated, and I felt sure that the CO was bound to start the push forward soon. There was a ground fog beginning to form, which was a sure indication that it would soon be daybreak. The fog would give some cover for A Company and maybe it was the opportunity the CO had been waiting for. Sammy Dougherty gathered us together and said, 'There's not much time to explain, but in about half an hour or so A Company will be ordered to fix bayonets and will begin pushing forward.' He said, shortly before A Company began their assault, 'We're going to position our guns on the lip of the bowl. Our task is to lay down covering fire for them.' We were given thousands of rounds of belt ammunition for our guns. I distributed the ammunition between Pte Tony Bojko, Pte Pete Maddocks and myself. We were now weighted down with belt ammunition. We laughed, as we resembled a trio of Mexican bandits.

Pte Pete Maddocks, 22 yrs – Anti-Tank Platoon attached to A Company

I watched as the first gun team from our section began crawling into the gun position. LCpl Ned Cameron shouted over to them, 'Keep your fucking heads down, lads.' Sgt George Duffus was acting as a spotter; Pte Terry Martin was the gunner, with his No. 2, Jim Fearon, and Cpl Joe Black as gun controller. They would be on our right. My gun team would be placed in position by Sammy Dougherty and consisted of Sgt Chris Phelan acting as gun controller, Pte Tony Bojko as gunner, myself acting as No. 2 and LCpl Graham Tolson acting as a spotter. We were in a slight dip in the ground just above the First Bowl, full of freezing cold water. I began to set up the belts of ammunition ready to feed the gun. Tony Bojko was adjusting his gun and getting into a comfortable firing position.

It seems everyone from the Support Group crawls out to assist in some way with the two GPMGs.

Sgt George Duffus

We set up and awaited Sammy Dougherty's command to engage the Argentine positions to our front. They were clearly visible from their muzzle flashes. Then, out of nowhere, Cpl Stewart McLaughlin crawled over to us with armfuls of belt ammunition for the guns and said, 'Here you go, George,' and passed us the ammunition. He then said, 'Can I help you, lads, is there anything you want?' I said, 'Scouse, fuck off, you've done your bit, go and have a fucking rest.'

We opened up for all we were worth. We gave A Company as much fire support as we could give from both GPMG positions. I am sure the covering fire we gave them provided that extra manoeuvrability on their initial assault. We continued up to and just after first light. Eventually my gun team was withdrawn back into the bowl.

Pte Tony Bojko, 21 yrs – Anti-Tank Platoon attached to A Company

Pte Terry Martin and I were firing at any likely enemy position to keep their heads down while A Company established a foothold on the top area. We were also directed to fire at various locations that were requested by 2 Platoon. We began to come under fire from small arms directly to the front of our position, and returned fire immediately. I did not have one stoppage. I think the weather helped, it was absolutely freezing, and cooled the barrels of our guns. We fired thousands of rounds across the area ahead of A Company. Eventually, as they approached the Full Back position, I was told to cease fire by Sammy Dougherty. He gave me a cigarette and although I don't smoke, I took it to calm down a bit.

LCpl Graham Tolson

We were in a slight hollow that was full of water that had iced over. We broke the ice and crawled in, not ideal, but we were protected from the sniper fire. Tony Bojko cocked the gun and began to double tap [firing in quick two-round bursts] at every Argentine muzzle flash he could see. Geordie Maddocks and I assisted in selecting targets, pointing and shouting, 'There's one.' Tap-Tap. 'There's another.' Tap-Tap. Sammy Doc suddenly stopped Tony from firing, and said, 'Watch up there.' He pointed to the right-hand side of the mountain. We took note: an Argentine was routinely moving between several places, firing one or two shots from each position. We watched as the Argentine started to go through his routine.

Sammy said to Tony, 'When he comes out, nail the bastard.' Tony said, 'Okay,' and pulled the butt of the gun tightly into his shoulder and waited. The man ran out onto the track, and as he did so, a mortar illumination round lit up the area. It took him by surprise and he froze. He then tried to scramble back to safety, but it was too late, a burst of about ten rounds hit him.

Major David Collett

I brought up 2 Platoon under the command of Lt Ian Moore and Sgt Gerry Carr; their 2 Section would be the first section to begin the advance. I spoke to Cpl Sturge and said, 'Look, we don't want to lose any more people on this. I want you to tell your section, take your webbing off, crawl forward on your stomach, do it carefully, do not rush, take your time.'

Pte Trevor Bradshaw

I remember Major Collett telling us to take off our webbing and put our magazines and grenades in our smock pockets. I felt this made a big difference in the way we were able to move about, once we got over the lip of the bowl and started working our way through the enemy positions.

Cpl Stewart McLaughlin asks if he can go with A Company, but is told to stay in the First Bowl with B Company.

Pte Bill Metcalfe

I moved up to the lip of the First Bowl and was watching for enemy movement, when suddenly a 7.62mm round passed through the instep of my foot. I fell back and landed on top of Cpl Mark Brown. He said, 'What the fuck are you doing?' I said, 'I've just been shot!' Pte Adam Corneille treated me, wrapping shell dressings around my boot. I was then helped down to the Regimental Aid Post by Mark Brown.

6.4   'It was a sight I shall never forget'

At approximately 09.30hrs (zt), there is a huge amount of firepower being directed at Full Back. Having had their main lines of defence overrun, and with the possibility of being surrounded, Major Carrizo Salvadores speaks by radio to Brigadier General Oscar Jofre and tells him that they can no longer hold the position. He receives permission to abandon Mount Longdon. Major Carrizo Salvadores then orders the destruction of documents and equipment in preparation for the final withdrawal.

Major David Collett informs the CO, who has by now located himself up on Fly Half, that 2 Platoon is on the eastern slope advancing towards Full Back:

09.40hrs (zt): from C/S 19 to C/S 9: 'Call Sign 1/2 has cleared and now manning high ground.'

Cpl Louie Sturge

I sent my gun team of LCpl John Reeves, Pte Dave Herbert and Pte Jimmy Young crawling out of the bowl to try and establish a protective firebase. I then went over with Pte Alan Sparrock, followed by the rest of my section. Behind us was Cpl Laurie Bland's section, followed by Cpl Mick Ferguson's section. When we first crawled out into the open top area, we attracted a lot of effective enemy fire. We found it difficult to move – we operated in pairs carrying out standard fire and manoeuvre tactics, and we could only move in short bounds.

I got on the radio and asked Sammy Dougherty to lay down fire forward of us. He was using his two guns and he also asked WO2 Thor Caithness to pull in fire from the SF gun teams on Fly Half. Major John Patrick and Lt Jon Lee were also calling in artillery. The noise was tremendous. It was a relatively small area and everything was dropping 'danger close'. I fired a couple of 66mm LAWs into an Argentine position to our front and said to the lads, 'Who's with me? – Let's go.' To a man everyone went charging towards the position. We were then instructed by Lt Ian Moore to drop down onto the northern side of the mountain and work our way east along the northern edge of Longdon.

LCpl John Reeves

I was told by Cpl Sturge that my gun team would be going out first to provide covering fire for the rest of the section. As we waited to go, I felt quite apprehensive. It felt similar to parachuting, i.e. standing in the door of a C130 and waiting for the green light and the air dispatcher to shout, 'Go!'

Pte Jeremy (Jez) Dillon

I moved forward with Pte Trev Bradshaw, clearing bunker after bunker. We [2 Platoon] had established a foothold and would now provide a firebase for 1 Platoon to move through us. I remember seeing Major Collett standing there in open ground trying to cock an Argy .50 Cal [Gun No. 3], but he just couldn't get it to fire, it was jammed solid. In the end he gave up. We could see them starting to break, which spurred us on. The bunkers still had to be cleared. We were not about to take any chances and even those who appeared dead were shot or bayoneted unless very obviously dead. The effect of artillery was absolutely devastating, bodies were torn apart. It was a sight I shall never forget.

At first light, at approximately 10.00hrs (zt), the Argentine withdrawal begins. Anyone who has not made it back to Company Headquarters on Full Back is assumed dead or taken prisoner. The wounded will leave first, followed by the able-bodied. Lt Dachary also orders that documents and equipment are destroyed; two columns of approximately 78 men begin to make their way towards Wireless Ridge, harassed by British fire.

Argentine Cpl Gustavo Pedemonte, 7th Infantry Regiment

I was in severe pain and alone and without the possibility of recovering my position. I tried calling for help, but my comrades had gone. With the severe pain in my legs, I was barely able to walk. I dragged myself about 50 metres and then rested for a moment. Two soldiers, Ruiz Diaz and Gonzalez, joined me and helped me back to the Company Headquarters. The place was hell. I was now able to reach the command post and report the status of my section. I met fellow soldier Felix Barreto, he asked me how I was and I rested with him. Then Major Carrizo Salvadores ordered the walking wounded to withdraw first. I eventually arrived at the former headquarters of the Royal Marines in Moody Brook, and from there I was transported to the King Edward Hospital in Port Stanley.

Pte Davie Barclay

As I waited to leave the bowl, it felt like something out of World War One. Sgt Gerry Carr and I would work as a pair. I remember someone shouted, 'Go!' and slapped me on the back. We both crawled out; I had a bolt-action sniper rifle, Gerry Carr was pointing out targets. The noise of small arms and artillery was deafening, my heart was racing.

Major David Collett

We had to take our time because there was very little cover. Basically, as one man moved forward, another man took his place. Once the section had gone through, another section followed. It was a very slow process. The CO wanted me to speed it up, but there was no way we could move any faster without risking further casualties.

LCpl John Reeves, 22 yrs – 2 Section, 2 Platoon

Cpl Sturge called for us to move to another position, which meant crossing a piece of open ground of about 20 metres. The rest of the section would provide us with covering fire. I said to Dave Herbert, who was the gunner, 'You go first, and if you get dropped [shot], Jimmy Young will pick up the gun [GPMG].' Dave Herbert set off and made it into the new position. Then it was Jimmy Young's turn to go. I looked over at him and he was rocking back and forth, building himself up for the run across, then away he went. I was next to go, I jumped up and began zigzagging across the open ground. As I reached halfway, I tripped and fell over. I hurriedly picked myself up. When I reached the new position, Dave Herbert and Jimmy Young were already engaging positions to our front. There were rounds bouncing off the rocks behind us. I'll never forget how close those rounds were.

Pte Dean (Jasper) Coady

I watched as our gun team went out. They were flat on their stomachs, crawling off into the darkness. I was thinking, Oh, fucking hell. Cpl Sturge said, 'Right, Coady and Bull, go now!' He was continually shouting orders and advice over the constant noise of battle: 'Coady, Bull and Sparrock, clear those positions to the left, move now!' I shouted back over the noise to Pte Mick Newbold, the radio operator, to get the gun group up for some covering fire. Then away we went; the training took over, we were tossing grenades into bunkers, pausing for a moment, then jumping in and firing at the slightest movement. We were hyped up with adrenaline flowing, the tiredness and cold were forgotten.

Ged Bull and I threw grenades into a trench and made the near-fatal mistake of being over-enthusiastic. With the grenade barely exploding, we both jumped up in order to dive into the trench, but we were caught by some of the blast and small pieces of shrapnel from our own grenades. Ged Bull received a piece of shrapnel to the tip of his finger and I was hit in the right arm. We carried on with Alan Sparrock and moved on to attack another position. My arm was starting to go numb, I asked Ged Bull, who was carrying an SMG, 'Can we swop?' I gave him my SLR and I took his SMG. Cpl Sturge had a quick look at my arm and told me to go back and get my arm treated, but I refused. We continued on and attacked one more bunker.

Pte Stu Dover

At the lip of the First Bowl, WO2 Sammy Dougherty was acting as a sort of 'dispatcher', saying, 'Okay, lads, there's trenches left and right that have been cleared, use them for cover, right, GO!' My section were to keep to the left, moving along the main ridge among the rocks. We moved in very short bounds, covering each other. A lot of the enemy had begun to break contact and were heading down towards Wireless Ridge. We carried on going through the process of clearing bunkers, all the way till we reached the far end of Full Back.

Pte Trevor Bradshaw

I left the bowl with Stu Dover. We ran over to the first piece of cover we could find. I had the night sight and could see figures in the distance, probably about eight or maybe ten of them. I could see that they were moving away from us. I felt fairly sure that they were Argentines, but I didn't fire on them, as I was concerned that they may have been men from our own platoon. I remember saying to Stu Dover, 'Shall I open up, to act as an indicator for the gun team?' But we decided they might be our lads, and that it just wasn't worth the risk.

As we were running across an area of open ground, two figures suddenly appeared in front of us. It turned out to be Dean Coady and LCpl Andy Allman, who turned and looked at me with big smiles on their faces. I don't think they realized how close they had come to me opening fire. We then moved through, clearing positions up to the far edge of Full Back. By then it was daylight and we were told to begin moving back and do a sweep through the area. There was now a ground mist.

Pte Davie Barclay

Cpl Louie Sturge led by example, firing 66mm's into many positions and encouraging the lads to follow him. We had to move across fairly open ground towards Full Back. As we reached it, I remember firing at an Argentine manning a SF machine gun; as I got closer, it became clear he was already dead, but the man had died still holding the gun. He was shot by a number of people who mistook him as a threat.

Major David Collett

Once 2 Platoon had established themselves on the ridge, I then sent 1 Platoon along the eastern slope, carrying out the same operation. By this time it was beginning to get light, and as 2 Platoon started getting closer to Full Back the enemy began to pull off the position. We started moving forward at a faster pace.

Sgt Manny Manfred

We briefed 1 Platoon, telling them that it would be 2 Platoon who would be first to leave the bowl, and that once they had a firm footing we would move out on to the eastern slope, followed by 3 Platoon. The platoons would all move in tactical bounds, supporting each other along to the Full Back position. Once there, we would go firm and form a defensive position.

Shortly after that, Captain Freer's gun group and the SF gun teams opened up. I remember someone saying what a bunch of noisy bastards they were. 2 Platoon then left the bowl. Our own artillery was still hitting Full Back, then it was our turn [1 Platoon], as we started down the eastern slope. We advanced in extended line; I was positioned on the left of the middle section and 2nd Lt Kearton was on the right of the middle section. It was still dark, but I could see the Platoon Commander in between explosions and muzzle flashes.

As daylight began to break, we saw the Argentines pulling out and beginning to run. At that moment we lost the tactical bounds and began to run after them, firing, caught in the excitement of the moment. The platoon ran past the end of the objective, they were in hot pursuit down the hill. It took a while to stop them chasing the fleeing Argies and get them back into a defensive position on Full Back.

Pte Mark (Chuck) Berry

We waited to be sent over in pairs – I would be skirmishing with Pte Jay Butler. I heard Lt Kearton shout to Cpl Paddy Barr, 'Corporal Barr, start sending your men over.' Paddy slapped my back and said, 'Are you ready? Go!' I quickly scrambled out and took up a fire position and began returning fire at green muzzle flashes. Soon the whole platoon was out across the eastern slope, skirmishing forward.

As daylight started to break, we saw them turn and run. We began to take larger bounds and completely passed our objective as we ran in hot pursuit. Lt Kearton and Sgt Manfred began shouting, 'Stop! Stop! Fucking stop, cease fire!' It was quite hard to stop as the adrenaline was pumping.

Pte Mick Carr

It was now our turn to move out of the First Bowl; it was starting to get light. I was looking out for any bits of cover. I was on the far right on the southern side of the eastern slope. There was still fire coming from Full Back. We moved forward slowly in pairs: I was with LCpl Gary [Gaz] Easter, with supporting fire from Pte Larry [Doc] Halliday's gun group. I could hear Sgt Jim McCallum constantly shouting at the top of his voice, 'Come on, 3 Platoon, keep pushing up, keep moving forward, and let's fucking show them,' and that's what we did.

Pte Stu Dover

There were a number of Argentines wandering about in a state of distress. I remember one looming out of the mist. He ran past me, stripped to the waist with cuts all over his upper body, clearly off his trolley, and he was being closely pursued by a member of 3 PARA with bayonet fixed. As we were moving back up the mountain, we noticed an Argentine SF team sitting in the rocks. We had somehow missed them during the advance as they hadn't fired a shot. They had just sat there, not wanting to attract attention. We took them prisoner and marched them off.

Cpl Mark Brown

When I returned from the RAP, I saw LCpl Pete Higgs and said, 'Pete, where's A Company gone?' He said, 'To be honest, Mark, I didn't see them go.' I sat down and decided to have a brew. While I was making some porridge an artillery round struck the rocks just above me. A substantial lump of rock fell off and landed on Pte [Jock] Wilson's chest – he moaned like fuck. Shortly after that there was a huge explosion on the other side of the large rock that we were taking cover behind. It was followed by the noise of people shouting urgently for a medic. Then someone said, 'Scouse McLaughlin's been hit!' Pete Higgs looked at me and said, 'Mark, can I go?' I thought, You're my 2ic, medic and radio operator, I don't really want you going missing. But I could see from the look in Pete's eyes, he was desperate to go and help. I said, 'Okay, Pete, but get straight back here.' That was the last time I saw him. I often think I should have said no.

Major John Patrick RA, 31 yrs – Forward Observation Officer, Battery RA

Our group moved down to join A Company, led by Major Pat Butler. We moved to a position somewhere between Fly Half and Full Back, slightly down the hill. We came under quite a lot of indirect fire, from what I thought were 105mm RCLs. They inflicted quite a lot of casualties amongst B Company. We ended up at the eastern end of Full Back and I got a good opportunity to accurately locate the enemy batteries: I could see the smoke from their guns and the three separate guns on the reverse slope of Sapper Hill. They were out of range of our own guns, but I was able to summon the Forward Air Controller and give him a fix. He subsequently managed to get an airstrike to go in. I also managed to engage a pack howitzer battery. One gun was on the forward slope and the remainder were behind a small hillock. I was able to neutralize them to the extent that the gun detachment pulled off the gunline and ran up into the hills. I could see the batteries on the Murray Heights to the south of Stanley: they were engaging us; you could see the smoke from their barrels quite clearly.*

Major Collett informs the CO that Mount Longdon is secure:

10.28hrs (zt): from C/S 19 to C/S 9: 'Now on position, very extensive position with Support Gun at end.'

10.28hrs (zt): from C/S 9 to C/S 19: 'Reorganize on north slope not on top or south.'

---

* Tape-recorded debrief from 1982 by Gen Sir Anthony Farrar-Hockley with Major John Patrick RA.

Major David Collett

Just after we reached Full Back the mist came down, but as we got to the edge of the feature we realized the extent of it. On our side of the feature was a 105mm recoilless which had been firing shells at us.

LCpl Graham Tolson

Sammy Dougherty decided to move us forward to another position. We followed him into the fog; it was so thick that if I allowed the man in front to get more than 5–6 feet away, we would lose contact with each other. After squeezing through a narrow opening in the rocks we stumbled upon a dead Argentine slumped over an anti-aircraft gun. Initially the Argentine soldier seemed to be alive, but when I got close to him I saw that he was full of bullet holes and his clothes were soaked with blood.

We arrived at the cliff face on the southern side of Mount Longdon and found a great place to set up the gun. The position overlooked the valley between Mount Longdon and Mount Tumbledown, although we couldn't see much because of the fog.

Sgt Manny Manfred

By now the last Argy stragglers were 800 to 900 metres away. We were instructed to pull off the southern side because there was a risk of direct fire coming from Mount Tumbledown. The threat was thought to be from .50 Cal and Cobra missiles, so we now pulled further back to consolidate and reorganize. I told 1 Platoon to get into cover. We then started removing the dead bodies out of the bunkers and climbing into them. We then started to take 105mm incoming fire from the racecourse in Port Stanley. The bunkers at this end of the mountain were full of all sorts of food, razors, toothpaste, cigarettes and drink. I watched as Captain James munched away on some liberated corned beef, while giving a fire mission at the same time, onto Argentines in the Moody Brook valley.

These positions are the Argentine B Company Headquarters.

Major David Collett

We occupied the Argentine positions, as they had been very well constructed – we then prepared for a counter-attack. There were large stocks of Argentine

7.62 ammunition in sandbags which we redistributed, and also large stocks of food and cigarettes. As the mist began to lift, the artillery barrage began in earnest. No one could move anywhere. It became lethal to move in the open, we just had to sit tight and make ourselves as comfortable as the situation would allow. The artillery was particularly heavy on our area and I tried to speak to Lt Col Pike, but he couldn't be reached. I spoke to Major Patton, who said, 'Do you want to pull the company back?' but I replied, 'No, we'll stay here.' This turned out to be fortunate, as the artillery fire switched further west onto Fly Half and the western slope. This went on for four or five hours; it seemed to go in waves up and down the mountain.

Pte Jeremy (Jez) Dillon
The area around Full Back was a scene of utter devastation, with smouldering abandoned kit, weapons and dead bodies lying around the area, some missing arms and legs. As we began moving back, Argentines were appearing out of small holes. I was sorely tempted to shoot one of them bastards as payback for Tim, but then common sense kicked in. These guys were beaten, some were in a very shocked and distressed state, wandering about in a daze, some were half dressed, clutching rosary beads. A mist had settled across the eastern slope – it was quite eerie.

Pte Len Baines
I was told to go back around to the northern side, where Major Collett had set up his command post. As I made my way around, I saw a leather belt with a pistol and a trench sword lying in between some rocks, and I thought, That's a nice souvenir. However, on closer inspection there was a wire attached to it: it had been booby-trapped.

I found a bunker near to Major Collett. My job now was to sort out any problems with radios. I noticed a dead Argentine lying nearby with his stomach hanging out and one of his legs almost blown off. His face was blackened; but he had a lovely pair of size ten boots on, and I thought to myself, They'll do me! But then I got called to go and sort out a problem with one of the radios. When I came back, I noticed the Argentine just had his socks on – someone had beaten me to the boots!

CSM Alec Munro

Full Back resembled a junkyard, with weapons and ammunition scattered all over the position. There was at least one .50 Cal, several shoulder rocket launchers, SAM-7 Grail rocket launchers, and dozens of FN rifles. I spotted some Argentines running along a gully to the north of our location towards Wireless Ridge. I asked Major Collett whether I should engage them. He said, 'Yep, crack on.' I fired a couple of rounds over their heads and they immediately went to ground. After a couple of minutes they got up and started running again, so then I fired a couple more rounds right in front of the lead man. It was then that RSM Ashbridge came over, screaming, 'Stop firing! You're shooting at C Company.' I was just ready for a head to head since I was of the opinion that he didn't have a clue what I was shooting at. Then someone shouted, 'They've stood up, they're surrendering.'

Pte Mick Carr

My group was located on the southern side of Full Back and had found a large shell hole in which Pte Doc Halliday, LCpl Gaz Easter and I took cover. While we were here Doc Halliday decided to start firing at Mount Tumbledown, but the return fire was tenfold and we decided to try and move back to another location. Doc Halliday was the first to go; he ran for it and only just made it. We decided it was too dangerous to try that, so we were now pinned down in this location for approximately four hours. There was constant machine-gun fire and sniper fire. We couldn't put our heads up without attracting incoming fire. The rest of A Company had been pulled onto the northern side of Full Back. In the end, we were only able to move with the help of Lt Jon Lee calling in artillery onto Tumbledown and dropping smoke. Lt Peter Osborne and Sgt Jim McCallum got the whole of 3 Platoon to give covering fire. We needed to move fast, so we decided to leave our webbing and just take our weapons and sprint back up towards Full Back and dive into the cover of the rocks. I returned later under cover of darkness and recovered our webbing.

Pte Len Baines

Some of D Company [Sgt Pettinger, Dickie Absolon, Jock Wilson and Zip Hunt] had come down to Full Back and began firing one of the Argy .50 Cals at enemy positions just north of Wireless Ridge, which caused the shelling to start again. They were told in no uncertain terms to stop firing, as you could hear the crump of the artillery being fired from Port Stanley, the whistle as they came in, and then the terrifying noise at the end as it rushed in to impact. I would close my eyes and brace for that split second and think, Is this it? Then it hits the ground with a huge explosive bang that shook the ground and the bunker, closely followed by the noise of shrapnel flying through the air and rocks and soil raining down. The artillery was truly the stuff of nightmares; sounds that I will never forget.

CSM Alec Munro

It was clear that we needed to rebrief for the defence phase. It was now broad daylight, and the mist had cleared completely. The Argentine artillery observers were having a field day.

We had to prepare ourselves for the possibility of a counter-attack. Major Collett ordered the Platoon Commanders and Platoon Sergeants to RV on Company HQ. No sooner had the Platoon Commanders and SNCOs closed in when there was a tremendous explosion just metres from our position. Whatever it was, it landed on the other side of some rocks, which protected us from the shrapnel. We were obviously being scoped [observed with binoculars] and it was agreed to disperse back to the platoon positions.

Later on, during a further lull, they returned for the briefing. The OC issued the tactical brief; I then briefed the SNCOs with regard to the reallocation of ammunition and equipment, an update on casualties, and any missing or damaged kit that needed replacing. It was important to clear the position of enemy bodies; I didn't want the lads sharing bunkers with corpses. I told them to search the bodies and take an item of identification off each one, so that we could put in a return for Brigade and pass on any intelligence gathered. They were instructed to put all the bodies into shell holes down the slope from the company area and cover them with ponchos. At this stage we didn't know how long we would be there.

Major David Collett

The Argies in this area were certainly well dug-in. They had store bunkers, clothing bunkers and weapon bunkers. The Company Commander's bunker, which I took over, was very secure. It had a .50 Browning outside it, and there were lots of weapons. We found SAM-7s, numerous SF GPMGs and dozens of FALs. The Argentine Company Commander had obviously left in a hurry as he'd left his pistol behind hanging up in the bunker. They had very good night-fighting capabilities; they had PNG goggles that were literally scattered around the position. They had weapon scopes, small NOD sights, and they also had the American version of the pocket scopes. We also found brand-new laser rangefinders in their boxes, virtually unused. The instructions were still in polythene.

LCpl Graham Tolson

CSM Sammy Dougherty turned up and said, 'Right, lads, you need to take your stuff and move around to the other side of here. Find some cover, and sort yourselves out.' We moved on to the northern side of Full Back and found a bunker. Its roof was constructed from solid slabs of rock. The inside was full of goodies; it may have been a QM store. We found bags of pasta, tins of corned beef, tins of fruit, candles, matches, batteries and thousands of packets of Jockey and Camel cigarettes. Tony Bojko sat down and started cleaning the gas parts of the gun. They were covered in carbon from firing thousands of rounds. Geordie Maddocks and I set about cleaning our rifles. I watched both of them, they were unusually quiet. They looked bedraggled and very tired.

Suddenly, we heard shouts of 'Incoming! Incoming!' It was like a ripple moving slowly towards us over the mountain, the explosions were getting nearer and nearer, louder and louder. We listened in total silence, holding our breath. We squinted up as dust fell from our vibrating roof. This went on for about two or three hours, and when it finished, I was worn out from automatically curling up in a ball each time I heard a loud explosion. It seemed to make every muscle in my body tighten with each near miss.

When the artillery took a break, we reappeared from our bunker. Sgt George Duffus appeared and said, 'How's it going?' 'Fucking shit,' I replied. He told us: 'The CO has ordered a clean-up operation. LCpl Tolson, I want you to take your gun group to the other end of the mountain to assist in the locating and collecting of our own dead.' For a moment I stared at him in almost disbelief. I squatted down and began to cry. I felt sick. Pete Maddocks helped me to my feet and ushered me away to the small bunker that we had found. For a minute or two we looked at each other in total silence. I was embarrassed by my behaviour because I was the NCO and he was a Private soldier. Geordie said, 'Do you want a brew?' 'Yeah,' I replied. I then said I was sorry about what has just gone on but Geordie said, 'Sorry for what, don't worry about it.' It was only after I had recovered my composure that I realized I had a condition called Battle Shock, something that affects many soldiers during a battle. Despite being debilitating, it was short-term and passed within a couple of hours.

Pte Tony Bojko

Our bunker was like an Aladdin's cave, it was full of all sorts of tins of food. We made a big meal of spaghetti and meatballs, and gorged ourselves, but it backfired as our stomachs couldn't stand the rich food. We ended up with 'Galtieri's revenge' [diarrhoea].

Sgt George Duffus

We were tasked to clear some small tents that were about 100 metres away, just north of the Second Bowl. Cpl Black reached the first tent and I shouted, 'Clear that tent, Joe!' He shouted a warning for anyone in the tent to come out, then fired about five rounds through the tent and shouted, 'Clear!' I said, 'That will do for me.' The tents were all empty, but just to the left of them was a trench. We looked in, and two Argentines stood up rather quickly. Pte Kev Darke, out of shock, punched the nearest one and knocked him out. The other one immediately threw his hands up.

Cpl Joe Black

Once the unlucky recipient of Kev Darke's right hook had came to his senses, we gestured to them to lie down. David Goldsmith and Jim Fearon watched over the two prisoners while Kev Darke and I thoroughly searched both of the prisoners, who were surprisingly clean. My trouser belt had just broken, so I gestured to one of the terrified Argentines to take off his trouser belt. The Argentine looked a bit alarmed, but complied.

Sgt George Duffus

We were tasked to look for any deceased members of 3 PARA. This task was allocated to us by the CO; he didn't want B Company having to pick up their own dead. It was a task that I didn't relish asking my blokes to carry out. But it had to be completed. This was a duty that was required to be done with dignity.

I shall never forget the discomfort we felt as we walked past the Third Bowl. I remember WO2 Sammy Doc Dougherty saying, 'Who is that?' On closer inspection, I discovered it was Sgt Ian McKay. He was lying head first, half in and half out of an Argentine trench. I instantly recognized him. In the trench with Ian were three dead Argentines with obvious fatal lower limb wounds, compatible with grenades exploding at ground level in the trench. Privates Kev Darke, Pete Maddocks, Tony Bojko and I lifted Ian out of the trench. Kev Darke removed Ian McKay's ID tags from around his neck and passed them to me. It was getting all a bit much by this stage. We then wrapped Ian in a poncho and carried him down to the RAP, where we placed him alongside our other dead.

Initially Ian's body had lain at the front of the Argentine bunker. However, as the night progressed that area was extensively shelled and also reoccupied by Argentine troops. We can only imagine they would have searched the bodies lying in that area, and somehow his body was either blown or placed into the bunker head first.

Pte Tony Bojko

One thing that will always stay with me was the smell of death on that hill. Unless you've been in that situation you cannot imagine what it's like. You often see photos of death and destruction, but the smell, it stays with you.

I came across Sgt Ian McKay. I nearly walked past the position, but then I noticed the British camouflage uniform. Also in the trench with him were a number of dead Argentines. There were Argentine weapons everywhere. I saw one of our blokes holding a prisoner by the neck and forcing him to go face to face with a dead British soldier. He was saying, 'Look what you've fucking done, you fucking bastard!' The prisoner was crying his eyes out.

Pte Ashley Wright

I rejoined A Company and broke the news that LCpl Chris Lovett was dead. To be honest, I was a little bit lost, as Chris and I were good friends. We had been together all the way across, and now I was on my own, without his cheery humour. Luckily, Pte Andy Broad and Pte Mark [Archie] Statham said, 'Come and join us in our bunker.'

Cpl Joe Black

Once we had found a solid Argy bunker with decent cover, we began making a brew. Most of the blokes were sitting eating Argy scoff, but I wouldn't eat any, as I still had some of my rations left. We were aware that Argentines were still being found hiding in all sorts of places. But there was no fight left in them.

As the rounds flew over us, I remember looking across at Cpl Louie Sturge, Cpl Laurie Bland and Sgt Gerry Carr, who were sitting talking with the CO, who was standing up with a mug of tea in his hand. The CO seemed to be quite unperturbed by explosions on the northern side. I popped my head back out and David [Goldie] Goldsmith shouted across to me, 'Joe, there's something wrong with my foot.' Kev Darke said, 'What's up, Goldie?' He said. 'I've been hit in the foot.' Kev replied, 'No, you haven't.' But Goldie insisted, 'I have!' 'Whereabouts?' said Kev. 'In my foot,' replied Goldie. Kev then got down to undo Goldie's bootlaces and blood started pouring out, so Kev left the boot on and told him to take his morphine but Goldie refused. They put a shell dressing around his boot and Kev piggy-backed him down to the RAP.

6.5   **'It just never seemed to stop'**

While they wait for a helicopter, a badly wounded member of C Company walks in. Pte Mark Blain's arm has been extensively lacerated by shrapnel from shoulder to wrist. They are both evacuated by helicopter at approximately 15.30hrs (zt).

Pte Trevor Bradshaw

Our platoon location was surrounded by rocks, so we felt a little bit safer. We thought we could judge by the whistle of the incoming rounds whether they would simply pass over us, or when we needed to dive for immediate cover, or when we had a few seconds to spare. People would hear the rounds coming in and say casually. 'Don't worry about that one, mate, it's going over.' But you could be so easily proved wrong.

Sgt Manny Manfred

I was getting quite annoyed with the lads. They were getting really blasé with incoming artillery fire. They could hear the crump of the rounds being fired and in their heads they thought they knew roughly the flight time. They would continue walking around, and at the last moment dive into cover. After a shell landed particularly close to one of the bunkers, we discovered that a piece of shrapnel had virtually cut someone's poncho roll in half. I think it was Pte Bob Dobson, who was the platoon 84mm anti-tank man. The guys seemed to take the artillery a bit more seriously after that.

Major David Collett

Having been away from the battalion for some time I'd arrived back with some trepidation of the standards of the younger soldiers, but the Falklands certainly taught me a lesson. Throughout the campaign they never complained, they were always saying, 'When are we going to Stanley?' 'When are we going to see the Argentinians?' When the time came, and we actually started coming under fire and assaulting positions, they always moved under orders, even when there was fire coming down. When A Company was heavily shelled the first day, they almost had a scornful disdain of artillery fire, partly through ignorance, I think, but also through sheer bravado. Their spirit was up the whole time and was very impressive.

Pte Tony Bojko

Later that day Sammy Dougherty said, 'Come and have a look at Stanley.' To me, after not seeing any built-up areas since we left Freetown in Sierra Leone, my first reaction was that it looked like a big metropolis, not some fishing village as I had first thought. It also seemed to me that we were within touching distance of victory.

Cpl Louie Sturge

I went forward for a good mooch around the enemy position just to see what trophies were to be had. Nineteen-year-old Pte Alan Sparrock came along with me.

There was an enemy observer out there somewhere on the ridge who had been watching us, and Alan and I heard the rounds being fired from the gunlines around Port Stanley. We had been occasionally shelled at our previous location [north of Mount Kent]. During that time, we had learned to predict the average point of impact, just by the tone of the shell flying through the air. Alan and I both looked at each other knowing that one of these might well have our names on it. We dived down behind a large boulder and squeezed close to each other.

Then, Whooomp, Whooomp, WHOOOMP, dirt and crap were landing everywhere; I was struck on the helmet by a huge sod of earth thrown up by the blast. My neck creaked and a pain shot straight up to the base of my skull. I realized that I was okay, but I had taken a good smack. I then became aware of Alan shouting, 'I've been hit.' I turned towards him and he was clutching his chest. I quickly unzipped his smock and pulled up his jumper to get down to the bare skin of his right side. A piece of shrapnel had ripped a large chunk out of the right sleeve of his windproof smock and jumper; it had glanced off his rib cage without drawing blood! Then it exited out of his top left-hand smock pocket, passing straight through a shell dressing, reducing it to shreds. What I then saw was the fastest-growing bruise that I have ever seen, it went from an egg size to saucer size in about ten seconds and it was getting bigger.

I decided we should make our way back to the platoon location. When we got back, Alan was told to make his way down to the RAP. I had a pounding headache and my vision was becoming blurred. I think it was Cpl Laurie Bland who put me in a bunker and told me to get some rest.

Pte Trevor Bradshaw
At one stage Stu Dover got one of the .50 Cals working and began firing short bursts of two or three rounds, but it kept jamming. Some bloke came up and said, 'I would stop that if I were you.' Stu said, 'And who the fuck are you?' The bloke said, 'I'm the FAC [Forward Air Controller] and every time you do that we're getting fucking shelled, now fucking stop it!'

One of the lads was due to go on stag but he didn't have a watch. Someone said, 'There's a pile of stiffs down there, go and see if one of them is wearing a watch.' So he went over to them, and after checking a couple of bodies, he found one wearing a wrist watch. He began taking the watch off, when the supposedly dead man moved and made a noise. The Argentine was still alive and had a very bad injury to his lower leg, and his foot was just about hanging on. Sadly, he died shortly after he was found.

CSM Alec Munro

I saw Pte John [Sid Vicious] Haire venturing out in front of the position and said to him, 'Where the fuck are you going?' He said, 'Sir, my stomach's in bulk, I'm going for a crap.' He was suffering badly with dysentery. He walked about 30 metres down the slope with his shovel, dropped his denims and squatted out in the open. I then heard the crump, crump, of artillery shells being fired from Stanley. You could hear them pass the culminating point as they started to whistle on the way down. These were going to land close and Sid must have thought the same. He judged it to the last second and then launched himself sideways into a shell hole, denims still round his ankles! I thought the worst for a moment, and then his head popped up from the shell hole, like a meerkat with a grin all over his face.

Pte Jeremy (Jez) Dillon

I remember sitting in a bunker and putting my arm around a member of A Company during one particularly bad period of shelling. He said, 'I fucking hate this,' and began to cry. I just said 'Don't worry about it, we'll be all right.' I'm not religious, but I remember praying to my dead father, praying that the next one didn't have our names on it. It just never seemed to stop. For me this was the hardest part of the battle.

CSM Alec Munro

As the day progressed Battalion HQ wanted me to send a return of enemy equipment found on our position. For some reason they wanted me to send a runner. It was a direct order of the 'You will' variety. I thought, Which half-wit, sat on his arse in Battalion HQ, wants me to risk someone's life to fill in a piece of paper?

I wasn't about to send any guys out to conduct an inventory check just to satisfy some bean counter, so arbitrary figures were plucked out of thin air. It made it all that more tense, as I waited anxiously to see if the runner had arrived back safely, after putting his life at risk to deliver a worthless piece of paper. There was still sporadic shelling on our position, but thankfully he got back okay.

We then got another request to send a resupply party to pick up rations. I said, 'We're under bloody shell fire here, we can survive.' I asked could it not be done under the cover of darkness, but was told they needed to clear the resupply area! Reluctantly, I asked the platoon sergeants to send a party from each platoon. It didn't take a genius to realize there was an artillery spotter out there who was directing fire down whenever someone presented a good target, particularly around the northern side of the feature. As a result of this idiocy, one of our men lost his life.

LCpl Kenny Watt, 24 yrs – 1 Section, 1 Platoon

Early on the Saturday evening, I was tasked by Sgt Manfred to take five members of 1 Platoon and join a resupply party which was made up roughly of a section from each platoon of A Company. On our arrival at the resupply area, A Company's resupply allocation had been laid out for collection. John Reeves and I gave the lads the ammunition first and warned them to be careful crossing any open ground. We sent them back to their platoon locations in pairs. Ged Bull was the last member of the resupply party to leave. He had a large ten-man ration box. There were only two of the 24-hour ration packs left, so I unzipped his smock and stuffed the two ration packs into his smock. I zipped it up and told him: 'Make sure you run like fuck when you reach the open ground.' He nodded and said, 'Will do, Kenny,' and away he went.

LCpl Graham Tolson

WO2 Sammy Dougherty asked Tony Bojko, Pete Maddocks and me to go down to the Regimental Aid Post, where a resupply area had been set up. We were to collect a dozen 24-hour ration packs, 2,000 rounds of belt ammunition and one water bottle per man. We took a water bottle off each member of our section and set off towards the resupply area.

We followed a narrow track which had been well used and was muddy. After 100 metres or so it disappeared and before me was a long slab of rock lying flat to the ground. I stepped up onto the slab and walked along its length to see that the trail continued at the other end. But the rock was thicker at the far end, so I jumped down. Protruding from the base of the rock was an arm, plus the head and shoulders of an Argentine soldier. The remainder of his body was out of sight under the rock. Pete and Tony caught up with me and we stood looking at the man. He was obviously dead and I saw a bubbly mixture of spit and blood seeping through the man's clenched teeth, forming a puddle on the ground. The colour of his face was ash white.

I led the patrol in the general direction of the RAP until we crossed onto Route 2. Just then I heard the sound of incoming. I screamed at the top of my voice, 'Take cover!' Other people were also shouting, 'Take cover.' But there was no cover. I dropped down and hugged the ground. The earth shook and trembled as the shells exploded one after another. Something thudded into the small of my back. It felt like I'd been kicked by a mule and I shouted, 'I've been hit!' Pete Maddocks ran over and knelt beside me, and said, 'Stay still, let me have a look.' He pulled my hand away from my back to assess my injury, then started laughing and said, 'You daft bastard, you've been hit by a lump of peat!'

We reached the RAP which was also a prisoner containment area. There were 20 or 30 Argentine prisoners, and a couple of them were wounded. I couldn't see any sign of the resupply area. Then I noticed Cpl John Sibley, one of the medics. He was changing a shell dressing on the head of one of the wounded Argentine soldiers. I watched as he removed the shell dressing that had been covering the soldier's head injury. What was revealed churned my stomach, and at the same time it made me marvel at the endurance of the human body. The young soldier had obviously been hit by either a bullet or shrapnel which had taken the side of his skull off, just above the ear. The hole was the size of my hand and I could see his brain through a yellowish sac. Surprisingly, there wasn't much bleeding, although his blond hair was matted with blood around the site of the injury. John began to redress the wound. While he was doing that, he looked up and asked me, 'What do you want?' 'Where's the resupply area?' I asked. He pointed saying, 'Around there.'

I looked ahead and saw Snowcat vehicles and trailers, with lots of people around them unloading stores. Eventually, having got our rations and filled the water bottles, I asked one of the QM's men, 'Where's the ammunition?' He told me, 'It hasn't arrived yet, but it won't be long. It's on its way as we speak.' We sat on the boxes of rations and waited. The battalion padre, Derek Heaver, stopped for a chat. He looked tired and drained, and from the redness of his eyes, I could tell he'd been upset. I told him about the soldier I'd seen with the head wound, and that he was expected to die, and that I felt sorry for him. He responded by saying, 'There's lots more like him and there's not much anyone can do except pray.'

The Snowcat finally arrived. We collected our ammo and started back the way we'd come. I heard the whistle of incoming artillery shells heading into the same area where they had landed in before. We took cover and looked towards the explosions. It was only a short exchange, so I decide to move on at speed and get back to our position before the next salvo came in. As I approached the Second Bowl, I was running along the sheep track with Pete Maddocks and Tony Bojko in hot pursuit. Suddenly I was confronted by the sight of a body dressed in British combat clothing lying face down in the grass. I went cold as I approached him. Tony and Pete followed, 'It's Ged Bull!' shouted Tony. I immediately told Pete and Tony to get into cover, and pointed over to the Second Bowl. I turned Ged's body over and realized immediately that he was dead. I became very emotional, my chest tightened, and I found it hard to breathe.

My attention was drawn by someone shouting loudly from the rocks above: 'Graham, Graham!' I looked up to see the silhouette of someone waving to me. He shouted, 'Quick, get your fucking arse up here!' I was jolted into the realization that we were still under mortar or artillery fire. I scrambled up into the Second Bowl to rejoin with Tony and Pete. I recognized the faces of Vincent Bramley, Steve Ratchford and John Skipper from the Machine Gun Platoon. As I reached the position, Vince grabbed my arm and helped me into his bunker. Down in the area I had just left, there were several explosions in quick succession. Vince said, 'You were fucking lucky there, mate.'

A Company report Pte Ged Bull's death to the RAP:

20.15hrs (zt): from C/S 1 to C/S 9A: 'Another fatality, Company Number A 107.'

Pte Mick Carr

At approximately 19.00hrs (zt), we were tasked to go and collect ammunition, rations and water from the resupply point. About halfway we were caught in an artillery or mortar barrage. We all took cover, and after the salvo ended, we picked ourselves up and carried on. At the resupply area, we loaded up with food, ammo or water and made our way back. Once again, we were caught in another barrage. We reached the platoon area and dropped our loads off, then made our way back for a second run. Again, we came under shell fire but this time they fell a lot closer to us. I was hoping that our luck would hold out as we picked up more supplies and began to make our way back.

I was behind Ged Bull, who was carrying a large ration pack, plus a number of individual ration packs stuffed into his smock. We reached the sheep track that ran between the First and Second Bowls. I stopped for a moment to adjust my load and shouted, 'Hang on, Ged!' but I don't think he heard me. Suddenly, a shell dropped really close by; there was a fucking big explosion. I thought, What the fuck was that? I couldn't hear anything. I was covered in shit. Then a couple more rounds dropped, and then it stopped as suddenly as it had started. I saw Ged lying on the ground. At first I found it hard to take in, like my brain couldn't absorb what I was seeing, his smock was torn and smoking and he was lying face down.

LCpl Kenny Watt

I climbed up into Pte Paul Audoire's sentry position, and he turned to me and said, 'Ged's dead.' I said in disbelief, 'Are you sure? Where is he?' He pointed to where Ged's body lay; I had just run past him, within perhaps 4 feet of him, and I hadn't even seen him. He was lying in the open and was clearly dead. I told Paul that I would tell the CSM [Alec Munro] and that he should inform Sgt Gerry Carr. On my return, I told CSM Alec Munro of Ged's death and gave him a rough description of where Ged's body lay. He then told me to go and get a brew on. I also told Sgt Manfred about what had happened. Pte Bob Taylor made me a brew, but I had only managed a few slurps of tea when Cpl Paddy Barr said, 'Manny Manfred wants to see you.'

Sgt Manny Manfred

I remember LCpl Kenny Watt returning and telling me that Ged Bull had been killed. I said, 'What happened?' He replied, 'Artillery, over by 2 Platoon's area.' I was really saddened by this and asked, 'Did anyone cover him up?' and he said, 'I don't think so.' I knew Ged Bull's body would have to be covered over, and asked Kenny if he would go back and do it. He asked me if somebody else could go. But I said, 'Kenny, it's nearly dark, and you know exactly where his body is.'

LCpl Kenny Watt

Manny said, 'Alec Munro wants you to go back and cover Ged's body.' I replied, 'Why me? Someone from 2 Platoon should do it.' Manny said, 'Ken, they're very close to Ged, they're his mates.' I was about to say, 'I was also his mate!' but I accepted the task and moved cautiously back along the feature to 2 Platoon's location, where I came across Cpl Laurie Bland standing with Sgt Chris Phelan and Cpl Louie Sturge. I told them what I had to do, and that I needed a poncho. Louie Sturge said, 'Kenny, I'll help you.' We found a poncho and made our way over to where Ged's body lay. Louie went to Ged's head and I took his feet. Ged had been very badly hurt and the task was extremely distressing, but we straightened Ged out, and treated him with dignity and respect.

Pte Davie Barclay

I'm not sure who told me, I just remember someone saying to me, 'Do you know Ged Bull's dead?' I couldn't believe it; I had only spoken to him about 30 minutes ago. I went back down towards the Second Bowl, where I saw a poncho covering a body. I pulled back part of it – I am not sure why, it may have been just for confirmation, but there he was. I was gutted, I knew Ged well. I had dated his sister and knew his mum and dad. I felt numb and made my way back and tried to compose myself.

That night we searched for anything that might help us keep warm. I found a bottle of Hennessy brandy and an extremely smelly blanket, so we passed round the brandy and then wrapped the blanket around ourselves and cuddled up for the night. We were shelled through the night, but I slept right through it.

Pte Trevor Bradshaw

As it began to get dark, I looked around for something to keep warm. I found a sleeping bag with a dead Argentine still in it. As it was bitterly cold, I took him out and climbed in. I later developed scabies, which I think I got from him.

LCpl Graham Tolson

I returned to our bunker and spent the next hour in total isolation and in the complete darkness of the bunker. I curled up in a ball, and closed my eyes, but I was so cold, and the prospect of going down with hypothermia weighed heavy on my mind. Pete and Tony returned from their sentry duty and crawled in alongside of me. They too were feeling the strain from the cold and we began to curse this place. Tony Bojko said that he'd had enough. He was going to go outside and search for something that might keep us warm. He returned some 20 minutes later with a couple of blankets. They smelled absolutely disgusting, but we didn't care.

The next morning, I woke up to see Pete and Tony sitting over a partially boiling mess tin of water. As I joined them, I noticed I had bloodstains on my trousers. 'Don't worry,' said Tony. 'It's from the blankets, we've both got blood on us.' I said, 'Where did you get them from?' 'A dead Argentine was wrapped up in them, but we needed the blankets more than him.'

6.6   'I remember thinking, I wouldn't like to be on the receiving end of that!'

SUNDAY 13 JUNE 1982

First light approximately 10.00hrs (zt).

Captain Adrian Freer

I spent most of Sunday under cover to avoid artillery fire. There was minimum movement. Men reinforced their positions and made them more comfortable. We were also busy cooking Argentine rations. Water was a problem. We had been spoilt at our last position as we'd had a stream running through the re-entrant. The previous day the company water party brought back the dirtiest water imaginable, to the extent that it defied purifying tablets. Sammy Dougherty and I were violently ill through the night.

Pte Ashley Wright

I woke to another freezing day, light snow, and more artillery bombardment. We could hear the artillery land at one end of the mountain, and then it would creep back along towards us. We could hear the explosions growing louder as they got nearer. The tension and strain on your nerves are very hard to describe. With each round I thought, This is the one; this is when I get it. This would be followed by the relief that you survived and the nervous laughter – till the next time. We stayed in our bunker all day.

LCpl Kenny Watt

CSM Alec Munro informed me that a Snowcat was coming forward to retrieve Ged Bull's body, and that a few of our radio batteries and ancillaries needed to be replaced. I was to take a 'Tom' with me to 2 Platoon's location and leave the kit by Ged's body. Then the equipment would be exchanged by the personnel in the Snowcat. I spotted Pte Phil Adkins and briefed him on what we had to do. We moved back towards 2 Platoon's position, where I was met by Cpl Mick Ferguson. I went over to Ged's body and placed the equipment by him. We then waited in a safe position where we could see Ged. The Snowcat arrived and DSgt Geoff Deaney jumped out. He then helped us to load Ged's body into the Snowcat.

11.55hrs (zt): from C/S 1 to C/S 0: 'With re-supply extra: 6 x 351 batteries / 8 x 349 batteries / 4 x 350 batteries.'

An Argentine soldier is found hiding up on top of the rocks at the Full Back position; he has been hiding there for the last 24 hours:

13.14hrs (zt): from C/S 9 to C/S 0: 'Be aware that 1 POW is being taken down to 9A, he is from the Command Post position which has just been located, awaiting brief from Acorn.'

['Acorn' is the code name for Intelligence Officer.]

LCpl Graham Tolson

We decided that we should go in search of sleeping bags, blankets or something similar. We couldn't go through many more nights like the ones we had just been through. We walked along the northern side by the Third Bowl. I noticed a group of soldiers putting Argentine bodies into shell holes, which they then marked by sticking the muzzle of a rifle into the ground and placing a helmet on the butt. I watched the youngsters from the work party, who were mucking about, pushing and shoving each other in a playful manner. I was amazed at their joviality since I was as glum as fuck.

A Company observe reinforcements being sent to Mount Tumbledown:

14.51hrs (zt): from C/S 1 to C/S 0: 'Considerable numbers of troops moving from Moody Brook to Tumbledown.'

Pte Jeremy (Jez) Dillon
I heard about Dickie Absolon, Mark Brown and Jerry Phillips being wounded, and later I saw 2 PARA Mortars moving up through Furze Bush Pass and watching airbursts exploding above them. We did nothing but stay in our area.

Cpl Stephen Hope dies on Sunday while on a ventilator in intensive care on board SS Uganda. *Unfortunately the exact time is not known.*

Sgt Manny Manfred
We received a message from CSM Alec Munro about clearing up our area, so I asked for volunteers to search for bodies and make up a burial detail. Pte Bob (Jock) Taylor and Pte John (Sid Vicious) Haire both volunteered. It was strange watching these two small men struggling with stretchers over the rough terrain with bodies that were now stiff with rigor mortis. I was doing something in my bunker when I heard someone laughing and looked out to see Bob Taylor and Sid Vicious standing with a laden stretcher, glaring over their shoulders as someone shouted, 'Fucking hell, it's Burke and Hare, the body snatchers.' They took the bodies to an area which was off to the northern side of Full Back, where there were some quite large 155mm shell holes and they placed approximately six or seven bodies in each.

I had a call of nature; I made my way to a quiet area behind a rock to drop my trousers. Suddenly, without any warning, there was a massive explosion really close to me. The shell buried itself into the ground, but the blast wave hit me, and blew my helmet cover off my helmet (it was only loosely attached). It rattled me to the core, and someone who had seen my helmet cover fly away popped his head over the rock where I was squatting and asked, 'Are you okay, Sarge?' I was still in a bit of shock and replied, 'I think so!' He shouted back over his shoulder, 'It's okay, he's alive.' I quickly realized that I had lost two fillings as a result of the near miss, but it could have been much worse.

Later that night, I looked on as Wireless Ridge was being attacked by 2 PARA. I told the lads to come and watch, as it was regimental history being made, and we had a grandstand view. I could tell by the colour of the tracer and the direction of the firing who was who. The defenders would fire at our guys and once the enemy positions had been identified, there would be a massive weight of return fire, and then it would go quiet for a while. The attack moved forward gradually, until the whole ridge was secured. I couldn't help thinking about what was to come. Moody Brook seemed a likely defensive position, and then the big one – Port Stanley.

Cpl Joe Black

I woke on Sunday to a light snow. We stayed in our area all day. Word came down that some members of D Company had been wounded, with one possibly fatal. Again, there was very little movement due to artillery fire. At about 21.00hrs (zt), Kev Darke came and told us that another member of the Anti-Tanks, LCpl Denzil Connick, had been severely wounded and would be extremely lucky if he survived, and that two other blokes had been killed in the same incident. We spent another freezing night on Longdon. We could hear 2 PARA and the Scots Guards attacking their objectives, but we never moved out of our bunker – it wasn't worth being out in the open.

CSM Alec Munro

We got the brief that Support Company would be moving down through us, later that night. They would be establishing a firebase just forward of 3 Platoon's position, to support 2 PARA during their attack on Wireless Ridge. That night I sat with CSgt Graham Markey in 3 Platoon's position. We had a grandstand view of the battle. I had spent over ten years in 2 PARA and watched, willing them on, as they put in their assault. The sky lit up with explosions, PARA illumination and tracer. The most impressive was the Argentine anti-aircraft cannon being fired in the ground role. I remember thinking, I wouldn't like to be on the receiving end of that! We could also hear the distinctive but surreal sounds of a C130 landing at Port Stanley Airport. Any member of the regiment would recognize it, since it was the aircraft we regularly parachuted from.

Pte Mark (Chuck) Berry

I carried out another ration run and managed to speak to LCpl Harry Wilkie, who said, 'Chuck, say nothing, but we're attacking Port Stanley tomorrow.' That night I was on a two-hour stag with Andy Broad when we heard a C130 landing at Port Stanley Airport. We reported it back to Company HQ.

22.23hrs (zt): from C/S 1 to C/S 0: 'Hear what sounds like a C130 at Stanley airfield, also lights at that location, a convoy of vehicles left Stanley for airfield 30 minutes ago.'

Argentine Cpl Gustavo Pedemonte, 7th Infantry Regiment

That evening I was taken to the airport and loaded on board a Hercules. This would be the very last transport plane to leave the Falklands Islands returning to mainland Argentina with its load of wounded.

23.35hrs (zt): from C/S 1 to C/S 0: 'Four–five vehicles moving Moody Brook to Stanley, C130 sounds as if it's taking off.'

23.45hrs (zt): from C/S 1 to C/S 0: 'Four to five vehicles now moving back from airport to Stanley.'

Pte Tony Bojko

I didn't do much on Sunday as the shelling was quite intense. It was too dangerous to go outside unnecessarily. That night, as 2 PARA attacked Wireless Ridge and the Scots Guards attacked Tumbledown, I was sat watching it all with my pants around my ankles, as I'd developed terrible dysentery and was being violently sick at the same time, thinking, Oh, fucking hell, I'm dying. I felt absolutely awful. I eventually crawled back into the bunker and snuggled up to the blokes for warmth.

MONDAY 14 JUNE 1982

First light approximately 10.00hrs (zt).

Pte Len Baines

Another cold morning, with sleet. There was still shell fire going both ways, but for once they didn't seem to be shelling us. It was noticeably quiet on Longdon. The OC, Major David Collett, and his Platoon Commanders were going for their orders group with the CO, for the forthcoming night attack. Surprisingly, we all seemed up for the last big push and hopefully it should be over soon.

Orders group held at 12.00hrs (zt).

During the 'O' Group, first report comes in concerning enemy troops moving back into Stanley:

12.10hrs (zt): from C/S 0 to C/S 9: 'Enemy withdrawing from Sapper Hill, unconfirmed report 300 enemy withdrawing.'

12.50hrs (zt): from C/S 0 to All Stations: 'All stations to be on 30 minutes notice to move.'

Rumour control now goes into overdrive.

CSM Alec Munro

The OC went off with Sgt Mac French for a CO's briefing. We already had an idea that it was going to be about attacking Moody Brook. I was sitting in a bunker with Lt Jon Lee, our FOO; we were scoping out the firing positions of the 155mm artillery pieces. While we were doing this we saw long lines of troops streaming off Tumbledown, and I thought, What's happening here? They're all going back towards Stanley. I got my binoculars out and there seemed to be hundreds of them. I said to Lt Lee, 'You had better get on to your guys and tell them they're all out in the open and they're withdrawing.' I got on the battalion radio and told the young signaller to get hold of the CO and tell him the Argentines were pulling off Tumbledown and pulling out of Moody Brook. I thought that whatever the brief was that was being given, it was rapidly being overtaken by events. Later, Dave Collett came running up to our location and said, 'Right, get the company ready to move, now!' I did a quick brief to the Platoon Commanders and sorted out the line of march. 3 Platoon would lead, followed by Company HQ then 1 and 2 Platoons.

A Company move off Longdon at approximately 15.30hrs (zt).

CSM Alec Munro

I could see that 2 PARA had reached the same conclusion as us and were already heading along Wireless Ridge toward Moody Brook. Regimental pride was at stake. There is no doubt both units wanted to be the first into Stanley. It was going to be a race to get there. As we reached Wireless Ridge, C Company of 2 PARA were virtually at the double trying to get in front of us.

As we moved on to the Ross Road we were intermingled with C Company from 2 PARA, but 2 PARA's D Company were ahead of us and stormed up the road towards the racecourse. We were just glad that the two battalions of the Parachute Regiment had the honour of being the first troops into Port Stanley. We reached the far end of the racecourse and were told to stop and go firm. Major Dave Collett said, 'Sgt Major, go and commandeer one of those houses for Company HQ.' I found a house in the line of bungalows that appeared to have been vacated, so we moved in. We got the platoons sorted out in the other houses and watched as the remainder of the two battalions came up the road.

Much later on, the first units of the Marines were coming down the road to pass through our positions. It's probable that Brigade had wanted the Marines to be seen as the liberators of Port Stanley. We had some friendly banter with them as they passed by, looking at our watches and saying, 'What time do you call this?' and other annoying phrases. They were not amused. That, of course, was the very effect we were looking for. The Marines later set up a flag-raising ceremony at Government House in front of the Press.

Pte Mark (Zip) Hunt, D Company

We had been told that 3 PARA would now pass through 2 PARA and attack the racecourse in Port Stanley. C Company would be leading, followed by A Company, and our patrol had been told to tag on to the end of A Company. Suddenly it got passed down the line by word of mouth that the Argentines had surrendered – even though I was carrying a radio, I heard it off the lads before it came over the radio. I was absolutely delighted, but at the same time we had been warned that we were now moving through an area that was mined, and I thought, Don't want to lose my leg now that it's over, but I thought to myself, If I am meant to stand on a mine, I will, it's fate. Ahead of us we could see 2 PARA moving off Wireless Ridge, so we cranked it up and then the race was on to be the first British unit into Stanley.

Captain Adrian Freer

3 PARA had been tasked to take Moody Brook supported by 2 PARA; the Welsh Guards and 40 Commando, backed by a troop of the Blues and Royals, were to take Sapper Hill. Suddenly, we were moving off Mount Longdon. Then we heard the first reports of an Argentinian surrender. Both 2 PARA and 3 PARA were the first units into Port Stanley. I was slowed down by the fact that I had to collect Argentine stragglers with my group. The pace had been very hot, but with the heavy support equipment that we were carrying, we could not keep up with the lead platoons.

On the way in we passed the Argentine gun positions that had given such a hard and unpleasant time on Mount Longdon. We picked up more prisoners by the FIGAS [Falkland Islands Government Air Service] hangar. When we arrived in Stanley no one quite knew what was happening. It turned out that the Argentines had apparently not surrendered and negotiations would not start till 20.30hrs (zt). We just sat around for some time before occupying some houses on Ross Road West.

17.08hrs (zt): from C/S 1 to C/S 9: 'We have got 5 prisoners, what do we do with them? Wait out, we will find out from Brigade.'

Pte Jeremy (Jez) Dillon

As we made our way to Wireless Ridge it started to get passed down the line that they had surrendered. I thought, Fucking hell, it's finished and I'm still in a minefield! We eventually passed over Wireless Ridge and down through Moody Brook. By then the guys were taking their helmets off and putting berets on. We were eventually stopped just before the old war memorial and then pulled back a bit. We all sat outside a line of bungalows and brewed up. Later we watched the Royal Marines arrive and they marched straight past us, while trying not to look at us. We were then told that we could commandeer a bungalow.

Cpl Joe Black

I distinctly remember seeing a white flare go up from Port Stanley, and shortly after that it came over the radio: 'They've surrendered.' Then it was helmets off, berets on, and the race for Stanley was on. Sammy Dougherty said to us, 'Listen in, you lot, we will be passing through a possible minefield, I want you to walk in the footsteps of the man in front, we don't want any more casualties now that it's finished.' As we moved towards Wireless Ridge, I was passing blokes who were just dropping their trousers, as quite a lot of blokes had dysentery and they just had to go whenever nature called.

It wasn't a sort of triumphant entrance. There was what I can only describe as a battle mist. A smoky haze hung in the air, the smell of cordite and smoke from damaged buildings. The place was a complete mess, there was no celebration. We were eventually told to halt; we all sat at the side of the road waiting for a decision to be made by higher up. Captain Adrian Freer and Sammy Dougherty then told us that we were to go into one of the houses that line Ross Road. We were to clean up and find a space to rest. The Mortar and Anti-Tank Platoons liberated quite a few crates of beer that night.

LCpl Graham Tolson

I'm not sure what the exact briefing was or who gave it, but the gist of it was, 'Prepare to move.' We were told that there had been reports of the collapse of the Argentine forces. We quickly began advancing towards Wireless Ridge. I was quite wary as I felt there was a likelihood that we were moving through a minefield. I noticed some of the lads in front were dancing and cheering, and I wondered what was going on. Pte Ilija Lazic shouted back, 'They've fucking surrendered!'

I looked towards Port Stanley and there it was: confirmation of the Argentine surrender. I could see an Argentine Huey helicopter flying low, circling the Sound, with a white sheet hanging from a weighted hawser. [This may have been one of the Argentine helicopters loading wounded Argentine personnel on board the hospital ship ARA *Almirante Irízar*.]

We continued our advance towards Moody Brook. 2 PARA were also heading into Moody Brook. My section had reached the track that leads up to the Ross Road West; in the distance I could see the Beaver hangar with its bright Red Cross symbols. Sapper Hill rose up to my right. The racecourse was in full view, with the Argentine 105mm Howitzers dug in just to the west of it. They stood silent, an ominous sight. We eventually walked to the edge of Stanley and went firm at the side of the road.

I had very mixed emotions at the time – I was proud of my unit and all it had achieved, but I was also saddened by the losses. I was physically and mentally shattered. 2 PARA had won the race into Stanley, but it didn't matter. At least the Parachute Regiment came first and second. After a short time we moved forward to the houses that were on Ross Road West. Tony Bojko, Pete Maddocks and I took up a position at the garden gate of one of these houses. We all huddled around a hexamine stove, making a brew, while sitting on the pavement.

The rest of 3 PARA continued to arrive. There was plenty of banter between us; there was an air of mutual respect between us all. Everyone appeared extremely relieved that the hostilities were over. I spotted a group of about ten people coming down the road; they stood out from the crowd. Their uniforms were relatively clean and they weren't wearing cam cream! As they got nearer to us, there was a bloke in a green waterproof jacket, smoking a pipe. He was clearly an important person [Brigadier Julian Thompson] with his entourage. As he walked past, he said, 'Well done the PARAs.' I thought, Yeah, that's fucking right.

Pte Len Baines

We were halfway between Longdon and Wireless Ridge when it came over the radio, 'White flags in Stanley.' Then shortly after we were told, 'Helmets off, berets on.'

When we reached Moody Brook we were told to 'make safe' our weapons and only to fire in self-defence. I noticed an Argentine sentry standing to attention, as if he was on a parade ground, with his rifle held tight by his side, gripping the pistol grip; he was guarding some oil drums as two Parachute Regiment battalions streamed past him! Eventually he was disarmed and taken prisoner. We stopped and searched some of the Argentinians at the field first aid station [Beaver Hangar] on the Ross Road. We disarmed them and then carried on down the road. We passed the Argentine 105mm guns that we later found out had previously been owned by the 7th Royal Horse Artillery, and continued into Stanley. We came to a stop somewhere along the coast road and then just sat at the side of the road waiting for orders as to what to do next. Eventually, we were told to occupy the bungalows along Ross Road. Shortly after we had moved in, three Argentine Huey Helicopters landed at the back of the bungalows. The crews all surrendered, the helicopters were then liberated for souvenirs. I managed to obtain one of the pilots' helmets, which I still have.

Sgt Manny Manfred

We were moving towards Moody Brook, while watching the ground very carefully, when the radio operator Pte Andy Broad, who was behind me, shouted to someone who was talking, to 'Shut the fuck up.' Then he spoke into his radio and said, 'One One Alpha, say again, over.' Then after a short pause, he said, 'One, One Alpha, Roger, out.' I turned to listen to what the message was, and Andy Broad smiled and said, 'They're saying that there's white flags flying in Stanley, they've surrendered.' There was a lot of cheering, but I thought to myself, Just our luck to be in a minefield when they surrender. I told the blokes, 'Do not switch off yet, it's still very dangerous.' But people were starting to accelerate, they could see 2 PARA streaming down from Wireless Ridge; it didn't take a genius to work out what was going on.

Sid Vicious [Pte Haire] had a bad case of dysentery and was struggling to keep up. I noticed a Snowcat vehicle passing, so I flagged it down and I told the driver I had a sick man who was struggling and needed a lift. They said, 'Okay, tell him to come over.' Sid made his way across and climbed in, but it was a very confined space in the Snowcat, and he stank of shit. After about 200 metres the Snowcat stopped, the door opened, and Sid was unceremoniously ejected, windmilling to keep his balance.

It seemed no time at all that we were on Ross Road West, heading into Port Stanley. Then we were told to stop. We sat at the side of the road waiting to be told what to do next, as no one seemed to know. Eventually CSM Alec Munro came along and allocated us various bungalows. My platoon went in and we rolled the carpets up so they wouldn't be damaged by our dirty boots and kit. My first visit was to the flush toilet. Unfortunately, the Argies had turned off the water and power the night we attacked Longdon, so I had to put it out of bounds until we could get buckets of water to flush it with.

Pte Trevor Bradshaw

We made our way to Wireless Ridge and down into Moody Brook. The barracks was devastated, it was a smoking ruin. It really felt and looked like a war zone. By now we had taken off our helmets and put our berets on, and at this stage people were in a lighter, jovial mood. I took some photos of our section on the Ross Road, but the NCOs were keen to keep us focused saying, 'Don't piss about, keep focused.' Smoke was drifting across the road. When we took over one of the bungalows, it was eerie, like someone had just got up and left the room. There was a half-eaten meal and the kettle was still warm.

CHAPTER SEVEN

'THIS ISN'T A FUCKING GAME!'

C COMPANY 3 PARA

'Almost immediately we began receiving fire'

FRIDAY 11 JUNE 1982

Major Martin Osborne, 36 yrs – Officer Commanding C Company

On 10 June I received my orders concerning the role that C Company would play in the forthcoming Brigade three-phase plan, to capture the high ground around Port Stanley. The battalion's mission was to capture Mount Longdon and my company's role would be to act as the reserve company. I was to move the company into a position where we could assist or reinforce either A or B Company. Once B Company had secured their objective, we were to exploit as far as possible along Wireless Ridge with A Company.

On Friday 11 June 1982 at approximately 15.00hrs (zt), C Company begin moving from their company location (grid reference 224786.) The order of march is 7 Platoon leading, followed by C Company HQ and 8 Platoon, with 9 Platoon bringing up the rear. They are to rendezvous at A Company's location, codenamed 'Apple Flake', which is a four-hour march away and situated 4 kilometres south-east of their present location (at grid 265767). 'Apple Flake' is to be the assembly area for the entire battalion.

The battalion begin leaving this area shortly after last light, with each company guided by members of D Company to the crossing point at the Murrell River

2 kilometres away. This area is also secured by elements of D Company. The river is to be bridged by 9 Squadron RE, and once across the river, they will march north, then east to an area (grid 304763) codenamed 'Slim Rag'. After they reach this location, they will continue east to the Furze Bush Stream (grid 314764). The stream runs north to south, it is quite shallow and can be easily crossed. Once across they will be on the Battalion Start Line, codenamed 'Jungle Boot'. The company will then push east to their reserve position (grid 330760). Once there the company will be positioned in such a way that it is out of contact, but will remain close enough to be able to react in support of the Battalion Command's plans or contingencies. They are to remain in this location until they receive any further orders.

CSgt Andy Gow, 27 yrs – CSgt C Company HQ

At the time, I was a spare senior NCO, having recently been the CQMS [Company Quartermaster Sergeant] for C Company and had been recalled from my pre-RMAS [Royal Military Academy Sandhurst] instructor course. I would be part of C Company Headquarters. As I had only just finished a first-aid instructor course, my role would be as part of the Company Aid Post team. Our task would be to set up a Company Aid Post area and deal with any casualties prior to their evacuation, and assist the CSM with any resupplies.

Cpl Richard (Dickie) Bishop, 26 yrs – D Company (Patrols) attached to C Company

My patrol Call Sign 43B would meet with C Company and guide them to the Battalion Start Line via a crossing point at the Murrell River. The only problem was the delay caused by the previous rifle companies crossing the Murrell River – as you can imagine, crossing a river in the dark, over a ladder with a plank strapped to it, is quite an awkward thing to do while carrying full kit and ammunition for a battalion attack.

Cpl Bishop's D Company Call Sign 43B consists of L/Cpl Joe McKeown, L/Cpl Pete Deakin and Pte Surinder (Raj) Rajput.

Cpl Boyd (Smudge) Smith, 22 yrs – D Company (Patrols) attached to C Company

The Murrell River is about 5 feet deep, and is fast flowing, although the river isn't very wide, only about 8–10 feet wide. The river banks are quite steep and about five feet high in places: wading across the river at night would not be an option. Eventually we located a suitable crossing point roughly 700 metres north of the Murrell Bridge. A temporary bridging structure was constructed using a scaffolding board and two ladders strapped together, which was then placed across the river.

With the makeshift nature of the structure, the task of shuffling across a scaffolding board in the dark carrying huge amounts of ammunition was taking longer than expected, and a number of soldiers fell in the river. I remember one lad being pulled out; he'd fallen in carrying his enormous Bergen and a GPMG, and by the time he was pulled out he'd half drowned. Finally, A Company were all across, they then marched off into the night. By the time B Company had crossed it was clear that the timings were running late.

Cpl Smith's D Company Call Sign 43C consists of Pte Mick (Robbo) Robson, Pte Gary (Gaz) Pullen and Pte Bruce (Aussie) Straughan.

Lt Barry Griffiths, 24 yrs – Officer Commanding 7 Platoon

I had taken part in a reconnaissance patrol of the Mount Longdon area the previous night, so I was familiar with the route. Unfortunately, when we reached the crossing point, there was a large backlog of troops waiting to cross the river, so we had to wait while B Company and Support Company crossed. Eventually we got C Company across and began moving at a fairly fast pace, but due to the battalion bottleneck at the river, we were now running late.

Due to the bottleneck crossing the river, it is not until approximately 22.50hrs (zt) that C Company finally manage to cross. They are still 3.8 kilometres from the Battalion Start Line, and a further 1.3 kilometres from their reserve position. The battalion H-Hour is 00.00hrs (zt).

SATURDAY 12 JUNE 1982

B Company and Support Company have been forced to divert from their intended route of march due to time delays at the river crossing.

B Company has reached their position on the Start Line:

00.30hrs (zt): from C/S 29 to C/S 9: 'Now across Jungle Boot [Battalion Start Line].'

On hearing B Company have begun their advance, the CO immediately orders A Company to begin their advance towards the Furze Bush Pass, where they will shake out into assault formation facing south:

00.31hrs (zt): from C/S 9 to C/S 19: 'Call Sign 1 move now.'

Support Company have just reached their firebase location:

00.31hrs (zt): from C/S 59 to C/S 9: 'Going firm (Free Kick) ready in five minutes.'

C Company are marching flat out trying to catch up:

00.31hrs (zt): from C/S 39 to C/S 9: '1000 metres from Jungle Boot.'

A Company have now reached a position approximately 800 metres north from Wing Forward. They are in dead ground and will form up into assault formation facing south and then begin advancing towards Wing Forward:

01.00hrs (zt): from C/S 19 to C/S 9: 'Now static.':

01.07hrs (zt): from C/S 29 to C/S 9: 'Contact wait-out.'

Shortly after C Company cross the Battalion Start Line; Cpl Milne of 4 Platoon steps on a mine located on the north-west corner of Longdon. Almost immediately there is a huge return of fire aimed at the north-western corner; C Company's position on the Start Line is at approximately a 45-degree angle from the north-west corner of Longdon, and they now begin to receive direct and indirect fire from Longdon; also the enemy defensive artillery fire is called on all possible approaches.

Cpl Richard (Dickie) Bishop

There was very little to navigate off other than Mount Longdon itself, so I used the left-hand shoulder of the mountain as a reference point, and kept it at the two o'clock position. Eventually we reached the area of Furze Bush Stream, which had fairly steep rocky sides. We had to scramble down some rocks to cross the stream, but they were nothing, only maybe 9 or 10 feet high. We crossed the stream and then moved towards our position on the Battalion Start Line. B Company's position on the Start Line was to be off to our right, but as we were running late, there was no one here, as both A and B Company had already started their advance. I remember saying to Lt Griffiths, 'Sir, this is the Start Line.' My patrol then received a message telling us [my patrol] to push forward, to provide extra protection for C Company HQ. I now met up with Cpl Paddy Rehill [MFC]; Major Osborne was off to my left. The battle on the mountain had now started, and the Argentine artillery began firing on their pre-registered DFs. Almost immediately we began receiving fire from Longdon.

Cpl Boyd (Smudge) Smith

When we arrived at the Start Line, both A and B Company had already started their advance. Cpl Bishop's patrol led 7 Platoon to the northern end of the Battalion Start Line. We now paused for a moment, when suddenly we began taking indirect machine-gun and small-arms fire from Mount Longdon. Although the fire was mainly passing overhead, it was quite intense as the rounds zipped through the air.

Unfortunately, C Company's position on the Battalion Start Line at grid 314764 had been identified and reported by D Company 3 PARA and was included in the Intelligence Summary No. 16 covering 060900 (zt) to 062100 (zt) June 1982 stating 'an SF DF was located at grid 314764'. But it was thought the entire battalion would have passed through this location before any contact had been made, and all of the rifle companies would have been in their respective positions.

Lt Barry Griffiths

Shortly after we moved on to the Start Line, we came under pretty heavy machine-gun fire, but fortunately it passed overhead.

Sgt Martin (Dickie) Bird, 29 yrs – Sergeant, 8 Platoon

Shortly after A and B Company engaged the enemy we came under an awesome amount of fire, which was probably the stuff that was being fired at B Company. It was bloody awful; we were lying in the open and it was sickening to hear the enemy small-arms fire passing just over the top of us.

Things are going relatively well for A Company. Although there is a large amount of small-arms fire being fired at them, it is passing overhead, and they are steadily advancing uphill towards Wing Forward.

01.25hrs (zt): from C/S 19 to C/S 9: 'We have not encountered any opposition.'

01.30hrs (zt): from C/S 9 to C/S 19: 'Are you too far forward for us to call down artillery fire on Rum Punch.'

01.30hrs (zt): from C/S 19 to C/S 19: 'No, we are clear.'

A Company continue advancing over the crest of the ridge leading to Wing Forward, when suddenly the small-arms fire becomes more effective and the decision is made to take cover in the peat banks to their immediate front. During this movement Cpl Hope is wounded. A Company are now approximately 600 metres from the base of Mount Longdon.

Major Martin Osborne

Artillery was also beginning to land around us, and I realized we were being bracketed by the enemy artillery. I decided to move the company to the northeast into lower ground, but we were bracketed once again. I then moved the company south and pushed further east. Eventually we reached our reserve position, where I carried out a battle appreciation and acted accordingly. Although we were in the slightly lower ground, it did not prevent us from continuing to receive small-arms fire.

At 01.40hrs (zt), after an extremely fast march, C Company reach their reserve position. They are now situated approximately 100 metres behind A Company. Major Osborne makes contact with CO Hew Pike, to find out if there is any task for C Company. He is told to 'go firm'. Major Osborne now calls in his Platoon Commanders to give them an update on what is happening.

CO Hew Pike informs Major Osborne there is no task for him at present:

01.40hrs (zt): from C/S 9 to C/S 39: 'Stay where you are. You will have some sport later on.'

Lt Barry Griffiths

It was shortly after this that all the C Company Platoon Commanders were called in for an 'O' Group. While I was away from 7 Platoon,, Sgt Robinson detailed one of the sections to recover a casualty from A Company, who lay wounded out to the front of 7 Platoon.

Cpl Boyd (Smudge) Smith

As we moved into the reserve position, my patrol had tagged on to 7 Platoon, who were now directly behind A Company. We could hear them urgently shouting for a medic, and we could see the silhouettes of people. I estimate A Company were roughly 100 metres to our front.

A Company now inform the CO that they have taken one casualty (Cpl Hope):

01.52hrs (zt): from C/S 19 to C/S 9: 'This Call Sign has one casualty; we are pinned down by sniper fire and are staying put until cleared by Call Sign 2.'

01.52hrs (zt): from C/S 9 to C/S 19: 'Roger.'

Lt Barry Griffiths

Not long after we moved into the reserve position we came under machine-gun fire; this fire was aimed at A Company as they had begun returning fire. However, the return fire was only just passing over C Company's position.

CSgt Andy Gow

We had now reached our reserve position, just to the rear of A Company. The area where we were located was rather boggy, and I noticed off to my left a slight hollow with a huge shell hole in it. This shell hole was fairly deep and wide, and I thought it would provide us with some extra cover. We decided this would be our Company Aid Post location, and our group now took cover in the shell hole. We decided that in the event of anyone being wounded, one of the two medics would attend, and then the casualty would be brought back to us and we would centralize any wounded here. I'm not sure how long it was until we heard someone shouting, 'Medic!' Dave Stott turned to me and said, 'I'll take this one.' I agreed and said, 'Okay, if you need help just shout.' He then crawled off into the darkness, across to where the shouting had come from.

LCpl Dave Stott crawls across to 7 Platoon. He is then detailed by Sgt Robinson to go forward with a section and recover a wounded member of A Company lying about 50 or 60 metres to their front.

Major Martin Osborne

The enemy artillery was repeatedly adjusting its fire onto us, and I had to keep the company moving continually during the night; I had them digging shell scrapes, and then moving before 'fire for effect' was called. This annoyed some of the younger members of the company. They thought they were being fucked about, as they were not aware of the process of bracketing.

Pte James (Scouse) O'Connell, 22 yrs – Anti-Tank Platoon attached to C Company

I could see the battle taking place on Longdon: there was tracer going in all directions and I remember seeing multi-coloured explosions up on Fly Half. Around us you could hear the noise of shrapnel and tracer whizzing through the air; it seemed to be passing only inches above us, it was incredibly close. Geordie Nicholson and I both began to dig shell scrapes. We had one digging tool between the two of us – Geordie had a pick, but you couldn't raise yourself up to swing the pick because of the incoming fire. We were hugging the ground and clawing at the sodden peat, trying to dig a hole with our hands.

CSgt Andy Gow

Shortly after Dave Stott had left the Company Aid Post, someone else began shouting for a medic. Cpl Harding-Dempster now crawled off into the darkness. At this stage, there were shells landing all around C Company's area.

Cpl Harding-Dempster makes his way to 8 Platoon; Pte Scott Fuller has sustained a leg wound. LCpl Stott's group now locates Cpl Hope.

LCpl Paul Read, 21 yrs – 7 Platoon

The Argentines began calling in defensive fire on their pre-registered targets to the north and north-west; they were also putting up illumination rounds to try to locate our positions. At some point a group of us [LCpl Dave Stott, Pte Tony Gregory, Pte Mark Blain and others] were tasked to go forward and recover a casualty who was just to the rear of A Company and about 50 metres to our front. We cautiously made our way out, moving to roughly where the shouting was coming from. The person who we were looking for had now gone quiet, then out of the darkness a voice called out, 'Don't shoot, I'm a medic from A Company.'

Pte Ashley Wright

I heard voices, and wasn't sure who they were. I thought, Fucking hell, I hope they don't shoot me, so I shouted out, 'Don't shoot, I'm a medic from A Company.' I then heard Dave [Stotty] Stott shout back, 'It's okay, we're C Company,' and then a group of C Company appeared. I said, 'It's Steve Hope, he's been shot in the head.' Stotty replied, 'Okay, I'll need to check him over.' He quickly got his pen torch out and did a quick check of Steve, and then applied more shell dressings.

While Stotty was doing this, mortar rounds were beginning to fall around us. He said, 'Right, lads, we need to get him [Cpl Hope] back to C Company.'

Cpl Martin (Taff) Richardson, 26 yrs – Anti-Tank Platoon attached to C Company

I shouted to my section to keep well spaced out, as artillery rounds seemed to be dropping all around us. I shouted, 'Who's carrying the IWS?' and Pte O'Connell replied. I said, 'Bring it over, I want to have a look and find out what the fuck's happening.' As I went to put my head up, machine-gun fire swept across our position – there seemed to be shit coming from everywhere. After a short while there was a bit of a lull, and then more incoming artillery. Suddenly a 155mm round dropped in among us; it buried itself deep in the peat, and there was an absolutely deafening explosion, throwing huge amounts of peat and bog water into the air. I yelled, 'Is everyone okay? Sound off.' Everyone began counting off, but when it got to Geordie Nicholson, he shouted, 'Scouse has been hit!'

Pte James (Scouse) O'Connell

I remember Cpl Taff Richardson shouting, 'Who's got the IWS?' I shouted back, 'Me.' He then warned me to be careful, and bring it over. I crawled across to his position and then crawled back to my half-dug shell scrape. The next I remember was being thrown backwards – something passing from forward left to right had glanced across my face. My helmet had come off, my front teeth were missing and my mouth was filling up with blood. I knew something was badly wrong with my face, and straight away, I put my hand to my face, and thought, Oh fuck! I felt across the right side of my face; I had a large hole in it; my cheekbone and right eye were missing. I ran my hand across the centre of my face and I couldn't feel my nose.

I heard Geordie Nicholson shouting, 'Scouse, are you okay?' Although we were not far apart, it was dark, and it was not safe to put your head up. I shouted back, attempting to sound calm, 'No, I've been hit.' He then asked, 'Where have you been hit?' and I replied, 'In the head.' He shouted back, 'Okay; I'll come over in a minute, just hang on,' as there was still tracer flying through the air and incoming rounds landing. He crawled over and said, 'Okay, Scouse, where've you been hit?' I said, 'It's my face, Geordie!' He took his small army torch out, shone it my face and said, 'Fucking hell!' I knew from his reaction it was bad.

7.2   'This is fucking madness!'

Meanwhile, back with Cpl Hope.

LCpl Paul Read

We managed to slide a poncho half-underneath Cpl Hope and then lifted him onto it, but almost as soon as we began to carry him we began to struggle. He was a heavy bloke, probably 16 or 17 stone. There were bits of shrapnel whizzing everywhere, tracer fire was passing overhead, and we had no choice but to take cover a couple of times. Somehow we managed to drag him back to C Company.

Lt Barry Griffiths

When I returned from the 'O' Group I saw Cpl Hope being brought back into C Company's position. The company at this stage had not been tasked, and had been told by the CO to stay in our reserve position in order to be able to react as required. We had to find any available cover from the incoming artillery fire, which was becoming more intense.

Pte Ashley Wright

When we arrived at C Company HQ with Cpl Hope, CSM Geoff Guest asked me, 'Who are you?' I replied, 'I'm a medic from A Company, I need to go back and rejoin A Company.' Dave Stott said, 'You can't move off on your own, stay here with us.' I protested, 'But I'm fucking supposed to be with A Company!' Geoff Guest said, 'Okay, that's fine, you'll catch up with A Company later, we're going to be moving through them later.' So I agreed to stay and help look after the wounded.

After a short while Dave came back and asked, 'Where's the medic?' I shouted, 'I'm over here.' He said, 'You come with me; I need a hand down here.' I asked, 'What about Steve?' [Cpl Hope] and he replied, 'He'll be okay, leave him here.' I followed Stotty, crawling and half running till we reached Pte O'Connell, but Dave had already done most of the work. We then moved him, and later Cpl Rehill, into a large shell hole. We then went back for Cpl Hope and carried him to the shell hole and I now sat with this group of wounded, basically just telling them not to fall asleep, and just reassuring them.

We were shelled constantly. The very soft peaty ground was acting as a sponge. The shells would explode deep into peat, throwing enormous amounts of peat into the air and showering us in watery mud. I said to Stotty, 'This is fucking madness!'

Cpl Martin (Taff) Richardson

I contacted 8 Platoon and told them we had a badly wounded man. We pulled Scouse O'Connell across to the huge shell hole and tried to establish the extent of his injuries; we got a poncho from somewhere and used it as a shield. Dave Stott got his torch out and said calmly, 'It's the right side of his head.' We swathed Scouse O'Connell's head in shell dressings.

Sgt Martin (Dickie) Bird

Lt O'Neill asked me to check on the Anti-Tank detachment. At this point there was tracer lashing all around. I crawled across and had a look at this guy [Pte O'Connell] who had blood rolling down his face and I quickly established it was a gunshot wound to the head, in fact entering through the eye and exiting through the side of his temple. I told him what had happened and he went very quiet and then later slipped into shock. We dragged him back down the hill and handed him to some guys behind.

CSgt Andy Gow

After what seemed only a short while there was another call for a 'Medic!' LCpl Stott immediately crawled off under small-arms and shell fire to locate the casualty.

LCpl Stott makes his way across to C Company HQ where he finds Cpl Rehill, who has been shot in the face.

Cpl Boyd (Smudge) Smith

The Argentine mortar illumination was now going up and we could clearly see the silhouette of Mount Longdon to our front. The Argentine machine guns were firing on all their defensive arcs. Cpl Rehill was just to my right when he was shot in the face. LCpl Dave [Stotty] Stott seemed to be with us almost immediately, as he had been located just to our rear. Pte Mick [Robbo] Robson and I crawled over to offer our assistance. The next thing I remember was that someone from A Company, who was located to our front, began shouting for a 'Medic!'

Cpl Paddy Rehill, 27 yrs – Mortar Platoon attached to C Company as MFC

I remember Major Osborne asking Cpl Dickie Bishop to push forward onto the top of the ridge line, so now we had Company HQ, Cpl Bishop's patrol, Major Osborne, Captain Pope the FOO (Forward Observation Officer) all up on the ridge. Shortly after this Major Osborne and Captain Pope went off somewhere.

I spoke to Cpl Ronnie Cooper and Cpl Terry McGlasson, who were on Longdon, to find out what was happening with B Company. They were saying they were meeting a lot of resistance, and that they were pulling back to an OP, to observe and report back to Major Dennison, who was still at the firebase, and to inform the CO, who was somewhere else observing. I got in touch with Cpl Leuan [Bully] Bullivant to ask what was happening on the Mortar Line, and he informed me that they had a problem; they had no ammunition and were waiting for it to be brought forward. I heard Ronnie Cooper ask for illumination, and then the CO came on the radio and said he did not want us to fire illumination.

Major Osborne now returned. We had Argentine illumination rounds falling to the rear of our position, and I said to Major Osborne that we were being lit up; this area was a DF [defensive fire]; we were also taking machine-gun fire and small-arms fire that was aimed at A Company but missing them and coming in our direction. Suddenly a bullet struck my radio boom microphone; it then entered my face through the left side of my jaw and lodged in the back of my throat. Someone began shouting for a medic, and after a short while LCpl David Stott and Cpl Steve Harding-Dempster appeared and began dealing with me. LCpl Chris Fitzgerald now took over my role as MFC.

After LCpl Stott has treated Pte O'Connell and Cpl Rehill, he then returns to Company HQ to bring Cpl Hope to the Company Aid Post.

Cpl Richard (Dickie) Bishop
Suddenly LCpl Dave Stott appeared and said urgently, 'I need some blokes to give me a hand, Steve Hope's been hit in the head, and we need to move him.' My patrol and other members of C Company took hold of the poncho that he was lying on, and we carried and half dragged him to a large recently made 155mm shell hole, which was actually still warm from the explosion. A couple of blokes climbed into the hole, and we lowered him in; he was snoring heavily. After that we were asked to go and help get another member of C Company who had been wounded [Pte Scott Fuller]; he was also brought across and placed in the shell hole.

Pte James (Scouse) O'Connell
I remember Dave Stott treating me; I remember his voice, but after that it's a bit of a blur, I seemed to drift in and out of consciousness. I remember speaking

to Sgt Dickie Bird at some point, and shortly after this, Cpl Steve Hope was rolled into the shell hole, he fell across me and I was trying to push him off, but someone warned me, 'Leave him alone, it's Steve Hope, he's been shot in the fucking head.' We had lots of incoming rounds landing extremely close – I honestly thought it was only a matter of time before this shell hole got hit again, and we all got blown to pieces.

Cpl Boyd (Smudge) Smith

There was a lot of incoming fire directed towards A Company, because they were returning fire at the mountain. Then some members of C Company, who were to my front right, also started firing. I yelled across to them to 'Stop fucking firing! They can't see you; they are firing at your muzzle flashes, so stop fucking firing!' I had to shout a couple of times – eventually they stopped.

Cpl Paddy Rehill

I was now in a shell hole, and at some time after this a member of C Company was brought in [Pte Scott Fuller]. The Argentine artillery fire was relentless; it was landing all around us, all through the night. I still had my radio headset on, so I sat and listened to the progress of the battle throughout the night.

Sgt Martin (Dickie) Bird

After leaving the wounded, myself and a few others crawled back up the hill, when, almost without warning, we were blown over by a 155mm shell which landed probably only 10 or 15 metres away. I remember being thrown onto my back, and sliding backwards and then looking up at tons of peat going up in the air, and I was thinking, This is going to bury me when it comes down, and it did, I got covered in all sorts of mud and peat; I was temporarily deafened, I didn't get my hearing back for about an hour.

7.3   ## 'It had just missed us by a matter of a few inches'

Major Argue assumes that C Company will be used to pass through B Company:

03.30hrs (zt): from C/S 29 to C/S 9: 'Roger, I am now with Call Sign 2/3 [6 Platoon] and there are a few well-sited automatic weapons, but believe little resistance left, do not think it necessary for Call Sign 3 [C Company] to pass through us yet; we will keep knocking the enemy bit by bit.'

CSgt Andy Gow

The shell hole was now quite full with wounded and their attendees. We still had artillery landing all around us; the noise was horrendous, as they were landing extremely close to us and then showering us with peat and filthy water. At some stage, another one of A Company's casualties was passed back to us, Pte James [Jock] Brebner; he'd received a shrapnel wound to his ankle. So we were quite busy trying to keep all the casualties warm, and were constantly checking on the most seriously wounded. We were anxious to get the casualties to the RAP, but at that time it just wasn't practical, there was too much incoming exploding all over the place.

Spr Stephen Smith, 20 yrs – 9 Squadron Royal Engineers

At one point during the night, I did a radio check with Cpl Scotty Wilson, who was attached to B Company, but he quickly told me to get off the air, as he was obviously busy. We were continually shelled, on one occasion a huge piece of shrapnel passed between me and Spr Mick Leather; it lodged in the peat and started smouldering. It had just missed us by a matter of a few inches.

Pte James (Scouse) O'Connell

I remember being constantly told to 'Stay awake, don't fall asleep' but it was so hard trying to stay awake; I remember asking, 'Where's the fucking choppers?' I have never felt so cold, I felt like I was freezing, I was just so cold and desperately wanted to close my eyes and sleep, but whenever I nodded off, someone would poke me, and say, 'Don't fucking fall asleep!'

Lt Barry Griffiths

I remember seeing the unmistakable silhouette of Captain Tony Mason as he passed in front of us, leading his group as they withdrew from Wing Forward and made their way to Mount Longdon.

At approximately 04.00hrs (zt), Captain Tony Mason withdraws from Wing Forward to make his way up to Fly Half.

Cpl George Pullin, 29 yrs – C Company, 7 Platoon

We were the right-hand section of 7 Platoon. When it all kicked off, there were some peat cuttings and my section quickly got into cover with the minimum of digging. The peat banks provided good protection from the small-arms fire to our front, but not much cover from artillery to our rear. We could see the dark feature of Mount Longdon to our front, but there was nothing we could do from this position; we just waited to be tasked.

I remember Cpl Alan (Jock) Burton made his way across to my position as he knew I had cigarettes, so Jock, my youngest Tom and I, were sharing a covert smoke when we heard the crump of the Argentine guns being fired from Port Stanley. We then noticed someone approaching from our left and I spotted it was the OC, Major Osborne, and I thought he'd smelt the tobacco or seen the flash of the match, and I expected a bollocking, but seconds later Major Osborne shouted, 'Incoming!' and took a flying leap into our trench. To this day, I don't know if the almighty crash was the sound of the shell, or the OC landing on top of us, but it was the closest I came to injury during the entire campaign.

Major Martin Osborne

I was informed that A Company would soon be withdrawing from Wing Forward as they had now been tasked to join B Company on Mount Longdon. I immediately made my company fully aware of this movement; furthermore, in preparation for their move, we accepted another casualty from A Company.

A soldier from HQ Company attached to A Company suffering from shell shock is passed back to C Company and is put into the shell crater with the rest of the wounded.

Lt Barry Griffiths

We then knew that B Company's attack had stalled, and that they had taken a lot of casualties, and seeing as A Company could not progress any further forward, it was then decided A Company should withdraw from Wing Forward and make their way to Longdon where they would pass through B Company.

C Company send the CO a situation report:

06.27hrs (zt): from C/S 39 to C/S 9: 'Situation Report: 2 x mortar casualties, 1 x spent round casualty, +3 x casualties from Call Sign 1 all stable, continual mortar fire, now digging in.'

06.30hrs (zt): from C/S 0 to C/S 99: 'Under mortar attack from grid 338748 on Call Sign 3.'

All the Platoon Commanders are now called into C Company HQ for an 'O' Group with Major Osborne at approximately 06.30hrs (zt).

A Company now move off Wing Forward passing, in front of C Company.

Major Martin Osborne

At approximately 07.00hrs (zt), A Company began withdrawing. Once A Company had fully withdrawn, I now repositioned the company to face south-east in case of a possible counter-attack.

CSgt Andy Gow

Eventually it was decided that the wounded would be moved across to the RAP at the base of Mount Longdon, for further treatment and for possible evacuation. Cpl Hope was the most seriously injured; the rest seemed stable once their wounds had been treated, in fact their survival may have been helped by the extreme cold. If I remember rightly, we got one section from each platoon – the majority of the blokes would carry the wounded and some would provide protection. That way the integrity of the company was still maintained. Shortly after the wounded left us, the company moved into a new position facing east. At some time before first light we began advancing east towards our new objective, Rum Punch, which was approximately 1,800 metres away.

LCpl Steve McConnell, 21 yrs – C Company, 9 Platoon

About an hour after A Company had withdrawn, someone announced, 'We need volunteers to move the casualties to the main RAP.' At this stage I wasn't aware of who had been wounded, but someone told me that Paddy Rehill had been hit, so I said, 'Okay, I'm your man.' We all went to the Company Aid Post; I don't remember being told to take anyone in particular. I went over to this bloke lying on the ground in a sleeping bag. I remember thinking, He's too big for that sleeping bag, how the fuck are we going to carry him? And I said, 'Hang on; we can't move him like that! We need a poncho.' Eventually, a poncho appeared and we slid Cpl Hope onto it. I think we were all quite apprehensive about carrying the wounded, as we knew we would be an easy target for anyone who happened to spot us. Our group would be led by Cpl Andy Mason.

Brigade informs 3 PARA HQ that a C Company Call Sign will be moving towards the RAP:

09.03hrs (zt): from C/S 99 to C/S 0: 'C Call Sign moving forward now, direct to casevac grid.'

This move will take quite a bit of manpower, as three of the wounded will be carried in ponchos. We are not sure how many assist, but it has been suggested about platoon strength.

Robert (Bob) Greasley, 17 yrs – 9 Platoon
I was one of the blokes that helped carry Cpl Hope across to the RAP; also with me was Andy Davidson. I remember that I was extremely nervous, as I was only 17 years old and was the youngest member of C Company. Cpl Hope was so heavy, and the poncho was very difficult to keep hold of; we often stumbled on the clumps of grass and holes full of muddy water. We were told our route had been checked for mines and marked with mine tape by 9 Squadron RE, but in the dark whilst trying to carry Cpl Hope, it was hard to keep to any route. What I remember most about Steve Hope was he was snoring like fuck all the time.

LCpl Steve McConnell
We were told to try to reach the RAP by first light, and also that the company was about to move position due to the fear of a possible counter-attack. The wounded had received only basic battlefield first aid and some were by then quite poorly. We split into small groups, and each group took one casualty; my group was carrying Cpl Hope. Before we moved out I remember Andy Mason

checking Cpl Hope's field dressings while I checked his pulse. Then someone said, 'Right, let's get these fucking blokes out of here now,' and off we went.

Steve Hope was a big lad, and I remember we had to keep putting him down as we were losing our grip on the poncho. I remember it got to the point that we were only making about 10 or 15 metres each go. With the bright moon, we could just make out the RAP; it was about 600 metres away. I was hoping we could make the rocks before first light, as we didn't want to get caught in the open. Andy Mason was constantly shouting at us all the way across, 'Come on, you fuckers, get a grip!' He wouldn't let up. I couldn't believe the determination and spirit shown by Andy Mason; he was the driving force in getting the wounded across to the RAP.

We were sinking up to our shins in the wet, muddy and boggy ground, it was absolutely exhausting work, and with the weight of Cpl Hope, we were truly on our chin straps, but Andy Mason kept pushing everyone. This went on for some time, lifting him and putting him down. The next thing I remember was a vivid crest of red light breaking from the east. We were still about 200 metres from the rocks when I heard the distant crump of the guns being fired. I counted three, and thought, There are three rounds in the air. About 20 seconds later they struck Longdon, at irregular intervals with a brief flash. I think two more fire missions hit Longdon; and I remember thinking, As long as the guns stay on Longdon, we can make the rocks. Then the guns switched to the open ground, and the next thing I remember is three rounds landing in quick succession. Two exploded with a dull thud, throwing peat, tufts of grass and water into the air. I remember sods of grass landing on the poncho and hitting me on the helmet. At that moment, I'd sunk up to my shins in peat and couldn't take cover because I was stuck. Cpl Hope was dropped, and the rest of the group all dived into cover.

The third round whistled in and landed about 15 metres away between Paul Wray's group and mine. It landed with a thud; fortunately it didn't explode, it made a hissing sound as it cooled down in the bog. Paul Wray came over to check if we were okay. The shelling continued with the odd sporadic round landing close, but they were now mainly going for C Company on Wing Forward, trying to zero the guns on their location. We continued, but only getting the odd drop-short.

LCpl Paul Wray, 21 yrs – 7 Platoon

I remember when the shells caught us out in the open. At this point everyone dived for cover, and I found myself left alone with Pte O'Connell. I grabbed him under the arms and started dragging him towards the RAP, slipping and sliding on the frozen ground. After about 20 yards, Steve McConnell appeared and grabbed his legs, and between the two of us, we carried him and dropped him a few times, but managed to carry him to the nearest piece of cover. After the shelling stopped, and with the help of the rest of the lads, we managed to get Pte O'Connell to the RAP.

Pte James (Scouse) O'Connell

I distinctly remember some incoming rounds landing around us; everyone seemed to scatter for cover, and I was dropped on the ground. The rounds exploded, throwing peat and general crap into the air. Paul Wray lay across me to cover me, which was extremely brave of him. This took place a couple of times before we eventually reached the RAP.

7.4 'Curb your natural enthusiasm and stay where you are'

A Company begin their advance towards Full Back:

09.40hrs (zt): from C/S 1 to C/S 9A: 'Call Sign 1/2 has cleared and now manning high ground.'

Major Patrick informs the Fire Direction Centre that C Company is being engaged by ZU5204, location unknown:

09.55hrs (zt): from C/S 79 to C/S 29FDC: 'C/S 3 engaged by ZU5204.'

First light at approximately 10.00hrs (zt).

Major Martin Osborne

I got a radio message asking me if I could send my Engineer Section [LCpl Mick Humphries, Spr Stephen Smith, Spr Mick Beeby and Spr Mick Leather] across

319

to Battalion HQ; the Engineers left at the double thinking they were going to sort out some sort of EOD [explosive ordnance disposal] problem.

Cpl Richard (Dickie) Bishop

On Saturday morning, I contacted Major Butler of D Company to find out if we were to stay with C Company. I was told to bring my patrol across to Mount Longdon, so we made our way over, and as my patrol came in, I remember seeing a wounded bloke being carried down to the RAP over another man's shoulder, using a fireman's lift. The Argentines were now starting to use air-burst shells.

The man being carried may have been LCpl Roger James.

Cpl George Pullin

As we began to advance east towards our next objective, we started taking heavy machine-gun fire from our forward right. Lt Barry Griffiths ordered my gun team to move to higher ground and start engaging. However, as we had previously been covering a re-entrant to our front, which was a likely Argentine route of re-enforcement or counter-attack, to move uphill would have put that re-entrant into dead ground, so I placed them into a position where they could still cover the re-entrant.

Cpl Donny McDonald, 26 yrs – C Company, 8 Platoon

We began to advance towards our next objective, Rum Punch, which was approximately 1,700 metres to the east and was overlooked by high ground on our forward right (Wireless Ridge). We moved off with two platoons forward, 7 Platoon left and 8 Platoon right; Company HQ would be centre but about 100 metres back, 9 Platoon left and rear. We began the advance in dead ground, but after about 500 metres we moved over a ridge and descended into open ground. My section was extreme right and closest to Longdon. At this stage A Company was still clearing positions along the northern side of Longdon. They were firing onto Argentines, some of whom were conducting a fighting withdrawal. At this point my section came under fire from A Company, until someone shouted, 'Stop fucking firing! It's C Company!'

Unbeknown to C Company they are now advancing through minefield number 75.

Pte Dave Gammon, 21 yrs – Anti-Tank Platoon attached to C Company

The only memory I have about moving forward is when we heard A Company clearing the northern side of Longdon. There were rounds flying everywhere – a couple landed at my feet, I heard the rounds go into the ground. I hit the deck and shouted, 'Fucking hell!' 'Jock the gob' [Cpl Alan Burton] called across to me and asked if I was all right. I said, 'Yes, I'm okay, but them fuckers over there are firing at us!'

Lt Barry Griffiths

Just after first light we came under what we thought was sniper fire from the east ridge of Longdon. This eventually stopped and we then moved off to advance towards Wireless Ridge.

A Company have now gone secure on Full Back:

10.28hrs (zt): from C/S 1 to C/S 9: 'Now on position, very extensive position with Sp Gun at end.'

The CO tells C Company to push forward:

10.50hrs (zt): from C/S 9 to C/S 3: 'Move forward to "Rum Punch" taking out anything past the gun that is firing.'

Cpl Donny McDonald

As my section was the furthest forward and on slightly higher ground, I saw to my front an occupied enemy position, about 1,000 metres away or maybe less. My section was moving across open ground and we had begun to receive accurate incoming shell fire. The situation was getting increasingly dangerous, and it would only be a matter of time before we would start taking casualties. I asked for smoke to cover us on the advance. The artillery fire increased, we continued advancing until I eventually took the decision to get my section into cover. It was at this point that Major Osborne and the FOO, Captain Pope, came forward and halted the advance. They pointed out various locations such as Wireless Ridge. After that Major Osborne said, 'The company will stop here.' He then told us to start digging in.

Lt Barry Griffiths

Shortly after this we were given orders to occupy the high ground, facing east. We were told basically, we are going across to that position over there, there are no enemy on it, and we are going to occupy it. However, as we reached the top of the ridge, we could see Argentines moving about on the position. I informed Company HQ, and after that Captain Pope and Major Osborne came forward and started bringing artillery down on them. We continued to push forward, but after only 15 or 20 minutes into the advance we began to come under heavy enemy artillery fire.

The Rum Punch objective is occupied by C Company 7th IR equipped with at least one 120mm mortar, a .50 Calibre HMG and a 105mm RCL.

CSgt Andy Gow

At some point, we began advancing east towards Rum Punch. The formation was the same: two platoons forward, one back, with C Company Tac HQ moving between the two forward platoons and our group approximately 100 metres behind Tac HQ. As we moved forward it was now fully daylight and we could clearly see occupied enemy positions in the distance. We began to receive enemy artillery fire; they were bracketing us, and it became rather accurate. If we had carried on, we would have taken a lot of casualties. It was decided, quite correctly, that we should pull back and dig in.

Major Martin Osborne

At some time after first light, I began to move the company forward; we were eventually parallel with Full Back. We were then ordered to push further forward to suppress a 105mm recoilless rifle that had been firing at the CO's location. As we came over the crest to our front, we came under artillery fire, and the CO told me to carry on, despite my concern about casualties. The 105mm recoilless was off to our forward right. It had now stopped firing, and we saw Argentinians running towards Wireless Ridge; we fired some GPMG at them, but it wasn't very effective.

I gave a situation report to the CO, which I ended by saying that I was preparing to continue to my primary objective. The CO said, 'Curb your natural enthusiasm and stay where you are.' So we began to dig in. I positioned C Company Tac HQ forward, so I could see the same ground as my lead platoons, 7 Platoon to my left and 8 Platoon right, with 9 Platoon left and rear as a committable reserve. The CO's decision to halt was correct, in that without a firebase and support along the ridge, C Company would have been pretty well chopped up while heading for Rum Punch in broad daylight. After that we were heavily and persistently shelled in this position until the battle for Wireless Ridge.

There is confusion over C Company's location.

3 PARA HQ inform Brigade that C Company 3 PARA are moving towards the northern end of Wireless Ridge (grid 345754) Rum Punch/Rough Diamond area of Wireless Ridge:

10.53hrs (zt): from C/S 0 to C/S 99: 'Situation report, Mount Longdon secure, Call Sign 3 moving forward to Wireless Ridge.'

Brigade now confirms it with 3 PARA HQ:

11.01hrs (zt): from C/S 99 to C/S 0: 'Confirm call sign 3 is moving on to Wireless Ridge.'

3 PARA HQ now confirm C Company are moving on to Wireless Ridge:

11.01hrs (zt): from C/S 0 to C/S 99: 'Confirmed.'

11.40hrs (zt): from C/S 3 to C/S 9: 'One of my sub units spotted a battery of guns, about to engage.'

Shortly after this last radio message an artillery fire mission is called on to Rum Punch:

11.45hrs (zt): from C/S 29FDC to C/S Arty: 'Call Sign 3 fire mission Bty ZU7914 [Rum Punch].'

This radio transmission may have led to more confusion over C Company's location:

11.50 hrs (zt): from C/S 29FDC to C/S Arty: '3 PARA up to Rum Punch.'

3 PARA HQ ask Brigade if they can move forward.

At 11.50 (zt), 3 PARA report a good view of Wireless Ridge and an opportunity to move forward. *

Brigadier Julian Thompson cautions against 'getting caught out on a limb' concerning the Argentine artillery. It becomes increasingly heavy and more accurate as the day wears on; clearly there will be no question of going forward on to Wireless Ridge. †

3 PARA HQ inform the RAP that two members of D Company are inbound:

11.51 hrs (zt): from C/S 0 to C/S 9B: 'Two D Call Signs en route to your location, two BV's, 1 going back to 9A.'

Cpl Boyd (Smudge) Smith

We heard a message on the battalion net saying something like, 'If there were any medics available, could they report to the RAP,' and they also mentioned that there were rations ready for collection, so I sent Pte Gary [Gaz] Pullen and Pte Mick [Robbo] Robson across. As they neared the RAP they came across an obvious casualty position; it was littered with shell dressings, bits of torn clothing, a set of webbing and a boot that was extremely badly damaged. They now realized they were in a minefield and needed to watch their step, and slowly moved off, scanning the ground ahead. As they neared the RAP they were fired upon by members of 3 PARA. Gaz Pullen roared, 'Fucking stop firing! We're D Company patrols.' Someone shouted back in a tired voice, 'Yeah, okay.'

12.05hrs (zt): from C/S 3 to C/S 0: 'Located battery position 365740 [Wireless Ridge, Moody Brook end].'

Cpl Martin (Taff) Richardson

At some stage we were told to expect a heliborne attack, so we lined up our section's two GPMGs and the Charlie G [anti-tank weapon] and waited. We began to take an enormous amount of artillery fire, but for some reason the

---

* From *The Official History of the Falklands Campaign* by Sir Lawrence Freedman.
† From *No Picnic* by Julian Thompson.

blokes had begun getting very relaxed about it, thinking they could judge the rounds by the whistle.

Lt Barry Griffiths

Shortly after going firm in our new location, we came under intense artillery bombardment. Pte Mark Blain was badly wounded in the arm, and was moved back to Sgt Paul Robinson and Cpl Paul [Ginge] Rogers' shell scrape. As I moved over towards their position to check on the situation, Captain Dwyn Starkey who was the company 2ic arrived with a medic. The medic gave immediate first aid and Mark was taken back to the Company Aid Post.

CSgt Andy Gow

We had been in this location for a couple of hours, and we were now used to the noise of incoming: every five minutes someone would be shouting, 'Incoming!' However, some of the soldiers thought they could estimate the flight times of the shells as they came in, and they seemed to be almost playing chicken. I yelled at a group of them, saying, 'This isn't a fucking game! Get yourselves into cover.' A short while later a round came thundering in, blew a huge hole and threw a great lump of peat the size of a three-piece suite into the air. I then heard someone screaming in agony; Pte Mark Blain had been hit by a piece of shrapnel, which had somehow ripped the flesh off the inside of his arm from his wrist to his shoulder.

14.50hrs (zt): from C/S 9 to C/S 9A: 'You do not need to collect casualty from Call Sign 3 yet.'

This is because C Company are under a heavy bombardment.

Lt Barry Griffiths

Lt Mike O'Neill and I had a routine throughout the campaign that, wherever we were, at about 16.00hrs (zt) we would meet up for a chat about how things were going within the company. On Saturday afternoon Mike O'Neill made his way across to my trench and we were chatting and enjoying a mug of tea, when we heard the ominous crump of rounds being fired. By now we thought we could judge the flight time and guessed that we still had a few more seconds before taking cover when this round came thundering in like a locomotive train right next to us. It landed less than 10 feet from us, plunged deep into the peat, and the blast threw us backwards. Mike and I were absolutely covered in peat and temporarily deafened. We were both shaken but otherwise unharmed. We were very fortunate with the terrain, otherwise this incident would have been without doubt fatal. Once I had picked myself up, I looked at the smoking shell hole and thought, 'That hole looks better than my trench,' and I decided it would be my new home.

CSgt Andy Gow

Later on Saturday afternoon, once the company had been sorted out, there was a bit of a lull in the shelling. CSM Geoff Guest and I made our way across to the RAP as we wanted to replenish our medical supplies and get an update on what had happened regarding battalion casualties. The RAP had now settled down a bit, the wounded had been evacuated and the prisoners were being processed. We met CSgt Brian Faulkner and he briefed us on the latest casualty figures. It was quite sobering to see the bodies of our dead colleagues placed to one side, covered over with various blankets and ponchos. I was saddened to hear that my best mate Ned Kelly had been badly wounded.

Pte David Gammon, 20 yrs – C Company, 3 PARA

I was on the very forward edge of C Company position; from here we could see Port Stanley in the distance. We were receiving a lot of artillery fire. A lot of the incoming shells were passing over us, but then one or two would come roaring in, and in those last terrifying one or two seconds, you didn't know if this was the one, and then there was the deafening noise of the explosions, followed by the relief that you were okay. But only until the next one. It's quite hard to explain unless you've actually been under shell fire; it's just so mentally draining.

At some time later on, Cpl Jimmy Cochrane gave us an update on the latest casualty figures. I particularly wanted to know if my mate Pete Hedicker was okay, but no one seemed to know. That night I couldn't get any sleep, what with intense cold, shelling and no sleeping bag, also I was concerned about a possible counter-attack. I was stagging on with a 17-year-old lad from 7 Platoon. I can't remember his name, but he hadn't been in the battalion long. I remember he kept repeating the password over and over, just in case anyone came over to us.

On Saturday evening, a situation report (Intelligence Summary No. 27) is sent from 3 PARA HQ to Brigade HQ with, among other things, all the various up-to-date company locations. Unfortunately, it states that C Company is located 1 kilometre further east, occupying Rum Punch at grid 345753. However, they are in fact located north of Full Back at grid 335753.

CSgt Andy Gow

That night we were supposed to be reserve for 2 PARA, who were building up behind us for the attack on Wireless Ridge. However, the attack was cancelled and everyone tried to settle down for another absolutely freezing cold night. I don't think anyone really slept – the enemy artillery, although it lessened, still fired on us right through the night.

Major Martin Osborne

Due to the freezing conditions, and with the entire company without sleeping bags for a second night, I found it impossible to sleep. I think it was that night when my signaller Cpl Ronnie Carlin got hypothermia.

SUNDAY 13 JUNE 1982

CSgt Andy Gow

On Sunday morning our position was covered in a layer of snow; we were all bitterly cold. There was nothing much to do, as we were keeping movement down to a minimum, as we didn't want to attract any more incoming fire. However, they knew where we were, and continued shelling us.

Major Martin Osborne

I received a message telling me the CO wanted to come across and visit C Company, but a route would have to be cleared first. 9 Squadron now spent quite a bit of the day slowly clearing a path through to our position. When the CO arrived, he informed me that we [C Company] would be the reserve company for 2 PARA, who tonight would be attacking Wireless Ridge, which would entail us being ready to move at a moment's notice to reinforce 2 PARA.

Spr Martin (Spike) Glover

At some time in the morning we were tasked to clear a route from Longdon through to C Company's position; we marked our route with white mine tape held down with six-inch nails. It was bitterly cold, and it took us about six hours as the company position was roughly opposite the Full Back position. I was glad to get back to my old position on Longdon, as all through the task we were constantly shelled. I felt safer on Longdon, as C Company was getting quite a bit of attention from the Argentine artillery.

Cpl Martin (Taff) Richardson

I think it was Sunday when they started putting air bursts up. In the afternoon I watched as some of the 9 Squadron Engineers were clearing a path from Longdon across to us. The shelling seemed to increase through the day, probably due to 9 Squadron. There was very little movement in our position and as the 9 Squadron blokes neared our position, I heard the familiar crump, crump, of incoming, and from the whistle I knew these were going to land really close. I screamed at them, 'Fucking run!' They all ran straight towards us and dived into the cover of a small peat bank. Shortly afterwards the 9 Squadron Section Commander came into my shelter and said, 'Fucking hell! You lot are getting some shit over here!'

CSgt Andy Gow

As we sheltered we could tell by the crunch or thud where the shells were landing: if they were hitting Longdon, they would crunch and have more effect, sending rock and shrapnel everywhere, and if they landed by us, they would thud into the ground, throwing up peat, mud and bits of shrapnel. The shrapnel made a noise similar to helicopter blades as it cut through the air, before landing with a thud nearby. But, like anything, we began to get used to it.

Pte Dave Gammon

On Sunday afternoon, I remember hearing the Skyhawks coming in. They came in from my left-hand side as I looked towards Mount Longdon.

15.10hrs (zt): from C/S 1 to All Stations: 'Air raid warning RED.'

15.17hrs (zt): from C/S 0 to C/S 9: 'Airstrike thought to be on Brigade HQ – now confirmed.'

15.22hrs (zt): from C/S 98 to C/S 0: '1 x Skyhawk [Captain Varela] hit trailing smoke heading north.'

15.22hrs (zt): from C/S 0 to C/S 98: 'Passed to Brigade.'

15.40hrs (zt): Note: 'No casualties suffered by Brigade, but 1 x Seaking with shrapnel through rotor blade.'

15.45hrs (zt): from C/S 99 to C/S 0: 'Air raid YELLOW.'

16.00hrs (zt): 2 PARA begin moving east through Furze Bush Pass in preparation for their forthcoming attack.

CSgt Andy Gow

We were once again warned that we would be reserve for 2 PARA's attack on Wireless Ridge, and that the SF machine guns were going to be brought across to our forward positions. Then it was discovered that we were not where Brigade thought we were! I'm not sure how that came about as during the day 9 Squadron RE had cleared a path to our location, the CO had visited us, we were only 500 or 600 metres from A Company – so how the confusion over our position came about, I simply do not know.

It is now early evening.

Major Martin Osborne

At some time on Sunday evening, Major Collett contacted me by radio and asked where my company position was. I ended up firing a mini flare, and he said that I was much further back than he thought I was.

CSgt Steve Knights, 31 yrs – Support Company

Sunday, at approximately 19.30hrs (zt), we were preparing to go out in support of 2 PARA, who would be attacking Wireless Ridge, when I spoke to Major Dennison. He was trying to confirm where everybody was, and he said to me, 'C Company are over there,' and I said, 'They're not there, they are over there, you can see them from the top of the hill.' And he replied, 'Well, there seems to be some confusion. What I'd like you to do is, can you go down to the CO and confirm with him, and update your map and his map.' I thought, Yeah I'll do that in a minute, I'll just get a brew on, as I'd been out all day, and then Denzil Connick said, 'Give me the map and I'll take it down.' And that's when he got hit.

Major Martin Osborne

I remember hearing over the radio something about Tac HQ needing a map from Support Company. Shortly after this, I remember watching two figures [Denzil Connick and Craig Jones] walking westwards, and then they suddenly disappeared in a puff of smoke.

20.00hrs (zt): from C/S 9A to C/S 0: 'We need two more stretchers; more casualties.'

20.00hrs (zt): from C/S 0 to C/S 9A: 'Roger.'

CSgt Andy Gow

Just before last light we came under mortar and artillery fire. I heard a piercing scream from quite a distance away, and then shouts for a medic, coming from what seemed like the full length of the mountain, and I thought, Fucking hell, some poor sod's got it [Denzil Connick]. His screams cut right through everyone. We now waited till late, and then watched as 2 PARA began their attack; we were willing them on. That night it was once again bitterly cold. It turned out that we were not called to support 2 PARA, but 3 PARA Mortars fired throughout the night in support of 2 PARA.

Major Martin Osborne

We were waiting to be called upon. I was stood with Captain Mike Pope and watching the progress of the battle for Wireless Ridge – I stayed in touch with 2 PARA's Tac HQ throughout the battle. Suddenly there was a loud 'splodge' as something landed in between Mike and me, it had buried itself in the peat, and we thought, 'What on earth was that?' I put my hand into the hole; I could feel the very hot tail fins of a mortar - we weren't sure if it was HE or illumination and did not want to find out! We rather quickly decided to change our position.

7.5 **'Shut the fuck up, and just keep walking'**

MONDAY 14 JUNE 1982

On Monday morning, 2 PARA are nearing the end of their battle for Wireless Ridge, and the Scots Guards are still fighting on Mount Tumbledown.

The following includes radio transmissions from various units which help to give an idea of what is happening:

(AAC = Army Air Corps; Arty = Artillery; R/L = Radio Log; 2SG = 2nd Battalion, Scots Guards; 1/7GR = 1st Battalion, 7th Duke of Edinburgh's Own Gurkha Rifles; 1 Troop RHG/D = Royal Horse Guards and 1st Dragoons)

07.20hrs (zt): AAC R/L from Brigade: 'Late entry. 2 PARA have clearance to advance with 1 Troop RHG/D south from Wireless Ridge on Moody Brook Camp as raid, but must return to high ground by first light. 2SG raid on position south of Mount William now ended. 2 dead and 9 wounded. Believed that 1 Welsh Guards have now extracted bodies by CVRT and casualties taken to Welsh Guards RAP 2SG believed pinned down on Tumbledown.'

07.37hrs (zt): AAC R/L from Arty to AAC: 'Report that C/S 4 2SG at east end of objective, are held up by machine-gun fire.'

07.58hrs (zt): Arty R/L from C/S 49 to C/S 50B: 'Fire Mission; Illumination grid 365750, Direction due east, Enemy position, Illuminate ASP for 3 minutes, be prepared for repeat.'

08.10hrs (zt): AAC R/L from DN to AAC: '2 Scots Guards having trouble with machine gun on Tumbledown, held up for 6 hours, 29 Cdo Bty 5 × rounds fire for effect against machine gun, 10 × Panhard AFV believed in area grid 3573 / 3673 Wireless Ridge: 2 PARA and Blues and Royals will attack Moody Brook camp but must return to high ground before first light, Scots Guards raid south of Tumbledown has now withdrawn with 2 × dead and 9 × wounded, Welsh Guards RAP assisting, no grid reference available.'

08.30hrs (zt): AAC R/L from 2 SG to AAC: 'From 2 SG Coy, the company has managed to pass through the machine-gun position and is pushing on position near ZU4231 grid 333723, many dead and prisoners taken.'

08.54hrs (zt): AAC R/L from Brigade: '3974-1 x Company 2 PARA 3574-1 x Company PARA'

[These two companies are C Company and D Company 2 PARA.]

09.12hrs (zt): AAC R/L from Brigade: 'Requesting PNG SK for casevac of 3 x Scots Guards from 295715, sitting cases, 1 possibly with head wound, no further details available.'

[Head wound is possibly Lt Robert Lawrence 2 SGs.]

10.00hrs (zt): AAC R/L from Brigade: '1/7 GR held up by arty barrage, now lifting and battalion moving forward.'

First light is approximately 10.00hrs (zt).

10.05hrs (zt): Arty R/L, from 29FDC: '29 [SGs] has secured objective, no prisoners not counted enemy dead, our casualties low. 49 [1/7GR] under heavy shelling, have moved off to an escarpment.'

10.15hrs (zt): Arty R/L from 29FDC: 'I4 [2 PARA] Cleared objective of snipers and other things.'

10.23hrs (zt): Arty R/L from 29FDC: 'I4 [2 PARA] at the moment counting prisoners they shelled every objective, and it appears the Argies did a runner.'

Brigade informs 3 PARA HQ of 2 PARA's success:

10.38hrs (zt): from C/S 99 to C/S 0: '2 PARA now firm on their objective.'

10.42hrs (zt): AAC R/L from 2F to 0: 'Finding way around snow shower.'

The C Company 3 PARA radio operator asks for confirmation of the location of Battalion 'O' Group:

10.50hrs (zt): from C/S 3 to C/S 9: 'Area of O Group?'

CO confirms RAP location:

10.50hrs (zt): from C/S 9 to C/S 3: '9A location.'

At approximately 11.15hrs (zt), there is an Argentine counter-attack against 2 PARA from Moody Brook Barracks. Lt John Page of D Company 2 PARA calls for fire support and the attack is broken up by a fire mission from all five batteries firing proximity rounds (air burst). The enemy then retreats in disarray; the fire mission also destroys what was left of the Royal Marines Barracks signals room, and officers' and sergeants' mess accommodation.

11.15hrs (zt): Arty R/L from 29FOC: '79 Battery engaged grid 367736 [i.e. Moody Brook].'

11.40hrs (zt): Arty R/L from 9Z: 'G19 reports small counter-attack from Moody Brook against 2 PARA 14 POWs taken.'

Scout helicopters are busy flying casevac missions:

11.48hrs (zt): AAC R/L from BM: 'All Scout Call Signs to remain on casevac stand by, task 004 postponed. Sit rep 2 Scots Guards – 2 dead, 9 wounded in south, 3 wounded in north, with 4 dead, up to 16 other casualties in north to be moved from 1/7GR/2SG.'

The situation begins to change.

CSgt Andy Gow
Major Osborne went across to Mount Longdon for an 'O' Group with the CO; we knew he'd be receiving orders for the next phase of the campaign and that C Company would now be the lead element of 3 PARA.

11.55hrs (zt): Arty R/L from FDC4, '97 Battery, finished on fire mission battery grid 350727 [eastern end of Mount Tumbledown] 110 rounds fired.'

Major Martin Osborne
I went across to an Orders group that was being held near the RAP on Mount Longdon at 12.00hrs (zt). This would be the warning orders for the attack into Port Stanley; it followed a familiar pattern: Situation enemy forces, Friendly forces, Task, Execution, and General outline etc. My company would now be the lead company.

3 PARA HQ informs the CO that the situation is changing!

12.10hrs (zt): from C/S 0 to C/S 9: 'Enemy withdrawing from Sapper Hill, unconfirmed report 300 enemy withdrawing.'

12.16hrs (zt): Arty R/L from 9Z: 'Reference troops withdrawing from Moody Brook, being engaged by Call Signs 1+2.'

12.20hrs (zt): Arty R/L from FDC29: 'Fire Mission 2 Battery – engaging with Call Sign 1, troops withdrawing from Moody Brook, plus Call Sign 3.'

12.22hrs (zt): AAC R/L from 2 S/Guards: 'Troops withdrawing from Mount William; artillery may engage shortly, troops about to surrender on Mount William. Large numbers of enemy moving from Moody Brook into Stanley, 300 men moving from Sapper Hill into Stanley unconfirmed.'

12.25hrs (zt): Arty R/L from 9Z: 'Reference Call Sign 1+2 engaging Call Sign 3 now joined them.'

Major Martin Osborne
Halfway through the orders, we suddenly got a message from 2 PARA saying something like, 'The enemy is running off the back of Mount Tumbledown.' The CO turned to me and said, 'Martin; you must go back across to C Company and get them ready to move. Let me know as soon as you're ready.' The intent was that C Company was going to be the assault company supported by 2 PARA. They [2 PARA] would hold Wireless Ridge while C Company [3 PARA] assaulted Moody Brook.

12.27hrs (zt): AAC R/L from LO: 'Mount William large numbers of troops moving back to Stanley RA may engage, looks like a number of troops about to surrender, mass withdrawal into Stanley, Moody Brook troops moving back, 300 moving from Sapper Hill.'

Lt Col David Chaundler, 39 yrs – CO 2 PARA
At the time of the Argentinian collapse only D Company and my Tac HQ were on the final objective overlooking Moody Brook.*

---

* Email correspondence, 7 November 2012.

12.32hrs (zt): Arty R/L from 9Z: 'Enemy also withdrawing from area forward of Sapper Hill.'

12.36hrs (zt): Arty R/L from FDC4: 'Fire Mission 2 x Batteries 348711 [Mount William].'

12.36hrs (zt): Arty R/L from FDC4 'Fire Mission 2 x Batteries 391717 [Sapper Hill].'

Lt Mike O'Neill, 25 yrs – C Company
When Major Osborne returned, he immediately called all Platoon Commanders together for an 'O' Group. The company was told to prepare to move. The OC gave his orders, explaining that we, C Company, would now be the lead company of 3 PARA, and our task was to attack the barracks at Moody Brook. We would be supported in this task by 2 PARA. The entire company was delighted at the chance to lead the battalion into battle; I then quickly briefed all my Section Commanders.

3 PARA HQ inform the battalion that they are to be on 30 minutes' notice to move:

CSgt Andy Gow
Not long after he had left, Major Osborne came running back over to C Company and he hurriedly called in his Platoon Commanders and SNCOs for a quick briefing. Our CSM was suffering with a knee injury, so he gave me his map, and I attended the briefing in his place. The gist of the briefing was that we were to make our way as fast as possible to Moody Brook; we would attack the barracks and clear it. We would be supported in this task by 2 PARA, who were at the moment positioned on Wireless Ridge overlooking Moody Brook. 8 Platoon will lead, followed by Tac HQ, then 7 Platoon and 9 Platoon. We were to move out in single file and we were warned we might be passing through minefields en route. As we got closer to the objective, we were to shake out into assault formation, A Company and B Company would follow behind us.

It was also decided to contact WO2 John Carey, who would take over the role as CSM, and a message was sent across to the RAP where he was based. However, such was our urgency to move out we decided to leave without the new CSM and hoped he would catch us up, but until then I would take over the role of

CSM. We were going to move on to an open forward slope in direct view of the enemy, then assault and fight through Moody Brook; we had visions of a stand-up fight and then progressing into Port Stanley, clearing house to house. We knew it would be hard work, but as a company we were really up for it.

13.20hrs (zt): AAC R/L from Arty: 'Welsh Guards move forward for attack on Sapper Hill.'

13.27hrs (zt): Arty R/L from FDC29: 'Situation report, C/S G19 states nobody between him and Stanley and in his opinion a good regimental shoot on Sapper Hill would clear.'

13.35hrs (zt): Arty R/L from FDC29: 'Under fire in Moody Brook, try and find out where it's coming from.'

13.36hrs (zt): Arty R/L from FDC29: 'Lots of smoke from the racecourse, plus bad visibility because of a snow storm.'

13.36hrs (zt): Arty R/L from FDC29: 'If possible don't use WP [white phosphorus], can if you want, but rather you would not.'

13.40hrs (zt): AAC R/L from Brigade: 'H-Hour assault on Mount William now 14.00hrs (zt).'

13.42hrs (zt): Arty R/L from FOC29: 'Fire Mission Battery (79) grid 370728 *** [word unclear] A888 DN360.'

[Grid 370728 = enemy gun positions west of Stanley.]

CO orders C Company 3 PARA to move to Moody Brook:

13.44hrs (zt): from C/S 9 to C/S 3: 'C Company now on 30 minutes, get ready now and close up behind 2 PARA, inform me when you're on the move.'

Cpl Boyd (Smudge) Smith

I remember Major Osborne saying to us, 'I want you to take me by the shortest route possible to Moody Brook.' We now took a direct line to Wireless Ridge, Pte Gaz Pullen would lead. We received small-arms fire from someone – we weren't sure whether it was an enemy or friendly fire [but] it came from the direction of A Company. However, we did not return fire.

Lt Barry Griffiths

When Major Osborne returned from his 'O' Group there was a sense of urgency. He told us that the Argentines were withdrawing off Tumbledown and we [C Company] were now going to attack the barracks at Moody Brook. We quickly loaded up and set off; we moved off at quite a rapid pace.

Cpl Boyd (Smudge) Smith

We carried on across the back of Longdon into an area of dead ground between Longdon and Wireless Ridge. We were aware that there was the possibility of minefields ahead. C Company followed behind us, and then as we got closer to Longdon someone behind us shouted, 'Are we in a minefield?' Gaz Pullen, who was the lead man, shouted back, 'Shut the fuck up, and just keep walking.' I looked back and there was a huge company snaking behind us, following in our footsteps.

Lt Col David Chaundler

I ordered the tanks and Machine Gun Platoon forward and they were firing down into the valley, also the Mortars were carrying out a searching shoot. The Battery Commander Tony Rice managed to get the artillery back and they were carrying out a regimental shoot. I had requested Fighter Ground Attack, but the weather was too bad for the Harriers to fly.*

14.15hrs (zt): Arty R/L from FDC29: 'C/S 3 Fire Mission Bombardment with G19 grid 387722 FUP [form-up point].'

Form-up point at base of Sapper Hill, codenamed Old Bill.

Scout helicopters from 656 Squadron collect SS11 missiles for forthcoming attack on gunline west of Port Stanley:

14.18hrs (zt): AAC R/L from AQ: 'From 656 echelon, Call Sign 1D at Echelon and Call Sign 2D, crew of 2D, awaiting collection of ASM [air to surface missiles], to move to Echelon to co-ordinate as part of task 012 C/S 1A on task.'

---

* Email correspondence, 26 September 2012.

Lt Col David Chaundler

I ordered A and B Companies forward onto the final ridge line. There was a big attack planned for that night, in which 2 PARA was to hold Moody Brook as the Start Line. However, I realized we must, and could, get into Port Stanley before the Argentinians had time to reorganize. I ordered a ceasefire, I think this was at something like 14.00hrs or 14.30hrs (zt) as we were slaughtering the Argentinians for no good purpose. However, communications with Brigade HQ were not good and I became frustrated that I could not get the message across that we must capture Port Stanley now.[*]

C Company 9 Troop of 40 Commando and the Welsh Guards begin moving forward by helicopter to a form-up position to assault Sapper Hill:

14.20hrs (zt): Arty R/L from 3J: 'Situation Report, C/S 49 and 1–2 moving out to phase 1 now, after that they will move forward to "Old Bill".'

Brigadier Thompson arrives by helicopter just behind Wireless Ridge and makes his way forward to meet Lt Col Chaundler, who is up on Wireless Ridge, and asks for a situation report.

Cpl Martin (Taff) Richardson

We now began moving off in a company snake. The Anti-Tanks were now located with Company HQ; I was quite wary as I knew from a previous briefing that we were moving through an area that was known to be mined. As we progressed towards Wireless Ridge a member of our section yelled, 'Taff, are we in a fucking minefield!' and I shouted, 'Shut the fuck up! And keep walking.' As we were already in the middle of it, and there was fuck all we could do about it, we might as well crack on.

Lt Barry Griffiths

As we approached Wireless Ridge, I remember spotting ankle-height wire, which I knew from previous intelligence briefings to be an indication that we were on the edge of a minefield. I then followed our Standard Operating Procedures for crossing a minefield when not in contact, which was to warn the platoon to follow in the footsteps of the man in front and spread out.

---

[*] Email correspondence, 26 September 2012.

British Forces are warned to be aware of Argentine helicopters loading casualties on board the hospital ship ARA Almirante Irízar in Port Stanley Harbour. The helicopters will have some form of Red Cross or white flag attached:

14.25hrs (zt): Arty R/L from U2: 'The Argentinian hospital ship will be loading in Port Stanley all afternoon; military helicopters will be used to ferry wounded soldiers; they are Not, repeat. Not to be engaged.'

14.25hrs (zt): Arty R/L from 9Z: 'C/S 3 End of Mission on FUP, many casualties, remainder hiding in rocks.'

Lt Col David Chaundler

It was at this time that Brigadier Julian Thompson arrived by helicopter behind the ridge. He was as frustrated as I was by the problems of communications. He crawled up onto the crest of the ridge. I was standing out on the forward slope feeling pretty pleased with events. He obviously thought, My God, I have already lost one CO from 2 PARA and rushed out and rugger-tackled me. As we got up I said, 'It is all right, Brigadier, we must get into Port Stanley.' He looked at the situation and agreed.[*]

Major John Crosland, 35 yrs – OC B Company 2 PARA

There was an 'O' Group on Wireless Ridge attended by Brigadier Julian Thompson, and we strongly suggested that we needed to keep the momentum going and not allow the Argentines to regroup in Port Stanley, as if they did, we would have a harder job fighting through them, which would result in inevitable civilian and military casualties. Brigadier Thompson agreed. It was decided that C Company and D Company plus elements of Support Company and the Tanks of Blues and Royals would provide fire support from Wireless Ridge, whilst B Company 2 PARA would advance into Moody Brook, clearing the barracks, and then move up onto the high ground to provide an element of cover for A Company 2 PARA, while they would move parallel to us along the road into Port Stanley.[†]

---

[*] Email correspondence, 26 September 2012.

[†] Email correspondence, 6 November 2012.

Brigadier Julian Thompson, 47 yrs

We stood and watched the Argentines fire what must have been one of the last artillery fire missions on the north side of Tumbledown. The shells crashed down, throwing up smoke and peat. Lt Col Chaundler told me that he had seen the enemy running away in large numbers from Moody Brook, Mount William, Tumbledown and Sapper Hill, nevertheless, the Argentine artillery was still effective, as had just been demonstrated. I told him to take his battalion and advance as far as the spur above the ESRO [European Space Research Organization] Building on the very edge of Stanley. I would then go back to my Tactical Headquarters and get the rest of the Brigade moving.[*]

14.30hrs (zt): (Argentine) C Battery of GAA4 fire their last 105mm round.

14.30hrs (zt): British artillery stops firing HE.

Brigadier Thompson makes his way north to RV with a helicopter which is inbound to take him back to Tactical HQ.

Brigadier Julian Thompson

As we waited, we saw three Scout helicopters fly in behind Wireless Ridge, line up and hover-taxi forward to fire their SS11 missiles at an Argentine gun position across the valley.[*]

Target, 4th Airborne Artillery Group GA4 located by the Felton stream, which is 1 kilometre west of the edge of Port Stanley.

Lt Col David Chaundler

Scout helicopters came up and fired SS 11s into the valley, but I ordered them away as they were attracting too much return fire from the Argentinians. I ordered A and B Company to close up onto the final ridge line.[†]

14.40hrs (zt) approximately: C Company 9 Troop of 40 Commando is landed by mistake, forward of Argentine troops on Sapper Hill. A firefight ensues, two Royal

---

[*] From *No Picnic* by Julian Thompson.

[†] Email correspondence, 26 September 2012.

Marines are wounded and three Argentine Marines, Roberto Leyes, Eleodoro Monzon and Sergio Ariel Robledo, are killed. This is the final clash of the war.

14.45hrs (zt): AAC Radio log from 1/7GR: 'On Mount William, no location, status or security status yet available, civilians not centralized in church in Stanley.'

CSgt Andy Gow
We advanced with caution across the western end of Wireless Ridge, and then swung east into Moody Brook valley. We could see that the situation was changing; Argentines were moving off Mount Tumbledown and running towards Port Stanley. As we progressed towards Moody Brook, the Argentines were abandoning their positions and running along the road towards Port Stanley.

Major Martin Osborne
As we got closer we could see the smouldering Royal Marine Barracks in Moody Brook – it was obvious that the Argentines had run off.

Lt Col David Chaundler
I ordered B Company down through Moody Brook and on to the high ground on the other side, to protect our right flank whilst A Company were to advance down the Ross Road into the town.*

Cpl Boyd (Smudge) Smith
We then moved into the Moody Brook valley. We were moving parallel to Wireless Ridge heading east, and we continued advancing towards Moody Brook Barracks. 2 PARA were still up on Wireless Ridge to our left, and Argentines were still leaving Moody Brook and Mount Tumbledown. Then B Company 2 PARA began moving down to clear the buildings in Moody Brook.

---

* Email correspondence, 26 September 2012.

Lt Mike O'Neill

As we were moving towards Moody Brook the Argentines in Moody Brook broke and ran. Then elements of 2 PARA started moving down off Wireless Ridge.

At 15.00hrs (zt), 2 PARA's Forward Observation Officer calls in a fire mission for smoke onto the gunline west of Port Stanley, to provide cover as first B Company, and then A Company descend into Moody Brook to clear and secure it:

Captain Robert Ash, 25 yrs – 29 Field Bty RA attached to B Company 2 PARA

I called a deliberate smoke mission using base ejection smoke rounds. The area to be blinded was the Argentinian positions to the west of Port Stanley, and the high ground dominating the road. But as to where the smoke canisters actually landed, I don't really remember, as it would have been dictated by the direction of the wind and its speed, which was usually pretty high.*

The weather has changed.

15.00hrs (zt): Two Harriers are launched from HMS Hermes*: Sqn Leader Harris (XZ997) and Flt Lt Gilchrist (XZ113) en route for Sapper Hill. The first Harrier is armed with two x 1,000lb LGBs (laser-guided bombs) and the second is armed with two CBUs (cluster bombs).*

15.00hrs (zt): General Menéndez contacts the President of Argentina, General Galtieri, by telephone asking for permission to surrender. After a short conversation his request is refused.

Doctor Alison Bleaney, Civilian GP at the King Edward VII Memorial Hospital

We'd actually kept a small transceiver in the hospital despite the Argentines raiding us to try and see if we had any communications. Suddenly I heard one of the British talking, first in English and then in Spanish, basically saying that they were ready to negotiate a surrender from the Argentinians, and if anyone was listening could they acknowledge so that they could proceed with it.

---

* Email correspondence, 12 November 2012.

I realized I had to go and find the senior Argentinian commanders. So I found the commander, Commander Menéndez, and said, 'Do you know the British are calling, they're prepared to negotiate a surrender, you have to do this.'

Such is the dire situation, General Menéndez gives permission almost immediately for Captain Hussey (Argentine Navy Translator) to contact British Forces (Lt Col Mike Rose) on his behalf. A phone line has been established for several days between British and Argentine Forces, and he indicates they want to talk about a ceasefire in accordance with UN Resolution 502 (immediate cessation of hostilities between Argentina and the United Kingdom and a complete withdrawal by Argentine forces). He also emphasizes they do not want British Forces to enter Port Stanley. He wants to meet at the Royal Marines Barracks in Moody Brook, but the barracks have been destroyed by artillery fire, and it is decided the meeting place will be the Secretariat building:

Lt Col Mike Rose, 42 yrs – 22 SAS

On Monday afternoon on 14 June, I was with D and G Squadron (22 SAS) located on the Murrell Heights. I agreed to fly into Port Stanley with Captain Rod Bell and a signaller; I spoke to the Argentine HQ who wanted me to fly into Port Stanley to talk about a possible end to hostilities.[*]

Lt Col Mike Rose

I said, 'I am coming in at a time agreed and will be coming in from that particular direction (the north) and I want "no funny business".' They said 'Fine' and they put out a message not to shoot at the helicopter.' I flew in aboard a Gazelle helicopter with a white flag trailing underneath.[†]

Smoke-shoot still ongoing:

15.09hrs (zt): Arty R/L from 9Z: 'W2 engaged on series of smoke shoots to cover move forward to Moody Brook as per the creeping barrage.'

---

[*] Email correspondence, 31 December 2012.

[†] From an article by Thomas Harding and Neil Tweedie, *Daily Telegraph*, 13 June 2012.

15.09hrs (zt): A strong firebase has been established on Wireless Ridge, consisting of C, D and Support Company 2 PARA (Machine Guns and Anti-Tanks); also further east on Wireless Ridge are the Blues and Royals, who will act as fire support; 29 Cdo Regt RA will be registering targets, as the advance progresses. 2 and 3 PARA Mortars are also on call. 2 PARA now begins to break out of Moody Brook. B Company 2 PARA will advance along the high ground towards the Argentine gunline and will provide covering fire for A Company 2 PARA who will advance along the Ross Road.

Sgt Ian Aird, 31 yrs – B Company 2 PARA

We moved off Wireless Ridge – A Company was on the left and B Company was on the right; on our far left was D Company who had hooked around in the early hours to give the Argies a sucker punch. At this stage we could see a huge amount of Argentines retreating back into Port Stanley. Eventually B Company was tasked to go forward and then move on to the high ground and advance east, clearing anything to our front. A Company was ordered to go down to the road and head east.

Lt Col Chaundler starts giving orders.

Lt Col David Chaundler

'I'm not having anybody going down that road unless the high ground is covered, so I'm getting B Company up there. The Blues and Royals will stay here and provide a firebase...' The first men of B Company were already threading their way through Moody Brook, and up the opposite hillside the Scorpions and Scimitars deployed along the ridge, so that their fire could cover the road for miles. A Company was to march straight up the road. I [Max Hastings] trotted after Major Dair Farrar-Hockley.*

Major Dair Farrar-Hockley, 35 yrs – OC, A Company 2 PARA

Our order of march along the Ross Road was Lt Mark Coe's 2 Platoon, with Cpl Tom Camp at point section; Company HQ, followed by Lt Jon Shaw's

---

* From *Going to the Wars* by Max Hastings.

1 Platoon, with Lt Guy Wallis's 3 Platoon in the rear. We straddled the road, to achieve the CO's clear order to press on and clear the road into Port Stanley.*

Captain Robert Ash

As B Company 2 PARA moved towards Port Stanley, I moved south of the road onto a ridge to cover the approach. I initiated a smoke fire mission, which I controlled with 'At my command'. My aim was to be able lay down smoke to cover [screen] our forces from any fire from Stanley. The guns duly reported 'Ready'; this meant that they were laid and loaded onto the targets that I had indicated. I am not aware that I ever gave 'End of mission', thus the guns should still be there awaiting my order to fire![†]

The airstrike is still inbound for Sapper Hill.

Brigadier Thompson has returned to his Command Post.

Brigadier Julian Thompson

At that moment the Brigade Air Liaison Officer, Lt Commander Callaghan, Royal Navy, reminded everybody in the Command Post that an airstrike on Sapper Hill with cluster bombs had been ordered and was due in minutes. With the Argentines surrendering, the last thing that was wanted at this stage was a massacre of the enemy. Fortunately Wing Commander Trowern, Royal Air Force, was forward in Brigade Tactical Headquarters; he grabbed the radio and stopped the strike as the aircraft were coming in.[‡]

15.12hrs (zt): Arty R/L from U2: 'Enemy are standing around; those in contact with our friends to the North [22 SAS] have asked that we fire only in self-defence. This is to be implemented. The offset task on Sapper Hill is cancelled.'

Airstrike on Sapper Hill is cancelled; however, the two Harriers remain over the target area for a further 30 minutes.

---

* Email correspondence, 11 January 2013.

† Email correspondence, 10 November 2012.

‡ From *No Picnic* by Julian Thompson.

Sgt Andy Gow

I noticed that elements of 2 PARA were beginning to move off Wireless Ridge and were heading down into Moody Brook. There now seemed to be a bit of confusion as to what was supposed to be happening, as 2 PARA were supposed to be giving us fire support. After a short while we began making our way into Moody Brook.

Robert Fox, journalist

Colonel Chaundler looked down from the eastern promontory of Wireless Ridge: 'I saw the Argentinians pouring down the hill into Stanley. They were like hundreds and thousands of black ants, pouring back.' His battalion prepared to follow, but first Brigadier Julian Thompson came to size up the position and then gave 2 PARA permission to move down the road into Stanley. With them was C Company 3 PARA, which had acted as reserve for Wireless Ridge.[*]

15.20hrs (zt): Arty R/L from U2: 'Relay to your Sunray, we are not to fire except in self-defence. Enemy to the north are giving up; those on Sapper Hill are standing up and not fighting, DO NOT fire except in self-defence.'

15.24hrs (zt): Arty R/L from U2: 'This last applies across the battlefield.'

Cpl Boyd (Smudge) Smith

Once the barracks had been secured by 2 PARA, C Company 3 PARA moved into the Moody Brook area; now members of both C Company 3 PARA and 2 PARA (2 PARA Tac HQ) stood chatting as we watched as the last of the Argentine stragglers ran towards Port Stanley. I was approached by a reporter/journalist [possibly Robert Fox] who asked, 'Who are you lot?' I replied, 'It's none of your business.' Everyone now waited for permission to advance forward into Stanley.

While C Company 3 PARA are in Moody Brook, they inform CO 3 PARA of the changing situation:

---

[*] From *Eyewitness Falklands* by Robert Fox.

15.24hrs: from C/S 3 to C/S 9: 'From Blue 2: the enemy appear to be surrendering, move down at best speed to Moody Brook.'

The CO 3 PARA, Hew Pike, orders his battalion to move off Mount Longdon and head for Wireless Ridge; the CO's Tac HQ follows A Company 3 PARA.

Major Martin Osborne

Moody Brook was deserted. I was aware of Major John Crosland of B Company 2 PARA moving down my right-hand side in order to get up onto higher ground. His company would advance towards the racecourse. I contacted the CO, Hew Pike, and updated him on the changing situation and he said, 'Martin, I want you to push on as far into Stanley as you can, before the enemy has a chance to regroup.'

15.27hrs (zt): Arty R/L from 59: 'From my Sunray, if he sees any enemy, fire one more gun at him, he will hit it with all he has got.'

15.27hrs (zt): Arty R/L from U2: 'Inform your Sunray that the order given was that firing in self-defence was permitted, but only self-defence.'

Sgt Ian Aird

As we progressed it became apparent that nothing was up on the high ground. However, there were a lot of anti-personnel mines scattered about, and it was decided by Major Crosland that we should move on to the Ross Road and follow A Company. From what I remember we were told to stop on the outskirts, but I remember hearing Major Hector Gullan protesting, 'No, push on.'

Lt Col Mike Rose

We landed on the Community School playing field. When we eventually arrived at the Secretariat a photo was taken by the local Port Stanley newspaper of us being escorted by Captain Melbourne Hussey into the Secretariat building. At this stage they were still not using the word 'surrender'.*

15.33hrs (zt): from AAC Radio log: 'Our friends are in Stanley and the enemy are putting up no resistance.'

---

* Email correspondence, 31 December 2012.

15.35hrs (zt): AAC Radio log from Brigade: 'Enemy on Sapper Hill, 45 Commando moving east down though Moody Brook, 2 PARA down Wireless Ridge. No move forward of 39 Easting. No fire to be opened except in self-defence. Guarantee given that no move east of 39 Easting as part of surrender terms.'

First report of white flag flying:

15.35hrs (zt): AAC R/L from Brigade: 'Urgent report of white flag flying over Port Stanley.'

15.35hrs (zt): Arty R/L from 9Z: 'G19 has just walked into a deserted enemy gun position 1500 metres along the road west from Stanley.'

15.37hrs (zt): AAC R/L from 0: 'From Div, no firing other than self-defence.'

15.40hrs (zt): AAC R/L from 9A: 'Call Sign moving east no resistance, possible surrender.'

Pte Bob Greasley, C Company 3 PARA

As we moved through Moody Brook, I was looking at some of the dug-in Argy machine-gun positions, thinking, Thank fuck we didn't have to attack this fucking place!

Cpl Donny McDonald

Moody Brook was surreal, with the smoke and smell of burning. The 2 PARA guys looked exhausted; the first person to speak to me was an officer from 2 PARA Tac HQ, who asked, 'What are 3 PARA doing here?' I said, 'Sir, we were told that we were to attack Moody Brook and then advance into Stanley.' He didn't reply; he just turned and walked off. Everything was happening so fast, then a white flare was fired up from Port Stanley and everyone seemed to think it was a signal that the Argentines wanted to surrender. The blokes were saying, 'That's it; it's over; they've jacked.' Shortly after that I heard someone saying, 'Okay, 2 PARA, let's get into Stanley.'

Lt Col David Chaundler

We had been joined with great rapidity by C Company 3 PARA, who'd come off Mount Longdon, and who I think were trying to race us. We encountered some small-arms fire, but I'd got the tanks and machine guns on the other side of the inlet ready with covering fire, and the artillery were silently marking targets as we proceeded, in case we got into trouble.*

15.46hrs (zt): Arty R/L from 9Z: 'From G19 leading B elements [B Company 2 PARA] now on the outskirts of Port Stanley.'

Lt Barry Griffiths

As we advanced towards Moody Brook, 2 PARA came off Wireless Ridge and cut in front of us, which we were quite annoyed about, so we stepped up the pace and as they moved into Moody Brook we all sort of intermingled with 2 PARA. After a short while we went into Stanley with them.

Lt Col David Chaundler now leads 2 PARA Tac HQ towards Port Stanley.

C Company 3 PARA will follow after them at a tactical distance into Port Stanley.

CSgt Andy Gow

It felt strange walking in, with all the smoke drifting across the road from smouldering bunkers and buildings. As we approached, the FIGAS building was on our left, and up on our right was the gunline of 105mm's that had given us such a hard time. It was weird seeing everywhere deserted and abandoned kit laying everywhere.

15.50hrs (zt): Arty R/L from 9Z: 'There is a white flag flying over Port Stanley, from B elements G19, Thank God.'

[B Company 2 Para.]

Major John Crosland

After negotiating several minefields, I eventually ordered B Company 2 PARA to move down from the high ground and on to the Ross Road, where we chased after A Company 2 PARA. We eventually went firm around the area of the Deputy's house, which we took over and set up as B Company HQ. At this point the situation was not at all clear as to whether the Argentines had agreed

---

* From *Forgotten Voices of the Falklands* by Hugh McManners.

to any 'Terms of Surrender'. B Company established a defensive position and I then instructed my soldiers that no one was to pass.*

15.50hrs (zt): AAC R/L from Brigade: 'Unconfirmed report of white flag flying over Port Stanley.'

15.54hrs (zt): Arty R/L from U2: 'From Sunray, inform G19 he is to tell Sunray his supported arm that he is NOT repeat NOT to cross the 39 Easting.'

3 PARA HQ inform the CO 3 PARA, who is marching towards Wireless Ridge, of a possible surrender:

15.54hrs (zt): from C/S 0 to C/S 9: 'Situation report: the enemy appear to be surrendering; lots of enemy standing on Sapper Hill, negotiations taking place between Higher Formation and Argies.'

Lt Mike O'Neill

I am not sure how long we were in Moody Brook, but it wasn't long before both C Company 3 PARA and 2 PARA were advancing down the Ross Road into Stanley. We were behind either one or two platoons from 2 PARA.

Major Martin Osborne

We now moved without orders, and indeed possibly against orders given by Brigadier Thompson, on to the Ross Road, and began advancing towards Port Stanley. We carried on, mixed in with elements of 2 PARA, passing the FIGAS [Falkland Islands Government Air Service] station. The road was covered with the debris of war: ammunition, weapons and various bits of kit.

Cpl Boyd (Smudge) Smith

We continued along the Ross Road as far the FIGAS building, as my patrol had completed the task of getting C Company to Moody Brook. I then asked Major Osborne did he want me to do anything else. He said politely, 'No, C Company will take it from here.' They then passed through us and advanced along the Ross Road, following 2 PARA. My patrol now went into the FIGAS building; it was empty, the Argentines had bugged out and made their way into

---

* Email correspondence, 6 November 2012.

Stanley. We cleared it and came back out onto the Ross Road. We saw some 2 PARA blokes walking down the road wearing berets, and they called over, 'It's "end ex", mate; they've surrendered.' It was now that we all took our helmets off.

16.00hrs (zt): Arty R/L from 9Z: 'G19 has stopped at the correct location, LO (Liaison Officer = Major Hector Gullan) from Higher Formation is with him.'

16.00hrs (zt): A and B Company 2 PARA have stopped and taken up defensive positions in the area around the racecourse grandstand. 2 PARA Tac HQ establishes its headquarters in the offices of the Argentine state airline Lineas Aeréas del Estado (LADE), which is approximately 500 metres east of the 39 Easting

Now that A and B Companies have established a firm defensive line, the Support element of 2 PARA is called off Wireless Ridge. D Company, C Company and Support Company 2 PARA are followed by the Blues and Royals.

16.15hrs (zt): Arty R/L from U2: 'Although calm prevails, a formal ceasefire has not yet been negotiated. We remain in a state of hostility to Argentine Forces outside the Falklands. Blackout is to remain in force; security is not to be relaxed, and normal operating procedures remain in force until further notice.'

Brigadier Julian Thompson has now returned by helicopter and has landed on the reverse slope of Wireless Ridge, where he encounters CO 3 PARA. Brigadier Thompson then joins the tail end of D and C Companies 2 PARA as they move off Wireless Ridge.

Brigadier Julian Thompson

I left to rejoin 2 PARA, taking Holroyd-Smith, Rowe and Marine McGuire, with a radio and Corporal Dean for close protection. The other key member of the R Group [Rover Group], Major Roddy MacDonald, was forward with 2 PARA already. It was with jubilation that we stepped out onto Wireless Ridge to join the tail of 2 PARA snaking their way downhill past Moody Brook.*

3 PARA HQ warn CO 3 PARA that there is no surrender yet:

---

* From *No Picnic* by Julian Thompson.

16.20hrs (zt): from C/S 0 to C/S 9: '1) Argies have not yet surrendered, 2) All units to remain on Full Alert, 3) Look out for air attack, 4) Watch blackout tonight.'

Sgt Martin (Dickie) Bird

As we advanced, my platoon was tasked with clearing the 105mm positions. I entered into a Command Post which had been completely wrecked by a direct hit from an SS11 missile. It was full of dead guys, but under some rubble we found a young-looking artillery officer, who had survived the carnage. At first he thought we were going to kill him, but when we offered him a cigarette, the look of relief on his face was unbelievable. We delivered him back to his own guys in Port Stanley about half an hour later. Before he left us, he gave me a tobacco tin which I still have.

16.25hrs (zt): from C/S 69 to C/S 0: '2 Call Sign have been in and are now clear.'

Cpl Donny McDonald

It was quite eerie as we came in, passing the bodies of dead Argentines and smouldering bunkers. There were all types of weapons and equipment scattered all over the road, there were shell holes everywhere, and smoke was drifting across the road, the smell of cordite; it is a sight that will always stay with me. 8 Platoon C Company entered with 2 PARA, but 2 PARA were slightly in front.

3 PARA HQ informs the CO that 42 Commando are being flown forward; this will give an incentive to the rest of 3 PARA to speed up:

16.27hrs (zt): from C/S 0 to C/S 9: 'From Brigade: 42 Commando now being flown into forward location.'

16.31hrs (zt): Arty R/L from 9Z: 'G19 has gone in with his Foxhounds and is on the racecourse, have we any tips for good runners?'

16.50hrs (zt): AAC R/L from Brigade: 'Unconfirmed report of white flag flying over Port Stanley.'

16.52hrs (zt): AAC R/L from 0: 'Argy Mercy Bird coming into Stanley escorted by two Harriers, do not shoot at it.'

Pte David Gammon

I think it came over the radio whilst we were on the Ross Road, that the Argentines had surrendered. It was a great relief; the blokes were just taking their helmets off and putting their berets on. I felt extremely proud of our achievement, but also saddened by the loss of such good blokes. I remember looking at artillery positions that had given us such a hard time and thinking, You bastards!

CSgt Andy Gow

We continued along the Ross Road and at some point 2 PARA were told to stop; however, as we had not received any order to stop, we continued on for 300–400 metres, passing the old war memorial, until we reached the bend in the road. We now received orders to 'go firm'. Just ahead of us was a crashed enemy Puma helicopter. We stopped here for a short while, but we received orders to pull back.

As no one has told C Company 3 PARA to stop, they continue advancing 500 metres forward of 2 PARA's stopping point before they are eventually ordered to stop, just before Government House.

Lt Barry Griffiths

As we moved towards the outskirts of Stanley there were smoking shell holes, equipment had been abandoned everywhere, but there was a sense of euphoria. I can only imagine it was similar to winning the World Cup. We had received no orders to stop, so we continued moving into Stanley and eventually stopped just short of Government House, but after a short time we were ordered to pull back by members of B Company 2 PARA. We eventually moved into the houses on the coast road. One thing I particularly remember is clapping the Royal Marines when they came in, it was like a rugby tunnel, with PARAs either side of the road, but they weren't too pleased. They then continued on to Government House, where they hoisted their Union Jack.

Major Martin Osborne

Eventually we reached the outskirts of Port Stanley. As we approached the old war memorial, we could see in the distance Argentines running away from us. I then noticed an Argentinian gun team in a ditch outside Government House;

they were looking at us with utter astonishment, and I decided to go across and speak with them. Also with me was Pte Paul [Scouse] Palmer. I ordered them to unload, which they did. I said to them firmly, 'Don't you dare move or my sniper will shoot you,' [meaning Pte Palmer] but as I glanced back to Palmer, he was looking over his shoulder looking for the sniper!

Someone from B Company 2 PARA appeared behind me, and said he wanted us to move back, but I protested: 'The CO has told me to push as far forward as we can get.' Fortunately, just at that moment I received a message from the CO ordering me to stop.

The CO orders C Company 3 PARA to 'STOP':

16.55hrs (zt): from C/S 9 to C/S 39: 'You must stop; you must not go any further forward, there is no surrender yet.'

Cpl Martin (Taff) Richardson

We eventually reached the town and continued on to just beyond the old war memorial, where we were ordered to stop. We then turned about and moved back. I thought Major Osborne was a good OC; he led from the front all the way across.

16.58hrs (zt): AAC R/L from Brigade: '1 Welsh Guards on Sapper Hill.'

3 PARA HQ informs CO 3 PARA, no move east of 39 Easting. C Company 3 PARA is approximately 900 metres forward of the 39 Easting:

17.00hrs (zt): from C/S 0 to C/S 9: 'From Brigade: No move east of 39 Easting.'

Lt Mike O'Neill

We eventually pulled back to link up with the lead elements of 2 PARA. I remember seeing Lt Geoff Weighell of B Company 2 PARA sitting in the front garden of a house having a brew.

Lt Geoff Weighell, 25 yrs – B Company 2 PARA

At that point we were joined in the gardens of houses running alongside the main road by elements of C Company 3 PARA. We were all sat around having a brew, waiting for next orders. I suddenly realized that the bloke opposite me –

who I didn't immediately recognize – was none other than Lt Mike O'Neill, my best mate! Under several weeks of cam cream and the effects of the preceding hard days of battle, neither of us recognized the other! It was a fine reunion.*

Major Martin Osborne

I was discussing what to do next when CO 2 PARA turned up, and after a short chat it was decided we should move back. We found ourselves some bungalows close to HQ 2 PARA, about 300 metres back down the road. I then spotted the unmistakable figure of journalist Max Hastings, who appeared, striding down the road with his walking stick; he was heading in the direction of Government House. I knew Max well, as he and I had played Scrabble aboard the SS *Canberra* many times. However, we didn't speak to one another as he went down the road, so I doubt he will remember the encounter.

Max Hastings has slipped the net!

17.15hrs (zt): from C/S 0 to C/S 9: 'Send location status for Brigade; and also no Press to go forward yet.'

CO 3 PARA has now caught up with C Company 3 PARA, who have moved back and are co-located with 2 PARA, who have set up Tactical HQ in the offices of the Argentine airline LADE.

CO 3 PARA now informs 3 PARA HQ of his location:

17.20hrs (zt): from C/S 9 to C/S 0: 'Co-located with C/S 3 in community centre talking to CO 2 PARA, rest of battalion at Moody Brook.'

17.22hrs (zt): AAC R/L from 9A: 'No info to be passed to Press.'

Cpl Boyd (Smudge) Smith

As we went past the gunline of 105mm Howitzers, there was smoke everywhere, discarded kit and weapons all over the place. It seemed as if, as the Argentines had been running down the road, they were gradually running out of steam; they were ditching anything that might have slowed them down. We then

---

* Email correspondence with Dair Farrar-Hockley, 4 September 2012.

came across what looked like a QM's bunker; it contained four Argentinians who immediately surrendered to us. One of them had a chest wound; either Pte Gaz Pullen or Pte Mick Robson treated him. We took them across to the Ross Road, where we gave them to members of A Company 3 PARA, who were now entering Stanley.

We then continued up to the first bungalows, where we found an abandoned Argentine jeep. We drove back to the Argy QM's bunker, where we collected some scoff, pasta and tins of meatballs in tomato sauce; we also found a few FALs with folding butts still wrapped in greaseproof paper. We then just waited for the rest of the battalion to catch up. C Company was told to move back from Government House to consolidate. We waited by the roadside near the jeep for the rest of the battalion to arrive, and as they did, we greeted them with much relief, as most of them we hadn't seen since we cross-decked from the SS *Canberra*.

Brigadier Julian Thompson
I remember having seen a helicopter coming into Stanley with a white flag hanging underneath, and I thought it may have been bringing in General Moore. I wanted to meet him and give him an update on Army and Commando units in and around Port Stanley. This is what made me ignore the stop order, and go forward with my small group to the Secretariat building. When I reached it, a smart Argentine officer, Major Carlos Doglioli, who recognized my badge of rank, asked me in perfect English, 'What do you want, Brigadier?' In return I asked him if my General was here, and he said, 'No, but mine is, and there are two British officers with him, do you want to come in?' However, I decided to leave, as I did not wish to break in on the delicate negotiations and risk their success by my interrupting.*

CSgt Andy Gow
By now the rest of the battalion was coming up the Ross Road. We waited at the side of the road for decisions to be made on what was happening, and for it to be confirmed if the Argentines had actually surrendered or not! Eventually we were told to occupy one of the bungalows; we moved into number 16 Ross Road West.

---

* Email correspondence, 18 September 2012.

Later a photographer, Paul Haley of *Soldier Magazine*, came along and asked could he take a photo of us outside the bungalow. Shortly after, I came across two very young members of B Company who seemed to be wandering around a bit shell-shocked. We brought them in and sat them down and made them a brew. I remember a couple of bottles of wine and Fray Bentos tins of steak appearing in the bungalow – and what a great scoff we had that night!

Pte David Gammon

I remember Cpl Alan [Jock the gob] Burton hunting high and low for alcohol. Eventually he made up an alcoholic brew, and I think he mixed it in a large trophy cup; it turned out orange and was the consistency of snot. We drank it from old jam jars, cups, anything we could find. There was Taff Richardson, Geordie Nicholson, Jock Burton, Karl [Ox] Oxbury and Paul [Johno] Johnstone. I remember watching Geordie Nicholson and Ox slowly sliding down the wall after a few mouthfuls. We all slept well that first night.

17.40hrs (zt): AAC R/L from C/S 2 to C/S 9: 'There are seven friendly bodies at C/S 9B location send either a V or Y call sign to pick up these bodies.'

17.57hrs (zt): AAC R/L from C/S 9 to C/S 9A: 'Could they have 30 minutes to prepare bodies for removal?'

17.59hrs (zt): AAC R/L from C/S 9A to C/S 9: 'A Victor C/S has already been tasked and will be leaving in five minutes.'

18.41hrs (zt): AAC R/L from Brigade: 'Brigade, expressed wish that SG [Scots Guards] move back to Bluff Cove.'

19.12hrs (zt): AAC R/L from Brigade: 'Scout to be tasked to pick up member of 1WG to try and find two WGs who are missing.'

19.26hrs (zt): AAC R/L from C/S 9A to C/S 0: 'Task to look for Welsh Guards cancelled.' [Due to weather conditions.]

Brigade to 3 PARA HQ:

19.32hrs (zt): from C/S 99 to C/S 0: 'All Sunrays to Government House by 20.30hrs (zt).'

20.18hrs (zt): AAC R/L from Brigade: 'Ceasefire agreed between Britain and Argentina.'

21.00hrs (zt): from C/S 0 to C/S 9: 'From Brigade: all units east of 39 Easting are now to withdraw to the west of this line.'

21.00hrs (zt): from C/S 9 to C/S 0: 'Roger.'

21.00hrs (zt): AAC R/L from Brigade: 'Situation report negotiations with Menéndez in Stanley continue, he has agreed to ceasefire.'

Lt Col Mike Rose

After some six hours of discussion, Menéndez finally agreed the surrender of all forces, at which point I asked General Moore to come to Port Stanley and sign the formal surrender document. I did not return to HMS *Fearless* until the next day, when I escorted Menéndez to captivity.*

3 PARA HQ inform CO that Brigade wants everyone to move west of 39 Easting:

21.45hrs (zt): from C/S 0 to C/S 9: 'From Sunray Higher Form: We are to move west of 39 Easting and inform Brigade when this has been done.'

21.45hrs (zt): from C/S 9 to C/S 0: 'CO informed.'

22.00hrs (zt): from C/S 0 to C/S 9: 'If you can give an assurance that no Argentinian will be rounded up, or disarmed, you may stay where you are, CO acknowledge.'

22.00hrs (zt): from C/S 9 to C/S 0: 'CO acknowledged.'

22.45hrs (zt): from C/S 99 to C/S 0: 'There will be a helicopter flying over Stanley at 23.30hrs (zt).'

CTF 317 General Jeremy Moore collects the surrender document and is then flown into Port Stanley:

23.07hrs (zt): Arty Net, Info: 'Commander Land Forces left to collect surrender document, he will then fly to Port Stanley to take surrender of the Falkland Islands.'

---

* Email correspondence, 31 December 2012.

TUESDAY 15 JUNE 1982

Brigade informs 3 PARA HQ on the condition of LCpl Denzil Connick:

00.54hrs (zt): from C/S 99 to C/S 0: 'LCpl Connick wounded in action, GSW. He is now on SS *Uganda*, condition not known.'

00.54hrs (zt): from C/S 0 to C/S 99: 'Ops Officer informed.'

01.15hrs (zt): from C/S 0 to All Stations: 'Surrender of both east and west Falklands.'

3 PARA HQ want to know where CO 3 PARA is located:

01.15hrs (zt): from C/S 0 to C/S 9: 'Send location status.'

01.15hrs (zt): from C/S 9 to C/S 0: 'LH ZTR [grid 388730].'

01.15hrs (zt): Arty R/L from NGS [Naval Gunfire Support]:, 'The Surrender has been signed! A long hard slog is over – God rest those who will always stay. '

This message is dated Tuesday 15 June 1982, signed WO2 SJ Absolon Royal Artillery, Land Forces, Falkland Islands.

The surrender document is signed at 01.00hrs (zt) 15 June, which equates to 9.00pm on the 14th local time.

01.17hrs (zt): AAC R/L from AAC-OC: 'The surrender was signed 30 minutes ago – no more details.'

01.20hrs (zt): Telex sent by Commander Land Forces 317 General Jeremy Moore:

HQ LFFI Port Stanley, In Port Stanley at 9 O'CLOCK PM Falkland Islands Time tonight 14 June 1982, Major General Menéndez surrendered to me all the Argentine Forces in East and West Falkland, together with all their impedimenta. Arrangements are in hand to assemble the men for return to Argentina, to gather in their arms and equipment, and to mark and make safe their munitions. The Falkland Islands are once more under the government desired by their inhabitants.

God Save the Queen.

Signed JJ Moore.

Message ends

02.00hrs (zt): from C/S 0 to C/S 9: 'Confirmed by Brigade; D 31 [Pte Dickie Absolon] now deceased.'

02.24hrs (zt): from C/S 0 to C/S 9: 'Argentine unconditional surrender of both islands.'

14.30hrs (zt): from C/S 9 to C/S 0: 'Can you confirm SP 104 [LCpl Denzil Connick] has died?'

14.30hrs (zt): from C/S 0 to C/S 9: 'Alive.'

CHAPTER EIGHT

'WE'LL TRY TO GET YOU OUT OF HERE AS SOON AS POSSIBLE'

MEDICAL AND EVACUATION
3 PARA AND ATTACHMENTS

8.1   'The mountain was alive with gunfire'

FRIDAY 11 JUNE 1982

The plan for the casualty treatment and evacuation was that there would be a member of each section who had done a basic medical course. On the journey south the entire battalion had refreshed their basic battlefield first-aid drills. There would be two battalion medics with each rifle company. The wounded personnel would be moved, when safe to do so, to the Company Aid Post. Once there, they would receive treatment from the company medic. Eventually the casualty would be moved to the Regimental Aid Post. They would be assessed by a doctor, who would be operating a triage system. The wounded man would be evacuated by a Snowcat vehicle (Volvo BV 202) to a helicopter landing site approximately 5 kilometres away for helicopter evacuation, and from there they would be taken to a Medical Reception Centre at Estancia House (Starlight 2). Here a Commando medical unit would act as a clearing station where they would triage the wounded, to avoid the Advanced Surgical Centres being overwhelmed with cases. Once assessed, the wounded would be transferred to an ASC [Advanced Surgical Centre] at Ajax Bay, Fitzroy or Teal Inlet, or taken directly to SS Uganda. For this task, there would be four helicopters equipped to fly at night, which would be based at Fitzroy. According to a report from 656 Squadron, the four helicopters did arrive at Fitzroy but, sadly, not one of them was equipped to fly at night.

The Regimental Aid Post Team would split into two groups: Captain John Burgess would lead the initial team and Captain Mike Von Bertele would lead a follow-up team. They would cross the Murrell Bridge once 45 Commando had crossed their Start Line at 01.00hrs (zt). Subsequently, they planned to arrive at Longdon at approximately 02.30hrs (zt). Then the Snowcats would begin the evacuation of any wounded personnel. The full RAP team would be two doctors, one padre, five medics and 18 stretcher-bearers; each man would carry his own personal weapon and ammunition plus 600 rounds of link ammunition. No Red Cross markers were used by anyone in 3 PARA. If the advance continued to Wireless Ridge, the rearward RAP would follow up behind in Volvo BV tracked vehicles with further stores, and would have the capability to move through the first RAP and set up independently.

Captain John (Doctor) Burgess, 26 yrs – Medical Officer

After extensive medical briefings, our group was moved up from Estancia House to an area occupied by A Company. During the move, news came through of our first casualty: Pte Lee Fisher of D Company. He was wounded in the back by a piece of shrapnel from artillery fire while waiting in the assembly area.

The battalion assembly area was about 6 kilometres from our objective. In the same area there were a large number of civilians. They very bravely agreed to help with the operation, by providing their own tractors to transport items such as mortar ammunition and medical supplies. Major Dennison gave a short talk to those under his command. As he did so, more shells started to fall close by, but it soon fell silent.

A Company contact 3 PARA HQ regarding Pte Lee Fisher:

16.00hrs (zt): from C/S 1 to C/S 0: 'Casualty report, D Coy 37, shrapnel wound in small of back, but walking, location Call Sign 1.'

3 PARA HQ update RAP Team:

17.45hrs (zt): from C/S 0 to C/S 83A: 'Casualty from C/S 1 [Pte Fisher] now back at Teal.'

Sqn Leader Peter Harris and Flight Lt Nick Gilchrist drop four cluster bombs on Mount Longdon at approximately 18.35hrs (zt).

18.40hrs (zt): from C/S 0 to All Stations: 'Two Harriers attacking Mount Longdon anytime now.'

At 20.30hrs (zt), the primary RAP group form up and takes its place in the Support Company column for the march towards Mount Longdon. Shortly after leaving A Company's position, the Support Company Group are in dead ground from Two Sisters, which provides some protection from enemy OPs. The march moves on steadily until the Murrell River is reached. The river is crossed and they continueeastwards. The stretcher-bearers suffer more than most on the march with their heavy loads. At approximately 00.31hrs (zt) on 12 June, the Support Company Group reach their firebase line, which was about 900 metres from the western edge of the mountain. It has been a dark night up until then. Then the moon begins to rise slowly above the eastern edge of the mountain, silhouetting the objective.

SATURDAY 12 JUNE 1982

Major Dennison informs the CO he is in position and setting up:

00.31hrs (zt): from C/S 59 to C/S 9: 'Going firm, ready in five minutes.'

Padre Derek Heaver, 35 yrs – Regimental Aid Post Team

We moved to Mount Longdon with Support Company. The equipment we needed meant that each man carried an almost excessive amount of weight. Being a non-combatant, my load was probably the lightest. Fortunately, I was able to relieve one of the soldiers by carrying some of his link ammunition, as he was buckling under the weight of his other equipment.

After approximately 40 minutes into B Company's advance, comes the first contact report:

01.07hrs (zt): from C/S 29 to C/S 9: 'Contact wait-out.'

01.15hrs (zt): from C/S 0 to C/S 99: 'Situation Report, A & B still advancing, B Coy hit mine, minor casualty.'

Captain John (Doctor) Burgess

I don't recall hearing the mine explosion, but I do recall the radios coming to life with reports of a mine explosion, followed almost immediately by small-arms fire on the mountain. Shortly after this we were despatched with a group of stretcher-bearers towards Mount Longdon to set up the Regimental Aid Post. We made our way as fast as we could, passing through what we now knew to be a minefield. When we eventually reached Longdon, I did a quick visual appreciation and decided to set up the RAP at the base of the north-west corner, keeping close into the rocks. The time was then approximately 01.40hrs (zt). The mountain was alive with gunfire.

Padre Derek Heaver

There was a huge amount of noise and tracer fire going overhead. Argentine illumination rounds were being fired into the air. There was a lot of confusion as to where people were. I can't remember how long, but it seemed quite a time before the first of the wounded was brought to us.

Pte Craig (Tommy) Onions, 19 yrs – Ammunition-Bearer/Stretcher-Bearer

There was a small explosion, which initiated the battle. Almost immediately, my group of ammunition-bearers was told to follow Captain Mason. With him were Cpl McCarthy's Milan detachment, Cpl Cook and LCpl Vince Bramley with their SF gun teams. We made our way as fast as possible across to A Company, who were situated approximately 600 metres away from us on Wing Forward.

Sgt Keith Hopper, 29 yrs – Ammunition-Bearer/Stretcher-Bearer

Our group of ammunition-bearers were under the command of Captain Mason. We were ordered to move to A Company's position on Wing Forward. Captain Mason moved off at a very fast pace, and we struggled to keep up. Once there, we were pinned down alongside members of A Company. The word went around that enemy snipers were also active. I searched around for some better cover and found a fold in the ground and lay next to another soldier [Jock Brebner]. We waited to carry ammunition in support of the SF machine guns, as and when the gun teams required it. I remember sitting there on the freezing cold, damp ground, listening to the sounds of battle.

CSgt Steve Knights, 31 yrs – Support Company

I received a message from Major Dennison to take my team of stretcher-bearers forward and set up at the base of the mountain. We made our way as fast as possible, in single file, to the base of the mountain. At about the same time, B Company came on the radio asking Major Dennison to send the stretcher-bearers, as they had taken casualties. Major Dennison told them that the RAP team and stretchers were already on their way. We reached the base of Longdon, and the RAP team began setting up to receive casualties. The stretcher-bearers dropped off their ammunition and found cover.

It is now approximately 01.40hrs (zt).

CSgt Brian Faulkner, 34 yrs – Regimental Aid Post Team

We began establishing ourselves, sorting out all our kit and waiting for the first casualties to arrive. There was gunfire coming from all areas of the mountain. We couldn't send the stretcher-bearers out, because we didn't know what areas were secure and where the casualties were.

At this stage, 6 Platoon have four dead and eight wounded:

01.50hrs (zt): from C/S 29 to C/S 9: 'Call Sign 2/3 [6 Platoon] has several casualties. Enemy still firing from high ground, am still advancing and clearing.'

3 PARA HQ give Brigade a situation report:

02.00hrs (zt): from C/S 0 to C/S 99: 'Situation Report from forward OC Mount Longdon. Casualties taken, warn off Hawkeye for later on.' (Possibly 3 serious.)

This last comment is in the log.

Major Roger Patton, who has been made aware of casualties and is anxious to move his convoy forward and begin evacuating wounded, contacts 3 PARA HQ:

02.05hrs (zt): from C/S 9A to C/S 0: 'Check with 45 Commando that it is clear for us to move forward.'

02.05hrs (zt): from C/S 0 to C/S 9A: 'Roger passed to 45 on other means.'

02.05hrs (zt): from C/S 0 to C/S 99: 'Call Sign Playtime request to move up track.'

However, X Company of 45 Commando are running late; they are struggling with their approach march. The following passage is from a book by Ian Gardiner of 45 Commando:

> My navigation team and I became confused and did not take the planned route. Instead, we found ourselves on the wrong side of a stone run. This was a major obstacle and it took ages to cross it safely.*

Brigade contact 3 PARA HQ, to tell them to move the convoy further back. Hopefully, the convoy will be able to move forward at 05.00hrs (zt):

02.15hrs (zt) from C/S 99 to C/S 0: 'Casevac move back by Playtime to secure area and also area of high ground, hopefully before five, grid 260765.'

Convoy is now 2 kilometres north-west of Murrell Bridge.

Padre Derek Heaver

It was in the early stages of the battle that Captain Burgess and I went up the western slope to find Pte Dodsworth, one of the B Company medics. We had been told that he had been wounded. We found him lying on his back. He was already being attended to by members of 6 Platoon. Even with all his medical skills there was nothing more the Doc could do there. We had to get him to the RAP.

3 PARA HQ is now informed by Brigade HQ that X Company 45 Commando are running two hours late, have only just reached their Start Line and have yet to attack and secure their objective, North Sister, codenamed 'Long Toenail'. Only then will Y and Z Companies of 45 Commando be able to begin their assault on South Sister, codenamed 'Summer Days'. Only then, when this attack has begun, will 3 PARA's vehicle convoy be allowed to cross the Murrell Bridge with their vital ammunition and medical supplies.

---

* From *The Yompers: With 45 Commando in the Falklands War* by Ian Gardiner.

02.55hrs (zt): from C/S 99 to C/S 0: '45 Commando at "FAST CAR" Rocky feature at grid 2672.'

[1 kilometre west of Murrell River.]

B Company contacts Support Company requiring stretchers:

03.00hrs (zt): from C/S 29 to C/S 59: 'Have taken quite a number of casualties and require a lot of stretchers, caused by heavy firefight.'

03.00hrs (zt): from C/S 0 to C/S 99: 'Situation report, Call Sign 1 under fire and going forward, Call Sign 2, after coming under heavy fire, but moving forward, ref casevac no numbers as yet, will inform when confirmed.'

At this time 3 PARA have a total of 24 wounded and eight dead. Four members of 6 Platoon's wounded have now been located:

03.20hrs (zt): from C/S 59 to C/S 9: 'Four casualties taken by Call Sign 59 stretcher party.'

These first four casualties are Pte Mark Dodsworth followed shortly by Pte Stuart Grey, Pte Den Dunn and LCpl Steve Wright; these will be the first wounded to reach the RAP.

Captain (Doctor) John Burgess

The first casualty to reach us was Pte Mark Dodsworth. He was conscious and we immediately began to check for entry and exit wounds. We located a chest wound and a thigh wound, applied a plastic seal over his chest wound and set up an intravenous drip. He was having trouble breathing and we checked his airway, and he seemed to ease. Shortly after this, three members of 6 Platoon arrived with various wounds [LCpl Steve Wright, Pte Stuart Grey and Pte Dennis Dunn]. However, at this stage, Mark Dodsworth was our number-one priority, he needed evacuating urgently.

CSgt Brian Faulkner

Pte Mark Dodsworth was 6 Platoon's medic and a friend of all of us in the medical team. Mark was in a terrible state, he had been shot a number of times. The team worked tirelessly to keep Mark alive in the most demanding of circumstances. Incoming artillery fire was landing on and near our position.

Our own artillery was passing overhead. Members of 6 Platoon told us that there were lots more wounded up on Fly Half. Sgt Pete Marshall and I made our way up onto the western slope to try to see if we could be of any assistance, but the majority of 6 Platoon's wounded were unreachable.

Pte Stuart Grey, 19 yrs – 3 Section 6 Platoon

I made my way down to the RAP, where I was checked over by Sgt Steve Bradley. Shortly after I arrived, Den Dunn also arrived. He was treated by John Kennedy. We were then told to find some cover, and that we would be called forward when the BVs arrived.

LCpl Steve Wright, 22 yrs – D Company Guide

I'm not too sure who led me down the western slope into the Regimental Aid Post area, but I was checked over by Doctor Burgess and told to find a place to shelter and wait until I'm called forward to be casevaced. I thought, So much for them saying, 'We'll have you on the SS *Uganda* within the hour.' [Gunshot wound right arm.]

LCpl Wright is referring to what a lot of soldiers remember being told: 'If you get wounded, the helicopters will fly you out to the SS Uganda within the hour.'

Major Roger Patton can wait no longer and decides to make his way on foot to Longdon to assess the situation. He details Captain Bob Darby to set up a night LS (Landing Site) at grid 273752 using a NATO 'T' configuration, then makes his way to Longdon leaving WO2 John Carey in command of the convoy.

CSgt Brian Faulkner

The vehicle convoy had still not arrived. It was now approximately 04.00hrs (zt) and there was still no sign of them. We urgently needed to get Mark Dodsworth evacuated. Major Roger Patton was constantly asking Brigade to let his vehicle convoy through, only to be told, 'No, 45 Commando has priority over the track.' It was chaos; the northern side of the mountain was still an unknown area as to what was happening.

At 04.16hrs (zt) on 12 June (Lt Col) Whitehead, conscious that he had to take advantage of the night, decided to advance without waiting for X Company to complete its attack.*

Moving Y and Z Companies off their Start Line would finally allow 3 PARA's vehicle convoy to cross the Murrell Bridge and begin its journey to the Mortar Line. Once there, they would drop off their mortar ammunition and continue on with the medical team and their supplies to Mount Longdon and begin evacuating the wounded, but this would be a journey time from the Murrell Bridge to Longdon of approximately 90 minutes.

Sgt Keith Hopper

We received orders to move from Wing Forward. Captain Mason told us to pack up, and that we were needed on Mount Longdon. We rapidly made our way across to the base of Longdon, where we dumped our ammunition and then reported to the RAP that by now had been established.

CSgt Derek (Dex) Allen, 38 yrs – Regimental Aid Post Team

Our group of ammunition-bearers/stretcher-bearers arrived at the RAP around 04.30hrs (zt). It was reported that voices could be heard out to the left of our position. LCpl Gary Teale, LCpl Alex Henderson and I went to investigate. After climbing down from some rocks, we found ourselves with flat ground ahead of us. We made contact by voice to somebody calling for help. We found Cpl Brian Milne being looked after by Pte Ron Duffy. Cpl Milne had already received first aid and was conscious. We retraced our steps and reported to Captain Burgess. He informed us that the 2ic, Major Roger Patton, would arrange for his evacuation as soon as the Snowcats arrived.

---

* From *The Official History of the Falklands Campaign* by Sir Lawrence Freedman.

Major Roger Patton, 40 yrs – 2IC Second in Command, 3 PARA, Headquarters Company (Vehicle Convoy)

When I reached Mount Longdon, Captain John Burgess and his team were located on Route 2, near the base of Mount Longdon. The RAP was in full view of the Two Sisters mountain that was now under attack. I decided to move them around to the north-west corner to a position that gave them a lot more cover from direct fire.

Captain John (Doctor) Burgess

Major Patton moved the RAP around to a more sheltered area just to the back of the rocks. Roger then took on the huge task of controlling the administration side of the RAP and the delegation of stretcher-bearers, along with radio communications regarding medical evacuation by BV and helicopter. Later, he controlled everything involving prisoner management and evacuation and the deceased. That left the doctors and medics free to treat the wounded.

Captain Mike (Doctor) Von Bertele, 26 yrs – Doctor RAMC (Vehicle Convoy)

Eventually, my team [Cpl Davie Wilson and Cpl Neil Parkin] reached Mount Longdon about 05.30hrs (zt). When we arrived, there was a bit of confusion over who was where and who was doing what. I had a discussion with CSgt Brian Faulkner, and it was decided that he would go off with a couple of medics onto the western slope to look for any further casualties. We were trying to get helicopters in. We kept calling; however, we didn't get any helicopter until well after first light.

CSgt Brian Faulkner

The vehicle convoy arrived shortly after Major Patton. We loaded Mark Dodsworth, along with a few of the other wounded, into a BV. Major Patton then got on the radio to liaise with Brigade HQ, trying to get a helicopter. Around that time, DSgt Geoff Deaney, WO2 Mick Shaw, WO2 Kenny Sargent and WO2 John Carey started to arrive individually, either on foot or with their BVs. It was during this time that the decision was made to use one of the BVs to drive into the minefield to try to recover Cpl Milne. Sgt Bradley volunteered to go, on board the BV. They hadn't gone far into the minefield when they detonated a mine. It shook up both the driver and Sgt Bradley. The driver thought it best to reverse out. They then struck a second mine. Eventually, the damaged BV limped back in. Both men were quite shaken but unhurt.

At 05.35hrs (zt), the first medical evacuation takes place. Pte Dodsworth and Pte Dunn are loaded into the first BV. LCpl Wright and Pte Grey are loaded into the second BV for the 5-kilometre trip. It takes approximately 1 hour 30 minutes, cross country, to the improvised helicopter LS manned by Captain Bob Darby and his team. The hope is that the helicopters will be there, as Estancia House is a further 9 kilometres away, over the most horrendous terrain.

Padre Derek Heaver

I remember Captain Burgess saying about Mark Dodsworth, 'There's nothing more we can do here. We must get him back.' It was heart-wrenching when we watched that slow-moving vehicle lurching from side to side over the rough terrain with the wounded in the back. We just watched them go off into the darkness.

05.35hrs (zt): from C/S 9A to C/S 0: 'Can we confirm that large Hawkeye [Wessex helicopter] will collect casualties from about 1k west of Broken Arrow?'

[Broken Arrow = Murrell Bridge.]

05.35hrs (zt): from C/S 0 to C/S 9A: 'Wait out.'

05.35hrs (zt): from C/S 0 to 99: 'Reference casualties: possibly require 2 x large Hawks. Could Hawks go to grid reference 273752 if not could you give a grid of how far forward they could go?'

Captain Burgess contacts 3 PARA HQ regarding at LS for urgent casevac:

05.45hrs (zt): from C/S 83 to C/S 0: 'We have immediate casevac. Can we give LS [Landing Site] for RV with BV?'

05.45hrs (zt): from C/S 0 to C/S 83: 'Wait out, 1 x Priority 1 stretcher [Pte Mark Dodsworth], 1 x Priority 3 Sitting [Pte Den Dunn], passed to Brigade.'

05.51hrs (zt): from C/S 0 to C/S 99: 'Immediate casevac 1 × Priority 1 stretcher, 1 Priority 3 sitting. Track from Murrell Bridge to the west of Murrell Bridge 1000 metres, LS pick-up point.'

[The text is underlined in the radio log.]

Captain John (Doctor) Burgess
The Regimental Aid Post became a sort of supply area and ammunition dump as well as assisting the wounded. All the stretcher-bearers and the BVs deposited their ammunition here to be redistributed to the various rifle companies.

Spr Tommy Trindall
We followed the tracks made by the BVs. As we descended into the open ground, passing through the western minefield, we were now very close to the hill. I took my steel helmet off as the knot in the liner string was drilling a hole in my head. Then I looked up and saw lines of tracer ricocheting off the rocks on the top of Longdon, so I decided to quickly put my helmet back on.

Spr Martin (Spike) Glover
We were told to make our way to Longdon as fast as possible as stretcher-bearers were needed. We moved into the RAP area; I saw a guy with a red torch dealing with someone in by the rocks, and I thought, One casualty – that's not too bad. We were then told to find defensive positions, which we did. Captain Robbie Burns then asked for volunteers to go out and look for Cpl Milne, who had been injured and was lying out somewhere on the north-west corner of Longdon, but we weren't sure where. So LCpl Paul [Ginge] Moore, me and one other guy from 2 Troop RE went out into the minefield, calling out, 'Cpl Milne, Cpl Milne,' which I thought was a bit daft, as we were either going to get shot or stand on a mine.

8.2 'I'm not sure, but I think he's dead'

Brigade warns of helicopters flying:

06.25hrs (zt): from C/S 99 to All Stations: 'Be warned that friendly helicopter will be moving into our area for pick-up of casevac.'

C Company now inform the CO of their casualty status; six wounded in their location:

06.27hrs (zt): from C/S 39 to C/S 9: 'Situation Report: 2 x mortar casualties: 1 x spent round casualty +3 x casualties from Call Sign 1 [A Company] all stable, continual mortar fire, now digging in.'

The B Company Aid Post has originally had ten wounded, but sadly Pte Neil Grose has died of his wounds, and after five hours Cpl Milne has still yet to be evacuated from the minefield; also the B Company Aid Post has not yet linked up with the Regimental Aid Post:

06.33hrs (zt): from C/S 29 to C/S 83: 'Approximately 10 casualties Call Sign 2 for BV Casevac.'

Brigade informed 3 PARA HQ that a Gazelle helicopter has been despatched. Although this small helicopter may not have been ideal it is greatly appreciated, and the pilots show great bravery flying at night in extreme weather conditions.

Call Sign designations: Charlie Zulu = Gazelle helicopter, Delta = Scout helicopter.

06.40hrs (zt): from C/S 99 to C/S 0: 'Hawkeye for casevac now airborne, Call Sign, Charlie Zulu.'

The Snowcat vehicle is struggling over the rough Falklands terrain, and the driver reports if for any reason he cannot reach the LS; he will guide the helicopter, via the radio, to his location:

06.42hrs (zt): from C/S 9B to C/S 0: 'I am moving with the casualty. If I cannot get to landing site, I will talk helicopter to my position.'

06.42hrs (zt): From C/S 0 to C/S 9B: 'Roger, helicopter to be briefed at landing site by MAST [Marine Air Support Team].'

3 PARA HQ inform Brigade that the Gazelle helicopter is at Estancia House:

06.50hrs (zt): From C/S 0 to C/S 99: 'Friendly Hawkeye CZ at "Starlight 2" now, Out.'

3 PARA HQ then inform the BV that the Gazelle helicopter is on its way to the landing site:

07.00hrs (zt): From C/S 0 to C/S 9B: 'Hawkeye now left this location to pick up casualties.'

A summary report for 656 Squadron's operations during the war states:

> It was agreed that any casualties from the Commando Brigade operation on 11/12 June would be evacuated to the field hospital in Fitzroy, and that four helicopters equipped to fly at night would be based at Fitzroy for the evacuation of casualties from the battle area. Four helicopters did arrive at Fitzroy before the battle, but not one of them was equipped to fly at night. A strong plea for the correct helicopters failed; the PNG helicopters were involved in other tasks. Casualty evacuation that night was far from satisfactory. The casualties of 3 PARA on Mount Longdon waited up to eight hours for evacuation.[*]

Brigade inform 3 PARA HQ that they are having trouble locating the casualty:

07.30hrs (zt): from C/S 99 to C/S 0: 'From Hawkeye. Once casualty in one place and we have accurate grid, they will send fleet of helicopters in.'

07.30hrs (zt): from C/S 0 to C/S 99: 'H E, *** [word unclear] will speak to call sign Charlie Zulu.'

3 PARA HQ tell Brigade to send the helicopter back:

07.35hrs (zt): from C/S 0 to C/S 99: '1 x VSI on way back call sign CZ will return and pick up 2nd casualty.' HQ 181 Pte Dodsworth!!

[The exclamation marks after Mark's name are written in the radio log like this.]

---

[*] Notes found in boxes 112 and 115 at the Museum of Army Flying, Middle Wallop.

Captain Bob Darby, 32 yrs – Air Adjutant, OC HQ Company

The BV arrived. The floor was sticky with blood and my boots squelched in it. I remember seeing Pte Mark Dodsworth lying there on a stretcher. He appeared to have a swollen left thigh where he'd been struck by a bullet, which indicated a possible broken femur. He was still alive, making the occasional groaning noise. I spoke to Call Sign Zero [Captain Robertson] back at Estancia. He had requested casevac helicopters, and said he would send them up straight away. It was still dark, and there was a heavy ground mist. I couldn't speak directly to the helicopter, but I could hear the sound of its rotors from far off, echoing up the valley. As it approached, I held up a red torchlight to guide the helicopter in. He seemed to be moving slow and cautiously, until eventually he emerged from the mist about 100 metres in front of me.

Trudi McPhee, 27 yrs – Civilian

Civilians Roddy McKay, Mike Carey and me were sent 1 kilometre west of the Murrell Bridge to help set up the helicopter landing site with Captain Bob Darby. The first BV contained a soldier [Mark Dodsworth] who had been shot in the chest and leg. As I helped him out he was clinging on to me, trying to say something, but he was so full of morphine his speech was quite slurred. I'm not sure if he even knew I was a woman. My heart went out to this poor boy. I just felt so bloody sorry for him.

I put my arms around him, saying, 'I'm sorry about this, love; you're okay now.' I wasn't quite sure what to say, but with the urgency of the situation people were being hurried out of the BVs. Someone was shouting, 'Hurry up, come on; we've got to go.' They needed to get back to Longdon and collect more of the wounded.

Captain Norman (Nobby) Menzies 42 yrs – Headquarters Company (A Echelon)

At approximately 08.00hrs (zt), seven hours after the battle began, we were told to expect our first casualties. One of them, battalion zap number HQ 181 [Pte Mark Dodsworth] was now en route in a Royal Marine Gazelle helicopter. He was very seriously wounded and would require urgent treatment. Sgt John Donovan and I waited with a stretcher team at the ready. As the first helicopter arrived, we rushed over, but the aircrewman said, 'I'm not sure, but I think he's dead.' A doctor was called for, and Mark was declared dead.

Major William McMahon, advisor on light helicopters, writes in a report after the Falklands:

> Aircrew were often in a position to render life-saving first aid. As a result of experiences in the Falklands, I understand that medical training is to receive new emphasis throughout the Army. In my Squadron, I am concentrating on improving the medical ability of aircrewmen. When they have achieved an acceptable level of theoretical proficiency, I intend sending them to help at civilian hospitals to reduce the shock which serious wounds produce on those unfamiliar with them. Even on training exercises aircrewmen are often in a position to render medical assistance to real casualties before the arrival of other trained personnel. I would recommend that all aircrewmen be trained to RMA3 [Regimental Medical Assistant] standard, as part of their Middle Wallop course.

Back on Longdon.

CSgt Derek (Dex) Allen

At around 07.00hrs (zt), I was asked to meet up with a BV evacuating Cpl Milne from the minefield. Cpl Paul Roberts, one of our cooks, and I made our way from the RAP back out into the minefield. We established contact with Pte Ron Duffy and told him that the BV would be here shortly. We were now joined by medic LCpl Chris Lovett, Cpl Joe Black and Pte Kev Darke to assist with Cpl Milne. I'm not sure if Roy Bassey was the driver or co-driver. However, as Roy stepped out of the BV, he stepped on an anti-personnel mine, which exploded and severely damaged his lower leg. At the same time another device went off, causing serious injuries to several men, including Paul Roberts, who had flash burns. Joe Black was temporally blinded, and Pte Darke was hit in the hand by a piece of shrapnel. We managed to get Brian Milne and Roy Bassey into the BV and got them evacuated. We returned to the RAP by the same route I had come in on.

Back with 4 Platoon's wounded.

Pte Mark Eisler

We had been in the B Company Aid Post for over three hours and we were all bitterly cold. I was sitting by [Pte Keith] Taff Parry, who had been shot in the knee and foot, and he had somehow had the sole of his boot blown off. Also sitting by me was [Pte] Dave Kempster, he had been very badly wounded in his left arm and leg, as well as a cauterized wound on the tip of his nose where a tracer round had just nicked him. I was wondering what had happened to the evacuation chain when RSM Lawrie Ashbridge and Sgt Ray Butters appeared. They were on their way to link up with B Company HQ.

RSM Lawrie Ashbridge

I remember hearing someone groaning, and then British voices coming from around the other side of some rocks. I went to investigate. I found a group of B Company's wounded. They were just sitting there, all huddled together in the dark. I particularly remember Cpl Kelly, Cpl Bailey and Pte Hindmarsh.

Cpl Ian Bailey

Someone stood on my arm, and I shouted, 'Who the fucking hell's that?' The RSM said, 'Who's that?' I replied, 'It's Cpl Bailey.' I then heard him shout, 'Why the fuck is this man lying here?' I heard a whispered conversation and someone said, 'Sir, he's dying, he's not going to make it.' The RSM then said, 'Well, pal, he's still alive, get him fucking out of here.'

Pte Pete Hindmarsh

I had been in the Company Aid Post for hours when the RSM appeared. He asked me how I was. I said, 'I'm okay, Sir, but I'm fucking freezing.' He took his gloves off and gave them to me, and said, 'There you go, pal, stick with it, we'll try to get you out of here as soon as possible.' [Gunshot wound to thigh.]

LCpl Paul (Ginge) Moore, 21 yrs – 9 Sqn RE

We were called over and told to take some boxes of ammunition [link] up the hill. I had to sling-carry my SLR and carry two heavy boxes of ammo up a pitch-dark gully. Suddenly, there was a large explosion. We all dropped to the floor. We were okay, so we got up and carried on to the top of the gully, where we met some 3 PARA lads. They told us that they were surprised we had come up the gully, as they thought there were some live or wounded Argies down in that area. We carried on taking ammo up and escorting 4 Platoon's wounded down to the RAP.

Pte Mark Eyles Thomas

It was members of 4 Platoon who took the first wounded to the RAP. We guided the stretcher-bearers back up to where the rest of the wounded were. Because they were unsure of the route, no one would venture up for fear of getting shot. I helped take Cpl Ian Bailey down to the RAP, then came back up and helped walk Cpl Ned Kelly to the RAP.

CSgt Brian Faulkner

Cpl Ian Bailey was one of the first people I remember being brought in from the northern side; he was followed shortly by Cpl Ned Kelly. Ned was being helped into the RAP by the cooks. He'd been shot in the guts, but still refused to get on a stretcher. We quickly began assessing his wound and applying more shell dressings.

Spr Tommy Trindall

The Troop reserve was based close to the RAP. During the night CSM Weeks asked our Troop Sergeant Taff Sweeney if we could help with the casualties. Several guys, including myself, came forward. We followed a guide from B Company up a gully and began helping to walk and carry 4 Platoon's wounded down to the RAP.

Padre Derek Heaver

I remember Cpl Kelly being brought into the RAP; he was seriously wounded. As I recall, he had been shot in the stomach. He was a good and tough soldier, and I was never really sure that he saw the relevance of a chaplain. But with wounds like his, now was not the time for talking. Quiet prayer seemed more appropriate.

Cpl Ned Kelly

It seemed to take ages to get to the Regimental Aid Post. When I eventually got taken down by the cooks, the first person I met was Major Roger Patton.

He immediately called Dr Mike Von Bertele over to treat me. He had a quick look and said, 'You're on the next BV.'

Major Roger Patton
I recall seeing Cpl Kelly. He was a bolshie bugger, but I liked him. I remember seeing him lying there and he said, 'Have you got any cigarettes, Sir?' It nearly reduced me to tears to see him in such a state.

Lt Andrew Bickerdike
All of 4 Platoon's wounded were now being moved to the Regimental Aid Post. I was the last one to be moved; I wanted my men to go first. [Gunshot wound to thigh.]

The medical team quickly deals with Lt Andy Bickerdike's gunshot wound to the thigh, Cpl Ned Kelly's gunshot wound to the stomach, Cpl Ian Bailey's multiple gunshot wounds, Pte Keith Parry's gunshot wounds to the foot and knee, Pte Mick Cullen's gunshot wound to the mouth, Pte Jeff Logan's gunshot wound to the hand, Pte Mick Swain's gunshot wound to the thigh, Pte Dave Kempster's multiple gunshot wounds and Pte Pete Hindmarsh's gunshot wound to the top of his right thigh.

Brigade wants to know casualty and POW numbers:

08.37hrs (zt): from C/S 99 to C/S 0: 'Request number of casualties and prisoners soonest.'

08.45hrs (zt): from C/S 99 to 0: 'Call Sign for casevac helicopters DN/DO.'

08.55hrs (zt): from C/S 99 to C/S 0: 'Helicopter LS under fog but helicopter will take off in five-minute intervals very shortly.'

Brigade informs 3 PARA HQ that a group of six wounded will be coming from C Company's location for urgent medical attention; in this group are Cpl Paddy Rehill, Cpl Stephen Hope, Pte James O'Connell, Pte James Brebner, Pte Scott Fuller and Pte 'Soldier':

09.03hrs (zt): from C/S 99 to C/S 0: 'C Call Sign moving forward now, direct to casevac grid.'

09.05hrs (zt): from C/S 0 to C/S 9B: 'Hawkeye on way to your location.'

The two Scout helicopters are having problems:

09.10hrs (zt): from C/S 0 to C/S 0B: 'Both DO & DN problems defrosting, with you ASP.'

A REME technician from 656 Squadron AAC at the Scout FRT (Forward Repair Team) notes in the 656 Squadron report that they measured the temperature during the morning of 12 June as −15° Celsius.

09.27hrs (zt): from C/S 0 to C/S 9B: '4 × casualties from 59, exact number not known.'

The above message relates to a 105mm HEAT round impacting on the western slope, killing Pte Pete Hedicker and fatally wounding Cpl Keith McCarthy and Pte Philip West. Also wounded in this incident are LCpl Garry Cripps, Cfn Clive Sinclair and Pte Chris Dexter, plus a number of people are caught in the blast and left shaken up.

Pte John Kennedy, 22 yrs – Regimental Aid Post Medic, Headquarters Company

I was in the RAP when I was called to go up on the western slope. A number of people had been hurt, and they needed a medic. The first person I remember seeing was the OC of Support Company, Major Peter Dennison. He said, 'They're over there.'

I immediately went to the person who appeared to be the most seriously wounded, Cpl Keith McCarthy. I cannot stress enough how seriously wounded he was. I was about to do CPR and began to turn him over, but I was that shocked at his wounds, I jumped backwards and fell and hurt my back on a rock. I picked myself up and continued treating Keith, but sadly, it was not a battle I would win. I began to treat others, but with the extent of people that were wounded, I began to run out of supplies. Someone asked me if the casualties were dead. I spoke with Major Dennison and I told him that I couldn't pronounce them as dead since I wasn't a doctor. They would both have to be pronounced dead by one of the doctors, either Captain Burgess or Captain Von Bertele.

Medics Cpl Neil Parkin and Cpl Davie Wilson are now on the western slope, and they help, treat and move the wounded around to the RAP.

LCpl Lenny Carver

I'm not sure how long I'd been unconscious. [He is still in the First Bowl.] I became aware of other people around me. There was someone's boot by my head, and I said, 'Who the fucking hell is that?' It was Cpl Graham Heaton, who said, 'All right, mate; I feel sick as fuck, they've given me morphine.' I noticed that Frank O'Regan had also been wounded. Someone had a hexamine block cooker going, they said to Frank and Graham, 'Do you want a drink?' And I said, 'What about me?' They replied, 'Sorry, mate, you're gut shot.' I said, 'Fuck off; I'm not fucking gut shot. Give me a fucking drink.' I reached up and grabbed the metal mug, but spilled the hot drink all over myself and passed out.

The next thing I remember, it was daylight and I was freezing cold. I recall seeing some 9 Squadron lads along with some of our cooks. They came up with two stretchers, full of ammunition. They said they were going to put me on one of the stretchers. I said, 'No, I can walk,' but truly I was in no fit state. They loaded Frank and Graham onto the stretchers and they were carried in front of me. I hobbled behind with a 9 Squadron guy. We'd reached halfway to the RAP when we heard the whistle of incoming rounds. The 9 Squadron guy threw me to the floor and lay on top of me. [Gunshot wound to the chest, punctured lung.]

Pte Mark Eyles-Thomas

CSgt Brian Faulkner helped me load Cpl Kelly into the back of one of the BVs that had arrived. Ned Kelly didn't look well; he was as white as a sheet. As I went to walk away Brian said, 'No, you stay with him, sit in the back and look after Ned, don't you dare let him fall asleep.'

09.30hrs (zt): from C/S 83A to C/S 0: '7 x casualties on board to 9B possibly more to be picked up.'

Two BVs have returned from dropping off the earlier wounded personnel and get loaded up with Cpl Ned Kelly (plus escort Pte Mark Eyles-Thomas), Cpl Ian Bailey, Pte's Dave Kempster, Keith Parry, Jeff Logan and Mick Swain. Lt Andy Bickerdike will wait for next BV.

Cpl Ned Kelly

I was loaded into a Snowcat vehicle by Mark Eyles-Thomas, WO2 Kenny Sargent and Brian Faulkner. Mark Eyles-Thomas was detailed by Brian to get into the back of the BV and make sure I didn't fall asleep. We began the long journey to the LS pick-up point [helicopter landing site]. It was only when sitting in the back of the vehicle that I began to realize how extensive my wound was. As I reached inside my smock to get a cigarette, I noticed a big hole in my jumper around the stomach area. When we reached the landing site a Gazelle helicopter turned up, and I was somehow squeezed into it. I was then taken to Teal Inlet where I was patched up by a PFA medic [Parachute Field Ambulance]. Then I was taken to Ajax Bay, where I was operated on [for a gunshot wound to the stomach].

Pte Mark Eyles-Thomas

I was quite nervous sitting across from Ned Kelly in the BV. He looked at me menacingly, and said, 'Don't let me fall asleep; if I fall asleep, I won't wake up.' He reached to get a cigarette but when he opened his smock I saw that his green army jumper was soaked in blood and there was a hole in it. Ned said to me, 'I want you to check my wound.' I thought, His guts are going to fall out, and he'll fucking kill me! I gingerly lifted his green army jumper and opened his shirt; I saw a tear in his stomach with a piece of intestine sticking out. I told Ned about the intestine and asked him if he wanted me to push it back in. Ned thought for a moment, then just nodded and raised his eyes to the ceiling of the BV. I pushed the intestine back in and Ned never flinched. I lowered his jumper and sat back with some relief.

Cpl Ian Bailey

The next thing I remember was waking up on board a BV and then somehow, I eventually arrived at Teal Inlet. I was taken to a building where they triaged the wounded. They began taking my clothes off, and I warned them, 'I still have a white phosphorus grenade in my smock pocket. Don't touch it.' I noticed somebody in camouflage uniform and I said, 'Give it to him; he will know what to do with it.' I was taken to an outside tent and left at the back of the queue. Some considerable time later, a medic came into the tent, lifted up the blanket and said, 'Fucking Hell!' He then ran off and told someone that I was still in there. Shortly after this I was loaded into a Wessex helicopter and flown to the SS *Uganda*. On arrival, I was taken immediately into the operating theatre.

[Time from wounding to theatre, possibly over ten hours.]

AAC Scout helicopters have lifted off from the helicopter landing site.

09.35hrs (zt): from C/S 0 to 9B: 'DN & DO left here with five passengers.'

Cpl Ian Mousette, 24 yrs – AAC Scout Helicopter Aircrew

On Saturday 12 June, shortly before first light, myself and Sgt Dick Kalinski sat in our Scout XR628, fuelled up and engines running, just waiting for the 'Go'. Suddenly, we were given the 'thumbs up', and we were off, racing to the landing site, flying fast and low. There were two Scouts tasked; the second aircraft was crewed by Captain John Greenhalgh and Cpl John Gammon. They were leading, and we were just behind. As we got closer, we dropped even lower, using our Radalt [radar altimeter] that we had just been issued with. We crept up to the LS, flying at roughly head height, until we saw the signal light held by Captain Bob Darby. We quickly found a piece of level ground to put the helicopter down, and stretcher-bearers immediately ran forward with the most urgent cases.

In reply to Brigade's earlier request, 3 PARA HQ now return their estimate of casualties:

09.42hrs (zt): from C/S 0 to C/S 99: 'Reference number of casualties, approximately, possibly two dead and 20 injured.'

09.50hrs (zt): from C/S 9A to C/S 9B: '2 x BV's leaving with 7 casualties. 2 more later, then possibly 5 more.'

8.3   'I won't ask again, leave the man alone!'

First light approximately 10.00hrs (zt).

C Company casualties have now arrived in the RAP area: Cpl Paddy Rehill, gunshot wound to the face; Cpl Stephen Hope, gunshot wound to the head; Pte James

O'Connell gunshot wound to the face; Pte James Brebner, shrapnel wound to the leg; Pte Scott Fuller, shrapnel wound to the leg; Pte 'Soldier', suffering from shock.

Captain Bob Darby informs 3 PARA HQ that he has seven wounded at the landing site:

10.10hrs (zt): from C/S 9B to C/S 0: '7 x total casualties my location.'

Captain John (Doctor) Burgess
I remember Cpl Hope arriving at the RAP. I immediately assessed him, but sadly, his head injuries were extensive. There was not a lot we could do for him; we had to categorize him as a priority four. He was moved to an area where he could be monitored, away from the survivable casualties. We later moved the dead, so that they were out of sight of the wounded.

LCpl Lenny Carver
When I reached the RAP, I was placed on my own; I found out later that they thought I might not make it, so I was moved to one side with Cpl Steve Hope. CSgt Brian Faulkner and Dr Mike Von Bertele came up. Mike did a quick check and said, 'Right, give him morphine.' Suddenly three artillery rounds landed quite close to the RAP: boom, boom, boom. I was starting to feel the cold so I asked for a blanket. Steve Hope was still snoring away. As blokes were being taken on board the BVs, someone would bring me the spare blankets and place them on me. The Argentine blankets were quite thick and heavy, and I was so weak I couldn't move under the weight of them.

Pte Robert (Bob) Greasley, 17 yrs – C Company, 9 Platoon
Now that we'd reached the RAP, my mate Pte Andy Davidson spotted a dead Argentine who looked as if he'd been shot through the throat. Andy noticed he had a nice set of boots on. He said, 'Fucking hell, Bob, look at those boots! I'm having them, give me a hand.' So we were in the middle of undoing the laces when an officer comes over and said, 'What are you two doing?' To which Andy Davidson replies 'Sir, my DMs are in a shit state and the Argy won't be needing his any more!' The officer said, 'Stop right now.' Andy said, 'But, Sir, my boots are fucked!' The officer then spoke with a bit more authority in his voice and said, 'I won't ask again, leave the man alone!'

LCpl Steve McConnell

It was now daylight. I came across Pte O'Connell propped against a small rock, and alongside him was Cpl Steve Hope. John Kennedy started to apply a field dressing to a casualty whom I didn't know. Pte [Mac] McFarlane went over to Cpl Hope and started to adjust his field dressing and check his life signs; at the same time I checked Pte O'Connell for life signs. I took his pulse and placed another field dressing over the wound. I removed his gloves and massaged his hands, trying to get circulation back into his fingers.

Pte James (Scouse) O'Connell

We eventually reached the RAP; I was drifting in and out of consciousness. At some point I blacked out, and I next remember being half-awake and being carried on a stretcher. I couldn't see anything because of the shell dressings covering my face. I was completely drained and too weak to move. I think I must have moved, because one of them said, 'Fucking hell, this one's alive!' His mate said, 'Who the fuck is it?' and the first one replied, 'I'm fucked if I know, let's take him back.' The next thing I remember was being placed in the back of a BV. Someone was taking names; he poked me and asked, 'What's your name?' I said, 'Scouse O'Connell.' I then heard Dominic Grey say, 'Fucking hell, Scouse! Is that you? Don't worry, mate, I'll look after you,' and he did. As we moved off, we began to get shelled. [Gunshot wound, loss of right eye and cheekbone.]

Cpl Davie (Jock) Wilson, 22 yrs – Medic, RAMC

I recall LCpl Neil Parkin from 23 PFA taking a jacket off one of the Argentine casualties in the RAP, and placing it on a 3 PARA soldier who was drifting in and out of consciousness and shivering.

Cpl Paddy Rehill

I managed to get in a BV commanded by WO2 Kenny Sargent. He began taking the names of the casualties in his BV. As we were being driven away we came under artillery fire. It was a creeping barrage. The driver stopped for a moment as rounds exploded around us, and then we continued on our way to the helicopter landing site. The site was just over 4 kilometres away and took approximately 90 minutes to reach. The terrain we had to cross was dreadful. [Gunshot wound to jaw.]

Pte Bill Metcalfe, 29 yrs – D Company Guide

I made my way to the RAP helped by Cpl Mark Brown. One of the first persons I remember seeing was Pte Dominic Gray, who had a huge bandage on his head with the bow tied under his chin. There was a large group of wounded who were waiting to be either attended to, or just waiting to be casevaced by BV. It was just getting light at this stage. I was eventually loaded into a Snowcat vehicle with Dominic Gray, Jim O'Connell and Lt Andy Bickerdike. [Gunshot wound to right foot.]

The RAP informs Captain Bob Darby at the LS that he has more casualties inbound:

10.21hrs (zt): from C/S 9A to C/S 9B: '6 x walking wounded, 2 x stretcher cases, leaving this location for yours in BV.'

Onboard the first BV are Lt Bickerdike, Cpl Paddy Rehill, Pte Jimmy O`Connell, Pte Unknown, Pte Bill Metcalfe and Pte Dominic Gray. Onboard the second BV are Cpl Stephen Hope on a stretcher and Pte Syd Fuller. Pte James Brebner will stay in the RAP. Pte 'Soldier' has now recovered from his initial shock and is assisting in the RAP.

Pte John Kennedy

I remember treating Pte Michael [Mushrooms] Bateman shortly after he was brought into the RAP; he had been shot in the throat and the round had exited out of his shoulder. With that type of injury there was not much more we could do. We just hoped he would get evacuated as soon as possible.

Pte Ashley Wright

We had both British and Argentine casualties arriving into the RAP. We began treating their wounds, locating blankets and giving them sips of warm tea; the Argentines were treated no different than our own. I remember speaking to Pte Michael Bateman, who, despite his terrible throat and shoulder injuries, still managed a smile as he sat up against a rock.

LCpl Roger James

The doctors had a quick look at my injuries and said there wasn't much they could do, as I already had shell dressings on, so they left the dressings alone

– it wasn't worth disturbing them. The padre was giving us sips of tea, and someone was giving out cigarettes. I remember hearing Major Patton on the radio saying, 'I want helicopters, and I want them now.' [Shrapnel wounds to foot, leg and back.]

Padre Derek Heaver

It was light, and I wanted to go and speak with the men. The ground I was crossing was reasonably open, when suddenly an incoming round landed close enough for me to catch some of the force of the blast. It didn't knock me over but it certainly shook me. I thought about it for a few seconds and then I returned to the reasonable cover afforded by the rocks of the RAP.

There were three stretcher teams under the command of CSgt Derek (Dex) Allen, Sgt Pete Marshall ACC and Sgt Keith Hopper. Cook Sgt Pete Marshall was blown up a number of times and carried on recovering the wounded.

Sgt Keith Hopper

We spent the day going up and down Mount Longdon bringing down the wounded to the RAP. There were some walking wounded, but the majority had to be stretchered down. It was quite a difficult task as some of the ground was rather steep and craggy, and sometimes slippery underfoot due to the frozen ground. We were trying not to jolt the stretcher too much, so as not to cause additional pain to the casualty, but at times it was difficult to keep your footing.

Pte Craig (Tommy) Onions

We were bringing Cpl Graham Heaton down to the aid post on a stretcher when we got caught in an artillery barrage. We all dropped to the ground. Pete Marshall and I lay across Cpl Heaton to shield him. Some of the peat and debris from the explosions landed on top of us. We judged when it was relatively safe to move, and then picked the stretcher up and began running. When we reached the RAP it was chaos. CSgt Faulkner shouted, 'Right, take him over there,' and pointed us to one of the doctors.

At that moment, I just slumped against a rock, and my emotions caught up with me. The tears ran down my face. CSgt Faulkner spotted me and shouted, 'What the fucking hell's up with you? Get back up there.' I couldn't talk; I'd really lost it. Dick Granger said, 'CSgt, he's just seen Chris Lovett killed, he's a bit upset.' Brian Faulkner was a good friend of Chris Lovett. He changed his tone completely and said to someone, 'Right, you, make him a brew and sit him over there.'

Pte Ashley Wright

Someone said, 'Ashley, sorry about this, mate, but they've just brought in Chris Lovett.' My heart sank. I went across to see him. Chris Lovett's body had been covered with a poncho; I recognized the long shape of his body, and his boots. I stared at him and felt empty. My world stopped for a moment. A cook stretcher-bearer was standing alongside me, and I asked him, 'What happened?' He said, 'He was caught in an explosion, he never felt a thing.'

Pte Simon Clark

As I got to the RAP the scene that greeted me was incredible. Wounded people seemed to be everywhere. Both of our doctors, Mike Von Bertele and John Burgess, were extremely busy with the most seriously wounded. The medics were dealing with people and trying to prioritize who required the most urgent treatment. Artillery rounds were still dropping around us. The padre was trying to give comfort to the wounded. The noise of the shells whistling over our heads was constant. However, we were in a relatively safe location, sitting with our back against a rock wall. I was classed as non-urgent since I could talk and wasn't in immediate danger of dying, as other people were. I just sat and waited for my turn. [Gunshot wound to left leg, later amputated.]

WO2 John Carey, 39 yrs – Vehicle Convoy, Headquarters Company

One thing I must say about all the wounded is that not one man complained, in fact some were in quite good humour. We had some badly wounded men, but there was nothing much we could do, except try to keep them warm, keep their spirits up and hope we could get some helicopters in to casevac them. I remember one man in particular, LCpl Roger James, who was wounded in the foot but desperate for a cigarette. His friend Pte Tony McLarnon came into the RAP, looking a bit bedraggled. His smock was torn and covered in small burn holes. He was carrying a rifle that had the stock smashed off. He looked quite comical and he said to me, 'Sir, can I have another rifle?' I said,

'What happened?' He replied, 'I've just been blown up, Sir.' I said, 'Are you okay?' Tony said, 'Yeah, I'm okay, don't worry about me, Sir, but I need another weapon, my rifle's knackered.' I gave him one of the weapons from a heap that had now accumulated from the injured, and then Tony made his way straight back up the hill.

CSgt Brian Faulkner

Sgt John Ross came to look for Cpl McLaughlin, who had been wounded within the previous half-hour. He had reportedly come to the RAP. John asked, 'Did Scouse McLaughlin and Ned Kelly get out okay? I said, 'Scouse hasn't been through, but Ned Kelly went about an hour ago.' John Ross said, 'Scouse must be down here somewhere, he was hit half an hour ago.' I said, 'John, I'm telling you, he hasn't been through here.' He replied, 'Maybe he's gone on a BV, and you've missed him.' I had to tell him, 'John, I know everyone that's gone out of here. He hasn't come in or gone out.'

LCpl Paul (Ginge) Moore

Spr Steve Thistlewhite and I moved up the gully towards the northern side. Someone called across to us and said, 'Lads, we need a hand over here.' We walked over to a quite exposed area where we saw the bodies of two 3 PARA blokes, laying face downwards. One still had his arm around the other. You could clearly see one had been helping the other walking down the hill. You could see the shell hole and the spoil just behind them. They had both been thrown forward and died immediately, almost as if they never knew what hit them.

CSgt Brian Faulkner

Two bodies were brought in by the cooks. I went over to check who they were and discovered one was LCpl Peter Higgs, and the other was the missing Scouse McLaughlin. We took the two bodies over to the storage area and covered them up. I walked back to the RAP, only to see Sgt John Ross walking towards me. I said, 'I'm sorry John, we've got Scouse.' My face must have said it all. He said to me, 'Brian, can you give me five minutes with him to say my goodbyes?'

Pte Julian (Baz) Barrett, 17 yrs – 3 Section, 6 Platoon

I was stretchered down from Fly Half to the RAP. I was relieved to see faces that I knew. I heard more news about who had been killed and wounded – Dean [Jasper] Coady from A Company told me of the deaths of Neil Grose, Ian Scrivens and Jason Burt. At that point my head really got fucked up; I pulled the blanket covering me over my head to have some time out. After a short while I heard someone yelling above all the noise. As he got nearer, I could hear him shouting about moving that body from the wounded area. He was very agitated and wanted it done immediately. Then someone touched me; he pulled off my blanket, and I said, 'What's up, I'm not dead!' He walked off cursing. [Gunshot wound to upper right thigh.]

To add more confusion to the Regimental Aid Post, a prisoner tries to escape and is shot dead.

CSgt Brian Faulkner

A group of prisoners were being escorted by a couple of 3 PARA personnel. They were being taken to a holding area, when I heard shouts of 'Stop, Stop!' A young Argentine had broken free from the group and he was running through the RAP. They shouted, 'Stop, or we will open fire,' then warning shots were fired. He still carried on running. Then deadly force was used. The young Argentine fell dead; his body was taken to one side and covered over with a blanket.

Padre Derek Heaver

I can't recall the time, but I know it was after first light when Captain Mike Von Bertele, our other doctor, asked me to come to the aid of an Argentinian soldier who was dying. He was lying across a flat rock not far from the RAP and had suffered terrible injuries. I was told subsequently that he had been manning a .50 Cal machine gun. I remember glancing at Mike and he at me. I then gave the man the last rites. [This man may have been a member of the Heavy Machine Gun crew No. 4.]

CSgt Brian Faulkner

The doctors began assessing the new casualties. I saw Grant Grinham and knew he would be priority one. The colour had left Grant's face, he was white, although surprisingly he was still in good humour, trading insults with people in the RAP. I knew that behind all the joking, this young man had to get out of here quickly, if he was to live.

Pte Grant Grinham

I remember asking for a drink, but they would only let me have a small sip of tea. I was absolutely freezing, so they began covering me in blankets. LCpl Neil Parkin kept talking to me and encouraging me to stay awake, and he was there for me when I needed it most. [Shrapnel wounds to both legs, right leg later amputated.]

Pte Kevin Eaton:

I was carried on the stretcher down to the RAP. I found myself sitting next to Simon Clark. I remember watching as they brought in Pte Baz Barrett, who had been shot in the upper thigh. He was lying face down on a stretcher. They put him on the ground and covered him with an Argentine blanket. CSgt Faulkner spotted me and said jokingly, 'Not another one of my rugby team injured, what am I going to do?' [Gunshot wound left thigh.]

11.04hrs (zt): from C/S 99 to C/S 0: 'Casevac helicopter put down due to poor visibility [snow storm].'

8.4 'It's a testament to my crap shooting that, luckily, I didn't hit anyone!'

Padre Derek Heaver

I didn't see the incident when the Argentinian soldier was shot trying to escape. Three of his friends were digging a shallow grave for him by a triangular-shaped rock about 40 metres out from the RAP. Although I spoke no Spanish, I was able to convey to them that I was a padre by pointing to the crosses on my collar and using the word '*padre*' [Spanish for 'father']. I remember their smiles of gratitude after I had taken a short field burial service for their dead colleague. We shook hands and there was no sense of animosity between us.

As others, including the three Argentinian prisoners, walked back across open ground to the RAP, Tom Smith [*Daily Express* photographer] and I remained by the rock talking. Suddenly, rounds began hitting the triangular rock. We ducked down behind the rock, and I remember the voice of CSgt Brian Faulkner leading the return of fire. It took about 40 seconds for the RAP to realize what was happening, when one of those firing at us raised a red beret on a rifle and shouted, '3 PARA!' It was a blue-on-blue. From about 100 metres away, Sgt Des Fuller had seen the three Argentinians walking freely and had assumed that the position had been retaken. Tom Smith and I were very grateful for that rock.

Captain John (Doctor) Burgess

We had a rather embarrassing episode when Padre Derek Heaver was conducting the funeral of an Argentinian. We were standing in the middle of the group when from another direction came Sgt Des Fuller and a group of 3 PARA soldiers escorting a group of prisoners. As they came around a clump of rocks, they saw our group of Argentines. They opened fire; our group broke and began to run. CSgt Brian Faulkner, who was in the RAP, heard the shots and rallied the cooks, medics and 9 Squadron to open fire on the group that were firing on the burial party. Luckily no one was hurt.

LCpl Paul (Ginge) Moore

I was in the area of the RAP when I heard shooting quite close to us. Someone shouted, 'Stand to, stand to!' and pointed in the general direction of the western slope. I took up a position on a rock ledge quite high up, and I could see four or five Argies crawling about. Then I saw a red beret being waved about, and above all the noise, someone began shouting, '3 PARA, 3 PARA!' I believe I was one of the first to cease fire and started to shout to the others to do the same. It's a testament to my crap shooting that, luckily, I didn't hit anyone!

Acting Captain Giles Orpen-Smellie, Intelligence Officer

I went down to the RAP sometime after first light. I stopped at the POW containment area for a brief chat with Sgt Graham Pearson about the prisoners. I bumped into Sgt Des Fuller, who was escorting some more prisoners down to the cage area. There were some Argentines milling about on their own further down the hill. Sgt Fuller called out to them in English but they ignored us. The next thing we saw was CSgt Brian Faulkner coming around a rock at the run and in absolute textbook fashion. He laid out a section of the RAP and began giving out perfect fire-control orders. Both Sgt Fuller and I, and the prisoners who were with us, took cover as best we could on a forward slope as rounds splattered into the peat around us. [Gunshot wound to the arm.]

Sgt Bob Whitehill, ACC

One of the first people I recognized in the large group of wounded huddled against the rocks was LCpl Roger James. He had various shrapnel wounds; he called me over and asked me for a cigarette. I didn't have one; but I managed to find one for him. While I was busy dealing with the blokes, a Snowcat vehicle was approaching to pick up some of the wounded. It had artillery rounds dropping all around it, but it just kept on coming. The Argentines were definitely trying to hit it. The 3 PARA Snowcat drivers were extremely brave; those slow-moving vehicles were a very easy target.

Major Roger Patton

We started sending the wounded back in the Snowcats. I remember WO2 Kenny Sargent arriving with some Snowcats. As they were making their way towards the RAP, Argentine shell fire was landing all around them. There were Argentine forward observation posts watching Longdon, directing the artillery fire. The Snowcats were legitimate targets, as they were bringing up ammunition and supplies. I remember watching as they approached our position: artillery rounds began landing closer and closer to the vehicle, and one of the drivers jumped out and took cover.

Captain Mike (Doctor) Von Bertele

We started to get overwhelmed. We desperately needed helicopters. We seemed to be continually going round rechecking the dressings, setting up intravenous drips and administering pain relief. My overriding memory was lots of legs and arms with holes and blood. We came very close to running out of stocks of shell dressings and drips.

11.15hrs (zt): from C/S 9A to C/S 9B: '2 x Stretcher cases left my location for yours about 10 more here; you must clear BV and send back.'

11.20hrs (zt): from C/S 9A to C/S 0: 'Must have more stretchers.'

3 PARA HQ inform Captain Darby at the helicopter landing site that their first casualty evacuation, Pte Mark Dodsworth, has died en route to Teal Inlet:

11.30hrs (zt): from C/S 0 to 9B 'Small Hawkeye to pick up casualty, large Hawkeye later with stretchers, 1st casevac died on way to TEAL INLET.'

3 PARA HQ ask Brigade to confirm whether Two Sisters is secure, to enable them to bring helicopters forward:

11.31hrs (zt): from C/S 0 to C/S 99: 'Confirm security state of Two Sisters as this will allow A/C to fly further forward.'

11.31hrs (zt): from C/S 99 to C/S 0: 'Confirmed firm by 45 Commando.'

3 PARA HQ inform the helicopter landing site that two Scout helicopters are on their way:

11.51hrs (zt): from C/S 0 to C/S 9B: 'Two D call signs en route to your location. Two BVs. 1 going back to 9A.'

Cpl Paddy Rehill

A Royal Marine Gazelle helicopter came in. Dominic Gray, Jimmy O'Connell and I were loaded into it. It took about 20 minutes flying time to get to Teal Inlet. We reached there at approximately 13.00hrs (zt), where we were helped into a tented area. We were assessed again and searched for any ammunition or grenades. They cut all our clothes off. Then we went into one of the houses with only a blanket for cover. Eventually, we were told to get on the next helicopter that came in, which turned out to be a Wessex helicopter. All eight of us made our way out and climbed aboard the helicopter bound for the SS *Uganda*. When we arrived, I was quite ill, my tongue had swollen up, and I couldn't speak, although I could still breathe through my nose. They X- rayed me and found that the 7.62mm bullet was lodged in the back of my tongue. [From wounding to hospital ship, 12 hours.]

Pte James (Scouse) O'Connell

Pte Dominic Gray, Cpl Paddy Rehill and I were squeezed into this small helicopter and were taken to Teal Inlet. When we arrived, I was carried into the Field Dressing Station where they cut all my clothes off as they looked for secondary injuries. From Teal Inlet, I was loaded on board a helicopter where I spotted my mate Pte Lee Fisher lying on the floor – he'd been wounded in the back. He looked up and mouthed, 'All right, Scouse?' and I said, 'All right, Lee.' It was quite surreal. I remember looking at the door gunner on the Wessex; he looked like he hadn't slept, washed or shaved in days. I then looked out the door of the chopper and watched as the coastline disappeared, and I thought, That's it, I've made it; I'm out of here. [From wounding to hospital ship, 12 hours.]

Lt Col James M Ryan RAMC, OStJ, FRCS, MCh, DMCC, Hon FCEM, Col L/RAMC(V)

The war in the Falklands was a watershed. It had more in common with the past; it harked back to the Great War and even the Boer War.*

WO2 John Carey

I remember CSgt Brian Faulkner coming up to me and saying, 'Bloody hell, you're not going to believe who's just been brought in, it's Ian McKay.'

3 PARA HQ contact Captain Darby and ask how many wounded at helicopter LS:

12.05hrs (zt): from C/S 0 to C/S 9B: 'How many casualties left in your location?'

12.05hrs (zt): from C/S 9B to C/S 0: '4 or 5.'

12.05hrs (zt): from C/S 0 to C/S 9B: 'WX call sign coming to you.'

12.15hrs (zt): from C/S 0 to C/S 9A: 'Reference Wessex call sign. Has he arrived, how many casualties have you got for him?'

12.15hrs (zt): from C/S 9A to C/S 0: 'Wessex no, Casualties quite a few.'

12.24hrs (zt): from C/S 99 to C/S 0: 'Confirm number of casualties still to be casevact.'

12.24hrs (zt): from C/S 0 to C/S 99: 'Just getting sorted out will answer ASP.'

---

* From 'A personal reflection on the Falklands Islands War of 1982' by James M Ryan *Journal of The RAMC*, 2007.

12.31hrs (zt): from C/S 9A to C/S 0: '14 stretcher cases in this location.'

12.32hrs (zt): from C/S 0 to C/S 99: 'Request Delta call sign for casevac. We have 14 stretcher cases forward.'

Captain Bob Darby confirms that 24 casualties have been lifted from the helicopter LS so far:

12.32hrs (zt): from C/S 9B to C/S 0: '24 Casualties taken from 9B today.'

CSgt Brian Faulkner

A couple of hours after first light I began the task of collating who was dead, who was wounded and who was missing. In addition, I also needed the figures on who had been evacuated and who had still to be evacuated. This information was taken to the Battalion CP [Command Post] and passed to Captain Kevin McGimpsey (the Adjutant). I was asked about Cpl Brian Milne, and I said, 'I haven't seen him, to my knowledge he hasn't come into the RAP.'

RAP updates 3 PARA HQ on latest casualty figures:

12.37hrs (zt): from C/S 9A to 0: 'X x 12, Y x 41, Z x Unknown.'

[X = Dead, Y= Wounded, Z= Missing]

3 PARA HQ update Brigade with latest casualty figures:

12.41hrs (zt): from C/S 3 0 to 99: 'Casualty Report, X x 12, Y x 41, Z x Unknown.'

The BVs are running short of fuel:

12.54hrs (zt): from C/S 9A to C/S 0: 'Urgent 10 x Jerry cans petrol 9A.'

Captain Adrian Logan

Shells were still landing just 20 or 30 metres out from the RAP. I recall Major Roger Patton fuming with rage on the radio, saying, 'This is not acceptable, where are our helicopters? We need them urgently.' Eventually, a Gazelle helicopter arrived, and I heard Major Patton saying about the Gazelle, 'That's no fucking use; we have stretcher cases here.' [Shrapnel wound to right arm.]

Captain Bob Darby is now told to close down his LS and relocate to Longdon:

13.01hrs (zt): from C/S 0 to C/S 9B: 'Move LS to 9A; Hawkeye will get up there now.'

Trudi McPhee

We were told to close the LS down, as the helicopters would be now picking up from the RAP. We drove over the Murrell Bridge towards Longdon to see if we could be of any help. As we got near to Longdon we bumped into Major Roger Patton, who said, 'Trudi, what the hell are you doing here? Get the hell out of here, this whole area is DF'd!' I replied, 'Well, thanks a bunch, pal; we've only come to help.' Roger explained that the helicopters would soon be lifting the wounded out, and it would be best if we made our way back to Estancia since it was too dangerous here. We had just begun to make our way back towards the Murrell Bridge when we began to receive incoming fire from a 120mm mortar.

The first helicopters begin to arrive at Mount Longdon; this helps considerably:

13.35hrs (zt): from C/S 9A to C/S 0: '3 x Stretcher cases own, 2 x Stretcher cases EN, 3 x Wounded.'

Sgt Keith Hopper

The scene around the RAP was a hive of intense activity with the doctors and medics treating the wounded. The helicopters were now flying up to Longdon to evacuate the wounded. Snowcat vehicles were arriving with supplies, and amidst all this we were taking a huge amount of incoming artillery and mortar fire. If one of the helicopters in the area of the RAP had been hit whilst being loaded with wounded, the effects would have been catastrophic.

Pte Dave Roe

I walked around to the RAP, and I saw CSM Weeks; I asked him about Mark Dodsworth. He said, 'I'm sorry, son; he didn't make it.' It felt like a hammer blow. I was still covered in Mark's dried blood. I remember breaking the ice on a small pool of water, sitting down and washing his blood off. I felt guilty. I felt like I could have done more. These things still go through my mind, even today.

Major Roger Patton

We cursed whoever it was that decided to assign Gazelle helicopters to evacuate the wounded. Some of our men could not be laid down because it was just not wide enough, and so we had to jam badly wounded soldiers, who were in great pain, into the helicopters as best we could.

LCpl Roger James

Eventually it was my turn; someone shouted, 'You're next.' Then some 9 Squadron guys helped me to the chopper. I was crammed into the back along with another casualty. They gave both of us sets of headphones to help drown out the noise, and off we went. Shortly after taking off there was a warning over the headset, 'Air-raid warning red!' We put down in a sheltered area, but kept the rotors going. We just sat there waiting for the all-clear. After a short while we got the all-clear and off we went again. We had only gone a short distance when we landed again in the middle of nowhere; the crew gave us no indication of why we were landing. It turned out we had landed at a forward helicopter-refuelling point. A guy appeared in front of the helicopter and quickly pulled back some camouflage netting, underneath were a load of 45-gallon fuel drums. The ground crewman had a hand pump and proceeded to start pumping as fast as he could go to fill the helicopter up. As soon as we were full, off we went. The next thing I remember is flying in over Teal Inlet.

Pte Ashley Wright

I was working on auto pilot, prepping people ready to go. Reassuring them, telling them that the helicopters were on their way, they wouldn't be long. No one believed me. A prisoner holding-area had been established not far from the RAP area. Eventually the helicopters began to arrive at the mountain and I remember helping to carry Julian [Baz] Barrett to one of the aircraft; he'd been shot in the hips. After that I decided to go back to A Company, as they now had no medics with them.

Cpl Ian Mousette, Aircrewman

It was quite a surreal scene. I was cocooned from the noise of battle with my flight helmet. Everything was done with hand signals and gestures. I quickly loaded the wounded on board while Sgt Dick Kalinski was keeping a lookout. Incoming artillery rounds were beginning to land extremely close to the helicopter. As soon as I'd fastened down the casualty pod on the side of the chopper, I gave Dick the all-clear [thumbs up], he immediately wound the throttle up and took off. He backed out of the RAP and then flew fast and low, contour flying so we wouldn't be silhouetted, and then set off at a pace.

The speed that people were loaded was amazing. We were on the ground for no more than two or three minutes at a time since we were a prime target for artillery and mortar spotters.

Acting Captain Giles Orpen-Smellie

I returned to the RAP and the first person I met was Dr John Burgess. He had a very quick look at my injury and told me to get on the next helicopter to Teal Inlet. I was then grabbed by Major Patton and put on the next Wessex that came in. He was quite impressive on that helicopter LS. Artillery rounds were landing close by at irregular but frequent intervals, but Roger Patton stood his ground, in the open, and directed helicopters regardless

Cpl Graham Heaton

I was carried to a Scout helicopter. I noticed that the pilot was my old next-door neighbour, Sgt Dick Kalinski from Salamanca Park in Aldershot. They loaded me into the stretcher pod and covered me with a blanket, although I was still extremely cold. They closed the pod and fastened it down. I looked out the small viewing window of the pod and saw Dick Kalinski smiling and mouthing, 'All right, Graham.' A couple of minutes into the journey, I noticed that some of the blanket was hanging out of the pod. It had started flapping in the slipstream and was gradually being pulled off me. The pod was beginning to shake violently, and my hands were freezing. I was trying to grip on to the blanket. I was thinking that if the blanket gets sucked out of the pod and gets tangled in the rotors, we're fucked! [From wounding to theatre, seven hours; right leg amputated.]

Pte Simon Clark

Someone shouted, 'Any walking wounded for the helicopter?' I shouted back, 'Me, I'll go.' Kev Eaton looked at me and said, 'You fucking good bloke!' in a good-humoured, 'Airborne' sort of a way. I got up and fell over, but Pte Harry Gannon and someone else picked me up, carried me to the chopper and lifted me in. I was taken to Ajax Bay, and then transferred to the SS *Uganda*, where I had a cardiac arrest. Luckily, I was brought back by the excellent team of doctors and medics of whom I cannot speak highly enough. [From wounding to theatre,14 hours; left leg amputated back in the UK.]

Pte Grant Grinham

I kept saying to myself, Don't fall asleep, but I did, a couple of times. The next thing I remember was waking up in a Scout helicopter pod and reading the yellow writing on the inside, explaining that I was being evacuated in a helicopter casualty pod. I remember that when we landed I was taken towards what looked like a shed. When we got inside it was nice and warm. They put me on a table; there was the padre at one end and a doctor at the other. I think while I was there I began to realize the full extent of my injuries. I resigned myself to the fact that my leg was coming off. [From wounding to theatre, four hours; right leg amputated.]

Spr Tommy Trindall

The Troop Commander, Captain Burns said, 'Right, lads, we need to go and get Scotty [Wilson].' A group of us made our way back to First Bowl and we carefully placed his body onto a stretcher. Then Cpl Jock Ferry, LCpl Derek Broadbent, LCpl Mick Humphries, Spr Mark Thomas, Spr Sam Robson and myself carried Scotty's body down to the RAP. It was solely 9 Squadron that manned the stretcher, carrying one of our own.

Cpl James Morham

During the reorganization, I saw groups of blokes gathering discarded weapons. I noticed a body being carried down on a stretcher, and I said, 'Who is that?' One of the Toms said, 'It's Jon Crow.' I thought, Oh no, not another bloke from the Anti-Tank Platoon. Then another stretcher came down, this time being carried by members of 9 Squadron with their steel Para helmets, looking very solemn with their heads bowed. I was good friends with all the 9 Squadron lads, and again I asked, 'Who's that?' They said, 'It's Scotty Wilson.' This was another blow. I was good friends with Scotty, and he was the brother in-law of Ginge McCarthy, who I had tried to give the kiss of life to earlier on. These two men were married to a pair of sisters, Linda and Jean, who would now be widows.

Padre Derek Heaver

It was when the body of Cpl Scott Wilson [9 PARA Sqn RE] was brought in that I decided to take care of the preparation and documentation of the dead. Our dead were being brought to an area on the far side of rocks, near but just out of sight of the RAP. As a sign of respect, I placed each man's beret in the body bag with him. With hindsight that was a mistake. When visiting next of kin after our return, the one thing that nearly all of them asked for was their loved one's beret.

LCpl Paul (Ginge) Moore

After I had found out about Scotty Wilson's death, I decided to go and tell his brother-in-law Cpl Keith McCarthy. I said to someone from 3 PARA, 'Have you seen Ginge McCarthy?' He asked why, and I said, 'Well, I've got a bit of bad news for him about his brother-in-law Scotty Wilson: he's been killed.' The lad just sat down and said, 'Fucking hell, mate, I've got news for you as well – I'm sorry, but Ginge McCarthy's dead as well.'

Spr Martin (Spike) Glover

As I surveyed the scene, there were bodies lined up, blokes being treated and helicopters coming in and going out with the wounded. We were still getting shelled. I saw one Sea King helicopter coming in to take out the wounded, but it had to be waved away as the artillery was too intense.

Major Roderick Macdonald of 59 Commando, accompanied by WO2 Pete Ellis, flies in to see Captain Robby Burns concerning the welfare of his men and to speak to Lt Col Pike regarding updates on obstacles and mines. They also go to Full Back to view the ground leading up to Wireless Ridge. They then make their way back to the RAP, where Roddy films, although only briefly, the wounded being taken out by helicopter.

LCpl Lenny Carver

I heard the noise of a Scout helicopter, and someone said, 'That's it; this is going to be the last chopper.' Then I heard CSgt Brian Faulkner saying, 'Right, lads, check the area, pick all those blankets up...' Then some bloke lifted the blankets covering me and said, 'Fucking hell, there's a bloke here.' I said, 'I've been here all the fucking time, you bastards!' Then there was a big flap on to get me out.

Someone ran across to the air crewman, Cpl Mousette, who in turn spoke to the pilot, Sgt Dick Kalinski. They had quite a few wounded crammed inside their chopper, so it was decided to put me in the stretcher pod on the pilot's side of the helicopter. As they shut the lid, I remember seeing a sign saying something like, 'You are not in a coffin, you are in a helicopter rescue pod.' I remember looking up towards Dick Kalinski, who did thumbs up and mouthed, 'All right, mate?'

As soon as we landed at Ajax Bay, I was taken into triage and put on a trestle table. They started cutting off my clothes and removing my personal possessions, my camera and my G10 army issue watch, etc. They were put into a plastic bag, and I never saw them again. On the table next to me was Kev Eaton. After triage, I was taken into the operating theatre, where I noticed a row of four operating tables, and quite a large bomb stuck in one of the walls! [Chest wound; from wounding to theatre, eight hours.]

Sgt Dick Kalinski, 33 yrs – AAC Scout Helicopter Pilot
On one of the trips to Ajax Bay, one of the wounded lads from 3 PARA, who had a chest wound, regained consciousness. In his confusion, he tried to climb out of the stretcher pod. He managed to break a couple of the retaining pins holding it down, but thankfully the other pins held him. We carried on evacuating all the 3 PARA wounded until eventually the task was completed. Then we started taking the Argentine wounded off. During one evacuation, I had to go back to the *Europic Ferry* [a roll-on/roll-off ferry requisitioned by the Task Force] to refuel. The ship's crew were amazed to see real Argentinians.

Sgt Keith Hopper
One of the last wounded soldiers I helped on to a helicopter was an Argentine soldier. His head was heavily swathed in bandages. He had lain quietly against some rocks for quite some time. A photograph of this soldier was taken by *Daily Express* photographer Tom Smith and appeared in various publications. I have no idea if he survived or not.

This man was Cpl Oscar Carrizo and he did survive.

Captain Bob Darby

Just after mid-afternoon on Saturday, I had relocated to Longdon. Finally, I had an opportunity to eat, having not done so for almost 18 hours. The prisoners sat in among the rocks, completely accepting of their situation, except for one, who spent most of his time staring angrily at me. I then noticed he was looking at my rifle. He looked at me, I stared at him, and he sat back down. To this day, I think he made a good call.

One of the badly wounded prisoners was lying on a stretcher close by me, watching me eat. I carried on and then realized that he must also be hungry, but I had no spare rations for him. This went on until out of frustration I gave him half of my mess tin, which he gobbled up. Eventually, when he was being evacuated on board a Wessex helicopter, he called over to me, 'Señor, señor.' He spoke no English, and I spoke no Spanish. He took my hand and pressed his rosary beads into it and said, 'Muchas gracias.' Then he was gone.

Pte Kevin Eaton

When I arrived at Ajax Bay, they began cutting all my clothes off me. I watched as an officer struggled to find a vein in my arm, then this little bloke, a Staff Sergeant from 16 PFA with 'bugger grips' and a big moustache, came up and said, 'Sir, I'll do that.' He said to me, 'Are you all right, son?' I replied, 'Yeah,' then he whacked my arm really hard and proceeded to rub 'Deep Heat' on it, saying, 'That'll be all right in a minute.' He waited a minute, and then whacked my arm again and a vein popped straight up! He nonchalantly said, 'There you go, Sir.'

I was moved on to an area where they categorized you. On my left was Lenny Carver and on my right was Frank O'Regan. To my surprise, an Argentine came around, handing out Benson & Hedges cigarettes! I thought, How the fuck has an Argy got Benson & Hedges cigarettes, and I'm using roll-ups? I got it into my head that he must have pinched them off one of our blokes. I grabbed him and he fell over, he fell onto Lenny Carver's ribs. Lenny punched the Argy, and the drips fell over. The medics came over and pulled us apart. They started shouting, 'We are all equal in here, there's no fighting, and everyone's treated the same.' I said, 'But he's got British fags, he must have nicked them off our blokes!' A medic said, 'No, he hasn't; I've just given him that packet to give to you lot.' [From wounding to theatre, 14 hours.]

The CO contacts 3 PARA HQ asking for our dead to be removed from the mountain:

13.55hrs (zt): from C/S 9 to C/S 0: 'Collection of fatalities from position, to be taken to a suitable place for temporary burial, or to a place Brigade suggest.'

13.55hrs (zt): from C/S 0 to C/S 9: 'Kestrel to arrange. Sending stretcher-bearers to centralize at 9A, Hawkeye to collect.'

['Kestrel' is the code name for the Operations Officer.]

14.00hrs (zt): from C/S 0 to C/S 99: 'Reference our DEAD we would like to remove them off the mountain, could we do a lift to Teal OKAY.'

Due to increasing mortar and artillery fire around the RAP, an echelon area is set up in the area where the Mortar Platoon had been located the previous evening. This will be manned by Captain Bob Darby and HQ personnel:

14.05hrs (zt): from C/S 9A to C/S 0: 'Send 9B to set up night LS on feature occupied by C/S 70 last night, approx grid 3075.'

Padre Derek Heaver

Caring for and documenting the bodies of our dead was difficult, emotionally. However, as one body followed another, I found myself getting almost hardened to it. I remember someone saying to me, 'Padre, don't do the next one, it's Chris Lovett.' It was very thoughtful of him.

Although I don't remember this next incident taking place, a Sergeant from the MT Platoon came up behind me and apparently said to me, as I was dealing with the body of his friend LCpl Dave Scott, 'How can you believe in God at a time like this?' He related it to me after we had returned to Aldershot. He didn't need to, but he also very graciously apologized. However, I must have been too absorbed with what I was doing.

Sgt Keith Hopper

Once all the wounded had been cleared, we were told to bring down our dead. I helped recover one body, I didn't know who it was, we carried the body to an area that had been designated for the dead. I saw Padre Heaver; I looked at his face, and I thought that nobody should have to do that on their own. I decided I would help him. A short time later, a couple of guys said, 'Can we help?' I declined their offer; I didn't think anyone else should be subjected to the task we were carrying out.

Soldier 01: ID disc, one notebook, one ruler, three letters, one toy bear, 32p in change, one toothbrush, one spoon, one pencil, compo [food], one Oris watch (broken).

Soldier 02: One P38 Walther pistol, two loaded magazines (one in leather case), one pair of glasses in leather case, one Charles cigarette lighter, two pens, one pencil, two batteries, two notebooks.

Soldier 03: ID disc, one torch, one pen, one notebook.

Soldier 04: ID disc, torch, two pens, one watch, one length of Para cord, one notebook.

Soldier 05: No possessions.

Soldier 06: ID disc, no possessions.

Soldier 07: ID disc, one pen, one black Para cap badge, one sewing kit, ring.

Soldier 08: ID disc, one fishing kit, one SOS talisman, three chains and one St Christopher medal, one pair of scissors, three letters, one watch.

Soldier 09: ID disc, one Seiko watch, £20.50p.

Soldier 10: ID disc, one optical cleaning cloth, one pack of playing cards, one fork, one whistle, three photos, one notebook.

Soldier 11: ID disc, no possessions, one army watch (signed by CSgt B Faulkner).

Soldier 12: ID disc, one pencil sharpener, five pens, one pencil, one whistle.

Soldier 13: ID disc, one photographic film, three letters, two drawings, one camera, one wedding ring, two pens, one notebook.

Soldier 14: ID disc, one Happy Eater toy, spoon, two pens, £4.00 to follow.

Soldier 15: ID disc, notebook, one Timex watch with leather case.

Soldier 16: ID disc, one cigarette lighter.

Soldier 17: ID disc, one photo, nine pens.

Soldier 18: ID disc, no possessions.

Sgt Keith Hopper

I began helping Padre Derek Heaver remove the personal effects from our dead, then placing the bodies into body bags. It was harrowing, as some of the fatal wounds sustained were quite horrific, and it hurt even more when I recognized a dead friend. Sadly, with one or two of the soldiers, there was precious little to identify them by, except for their identity discs. Of all the personal effects removed from them, I shall never forget the toy bear that one young soldier carried.

Captain Mike (Doctor) Von Bertele

On Saturday afternoon, I delegated two men to go and dig a latrine about 40 metres from the RAP area, it was a hole just in between two rocks. When they had finished, I decided I would go and christen it. As I was leaving the RAP, a salvo of artillery rounds came rushing in and one scored a direct hit on the latrine. The Argentine artillery observers had obviously watched the men working and by the grace of God, they had just finished and had walked away, but a close call indeed.

Sgt Bob Whitehill

Padre Derek Heaver asked if I and a couple of the cooks could double-check the deceased personnel for any personal effects, photos, etc., that may have been missed. He also wanted us to double-check name tags against the names on the bags. I spoke to the lads and told them, 'Look, I've never done this before, but it's a job we've got to do, so brace yourselves and let's get on with it.'

CSM Johnny Weeks walked past and asked us how we were. I said, 'We're okay,' but in truth, we weren't, it was probably the most awful task I have ever done. I noticed that all the senior ranks, the CO, RSM and CSM Weeks, were more human after the battle. They were speaking to people by their first names as if somehow we had all been made equal.

Evacuation of enemy prisoners.

14.25hrs (zt): from C/S 0 to C/S 99: 'Reference POWs 39 to be flown back.'

14.34hrs (zt): from C/S E16 to C/S 0: 'Inform our Molar, our number 9223 is fatal [Cpl Scotty Wilson].'

[Molar is the code name for Admin staff.]

14.34hrs (zt): from C/S 0 to C/S E16: 'Passed to Molar.'

14.35hrs (zt): from C/S 99 to C/S 0: 'Reference POWs, Sunray watchdog [Officer Commanding Provost staff] will be coming up there shortly to coordinate prisoner movement back. He will give RV when organized. It will be your responsibility to get prisoners held to the RV. 42 Commando will then take them off your hands and move them back to the Welsh Guards for onward escort to Fitzroy.'

Three more casualties, all shrapnel wounds: Pte Mark Blain, C Company; Pte David Goldsmith, Support Company; and Pte Alan Sparrock, A Company.

14.50hrs (zt): from C/S 9 to C/S 9A: 'You do not need to collect casualty from Call Sign 3 yet.'

Brigade HQ need more information on casualties:

15.01hrs (zt): from C/S 99 to C/S 0: 'Appreciate that there is a lot going on but we are being pestered from above. Forward accurate as possible casualty report: known dead, stretcher cases, walking wounded, and missing.'

3 PARA HQ then pass the message to the Regimental Aid Post:

15.10hrs (zt): From C/S 0 to C/S 9A: 'From Higher formation: Send consol return of walking wounded, stretcher cases and clear picture of our dead.'

15.10hrs (zt): from C/S 9A to C/S 0: 'Will take about 2 hours.'

CO is not happy and demands that Brigade are informed of our situation:

15.15hrs (zt): from C/S 9 to C/S 0: 'Mount Longdon under continual heavy shell fire and we are sustaining further casualties, <u>Sunray Higher Form to be informed</u>.'

[This text is underlined in the radio log.]

15.15hrs (zt): from C/S 0 to C/S 9: 'Brigade informed.'

16.03hrs (zt): from C/S 99 to C/S 0: 'Can we have update on artillery bombardment and casualties.'

Pte Alan Sparrock waiting for casevac:

16.03hrs (zt): from C/S 0 to C/S 99: 'Three casualties, two of which have been casevact.'

WO2 John Carey

I said to Major Patton that the Argentine spotters were using the larger Wessex helicopters as an aiming reference. Because the Wessex helicopters were flying in at higher altitudes and then descending towards our position, they were more noticeable. As soon as the Argentines saw them, they called in a 'fire mission'. It happened every time.

The CO gives a more detailed update on the details of the battalion's dead (X) and wounded (Y):

17.12hrs (zt): from C/S 9 to C/S 0: 'Casualty report: X 18/Y 39 including 3 officers Captain Logan/Captain Orpen-Smellie/Lt Bickerdike.

> X details:
> HQ 56 = Pte Greenwood.
> B 48 = Sgt McKay.
> B 05 = Pte Burt.
> B 24 = Pte Scrivens.
> B 94 = LCpl Murdoch.
> B 07 = Pte Grose.
> D 30 = LCpl Higgs.
> SP 112 = Pte Crow.
> HQ 95 = LCpl Lovett.
> E 9223 = Cpl Wilson.
> A 102 = Pte Jenkins.
> SP 200 = Cpl McCarthy.
> SP 215 = Pte West.
> SP 218 = Pte Hedicker.

HQ 181 = Pte Dodsworth.
HQ 169 = LCpl Scott.
SP 119 = Pte Laing.
B 43: missing/dead Cpl McLaughlin.'

Brigade are trying to evacuate the prisoners:

18.50hrs (zt): from C/S 99 to C/S 0: 'Reference POWs, we are to escort them to Grid 290703 where Company of 1 Welsh Guards will take them to Fitzroy.'

18.55hrs (zt): from C/S 99 to C/S 0: 'Reference Bergens, where are they, are they netted and where do you want them taken to?'

19.20hrs (zt): from C/S 0 to C/S 99: 'We have moved figures 10 POWs by Wessex Call sign and have 29 POWs left to move, also 18 of our own dead for movement to Teal.'

19.20hrs (zt): from C/S 99 to C/S 0: 'POWs priority one, Dead may not be moved till tomorrow.'

Lt Pete Skinner, 847 Naval Air Squadron

On Saturday 12 June, I was Flying Wessex 5, XT461, with my crewman, PO Harry Worth. We arrived at Mount Longdon late in the evening and were marshalled in by a Para in camouflage to a landing site facing east. We were given the task to move 39 POWs to a point out in the boonies, just north of Fitzroy. I elected to lift three sticks of ten and one of nine. During the fourth lift we had only managed to get three POWs on board when we came under some pretty well-aimed shell fire. I think one of the BVs was hit, rocks and peat showered the aircraft, but the Para marshaller was as cool as hell and signalled us to take off. I said to Harry something like, 'It's getting a bit hot; we're getting out of here.' We took off, leaving the final six prisoners behind, intending to return later for them. We dropped the three with the rest, and then got re-tasked. We forgot all about the final six.

Major Patton delays the lift of Bergens due to Argentine artillery fire targeting the RAP.

20.00hrs (zt): from C/S 9A to C/S 0: 'We would like our Bergens tomorrow if possible, but do not worry if it cannot be done – dubious of helicopters flying into our area.'

Pte Gerald Bull from A Company has just been killed returning from a ration run:

20.15hrs (zt): From C/S 1 to C/S 9A: 'Another fatality, No. A 107.'

Helicopter is refused permission to land at RAP:

20.35hrs (zt): from C/S 99 to C/S 0: 'Why is helicopter being sent away from your area?'

20.35hrs (zt): from C/S 0 to C/S 99: 'Position under fire helicopter unable to land.'

Pte Mark (Boots) Meredith is wounded by shrapnel to stomach:

20.50hrs (zt): from C/S 9A to C/S 0: 'One minor casualty, B 44, graze to abdomen by shrapnel, casevac to Teal.'

Pte Rick Westray has slipped on the frozen rocks and badly injured his neck:

21.40hrs (zt): from C/S 59 to C/S 83B: 'Suspected broken neck at my location.' [SP 206.]

Everyone settled in for another extremely cold night with whatever warm kit they could find.

Sgt Bob Whitehill

As night fell, I was mentally and physically exhausted. Our group was needed for stag [guard] duty from 21.00hrs (zt) till 24.00hrs (zt). I had no sleeping bag as our kit had still not arrived. I found an Argentine blanket and curled up and tried to sleep, but it was freezing, and with the artillery still landing on the mountain, I didn't get any sleep that night.

CSgt Brian Faulkner

We set up small shelters to prepare for the cold night ahead. That Saturday night on Longdon was brutally cold, absolutely freezing. I don't think I slept all night; I was just lost in my own thoughts.

22.35hrs (zt): from C/S 0 to C/S 9A: 'Are you moving the prisoners to 9B tomorrow?'

22.35hrs (zt): from C/S 9A to C/S 0: 'First light.'

22.35hrs (zt): from C/S 0 to C/S 9A: 'Is Padre moving with the bodies?'

22.35hrs (zt): from C/S 9A to C/S 0: 'Tell you later.'

Funeral service will take place tomorrow at 19.00hrs (zt) at Teal Inlet, CO to inform Padre that Brigade will attend:

00.35hrs (zt): from C/S 85B to C/S 0: '19.00hrs (zt) service, Dogfish, 9 to inform Brimstone, Sunray Higher Formation will attend.'

['Dogfish' is the code name for Teal Inlet.]

WO2 John Carey
Saturday night, I tried to sleep under some Argentine blankets, but mainly shivered all night.

Pte John Kennedy
Saturday evening Cpl Davie (Jock) Wilson and I were tasked to go out on a patrol with the Snowcat vehicle. Something was going on, and they needed medical cover. When we came back I went on stag. I did a two-hour stag between 04.00hrs (zt) and 06.00hrs (zt). There was a light covering of snow, it was absolutely freezing. I remember looking out and thinking this is a beautiful place, but then I had a sort of panic attack. My mind began to race and I was confused as to where I was, what was I doing here and what had been happening. It lasted only seconds and then passed, but it shook me for a moment.

8.5 'Listen to me, I don't want you to fall asleep, understand?'

SUNDAY 13 JUNE 1982

First light approximately 10.00hrs (zt).

CSgt Brian Faulkner

On Sunday morning there weren't as many people moving about. It was just too dangerous to be caught out in the open.

Pte Mark Eyles-Thomas

I was violently sick, but I wasn't sure whether it was the liberated Argentine food or contaminated water, or just simply shock. It was decided that I needed to be put on an intravenous drip to replace my lost fluids. By then I had begun to feel really cold. They put me into a sleeping bag. I fell asleep for a couple of hours, and was then loaded into the back of a BV. At this stage I was really drowsy and wasn't sure what was happening. I went into a deep sleep. I'm not sure how long I slept for, but when I woke up I was at a Field Dressing Station. To this day I don't know where I was.

Cpl Sturge reports to the RAP:

11.04hrs (zt): from C/S 0 to C/S 9A: 'Have you any immediate casevac in your location?'

11.04hrs (zt): from C/S 9A to C/S 0: '1 immediate casualty.'

11.30hrs (zt): from C/S 9 to C/S 9A: 'One person from Call Sign 1 transfer to Teal from 9A.' (A 120)

11.56hrs (zt) from C/S 9A to C/S 0: 'Need foam-filled tension wheel; need more body bags as well.'

11.57hrs (zt) from C/S 99 to C/S 0: 'For Seagull from Manhole: Ensure when battle permits that enemy dead are buried correctly forward field burial forms (names and locations) to FRO.'

[Seagull = Adjutant; Manhole = Admin Staff; FRO = Field Registration Officer.]

RAP requests the casevac of Pte Westray, who has been injured the previous evening:

12.05hrs (zt): from C/S 9A to C/S 0: 'Casevac SP 206 possible broken neck.'

3 PARA HQ relay Brigade instructions regarding field burial:

12.05hrs (zt): from C/S 0 to C/S 9A: 'For Seagull from Manhole. Ensure when battle permits that enemy dead are buried correctly forward field burial forms (names and location of grave) to FRO.'

12.36hrs (zt): from C/S 99 to C/S 0: 'Reference Heliquest, 01/13 casevac, do you require a large or small aircraft?'

12.36hrs (zt): from C/S 0 to C/S 99: 'We require a Delta call sign.' [Scout.]

13.05hrs (zt): from C/S 9 to C/S 0: 'Situation determines that no 3 PARA personnel on forward positions to attend funeral, representation from 85B.'

13.10hrs (zt): from C/S 9B to C/S 0: 'All 6 POWs taken back.'

13.10hrs (zt): from C/S 0 to C/S 99: 'What time will we get our Scout for casevac?'

An Argentine soldier is found hiding on top of the rocks in A Company`s Full Back position. He has been there since the early hours of Saturday morning. He will be debriefed by the Intelligence Officer:

13.14hrs (zt): from C/S 9 to C/S 0: 'Be aware that 1 POW is being taken down to 9A. He is from the command post position which has just been located, awaiting brief from Acorn.'

['Acorn' is the code name for Intelligence Officer.]

13.20hrs (zt): from C/S 99 to C/S 0: 'Reference casualty request none received, MQ / 01.'

13.30hrs (zt): from C/S G79 to C/S 0: 'Enemy OP on Tumbledown which are observing helicopters landing.'

13.30hrs (zt): from C/S 9A to C/S 0: 'No more large helicopters forward of 9B.'

Doctor John (Doctor) Burgess
Suddenly there was an explosion just to the rear of the RAP and the cry went out for a medic. Doctor Mike Von Bertele and Pte John Kennedy immediately raced to the scene.

WO2 John Carey
I was CSM of Support Company before the Falklands, so when I saw some members of the old Patrol Platoon coming in I recognized them instantly. They walked in and passed to the rear of the RAP, when suddenly there was a terrific explosion followed by a terrible screaming.

Patrol Platoon used to be part of Support Company but has evolved into D Company.

Pte John Kennedy
On Sunday, I saw a patrol from D Company coming in; they were using the tracks left by the BVs through the minefield. Once out of the minefield they passed out of sight, moving up towards Battalion Tac HQ. We started getting shelled, and then there was an almighty explosion on the other side of a rock divide. Someone started shouting, 'Medic!' I ran towards the direction the patrol had just gone. Cpl Phil Probets got to the injured men just ahead of me and was treating Cpl Jerry Phillips, who was in extreme pain, his arm was very nearly severed and he was in a right state. Cpl Mark Brown and Pte Richard [Dickie] Absolon had also been injured.

As I was treating Mark Brown, Pte Pat Harley was treating Dickie Absolon, who was now fitting. As I looked around, I realized there was someone missing, I could only see five men out of the six-man patrol. I shouted, 'We've got one missing!' After we'd finished treating the casualties, I said, 'There's another one,' but was told, 'No, they're all accounted for.' However, I was sure there was another one; I started walking around looking among the large rocks and boulders. After about five minutes of searching, I found Pte John [Jock] Wilson concussed and wedged under a large rock. We pulled him out; he was as white as a ghost and in severe shock. I was quite stressed at this stage. I told Major Patton in no uncertain terms how I felt.

13.34hrs (zt): from C/S 9A to C/S 0: 'Just had more casualties inform Brigade this area has had two more casualties, this is an unacceptable delay.'

13.36hrs (zt): from C/S 9A to C/S 0: '1st casualty brought in with head injury.'

13.36hrs (zt): from C/S 0 to C/S 9A: 'Delta Call Sign coming.'

Cpl Mark Brown

As we reached the aid post, more rounds started exploding around the same area. I have never been so afraid in my life; I tried to dig myself a hole. I next remember seeing Dickie Absolon and Jerry Phillips as they were carried in. I'm not sure how long we waited there, but I do remember seeing two Scout helicopters racing in fast and low. The first one landed and the aircrewman jumped out and quickly began to help load Jerry Phillips into his aircraft, then immediately it lifted off. The second one landed, flown by Sgt Dick Kalinski. His aircrewman, Cpl Ian Mousette, immediately jumped out and began to organize the loading of his helicopter. It was decided that Dickie Absolon would be loaded into the stretcher pod on the side and I was loaded into the back. I noticed that Dick Kalinski was watching Ian Mousette, waiting for the thumbs up. Then a mortar round landed just forward of the helicopter, throwing peat and mud up into the air, which fell back down through the rotating blades of the helicopter. The pilot then shouted something out of the window. The aircrewman quickly jumped on board, followed by Cpl Louie Sturge, and we were away.

I was beginning to feel drowsy. I felt a sharp pain as Louie Sturge pinched me. I cried out, and Louie said to me, 'Listen to me, I don't want you to fall asleep, understand? You do not go to sleep!' We were taken to the 16 PFA Advanced Surgical Centre at Fitzroy. Once there, they began to strip me. They took off my smock which contained six magazines, two HE grenades and one white phosphorus grenade. As they were removing my smock the white phosphorus grenade fell on the floor and rolled across the room, which caused a bit of concern to the orderly who was removing my clothes – he nearly hit the roof!

I was then moved into a building where it was extremely warm. They put me on a table and cleaned me up. I looked across at this guy who had half-moon glasses, like an old school teacher. I recognized Dickie Absolon with his feet towards me. After he'd finished with Dickie, he came over to me and said, 'Do you know that young man?' I said, 'Yeah, it's my mate, Dick Absolon.' He said, 'I'm sorry, but I don't think he will survive. Right, what's wrong with you?'

The next thing I remember is waking up on a Wessex helicopter with a splitting headache. It felt like I'd been on the piss for a week. Then I noticed Dickie Absolon laid next to me with his head swathed in bandages, like a huge turban. I said, 'Dick, Dick, are you all right?' The Loadmaster said, 'Don't talk to him, he's not very good.' He must have been able to hear me, he made a noise. After that I remember waking up on the SS *Uganda*. Next to me was an Argentine, and on the other side was Cpl Jerry Phillips, who was unconscious.

The second incoming Scout helicopter carries CO 2 PARA David Chaundler and his Battery Commander Major Tony Rice, who are coming forward to recce Wireless Ridge.

Major Roger Patton
I was constantly busy. I remember at one stage on the Sunday, it sounds ridiculous, but I stopped for a moment and sat on a rock. I got this strange feeling, it was as if I had left my body and I was up above the RAP, looking down on that terrible scene. It was probably due to lack of sleep, and stress. I hadn't got much sleep over the time we were on Longdon; all I managed was the occasional cat nap.

LCpl Paul (Ginge) Moore
On Sunday my section of 9 Squadron was tasked to go round to the southern side of Longdon and clear the bunkers of Lt Enrique Neirotti's 3 Platoon. We looked for booby traps, and I disarmed a Mamba missile. There seemed to be ammunition, kit and just general shit everywhere, they had obviously left in a hurry.

14.35hrs (zt): from C/S 9A/B to C/S 0: 'No bodies have yet been removed from this location.'

It is decided by Major Patton and WO2 John Carey that it will take too long and be too dangerous to load the 3 PARA bodies on to helicopters in the RAP – the large Wessex helicopters will immediately draw mortar or artillery fire. The decision is taken to place the dead into the BVs and send them to Captain Bob Darby's echelon area, located 1.5 kilometres west of the RAP. It is hoped that it will be safer to lift the bodies on to the aircraft from there. It will be done under the supervision of WO2 Carey and CSgt Faulkner. Thirteen bodies are placed into two BVs and five are left in the RAP waiting for one of the BVs to return.

WO2 John Carey
I organized a group of cooks and anyone who was available to load the bodies into the BVs. I felt it was so undignified; it was something that I will never forget.

15.10hrs (zt): from C/S 99 to All Stations: 'Air-raid warning RED.'

CO confirms his helicopter for Brigade 'O' Group:

15.16hrs (zt): from C/S 9 to C/S 0: '16.30hrs (zt) for pick-up from 9A's location.'

15.16hrs (zt): from C/S 0 to C/S 9: 'Airstrike thought to be on Brigade HQ – now confirmed.'

LCpl Cliff Legg, 29 yrs – C Company
I didn't take part in the initial attack as I had injured my ankle. I was taken back to Estancia, where I stayed until Sunday the 13th. I was then taken by helicopter up to an echelon area. Whilst en route we were caught up in an air raid, the helicopter pilot dropped into cover as they waited for the all-clear. Eventually, we continued our way to the echelon area, which was about 1.5 kilometres west of Longdon. The area was run by Captain Bob Darby, who asked what I was doing there. I said, 'I'm trying to get forward.' I was told by Sgt Bryan Washington to wait there for transport.

A short time later a BV arrived, loaded with mortar rounds. It was driven by Cpl Dave Hobson. As soon as the BV stopped, Argentine 120mm mortar rounds came whistling in. I said to Pte Tony McMenamin, 'Mac, get away from that BV, if that gets hit there'll be fuck all left.' We took cover behind some rocks, and shortly after that I noticed the bodies of about thirteen members of 3 PARA laid out in body bags.

Pte Chris Davey called over to me, 'Cliff, Dave Scott's over here.' I had already heard that Dave had been killed when I was at Estancia House. I said, 'Which one?' I went over and I said a few private words. Shortly after, a Wessex helicopter came in. We were told to lift the bodies on board as fast as possible. It all happened so fast, in fact, the only two I can remember were Dave Scott and Ginge McCarthy. There were two lifts almost immediately after each other, so it was all a bit of a blur. After that I made my way towards Mount Longdon.

The casualty status of LCpl Roy Bassey HQ 133 seems to have gone unrecorded:

15.25hrs (zt): from C/S 9 to C/S 0: 'Confirm Number HQ 133 is working with call sign 85B.'

15.25hrs (zt): from C/S 0 to C/S 9: 'Wait-out.'

This next radio message will bring REME Cfn Alex Shaw (Bluebell) to Mount Longdon:

16.45hrs (zt): from C/S 50B to C/S 0: 'We require as many charge 7 and 8 augmenting cartridges ASAP + bluebell this location, 3 containers.'

After LCpl Cliff Legg leaves the echelon area, five more bodies are brought forward to that area:

16.50hrs (zt): from C/S 9B to C/S 0: 'Only five bodies now to go back there.'

17.15hrs (zt): from C/S 99 to C/S 0: 'Funerals will now not take place – new date and time ASAP.'

17.15hrs (zt): from C/S 0 to C/S 99: 'Kestrel [Ops Officer] informed.'

LCpl Roy Bassey is now located:

17.20hrs (zt): from C/S 9 to C/S 0: 'HQ 133 has now been confirmed as a casevac and was casevact on the night of the attack and he can now become one of the Y returns.'

17.20hrs (zt): from C/S 0 to C/S 9: 'Sgt Bonham to be informed.'

Pte Paul Bachurzewski, 19 yrs – D Company

Late on Sunday afternoon, Sgt Mick Quinn, LCpl Bob Hunter, Pte Colin Charlton and I finally got orders to make our way to Longdon. We would be taking part in reconnaissance patrols for the next phase of operations.

On arrival we were met by CSM Kenny Sargent, who said, 'Lads, you'll have to walk from here, the choppers are attracting too much artillery fire.' He asked us to hang on for the moment as a Wessex would be coming in shortly to pick up the last five bodies of our dead. We were told that we would need to move as fast as possible as there were Argy spotters out there watching and they would call a 'fire mission' in as soon as they spotted the chopper. The pilot wouldn't want to hang around, so no fucking about. We moved over to where the five silver body bags were lined up. I looked at the bags marked with names; I knew every one of them.

The chopper touched down and the pilot gave the thumbs up. Colin Charlton, Bob Hunter, Sgt Mick Quinn and I picked up one of the bodies and began running towards the chopper. The noise of its twin engines was deafening. We passed the body in as gently as possible to the aircrewman, who placed it to one side, ready for the next one. We turned and ran back, then watched as the last body was being lifted on to the aircraft. Without fail, the noise of incoming artillery rounds could be heard. There were cries of, 'Incoming!' and 'Take cover!' The 3 PARA marshaller signalled the chopper to lift off. The pilot didn't need telling twice. Rounds were now landing in the peaty soil, throwing huge amounts of peat into the air. The pilot acknowledged and eased his aircraft into the air, dipped the nose, began to bank to the left and accelerated off to the west.

17.24hrs (zt): from C/S 9 to C/S 0: 'The Wessex Call Sign arrived at this location. Have loaded last five bodies for movement back. Own dead now clear of this location.'

18.00hrs (zt): from C/S 99 to C/S 0: 'Reference funerals – will now take place as planned at 19.00hrs (zt).'

18.00hrs (zt): from C/S 0 to C/S 99: 'Ops officer informed.'

Padre Derek Heaver

I left Mount Longdon to conduct a funeral service at Teal Inlet for the 19 men killed on Mt Longdon. The service was planned for 19.00hrs (zt), but when I arrived the long grave was still being dug. Padre Wynne Jones, 45 Commando, had made the arrangements and also had a number of his own men to bury. In all, there were 25 dead. Since the majority of the dead were from 3 PARA, Wynne Jones suggested that I lead the service with him assisting. I found Wynne to be a calming strength at that difficult time. Because of the delay in the burial timings, it was getting dark by the time I began my return journey. When I reached Estancia, the helicopter pilot would not fly any further in the darkness. So I spent the night at Estancia House, the home of Tony and Ailsa Heathman, who made me very welcome.

Captain Norman (Nobby) Menzies

WO2 David Rowntree, the chief clerk, was the man in charge of identifying the bodies and preparing them for field burial. I had to sign off that the deceased had died in the Falklands. The rules at the time were that the bodies would be buried in the Falklands. So WO2 Ian Hutchinson and I selected a piece of land that overlooked the inlet, and Ian Hutchinson then arranged for engineers to blow a large hole, then dig it out. It was a very sad moment for all involved. Wooden crosses, made by B Echelon, were placed out.

Dr John (Doctor) Burgess

A helicopter came in to take a sole Argentine prisoner away. It touched down, but then almost immediately took off again, due to the artillery fire. The prisoner, who was desperate to be taken away, ran and jumped up, clinging to the footplate of the helicopter. Luckily, he fell off before it rose too high.

Spr Steve Tickle, 9 Sqn RE

On Sunday evening we were dug in close to the RAP, when suddenly they began shelling us again. I was caught out in the open; I ran but couldn't make it into cover. Apparently one landed uncomfortably close and I was knocked out. I regained consciousness a few hours later in the back of the medics' BV with an artificial airway shoved down my throat. As they say, you never hear the one with your name on it.

The echelon area is now coming under increasing artillery and mortar fire due to helicopters bringing in supplies:

18.25hrs (zt): from C/S 9B to C/S 0: 'Coming under adjusting artillery fire, no more re-supply to this location, all further re-supply to go to Murrell Bridge.'

18.25hrs (zt): from C/S 0 to C/S 9B: 'Passed to echelon. 9B asked to supply GR at Broken Arrow.'

18.53hrs (zt): from C/S 9B to C/S 0: 'Will be establishing alternative landing site tonight.'

19.50hrs (zt): from C/S 5 to C/S 0: 'It is confirmed that Support Company No. 200 [Cpl McCarthy] died yesterday.'

A report of a casualty comes in: Cfn Alex Shaw has been wounded on the northern side of Longdon just below Fly Half:

19.55hrs (zt): from C/S Z9 to C/S 9A: 'We have just taken one casualty.'

19.55hrs (zt): from C/S 9A to C/S Z9: 'Roger.'

Captain John (Doctor) Burgess

It was on Sunday evening that the cry went out for a medic. Someone had been very seriously wounded and needed urgent medical attention. Dr Mike Von Bertele and Pte John Kennedy went racing up the northern side of the mountain and the helicopter was immediately called.

No sooner has the report come in of one casualty, when a second radio message comes in telling the RAP that two more have been wounded, LCpl Denzil Connick and Pte Craig Jones.

20.00hrs (zt): from C/S Z9 to C/S 9A: 'We need two more stretchers, more casualties.'

20.00hrs (zt): from C/S 9A to C/S Z9: 'Roger.'

LCpl Cliff Legg

I'd just got a brew on with Pte Johnny Joyce. There was a shout of 'Incoming!' We all took cover as a number of rounds came in. One shell exploded just out from the RAP and a piece of shrapnel struck the rock by us and ricocheted off; it clipped my smock, and then hit Johnny Joyce in the thigh. Thankfully, its energy was spent, and it just whacked him. There were reports that someone had been wounded and immediately the doctor and John Kennedy went running from the RAP. Someone shouted at us to grab a stretcher and follow them. Four of us now went running up the gully after the doctor. When we reached Cfn Alex Shaw, there were more shouts of 'Medic!' coming from further along the mountain. The doctor and John Kennedy quickly treated Alex, then they left us to go and treat the other casualties. I remember there was a REME bloke [Michael Hall] helping us to carry the stretcher. As we made our way back, I seem to remember LCpl Denzil Connick's stretcher being carried at the same time as us. We virtually came into the RAP together. I remember Denzil was saying, 'Don't let me die, lads, don't let me die, I don't give a fuck about my legs, just don't let me die.' Next to him, Alex Shaw was thrashing about saying, 'Mum, Mum.' It was heartbreaking, as I knew Alex's father.

The first reports suggest that Alex Shaw is not thought as badly wounded as the other two:

20.10hrs (zt): from C/S 9A to C/S 0: 'Two stretcher and one walking wounded. Need casevac. Urgent.'

Spr Tommy Trindall

Just as we were getting some scoff, we got shelled again. I heard someone shouting for a medic and I ran over to help. Alex Shaw was bleeding heavily and we applied five or six shell dressings on him, then medic Pte John Kennedy turned up and began trying to get a drip into him. A stretcher arrived and we hurriedly placed him on it, and we carried him down as fast as we could to the RAP.

Pte John Kennedy

On Sunday, I had been called to treat Cfn Alex Shaw. I ran as fast as I could up Route 3. A shell landed to my immediate left and buried itself deep in the peat. The blast from it blew me over. I picked myself up, checked myself and carried on to where Alex was. He had been sheltering in an alcove in the rocks just below Fly Half. I quickly applied shell dressings and applied a drip.

Cpl Phil Probets and the stretcher-bearers had just arrived. Then, there were shouts of 'Medic!' coming from further along the mountain. So I quickly jumped down from the rocks and ran to the scene of the second explosion, where I came across Pte Pat Harley and LCpl Vince Bramley. They were trying their best to stem the bleeding from Denzil Connick. Denzil started saying, 'Don't give me morphine, give it to him' [meaning Craig Jones]. I said, 'Denzil, you need it just as much as he does.' Craig Jones had gone into peripheral shutdown [collapsed arteries; both casualties had sustained bilateral femoral fractures]. I was struggling to get an IV [intravenous] line into him. I'm not sure how much time had passed, but Craig died from extensive blood loss.

I turned my attention to Denzil. I said to Pat Harley, 'Try and put a tourniquet as far up the stump as possible,' but there was very little stump. I tried to put a 'Venflon' into Denzil but he was also suffering from peripheral shutdown. So we rolled him over and put the IV drip up his backside. We needed to get fluids back into his body fast. He was dying in front of us. Mike Von Bertele and I were there for quite a while stabilizing him.

Charlie Call Sign = Gazelle helicopter/Delta Call Sign = Scout helicopter:

20.19hrs (zt): from C/S 9A to C/S 0: 'Charlie C/S 2 minutes, Delta C/S 10 minutes, confirm now three stretcher cases.'

Pte Craig Jones is now reported as dead:

20.40hrs (zt): from C/S 9A to C/S 0: 'Reference Casevac: 3rd helicopter not required; casualty is now a fatality.'

Pte Craig (Tommy) Onions

We got to Alex Shaw but he was already being treated, so we passed him and reached Craig Jones and Denzil Connick. Both men were in an extremely bad way. It took quite a bit of time, but eventually Denzil was loaded on to my stretcher.

We reached the RAP and the medics began further treatment on Denzil. I looked over at Alex; he was also in HQ Company, the same as me. I went over and sat by his head and leaned in to try and comfort and reassure him. He was in great pain, and was struggling. The doctor was desperately trying to find a vein to get some fluids into him. He was saying, 'Alex, listen to me, try and keep still,' but Alex couldn't keep still. Eventually, Alex could no longer fight, and slowly gave up the struggle. I was quite shocked by the emotion of it all.

Captain John (Doctor) Burgess

As soon as Alex was brought in, with shrapnel injuries lacerating one femoral artery and fracturing the opposite femur, we began to treat him. He was struggling and I was asking him to keep still, but he couldn't. As it was after dark, we had to use torches. I instructed two of the stretcher-bearers to hold a poncho over the top of us to shield the light of the torches since the Argentine artillery observers would strike at any opportunity. After a short time Alex gradually gave up the struggle for life. I then turned my attention to LCpl Connick, but there was not much we could do with him; just administer morphine, put fluids back into him and put more shell dressings on the numerous injuries on his one remaining left leg, and a tourniquet on what little was left of the stump of his right leg. We could do nothing fancy, it was all just basic first aid.

CSgt Brian Faulkner

I was gutted to see Denzil Connick with a leg missing and the horrendous damage to his other leg. I was thinking that it wasn't looking good for Denzil. While he was being treated by Dr John Burgess he kept insisting he needed to deliver a map; he kept saying, 'I've got to give them the map, it's important!' I said, 'Denzil, don't worry about the map.' All of the colour had drained from his face. Again he said, 'This map is really important.' I said, 'Right, give it to me, and I'll see to it.' I knew he was dying and I knew that he knew it.

LCpl Denzil Connick

I remember people all crowding around, trying to help me, I watched as Dr Von Bertele was trying to put a drip in my arm, he was slapping my arm trying to find a vein, and I was thinking, 'Hurry up, you twat!' My veins had started to collapse and I was dying. Eventually, they put an anal drip in. As all this was happening shells were still landing on the mountain.

I next remember I was bouncing along on a stretcher at great speed to the RAP. I knew I was in a bad way. Brian Faulkner came up to me and said, 'Well, I've seen it all now, Denzil. I know you've always wanted to run the rugby club bar, now you're just the man for the job.' I spotted Harry Wilkie and shouted, 'Harry, give me a fag, I'm gagging.' Dr Burgess then gave me an injection which eased the pain quite a bit. Luckily for me, a helicopter had been scrambled and it was already racing towards Mount Longdon.

A Scout helicopter once again comes to 3 PARA's aid. Flown by Sgt Dick Kalinski and Cpl Ian Mousette, it comes out of the darkness guided in by Major Roger Patton. However, there is a problem with the pod, so it is decided to take the door off the helicopter. After a bit of a struggle Denzil is loaded on board to be taken to Fitzroy Aid Station, a 20-minute journey. He is semi-conscious and quite incoherent. When he reaches Fitzroy he has a heart attack and for a short time shows no signs of life, but once again, through the fantastic skills of the medical staff, he will live.

Sgt Kalinski approaches Fitzroy Field Dressing Station and warns off ground troops:

20.45hrs (zt): from AAC radio log: 'One aircraft inbound with casualty; ask ground staff not to shoot at it.'

21.08hrs (zt): from C/S 0 to C/S 99: 'Reference casualty request A/C, Please ensure A/C have pods as with the long journey a wounded man in the open will suffer, also helicopter must go onto VCN frequency.'

21.25hrs (zt): from C/S 9A to C/S 0: 'One of the wounded: HQ 172 Pte Jones 627 died, HQ 171 Cfn Shaw died, SP 104 LCpl Connick wounded.'

CSgt Brian Faulkner
After all the goings-on in the RAP over the last hour or so, I made myself a brew and took myself to one side to contemplate my thoughts, just to be on my own. Suddenly another salvo of shells came in and one landed by me; fortunately it penetrated down into the peat, but the blast blew me through the air and knocked me unconscious.

Captain John (Doctor) Burgess
The shelling of the position continued. One shell blew a medical assistant off a rock, which resulted in a slight injury, but an even closer burst knocked out CSgt Brian Faulkner and he could not be found for some time.

Captain Mike (Doctor) Von Bertele

The artillery changed to mortars, and rounds started to fall around us. We huddled under a large boulder and prayed, until the familiar cry went up: 'Medic!' A soldier had been blown through the air by the blast from an exploding round and was unconscious. John Burgess and I debated whose turn it was to go. I lost, and ran, terrified, across the open ground to pull the casualty into cover. Now it was safe to use a torch, but a detailed examination revealed no injury. We concluded that the blast had literally knocked the breath out of him. Sure enough, he slowly came round, deaf, but otherwise unhurt, apart from a very sore back from where he had landed on a rock.

Spr Tommy Trindall

I was detailed to guard the prisoner who had missed being evacuated earlier. We shared a shell scrape, he just wanted to keep warm and not be killed, and it was as simple as that. It was bitterly cold and he was shivering and gibbering, and I wasn't much better off. I had given him a poncho earlier to wrap himself up in. As the night progressed it began to snow and the cold intensified, we were both frozen to the core. I thought, Fuck this. I got up and took the poncho off him; he looked shocked, but I indicated we should both share the poncho as the heat from both of us would keep us warmer. We spent the rest of the night like that.

8.6   **'Padre, there's a rumour going round that they've surrendered'**

MONDAY 14 JUNE 1982

Over the evening of 13/14 June, 2 PARA attack Wireless Ridge. The Scots Guards attack Mount Tumbledown, but most of 3 PARA who are not involved in supporting 2 PARA are just trying to keep warm and get some sleep.

Captain Julian James injures his back while acting as an MFC for 2 PARA:

02.01hrs (zt): from C/S 50B to C/S 9: '50 has been hit are stretcher-bearers coming from us or 2 PARA?'

02.01hrs (zt): from C/S 9 to C/S 50B: 'Casevac by 2 PARA system, did 59 know C/S 50 was with 2 PARA?'

02.12hrs (zt): from C/S 50B to C/S 9: 'Sunray 50 was not travelling with 2 PARA; he was in OP, trying to get Grid now.'

02.12hrs (zt): from C/S 9 to C/S 50B: '50 now making his way back to 9A (is it Sunray 50?) with back injury.'

02.30hrs (zt): from C/S 50B to C/S 9A: '50 OP party have minor injuries and will stay where they are until morning.'

03.00hrs (zt): from C/S 0 to C/S 85: '30 blankets required by RAP, can they be delivered in daylight?'

03.00hrs (zt): from C/S 85 to C/S 0: 'Roger, passed to 85B.'

03.40hrs (zt): from C/S 0 to C/S 99: 'Casevac helicopter flying, will be flying west of your location.'

03.50hrs (zt): from C/S 0 to C/S 99: 'Warning Order 3 x casualties 22 SAS details to follow shortly.'

03.45hrs (zt): from C/S 69 to C/S 0: 'Standby for casevac, 3 casualties, details to follow.'

03.45hrs (zt): from C/S 0 to C/S 69: 'Brigade warned, grid 415784.'

03.55hrs (zt): from C/S 69 to C/S 0: 'Now 4 casualties, 2 x seriously injured walking with assistance (mortar splinters); 2 x minor, checking grid now 398781.'

03.55hrs from C/S 0 to C/S 69: 'New details passed to Brigade.'

First light approximately 10.00hrs (zt).

Following a very quiet, but intensely cold night for the bulk of 3 PARA, the morning of 14 June proves to be another bitterly cold start. There is a thin layer of snow on the ground and at about 10.30hrs (zt) it begins snowing. The medical team begin to treat members of the battalion who are now starting to feel the effects of three weeks in freezing conditions and suffering from hypothermia.

CSgt Brian Faulkner

It was decided that for the next phase of the operation, our team would consist of Major Roger Patton, Captain Burgess, WO2 Kenny Sargent, Sgt Steve Bradley and Pte John Kennedy who would ride in the BVs. Captain Mike Von Bertele's team of Cpl Davie Wilson, Cpl Neil Parkin and Padre Derek Heaver plus a team of stretcher-bearers would move on foot with the battalion for the big push into Stanley. The BVs carrying all the extra medical supplies would bring up the rear.

11.05hrs (zt): from C/S 9A to C/S 0: 'Send Brimstone to my location.'

['Brimstone' is the code name for Padre.]

Padre Derek Heaver

When I arrived back on Monday morning from Estancia House I asked how things had been on the previous day. CSgt Faulkner replied, 'Padre, it was bad, you wouldn't have liked being here.' I was now beginning to think about what would lie ahead for us, during the battle for Port Stanley.

Cpl Phil Probets

The battalion's next objective was Moody Brook, so I restocked all my medical supplies ready for the next push. I had also found quite a bit of Argentine medical kit. By then, I was thinking that I had become quite numb to all the death and destruction that had happened over the past couple of days. I was just resigned to the fact that we were going to do it all over again.

Captain (Doctor) John Burgess

It all began to quieten; the shelling was becoming less frequent and certainly less accurate as the enemy OPs were destroyed. The CO then began to brief his officers on the forthcoming attack on Moody Brook. He covered the advance into Stanley itself, at least as far as the racecourse. During the 'O' Group held on the side of the mountain, the snow continued to fall. Everyone wondered how the attack on Stanley would result with regard to casualties.

Pte John Kennedy

On the Monday morning, we were told our next battalion objective would be an attack on Moody Brook, and then on to the racecourse. We loaded up with shell dressings, intravenous drips and extra blankets. We needed the blankets because it was so bitterly cold and we were desperately short of warm kit. But, fortunately, today we obtained from somewhere a load of multicoloured blankets, reds, greens and white, which we packed into MFO boxes and put in the back of the Snowcat vehicles. The vehicles were so crammed full of supplies it almost left no room for the medics.

WO2 John Carey

The 2ic Major Patton briefed me on the forthcoming push into Stanley. We loaded the bodies of Pte Craig Jones and Cfn Alex Shaw into a BV for evacuation to Teal Inlet. Then the OC of C Company, Major Osborne, contacted me and asked me to take over the role of CSM of C Company as their CSM had hurt his knee. I made my way over to meet up with them and take up my new role.

LCpl Cliff Legg

After a sleepless freezing night, I made my way across to rejoin C Company on Wing Forward. They said, 'Where the fuck did you come from?' I said, 'From that big hill over there.'

CO's 'O' Group is held in the RAP area at 12.00hrs (zt).

Major Roger Patton

On the morning of the 14 June, we were holding an 'O' Group in my area. It was snowing and very cold. The Commanding Officer and all the Company Commanders were present. During the 'O' Group, one of the signallers, in fact, my signaller, LCpl Harry Wilkie, came up and stood at the edge of the 'O' Group. The CO was slightly irritated by his presence, as he was in the middle of his 'O' Group. He was very persistent, this young LCpl, he interrupted the Commanding Officer and said, 'Sir, I've just received a message from Formation Headquarters that we are to be ready to move in 30 minutes.' The information was somehow quickly evident to us that the Argentinians had begun to withdraw, and shortly after the cessation of that 'O' Group the battalion was on the move.

We were pushed on as fast as possible by the CO. I packed up the RAP and we moved all the vehicles round to the northern side of Mount Longdon and across to Wireless Ridge, which was 2 PARA's objective the night before.

12.10hrs (zt): from C/S 0 to C/S 9: 'Enemy withdrawing from Sapper Hill, unconfirmed report 300 enemy withdrawing.'

12.50hrs (zt): From C/S 0 to All Stations: 'All Stations on 30 minutes to move.'

14.08hrs (zt): from C/S CK to C/S 0: '1 wounded to go back, D 40: frostbite.'

Pte Craig (Tommy) Onions
On Monday we were told to get all our kit together and that we may be moving off at any moment. From the experience of the last few days, I packed as many shell dressings as I could. We then just hung around waiting for the word to go. Eventually we moved off, making our way along the northern side of Longdon. As I walked along my boot clipped something, I looked down to see an AP [anti-personnel] mine. It seemed to roll away in slow motion, into the heather, and luckily, for some reason it failed to explode.

Spr Tommy Trindall
I think we heard it over the radio that there'd been a ceasefire. We were moving in single file and could see AP mines to the left and right of us. All the tops were exposed. The Troop Commander put his hand up and signalled for us to stop. It was at that moment the signaller, Spr Willie MacDonald, told Captain Burns, 'Sir, there are reports that the Argies are surrendering.'

Padre Derek Heaver
We began to move off Mount Longdon and Sgt Hopper said, 'Padre, there's a rumour going round that they've surrendered.' I said, 'Let's not speculate.' Then, a short while later, someone said, 'They have surrendered!' I replied, 'We need to hear it officially.' Then it came down the line, 'Helmets off, berets on!' Then I believed it.

15.15hrs (zt): from C/S 9A to C/S 0: 'Sgt Bradley (HQ) / Pte Hardwick (SP) – stomach pains / Spr Tickle (9 Sqn) brought to our location, plus one enemy prisoner.'

Pte John Kennedy

The mood changed completely. Just outside of Stanley we found a wounded Argentine lying on the floor. He had been shot in the chest and was in a bad way, and he was to be the last casualty of the war that I treated. We loaded him into the Snowcat and took him into the medical centre in Port Stanley. Then the battle for accommodation began. Once in Stanley we started to treat all manner of problems, ranging from trench foot to piles, and diarrhoea and vomiting which were caused by either contaminated water or eating Argentine rations.

LCpl Paul (Ginge) Moore

As soon as we went over the top of Wireless Ridge we could see Argentine troops streaming off the hills on the other side of the valley. We soon caught up with the lead company of 3 PARA [C Company] and then came across some 2 PARA lads sat by the side of the road. We continued up to the war memorial on the seafront, but we were told not to go any further whilst negotiations were ongoing.

CSgt Brian Faulkner

We decided that it would be too dangerous to have all of us in one vehicle because of the danger of a mine explosion. We would walk in the tracks of the vehicle at a safe distance. We slowly made our way along the northern side of Longdon, in the low ground heading towards Wireless Ridge. Suddenly, Major Patton told the RAP team driver to stop the vehicle. I said, 'What are we stopping for?' He replied, 'There are white flags flying in Stanley, it's all over.'

We then waited for the battalion flag to be flown forward in a chopper, which was en route to us. While we waited, we looked for something we could use as a flagpole. The only thing we had was a six-foot length of Bangalore torpedo. Shortly after the chopper turned up with the flag, we attached it to the Bangalore torpedo and had a group photo taken. If you look closely at the photo, you will see yellow stencilling three-quarters of the way up our flagpole saying, 'Bangalore torpedo MK1'. We were quite elated as we advanced along the Ross Road waving the flag, with the blokes cheering us along.

Captain John (Doctor) Burgess

We received the order to advance at full speed to Stanley. During the move, it was learned that there had been reports of white flags to be seen over Stanley. We moved down into Moody Brook. The snow had melted by this time, the sun was shining, but clouds of smoke were clearly visible coming from the western edge of the town, and from the Moody Brook Barracks. The RAP vehicle was the first of the BVs to get into Stanley. We were ordered to stop, while a helicopter brought forward the 3 PARA flag. It was attached to a Bangalore torpedo and carried high above the BV victoriously along the Ross Road into Stanley.

Padre Derek Heaver

I was walking along the Ross Road towards Port Stanley, sharing conversations with as many of 3 PARA as I could see. One of the signallers left the friends he was with and walked over to me. I remember that he had a huge smile on his face. He put his hand out to shake mine and said, 'Padre, I would never have admitted it before, but on Mount Longdon I prayed, and I prayed, and I prayed.' I told him he was not the only one.

That evening, I decided to seek out the Rev. Harry Bagnall, the minister in charge of Stanley Cathedral, because I was sure we would need his church for a service. It was dark when I began walking along the Ross Road toward where I knew his church must be. In retrospect, it was a rather naive thing to do. It wasn't long before I realized that I had strayed out of the British area and was now in an area where I heard Argentinians laughing, shouting and looting food and drink from containers. I noticed two Argentinian military policemen close by, and trying to appear casual, I went up to them and said, 'Excuse me, do you know where the church is?' They smiled, and were very courteous, and they replied in perfect English, giving me the directions. I said, 'Thank you, I will visit it tomorrow.' Then I beat a reasonably hasty retreat.

Pte Ashley Wright

I moved into a bungalow with fellow medics Cpl Steve Harding-Dempster and LCpl Dave Stott. Steve commandeered a Mercedes jeep and said, 'Does anyone want to go for a joyride?' We drove down to the airport and had a look around, and then later helped out in the King Edward VII Hospital treating Argentine soldiers and civilians.

Captain Norman (Nobby) Menzies

I was still at Teal Inlet when I got the message that the battalion was on the move heading to Stanley. I thought, 'My place is in Stanley, I am not missing out on this.' I was told I would be moved by landing craft the next day, but I couldn't wait that long. So we got hold of a great big piece of cardboard and wrote on it '3 PARA, Help.' I got the Landing Site Sergeant to hold it up; a Chinook helicopter pilot spotted it and landed with an SAS patrol onboard. He said, 'What's the matter?' I said, 'We need to get into Port Stanley now!' He asked, 'How many of you are there?' I replied, 'About ten and a bit of kit.' 'Okay, get in,' was the reply and we flew into Stanley and landed on the racecourse. It was chaos; people were liberating food from an Argentine food store, eating steaks that hadn't been cleared. The cook, Sgt Major [Smudge] Smith, took one whiff of the meat and straight away said most of it's rotten. It was, in fact, contaminated and should never have been eaten.

Captain John (Doctor) Burgess

The city was a mess, with no sewerage, water or electricity. With no food provided, many men began looting the Argentinian food sources until further supplies could catch up with the advance. Luckily, there was no shortage of Argentinian food in Stanley itself, the frozen steak being a favourite of 3 PARA. Unfortunately, a lot of the battalion who had been based on the eastern end of Longdon suffered from a lack of fresh drinking water. Troops had been getting water from puddles in the peat and boiling it. This was insufficient to kill off all the bacteria, and with the inadequate sanitation, most of the battalion went down with diarrhoea and vomiting.

On the first evening in Stanley, Mike Von Bertele and I, along with two guards, crossed the 'White Line' that separated the opposing forces in the city. We went up the road to the King Edward VII Hospital. We were the first British soldiers into that area, and the welcome bestowed on us will always be remembered. It was one of my proudest moments of being a member of 3 PARA. It is impossible to convey in words those embraces and messages of thanks from the medical staff and other civilians sheltering in the hospital.

WHEN THE FIGHTING IS OVER

The Third Battalion, The Parachute Regiment, left the Falkland Islands on Thursday 24 June 1982 onboard MV *Norland* bound for Ascension Island. From there they were flown back to the UK to RAF Brize Norton in Oxfordshire where, astonishingly, the soldiers immediately left the airport to go on leave.

The wounded were taken by ship to Montevideo in Uruguay, and from there were flown to RAF Brize Norton and then taken to RAF Hospital Wroughton where doctors would assess whether specialist hospital treatment was needed, or whether soldiers could be allowed home for the weekend. I was told I could go home but was asked to return to the hospital for assessment the following Monday morning.

On my way home, I asked my father if we could stop at a pub. We walked in and everyone was acting normally, chatting, as if the war had never happened. The barman poured a pint, which I paid for. Standing in my naval uniform with my head swathed in bandages, it was almost like I was from another world.

I spent the following four months in and out of hospital, eventually returning to my battalion in November 1982. On my return, something in the battalion had changed. I learned that some soldiers simply never returned to the army and were never seen again – the Falklands campaign had just been too much. A few soldiers were admitted to the psychiatric ward at The Queen Elizabeth Military Hospital in Woolwich, and I met several of them during my time in the burns and plastics unit. It was quite upsetting to see friends behaving really quite strangely, but, in hindsight, I think we were all acting oddly in our own way, whether that was excessive drinking or by challenging authority. My mother and father put up with my own various antics and helped support me.

Within two years, many of the Falkland veterans left the army – their mindset had changed. Of those who stayed, several went on to rise to very senior ranks.

For many years, Falklands veterans met only occasionally, usually in Aldershot on Airborne Forces Day, which is celebrated annually on the first weekend in July. Communication in 1980s and 1990s was very limited, but now, with the help of modern technology, we are all able to keep in contact on a daily or weekly basis. I have found it particularly reassuring to know I can just reach out to a fellow veteran with any problems, and he to me.

Over the years we have sadly lost a few veterans due to physical or mental health problems brought on by their time in service, and nearly all of us suffer with knee, back or hip conditions. Serving your country can take quite a toll on your mind and body, but we will always be there for each other.

APPENDIX I

BRITISH FORCES ROLL OF HONOUR

Pte Richard Absolon MM

Pte Gerald Bull

Pte Jason Burt

Pte Jon Crow

Pte Mark Dodsworth

Pte Anthony Greenwood

Pte Neil Grose

Pte Peter Hedicker

LCpl Pete Higgs

Cpl Stevie Hope

Pte Tim Jenkins

Cpl Scott Wilson 9 Sqn RE

Pte Craig Jones

Pte Stewart Laing

LCpl Chris Lovett MID

Cpl Keith McCarthy

Sgt Ian McKay VC

Cpl Stewart McLaughlin

LCpl James (Doc) Murdoch

LCpl David Scott

Pte Ian Scrivens

Cfn Alex Shaw REME

Pte Philip West

ARGENTINE FORCES ROLL OF HONOUR

S/C62 Eduardo Elbio E Araujo

S/C62 Miguel A Arrascaeta

S/C 63 Claudio Bastida

Lt Juan Baldini

S/C62 Angel Benitez

S/C62 Omar Anibal Britos

S/C62 Sergio A Carbadlido

S/C62 Luis Alberto Diaz

S/C62 Miguel Angel Falcon

S/C62 Aldo Omar Ferreyra

S/C62 Alfredo Gattoni

S/C62 Miguel A Gonzalez

S/C62 Nestor M Gonzalez

S/C62 Donato M Gramisci

S/C62 Guillermo E Granado

S/C62 Ricardo Herrera

S/C62 Jose Luis Del Hierro

S/C62 Carlos A Hornos

S/C62 Alberto M Juarez

S/C62 Julio Hector Maidana

S/C62 Marcello D Massad

Cpl Pedro A Orozco

S/C62 Rolando Pacholczuk

S/C62 Miguel Angel Pascual

Sgt Dante Luis S Pereyra

S/C62 Alberto D Petrucelli

S/C62 Ramon Omar Quintana

Lt Rolando Alberto Ramos

Cpl Dario Rolando Rios

S/C62 Isaac Erasmo Rocha

S/C62 José Luis Rodriguez

S/C62 Macedonio Rodriguez

S/C62 Victor Rodriguez

S/C62 Julio Romero

Sgt Jorge Albert Ron

S/C62 Enrique H Ronconi

S/C62 Alejandro P Vargas

S/C62 Pedro Vojkovic

S/C62 Manuel A Zelarrayan

S/C62 Luis Fernandez (ARA)

S/C62 Sergio Giuseppetti (ARA)

S/C62 Jorge Inchauspe (ARA)

S/C62 Jorge Maciel (ARA)

S/C62 Claudio Scaglione (ARA)

BRITISH AWARDS

Sgt Ian J McKay	Victoria Cross
Lt Col Hew W R Pike	Distinguished Service Order
Major Mike H Argue	Military Cross
Major David A Collett	Military Cross
Captain Willie A McCracken, 29 Cdo	Military Cross
Sgt Brian Faulkner	Distinguished Conduct Medal
Sgt John S Pettinger	Distinguished Conduct Medal
Pte Richard J de M Absolon	Military Medal
Cpl Ian P Bailey	Military Medal
Sgt Desmond Fuller	Military Medal
Major Peter Dennison	Mentioned In Dispatches
Captain Matthew Selfridge	Mentioned In Dispatches
Lt Mark Cox	Mentioned In Dispatches
2nd Lt Ian Moore	Mentioned In Dispatches
Sgt Dick Kalinski	Mentioned In Dispatches
Sgt Peter Marshall ACC	Mentioned In Dispatches
Cpl Thomas Noble	Mentioned In Dispatches

Cpl Jerry Phillips	Mentioned In Dispatches
Cpl John Sibley	Mentioned In Dispatches
Cpl Steve Harding-Dempster	Mentioned In Dispatches
Lance Cpl Lenny Carver	Mentioned In Dispatches
Lance Cpl Christopher Lovett	Mentioned In Dispatches
Pte Kevin Connery	Mentioned In Dispatches
Pte Adam Corneille	Mentioned In Dispatches
Pte Darren Gough	Mentioned In Dispatches
Pte Dominic Gray	Mentioned In Dispatches
Pte Pat Harley	Mentioned In Dispatches
Captain Norman Menzies	Member of the Order of the British Empire

My friend and colleague John Kennedy somehow missed out on an award, but received a Certificate of Commendation, which I think is worthy of mention:

Commander of the Task Force 317 Commendation:

Presented to Private J J P Kennedy of Third Battalion the Parachute Regiment.

Pte Kennedy was a medical assistant working in the Regimental Aid Post throughout the campaign. His courage and outstanding energy in tending to casualties during the battalion's attack on Mount Longdon on the night of 11/12 June, and subsequently during the defence of the position were beyond praise and in the highest tradition of the Army. Using initiative and authority far beyond what could be reasonably expected from one of his rank and experience, he rendered incalculable support in the work of running the Regimental Aid Post. He was constantly to the fore, his skill and confidence priceless in the tending of casualties, organizing of stretcher-bearer parties, and swift reaction to immediate calls after shelling. Under continual artillery and mortar bombardment, he displayed the utmost bravery and utter disregard for his own safety. No matter where the casualty occurred, Kennedy seemed always to be there to assist, frequently taking complete command of the situation.

His personal courage was matched by his fine medical skill under the most demanding and unpleasant conditions, and lives of wounded men were certainly saved by his constant bravery and superb application of his training. This young soldier was an inspiration to many and conducted himself magnificently throughout a fierce battle and the subsequent days of artillery fire. I commend him for his skill and courage, which was in the finest traditions of Her Majesty's Armed Forces.

Admiral John David Elliott Fieldhouse, 11 October 1982

ARGENTINE AWARDS

Unfortunately, we have not been able to gather a full Argentine awards list.
However, these are the ones we have managed to locate.

Army

Sub-Lt Juan Baldini	Medal of Valour in Combat
Lt Raul Castaneda	Medal of Valour in Combat
Lt Francis Galindez	Medal of Valour in Combat
Sgt Rolando Spizuocco	Medal of Valour in Combat
1st Corporal Dario Ríos	Medal of Valour in Combat
1st Corporal Manuel Medina	Medal of Valour in Combat
CC62 Leonardo Rondi Marine	Medal of Valour in Combat

Marine Infantry

Lt Sergio Andres Dachary	Honour and Courage in Combat
Cpl Carlos Rafael Colemil	Honour and Courage in Combat
Cpl Domingo Lamas	Honour and Courage in Combat
CC62 Osvaldo A Colombo	Honour and Courage in Combat

APPENDIX II

BRITISH PERSONNEL

The Third Battalion, The Parachute Regiment and Attachments

CO Lt Col Hew Pike
2ic Major Roger Patton
RSM Lawrie Ashbridge

A Company
Commanded by Major David Collett / CSM Alec Munro

1 Platoon
2nd Lt John Kearton / Sgt Manny Manfred

2 Platoon
Lt Ian Moore / Sgt Gerry Carr

3 Platoon
2nd Lt Peter Osborne / Sgt Jim McCallum

B Company
Commanded by Major Mike Argue / CSM Johnny Weeks

4 Platoon
Lt Andrew Bickerdike / Sgt Ian McKay

5 Platoon
Lt Mark Cox / Sgt John Ross

6 Platoon
Lt Jonathan Shaw / Sgt Pete Gray

C Company
Commanded by Major Martin Osborne / CSM Geoff Guest

7 Platoon
Lt Barry Griffiths / Sgt Paul Robinson

8 Platoon
2nd Lt Mike O'Neill / Sgt Martin Bird

9 Platoon
2nd Lt Nicholas Tscharner-Vischer / Sgt Bill Hayward

D Company
Commanded by Major Pat Butler / CSM Ernie Rustill
Captain Matthew Selfridge / Sgt Johnny Pettinger

Support Company
Commanded by Major Peter Dennison / CSM Thor Caithness

Anti-Tank Platoon
Captain Anthony Mason / CSgt Steve Knights

Signals Platoon
WO2 Graham Mills / CSgt Chris Williford

MMGs / Drum's Platoon
Lt Mike Oliver / DSgt Major Geoff Deaney

Mortar Platoon
Captain Julian James / SNCO CSgt Dave Robson

A Company Detachment
MFC A – Cpl Steve Baxter (Mortar Fire Controller)
MFC B – Cpl Mark (Geordie) Crowne
Battery Carrier – Pte Steve Fitton
CPO – Cpl Leuan (Bully) Bullivant (Command Post Operator)
ACPO – Pte David (Bert) Hughes (Assistant Command Post Operator)

Detachment 1
No.1 – LCpl Stephen Hoy-Priest
No.2 – Pte Peter (Ghost) Harvey
No.3 – Pte Andrew (Scouse) Ashworth

Detachment 2
No.1 – Pte Michael (Mac) McMenamin
No.2 – Pte Robert (Bob) Wade
No.3 – LCpl John Hunter

B Company Detachment
MFC A – Cpl Terry McGlasson
MFC B – Cpl Ronnie Cooper
Battery Carrier – Pte Neil (Midge) Mason
CPO – Sgt Dave Hallas
ACPO – LCpl Kevin Robison

Detachment 1
No.1 – Pte Duncan Watts
No.2 – Pte Kenny Fitzgerald
No.3 – Pte Andy (Taff) Williams

Detachment 2
No.1 – LCpl Terry (Tex) Grogan
No.2 – Pte Mal Whitaker
No.3 – Pte John (Taff) Ellis

C Company Detachment
MFC A – Cpl Paddy Rehill
MFC B – Cpl Christopher Fitzgerald
Battery Carrier – Unknown
CPO – Cpl Johnny Mountford
ACPO –LCpl Stephen Tucker

Detachment 1
No.1 – Pte Pete Cawse
No.2 – Pte Nigel (Nobby) Brandish
No.3 – Pte Michael (Naz) Nazroo

Detachment 2
No.1 – LCpl Charles Castledine
No.2 – Pte Anthony Hields
No.3 – Pte Stewart Murrant

HQ Company
Commanded by Captain Bob Darby / WO2 John Carey
Includes various support elements: MT, ACC, RAPC, Admin, Provo, Int Cell.

16 Field Ambulance
Commanded by Captain Mike Von Bertele / Cpl Davie Wilson /
Cpl Neil Parkin

2 Troop, 9 Squadron RE
Commanded by Captain Robbie Burns / SSgt Pete Guerin

29 Commando Regiment RA
Battery Commander Major John Patrick, 6 x 105mm Pack Howitzers

HMS *Avenger*
Captain Hugo White, 1 x 4.5 inch gun

Naval Gunfire Forward Observation Officer
Captain Willie McCracken

ARGENTINE PERSONNEL AND POSITIONS

7th Mechanized Infantry Regiment and Attachments

CO Lt Col Omar Gimenez

A Company based on Wireless Ridge

B Company based on Mount Longdon

C Company based on Wireless Ridge north

B Company Headquarters
Based on Full Back:

2ic Major Carlos Carrizo-Salvadores, in charge of Mount Longdon 'Silver Sector 2'.

Captain Eduardo Lopez, Officer Commanding 120 men of B Company.

Lt Hugo Quiroga, Officer Commanding 46 men of 10th Combat Engineers.

Lt Sergio Dachary, Officer Commanding 34 men of Marine Infantry Anti-Aircraft Platoon.

2 x Heavy Machine Guns manned by Marine Infantry located on Full Back, Gun number 2 facing north and Gun number 1 facing south.

Sgt Pedro Lopez, HQ Group in charge of 2 x 120mm mortars.

4 x Blowpipe anti-aircraft missiles.

On 16 May 1982 the Marine Infantry AA Platoon received:

6 x passive night-vision sights marked 'Mizza' for the Heavy Machine Guns.

3 x Head-mounted passive night-vision goggles marked 'Litton'.

3 x Rifle-mounted passive night-vision sights marked 'Litton'.

1 x 81mm mortar detachment. 1 x 120mm mortar detachment.

1 Platoon
Based on and around Fly Half:

Commanded by Sub Lieutenant Juan Baldini.

The platoon headquarters was based in 'First Bowl', the platoon area of responsibility was the western slope and north-west corner of Longdon.

1 x 105mm recoilless rifle commanded by Cpl Rios. (Fortunately, no ammunition had been delivered.)

8 x Cobra anti-tank missiles. 2 x 81mm mortars.

2 x 50 Calibre Heavy Machine Guns manned by Marine Infantry, Gun number 5 located on Fly Half facing west, Gun number 4 located on the northern edge of western slope facing north.

Based on and around the western slope:

Lieutenant Alberto Ramos, Artillery Forward Observation Officer, Sergeant Quinteros and radio operator from GA 3.

1 x Rasit radar facing west under the command of Sergeant Nista Roque.

1 x Sniper Sgt Cabral.

2 Platoon
Commanded by 1st Sgt Raul Gonzalez.

The platoon HQ was located in Second Bowl, and the platoon area of responsibility was the low ground along the northern side in front of the Third Bowl. The platoon was positioned facing north as this was thought to be the main threat; positioned with them was 1 x Rasit radar, located outside the entrance to the Second Bowl facing north. On the high ground behind them on the main ridge was a Marine heavy machine-gun position, Gun number 3, and further to the east of the Third Bowl was a 120mm mortar.

3 Platoon

Commanded by Lt Enrique Neirotti.

The platoon was located on the rocky south-west corner of the mountain. They were strengthened by 1 x 105mm recoilless rifle, 2 x 81mm mortars and a Marine heavy machine gun, Gun number 6. This platoon was not engaged.

Artillery Support: GA3 A and B Battery, 10 x 105mm Howitzers, Lt Ramos FOO.

GLOSSARY

2ic – Second in Command

2 PARA – 2nd Battalion The Parachute Regiment

3 PARA – 3rd Battalion The Parachute Regiment

2SG – 2nd Battalion Scots Guards

66mm – Disposable light anti-tank weapon

7.62mm (FAP) – Argentine heavy-barrelled automatic rifle

AA – Anti-aircraft

AAC – Army Air Corps

AB biscuits – hard biscuits

ACC – Army Catering Corps (cooks)

ASC – Advanced Surgical Centre

ATGW – Anti-tank Guided Weapon

Basha'd – A term used for erecting a tarpaulin shelter

Basher – Improvised shelter

BC – Battery Commander

Bergen – Large pack

BIM 5 – 5th Naval Infantry Battalion (Argentine Marines)

Bn – Battalion

Bde – Brigade

BM – Brigade Major

Brew – Make tea

Brig Gen – Brigadier General

Brimstone – Padre

BV – Volvo Bandwagon 202, a Swedish-made tracked vehicle, also known as Snowcat

CAP – Company Aid Post

Carl Gustav – 84mm light anti-tank weapon like a bazooka

Casevac – Casualty evacuation (pronounced Caz-evac)

Casevact – Casualty evacuated

CBU – Cluster bomb unit

CO – Commanding Officer

CP – Command post

Coy – Company

Cpl – Corporal

CPR – Cardio-pulmonary resuscitation

CQMS – Company Quartermaster Sergeant

Crack on – Just keep going

Crap Hat – What Paratroopers call regiment or corps not wearing the maroon beret

C/S – Call sign

CSgt – Colour Sergeant

CSM – Company Sergeant Major

D-Day – Day of operations

Danger close – Indicates friendly forces are within close proximity of the target being engaged

Det – Detached

DF – Defensive fire

Doss Bag – Sleeping bag

DSgt – Drum Sergeant

Echelon area – Grouping area for evacuation

Endex – End of exercise

FAC – Forward Air Controller

FAL – Belgian-made automatic rifle used by Argentine forces, fires 7.62mm ammunition, similar to British SLR

Field Dressing – Sterile absorbent pad with bandages attached

Fire for effect – The first artillery ranging rounds fired to check the target area is being hit

FGA – Fighter ground attack

FLOT – Forward location of own troops

FOO – Forward Observation Officer

Foxhound – Infantry

FRV – Final rendezvous

FUP – Forming-up point

Gazelle – Light reconnaissance helicopter

GPMG – General-purpose machine gun

Hawkeye – A helicopter

H-Hour – The time at which the first wave of troops cross their Start Line

HE – High explosive

Head sheds – Senior officers

HEAT – High-explosive anti-tank warhead

Hexamine stove – Small metal disposable cooker

HLS – Helicopter landing site

HMG – Heavy machine gun (.50 Cal)

Holdfast – Engineers

HQ – Headquarters

IO – Intelligence Officer

Int Cell – Intelligence Cell, a platoon sized cell that gathers and collates information regarding battalion threats as well as present and future operations

Int Sum – Intelligence summary

IWS – Individual weapon sight, a British first-generation image intensifier which can be clipped to rifle or GPMG for shooting or observing

Jacked – Given up

Kestrel – Operations officer

LADE – Lineas Aeréas del Estado, Argentine state airline

LAW 66mm – Light anti-tank weapon

LCpl – Lance Corporal

LGB – Laser-guided bomb

LO – Liaison Officer

LOE – Limit of exploitation. The furthest you advance or have advanced

LT – Local time

Lt Col – Lieutenant Colonel

LUP – Laying-up point

LS – Landing site

LSL – Landing Ship Logistics

MAG – 7.62 machine gun used by Argentine forces

Manhole – Logistics

MFC – Mortar-fire controller

MFO Box – Military Forces Overseas packing crate

Milan Post – Rocket launcher. It fires a Milan missile

Milan – Wire-guided anti-tank missile

MMG – Medium machine gun

MO – Medical Officer

MRC – Medical reception centre. Medical triage centre which grades and prioritizes the casualties

MT – Motor transport

NBC boots – Nuclear, biological and chemical warfare clothing – rubber boots

NCO – Non-Commissioned Officer

NGFO – Naval Gun Fire Observer

NOD – Night-observation device

NOK – Next of kin

OC – Officer Commanding

'O' Group – Order Group

On Stag – On guard duty

OP – Observation post

Playtime – Transport

PNG – Passive night goggles

Poncho – Rubberized sheet of canvas about 7ft square that can be used for shelter or as a stretcher

Pte – Private

PR – Public relations

Provo – Provost Staff

RAMC – Royal Army Medical Corps

RAP – Regimental aid post

RAP team – Medical team

RAPC – Royal Army Pay Corps

Rasit – Portable ground-surveillance radar system

RCL – 105mm recoilless rifle

REME – Royal Electrical & Mechanical Engineers

RFA – Royal Fleet Auxiliary

R/L – Radio log

RSM – Regimental Sergeant Major

Rubber dick – Hoax or wind-up

RV – Rendezvous point (meeting point)

Sangar – Construction built to give cover from enemy fire

SAS – Special Air Service

Seagull – Adjutant

Shell scrape – A hole in the ground, precursor to the full battle trench

SF – Sustained Fire

SF machine gun – Sustained-fire machine gun (mounted on a tripod)

Sit Rep – Situation report

SLR – Self-loading rifle

SMG – Submachine gun

Smock – Army jacket

SNCO – Senior Non-Commissioned Officer

Spr – Sapper

Sqn – Squadron

Stagging – Guard duty

Starlight 2 – Field dressing station at Estancia House

Start Line – A line on the ground, usually a natural feature, stream, fence or bank

Sunray – Unit leader

Syrette – Small morphine ampoule

TAB – Tactical advance to battle: typically a long march

Tabbing – Fast walk with weight on back, cross country

Tac HQ – Tactical headquarters

Toms – Rank of Private soldiers in the Parachute Regiment

Tubes – Mortars

U/S – Unserviceable

Watchdog – Military police

Wessex – Medium-support helicopter to transport troops and equipment

Wilco – Will comply

WO – Warrant Officer

ZU### – Zulu Uniform map grid references indicating enemy target locations, used in radio log calls

Zulu Time (zt) – Greenwich Mean Time

INDEX OF PERSONNEL

ACKNOWLEDGEMENTS

I would like to thank everyone who has taken part in this project:

Ian Aird, Sulle Alhaji, Derek (Dex) Allen, Lawrie Ashbridge, Paul Bachurzewski, Ian Bailey, Len (Basher) Baines, Dave Barclay, Tony Barlow, Julian (Baz) Barrett, Mark (Chuck) Berry, Andrew (Bix) Bickerdike, Martin Bird, Richard (Dickie) Bishop, Joe Black, Tony Bojko, Terry Bowdell, Trevor Bradshaw, Mark Brown, John Burgess, John Carey, Mike Carr, Lenny Carver, Colin Charlton, Simon Clark, Martyn Clarkson Kearsley, Dean (Jasper) Coady, Kevin Connery, Graham Colbeck, Carlos Colemil, David Collett, Denzil Connick, Mark Cox, John Crosland, Mick Cullen, Sergio Andrés Dachary, Duncan Daly, Bob Darby, Kevin Darke, Jeremy (Jez) Dillon, Stuart Dover, George Duffus, Andy (Stretch) Dunn, Kevin Eaton, Colin Edwards, Mark Eisler, Gordon Ellse, Mark Eyles-Thomas, Dair Farrar-Hockley, Brian Faulkner, Adrian Freer, Steve Gaines, Dave Gammon, Harry Gannon, Martin (Spike) Glover, Ben Gough, Andy Gow, Robert Greasley, Stuart Grey, Grant Grinham, Barry Griffiths, Michael Hall, Charlie Hardwick, Pat Harley, Craig (Harry) Harrison, Derek Heaver, Graham Heaton, Pete Hindmarsh, Keith Hopper, Chris Howard, Mark (Zip) Hunt, Paul Hutchinson, Roger James, Dick Kalinski, Ned Kelly, John Kennedy, Steve Knights, Cliff Legg, Gareth Lewis, John (Lewi) Lewis, Adrian Logan, Roderick (Roddy) MacDonald, Donny McDonald, Peter Maddocks, Manny Manfred, Tony Mason, Chris Masterman, Steve McConnell, Kevin McGimpsey, Clint McMillon, Norman (Nobby) Menzies, Bill Metcalfe, Paul (Ginge) Moore, Jimmy Morham, Trudi Morrison (née McPhee), Ian Mousette, Alec Munro, Mike O'Neill, Craig (Tommy) Onions, Giles Orpen-Smellie, Martin Osborne, Chris Parris, Keith (Taff) Parry, John Patrick, Roger Patton, Gustavo Pedemonte, Johnny

Pettinger, Hew Pike, Jerry Phillips, Phil Probets, George Pullin, Mark (Rolly) Rawlings, Paul Read, John Reeves, Paddy Rehill, Steve Richards, Martin (Taff) Richardson, Kevin Robison, Dave Roe, Nick Rose, John Ross, Ernie Rustill, Jonathan Shaw, Phil Simpson, Phil Skidmore, Peter Skinner, Morgan Slade, Boyd Smith, Stephen Smith, Mick Southall, Andy Steadman, Vernon Steen, Andy Stone, Louie Sturge, Peter (Tomo) Thompson, Steve Tickle, Graham Tolson, Tommy Trindall, Mike Von Bertele, Kenny Watts, Johnny Weeks, Bob Whitehill, Trev Wilson, Paul Wray, Ashley Wright, Quintin (Q) Wright, Steve Wright.

I would also like to thank the Falkland Islanders who assisted us during the battle, as without their help and bravery our task would have been made so much more difficult: Terry Betts, Trevor Browning, Mike Carey, Maurice Davis, Don Davidson, Margaret Davison, Pete Gilding, Ailsa Heathman, Tony Heathman, Mike Luxton, Bruce May, Connie May, Kay McCallum, Roddy McKay, Trudi McPhee, Philip Miller, Patrick (Pappy) Minto, Alistair (Ally) Minto, Claude Molkenbur, Ray Newman, Terry Peck, Terrance Phillips, Angus Robertson, Andrez Short, Vernon Steen, Richard Stevens, Toni Stevens, David Thorsen, Neil Watson, Keith Whitney, Pat Whitney.

Also, thanks to Mark Meaton for his assistance regarding Army Air Corps information, to Jon Baker and his team at IWM Duxford ParaData archive and to Paul Evans at the 'Firepower' Royal Artillery Museum archive in Woolwich.

All members of 3 PARA battle group would like to thank photographer and Mount Longdon veteran Tom Smith for the use of his black and white photographs.

I would like to thank Jake Lingwood for having faith in our story – it means a great deal to us.

REFERENCES

Although the majority of this book is based on interviews with veterans of the battle, additional material was provided, some published and some unpublished. I would like to thank the following for permission to reproduce copyright material:

Max Arthur, *Above All, Courage*, Orion, 2002

Lt Sergio Andrés Dachary, *Marine Infantry ARA, La 2ª Sección en Longdon*

Robert Fox, *Eyewitness Falklands*, Mandarin, 1992

Sir Lawrence Freedman, *Official History of the Falklands Campaign, Vol. II*, Routledge, 2005

Max Hastings, *Going to the Wars*, Macmillan, 2000

Ian Gardiner, *The Yompers*, Pen & Sword, 2012

Captain Ian Inskip of HMS *Glamorgan* (email communication)

Christian Jennings & Adrian Weale, *Green-Eyed Boys*, HarperCollins, 1996

Hugh McManners, *Forgotten Voices from the Falklands*, Ebury, 2007

Lt Col James M Ryan RAMC, 'A personal reflection on the Falklands Islands War of 1982', in Falklands War 25th Anniversary, *Journal of The RAMC*, Volume 153 (3), 88–91, 2007

Julian Thompson, *No Picnic*, Pen & Sword, 2009.